Eroticism, Spirituality, and Resistance in Black Women's Writings

UNIVERSITY PRESS OF FLORIDA

Florida A&M University, Tallahassee
Florida Atlantic University, Boca Raton
Florida Gulf Coast University, Ft. Myers
Florida International University, Miami
Florida State University, Tallahassee
New College of Florida, Sarasota
University of Central Florida, Orlando
University of Florida, Gainesville
University of North Florida, Jacksonville
University of South Florida, Tampa
University of West Florida, Pensacola

Eroticism, Spirituality, and Resistance in Black Women's Writings

Donna Aza Weir-Soley

University Press of Florida
Gainesville/Tallahassee/Tampa/Boca Raton
Pensacola/Orlando/Miami/Jacksonville/Ft. Myers/Sarasota

Copyright 2009 by Donna Aza Weir-Soley
All rights reserved
Printed in the United States of America on acid-free paper

22 21 20 19 18 17   6 5 4 3 2 1

First cloth printing, 2009
First paperback printing, 2017

Library of Congress Cataloging-in-Publication Data
Names: Weir-Soley, Donna, author.
Title: Eroticism, spirituality, and resistance in Black women's writings / Donna Aza Weir-Soley.
Description: Gainesville : University Press of Florida, c2009. | Includes bibliographical references and index.
Identifiers: LCCN 2009019220 | ISBN 9780813033778 (cloth: alk. paper) | ISBN 9780813054780 (pbk.)
Subjects: LCSH: American literature—African American authors—History and criticism. | American literature—Women authors—History and criticism. | African American women authors—Intellectual life. | Eroticism in literature. | Sex in literature.
Classification: LCC PS153.N5 W36 2009 OVERFLOWA5S | DDC 810.9/928708996073
LC record available at https://lccn.loc.gov/2009019220

The University Press of Florida is the scholarly publishing agency for the State University System of Florida, comprising Florida A&M University, Florida Atlantic University, Florida Gulf Coast University, Florida International University, Florida State University, New College of Florida, University of Central Florida, University of Florida, University of North Florida, University of South Florida, and University of West Florida.

University Press of Florida
15 Northwest 15th Street
Gainesville, FL 32611-2079
http://upress.ufl.edu

To the late Dr. Barbara Christian,
beloved mentor and friend,
and
to my beautiful children:
Chenjerai Christopher, Iyah Miguel,
and Kai Akili Christian

Contents

Acknowledgments	ix
Preface	xiii
Introduction: Spirit and Flesh: Black Female Aesthetics	1
1. The Cult of Nineteenth-Century Black Womanhood	12
2. Literary Interventions in *Their Eyes Were Watching God*	39
3. Contradictory Directives and the Erotics of Re-membering: New World Spiritual Practices and Black Female Subjectivity in *Beloved*	79
4. The Erotics of Change: Female Sexuality, Afro-Caribbean Spirituality, and a "Postmodern" Caribbean Identity in *It Begins with Tears*	141
5. Power, Eros, and Genocide: Capitalism and Black Female Subjectivity in *The Farming of Bones*	184
Epilogue	223
Notes	227
Works Cited	249
Index	261

Acknowledgments

Many people and institutions contributed to the development of this book. My gratitude first goes to the readers who critiqued the chapters of this project: Opal Palmer Adisa, Susan Schweik, David Lloyd, Margaret Wilkerson, and especially the late Barbara Christian—to whom this book is dedicated. A Career Enhancement Fellowship from the Woodrow Wilson National Fellowship Foundation allowed me to take a year's leave from teaching in order to begin this manuscript in its current evolution. I would like to thank Richard Hope, Sylvia Sheridan, and William Mitchell at Woodrow Wilson, as well as Lydia English at the Mellon Foundation, for their support of that program and for providing mentorship and support over the years for me and for the thousands of Mellon fellows in graduate schools and academic positions across the nation. Neither my career nor this book would have been possible without the support of the Mellon and Woodrow Wilson Foundations. Thanks go out, as well, to Florida International University for providing partial support for my Career Enhancement Fellowship year and to Dean Furton, Provost Berkman, and Vice-Provost Wartzok for their generous support of this book and of my career at Florida International University.

Many people read different versions of this manuscript as it underwent various revisions, and I am grateful to all of them for their loving energy, outstanding collegiality, and firm commitment to seeing me complete a project they sincerely believed in. Critic Houston Baker's incisive comments encouraged me to push beyond my comfort zone and to settle for nothing short of excellence. I am grateful to my colleagues Candice Jenkins, Arlene Keizer, and Kwame Dawes, who offered significant insights. In addition to writing brilliant critical texts to which my own work is much indebted, both Candice and Arlene have been especially generous and careful readers. I thank also my former teacher, the late Myrna D. Bain, who first made me aware of the critical connections between Afro-Jamaican spirituality and other African-derived spiritual practices in the black diaspora. Similarly, other Hunter College professors (Frank Kirkland, Audre Lorde, Dona

Marimba Richards, Melinda Goodman, Louise DeSalvo, Alan Brick, and Richard Barickman) were all instrumental in setting me along the path I am traveling today.

To my colleagues Kathleen McCormack, Tometro Hopkins, and Mary Free in the English Department of Florida International University, whose support for this project and for my career have been unwavering since the first day I met each of them, I extend my sincere gratitude. My colleague Meri-Jane Rochelson also read this manuscript in various stages of its development and never refused me when I called on her for feedback on a section or chapter that was particularly challenging. In addition to her professional support, Meri-Jane's support of me personally cannot be over-stated. I feel very blessed to have both her and Kathleen as dear friends and colleagues. Thanks go out to all of my colleagues in Arts and Sciences at Florida International University, and especially to my colleagues in English and African New World Studies. I am also grateful for the support of the F.I.U. libraries and staff and, most especially, for Steve Switzer and George Pearson who went above and beyond the call of duty to assist me in my research.

The University Press of Florida, and especially my acquiring editor, Amy Gorelick, believed in this project before it reached maturity and carefully shepherded me through every stage of its development. I value Amy's dedication, professionalism, and the meticulous care she took to ensure that this manuscript found fair and capable readers. I also appreciate—and have responded to—the insightful comments made by the anonymous readers of my manuscript. Carine Mardorossian went above and beyond the efforts of many readers. Her meticulous reviews, incisive queries, and generous praise for the project helped to shape and sharpen my critical thinking and writing. Because of her generosity as a critic this book is a much improved product. Thanks also to Michele Fiyak-Burkley and Ray Brady who painstakingly edited the final draft of this book.

Toward the end, when I needed support to finish well, Tiffany Pogue and Simone Bailey came through for me like true sister-friends. I also appreciate the proofreading skills Paulette Kerr offered at the earlier stages of this project. Thanks go out as well to a wonderful research assistant, Alisha Grines, who was a great resource during a critical stage in the life of this project. Former student Ray Infante was also a constant source of spiritual and emotional support, and Raydel Hernandez was truly a godsend.

For anyone whose name I forgot to mention, blame my omission on fatigue and not on ungratefulness. I am truly thankful to each and every person who offered support and encouragement at every stage of this project.

Special Thanks

I carry my family with me always. For those who have prayed for me, encouraged me, and celebrated my accomplishments, I am grateful for your love and support. Special thanks to my mother (Daisy), stepmother (Iris), and dad (Kenneth); my cousins Loris Kirkpatrick, Ricklann McCalla, and Curene Clarke-Ervin; and my sisters, Judene and Chloe Weir. To my husband, Cush, and my beloved sons, Chenjerai, Iyah, and Kai: your prayers have been answered, and the book is now a reality. I pray that you will all grow to believe in yourselves as you have believed in me, and as I believe in all of you. My beloved friend and colleague Heather Russell knew where I was going with this book before I did. Because of her insightful readings of my chapter on Opal Palmer Adisa's novel, I was forced to begin a brand-new project that culminated in this book. At every step of the writing process, Heather was there to offer critical feedback, a shoulder to cry on, a candle when I needed light and energy, and important downtime when I could not stand another minute at my desk. Heather is a brilliant critic, and her insights led to significant revisions that have made this book a much better product. In every conceivable way, her friendship challenges me to be my best self. Claudia May also read sections of this book and offered generous praise and support in this and in many other areas of my life. For including me in her prayers when I asked and when I forgot to ask, for loving and supporting me as a mother, poet, and scholar, and for being family to my children and a sister to me in every conceivable way, I thank God for the gift of a sister-friend like Claudia. Opal Palmer Adisa has been familiar with at least two chapters of this book from the embryonic stages of the endeavor. Opal is a source of inspiration as a mother, critical writer, fiction writer, and fellow poet. As someone who does it all, Opal's presence in my life is a constant deterrent to any impulse I may get to make excuses. I am grateful to her for the constant light, the sweet energy, for being the best godmother my son could have, and for believing. I am honored to call her Macomére. Meredith Gadsby read sections of this book in the very early stages and gave me invaluable feedback. Meredith and I have walked parallel paths in this journey: we have five beautiful sons between us in a career that does not always honor motherhood. But because of these precious children and the legacies we are determined to leave them, all of the sacrifices have been worthwhile. I am thankful for Meredith's positive presence in my life. Ifeona Fulani, with whom I have spent countless phone hours swapping family stories for well over a decade, became an excellent sounding board for my first chapter toward the end. I am grateful to Ifeona and to Carolyn Cooper for extending the hand of friendship and sisterhood to me over the years. I am thankful for Kim Lyons and Dorothea Smartt, sister-friends for over twenty years. Their love, laughter, and friendship have sustained me in difficult times and honored me in good ones. Pepper Black has been a wonderful "Auntie" to my children and the best co-mother I could ask for, supporting me and my children emotionally and spiritually in ways too numerous to mention here. She has become a beloved member of my extended family. I am grateful for and humbled by her friendship. Pastor Peggy Carter, who sends me a word of spiritual wisdom every day, is my prayer partner and sister-friend. She has prayed me through times of real doubt when I did not know if I could summon the energy or the faith to see this project through. My faith has been strengthened because of our friendship. I thank my ancestral guides for coming and for sharing their wisdom. This book is nothing less than my homage to them.

Last and foremost, I thank my Creator who is so much bigger (and better) than religion. Without God's guidance and protection, my life, my work, and this book would not have been possible.

Preface

"Black females are valued by no one."
—Motivational Educational Entertainment

In "The Height of Disrespect," Thulani Davis emphasizes the objectification of young black women in hip-hop lyrics and videos and chronicles the relationship between the way these women are portrayed and what Davis views as the lack of self-respect exhibited by many of these performers. Davis's concerns are shared by many cultural critics who believe that hip-hop culture disproportionately contributes both to the exploitation of black women and to the dehumanizing exhibition of black female bodies.[1]

Conversely, in *Sound Clash: Jamaican Dancehall Culture at Large*, Carolyn Cooper argues that Jamaican dancehall culture (a space akin to hip-hop culture) in fact allows women a "potentially liberating space" for erotic exploration (17). There is a definite corollary between the discourse around dancehall and the controversies surrounding hip-hop, with respect to the violent and overtly sexual language as well as the physical and verbal portrayal of black women in both spaces. Nevertheless, Cooper warns against the tendency to overstate the exploitation of the black female body in such a space: "the joyous display of the female body in the dance is perceived as a pornographic devaluation of woman" (17). Cooper argues that such an analysis misses the point and suggests that it denies women agency and the freedom to choose what to do with their bodies. Cooper goes even further, arguing "transgressively for the freedom of women to claim a self-pleasuring identity that may even be explicitly homoerotic" (17).

However, for the black woman, any performance of sexuality, no matter how liberating, is already preconditioned by historical baggage. Both positions reveal the almost antithetical ways in which black women's sexual performances have historically been read. Black women are either fully appropriated victims of patriarchal sexism or fully empowered subjects confidently challenging bourgeois respectability. While both Cooper and Davis make critical interventions into this disputation, neither position, I would argue, tells the full story.

The opening epigraph is shocking not merely because it is an overstatement but because it represents, arguably, an over-simplification of the facts.

Long before the emergence of hip-hop culture, black females were devalued, dehumanized, and disgraced in both private and popular arenas, and at the same time black women have gone to great measures to contravene, resist, and frustrate the devaluation of their identities since their arrival on the New World stage.

Given the legacy of the physical and sexual exploitation of the black female body and image, the earliest black women writers and activists were conflicted about how to represent black women as both moral and sexual beings. Overwhelmingly, they chose *not* to represent black women as sexual beings. Such drastic measures were deemed necessary to counter the damaging stereotypes of the black woman as hyper-sexual and/or sexually deviant. This unbalanced representation of the black woman continued well into the twentieth century until Zora Neale Hurston broke the pattern with her character Janie in *Their Eyes Were Watching God*. Indeed, *Their Eyes Were Watching God* represents a revolutionary shift in the representation of the black woman, a shift that recognizes what Audre Lorde dubs "the power of the erotic"—the ability to form a creative and productive alliance between sexual and spiritual energies. In this study, I chart the development of this new representation of the black woman in the works of black women writing across the diaspora. I argue that works such as Toni Morrison's *Beloved*, Opal Palmer Adisa's *It Begins with Tears*, and Edwidge Danticat's *The Farming of Bones* echo Hurston's *Their Eyes Were Watching God* in their evocation of black female empowerment through a form of embodied spirituality that recognizes the centrality of the erotic.

Notes

Epigraph: This quotation is attributed to the authors of a study conducted in 2004 by Motivational Educational Entertainment, a Philadelphia communications firm that researches and markets to urban and low-income groups.

1. See Ayanna's "The Exploitation of Women in Hip-Hop Culture." See also Kimberlé Crenshaw's article "Beyond Racism and Misogyny: Black Feminism and 2 Live Crew," for a cogent critique of the case against the rap group 2 Live Crew who were arrested and charged under a Florida obscenity statute after appearing in a Florida nightclub in 1990. Crenshaw wonders whether Henry Louis Gates was wrong-headed in citing the differences in African-American vernacular expression in his defense of 2 Live Crew. She states, "Ultimately, however, little turns on whether the 'word play' performed by 2 Live Crew is a postmodern challenge to racist sexual mythology or simply an internal group practice that has crossed over into mainstream America. Both versions of the defense are problematic because they each call on black women to accept misogyny and its attendant disrespect in service of some broader group objective" (iv).

Introduction

Spirit and Flesh: Black Female Aesthetics

Since their emergence on the literary stage, New World black writers have faced the challenge of representing a worldview that is inherently syncretic while using a literary model that privileges Western theoretical and epistemological precepts. In *Black Subjects,* Arlene Keizer argues that during slavery black identities were invented out of the conflict between two competing ideologies: the capitalist and patriarchal system of American slavery and "the subjugated system of West African beliefs and practices" that continued to lay claim to these captive Africans and their descendants (23). Despite the putatively dominant Eurocentric ideology that undergirded the slave system, Keizer argues that West African cosmology fostered "a culture of resistance" within the slave communities that ultimately culminated in the synthesis of Western and African worldviews that characterizes New World black identity. Evidence of this syncretism can be observed in early African-American writings.[1]

However, having come to literacy (and to subjectivity) under the aegis of a dominant and hegemonic Eurocentricity, New World black writers have chosen from among accommodation, assimilation, denigration, denial, or repression of their African sensibility in their texts.[2] One of the literary repercussions of this has been the assignment of certain themes to the secular and others to the spiritual realm, as well as an apparent inability to integrate the two (secular and sacred) as overlapping or interrelated categories.

While Western epistemology locates the sacred and the secular in separate and even opposing realms, the African worldview recognizes no such separation. For instance, to the extent that sexuality has been discursively constituted within the framework of Judeo-Christian morality in the West, and given that Christianity allows very little latitude for the full exploration (either discursively or ritually) of human sexual expression, any engagement with the subject of sexuality in Western literature is necessarily shaped by ideas that coalesce around concepts of "sin" and "immorality." Plainly speaking, although sex is sanctioned within marriage between a man and a woman, outside of these narrow parameters it is considered "sinful" according to traditional Christian doctrine, and this sinfulness is constitutive of how we read and write about sex in the West. Understood within the context of a Western paradigm that is informed by Judeo-Christian notions of morality and propriety, this dichotomy between the spiritual and the sexual has its corollary in the separation of the secular from the sacred in our discursive traditions.

By contrast, in many West African–based spiritual traditions, sexual expression is an integral part of the spiritual experience. The dramatization of human sexuality can be observed and practiced through rituals, prayers, and deities who present as sexual beings, either overtly or covertly. But if contemporary as well as historical black Christianity is to be taken at its basic doctrinal level, it appears that the separation of the sexual from the spiritual was one of the earliest adaptations of the black subject to his New World environment.

For the black female subject in the New World, this separation between the sexual and the spiritual had to be maintained within the framework of black women's historical subjugation, not just physically, but more significantly, sexually. Therefore, the central challenges for black women writers have revolved around the issue of how to represent black female characters as both sexual and spiritual beings while working within the constraints of a discursive tradition that historically maligned black women as sexual deviants.

Nineteenth-century black women writers formulated a dual strategy for addressing this issue: they internalized the moral standards of Judeo-Christian theology to support the maintenance of this separation, while simultaneously claiming that due to their condition of sexual servitude, black women were incapable of living up to the Victorian standards of sexual purity that the cult of true womanhood demanded. Black women's responses to charges of sexual immorality resulted in further institutionalization of the separation between the sexual and the spiritual spheres as evidenced by nineteenth-century texts written by black women.[3] Female characters who adhered to strict moral and sexual standards of propriety were forced to repress their sexuality, while those who did express themselves sexually were denied all legitimate claims to the redemptive and liberating potential of an empowered and empowering spirituality.

Beginning with Zora Neale Hurston's *Their Eyes Were Watching God*, twentieth-century black women writers have attempted to heal this rift and reestablish the interdependence between spirituality and sexuality that is central to the formation of black women's identities. They have done so by relying on the inscription of a symbolic, discursive, literal, and theoretical framework based on the spiritual precepts and epistemology of West African belief systems. Janie Crawford's liberating reclamation of her sexuality provides (in part) one noteworthy contravention to the most notorious example of how the black woman's body was historically appropriated to disenfranchise her of human dignity: the haunting episode of Sara Baartman, who was literally placed on display like a circus animal, first in public exhibitions in London, and later in similar venues in Paris, where she eventually died at the age of twenty-five. Upon her death, Sara's buttocks and genitals were embalmed and displayed in the Musée de l'Homme in Paris . . . and there they remained for 160 years. In 1974, her private parts were removed from public view. She was called the "Venus Hottentot," but the fascination she held for Europeans had nothing to do with adoration. Sara's tragic story stands as a warning to today's black women about the treacherousness of the objectifying gaze.

As Keizer convincingly argues, "the black slave in rebellion against white domination is the prototype for a black resistant subjectivity, a founding model of African-American and Afro-Caribbean subjectivity"(9). Implicit in Keizer's cross-gendered analysis is the recognition that these forms of resistance had to be multilayered, multidirectional, and multifaceted precisely because white domination took place (ubiquitously) upon multiple discursive and material planes. In *Their Eyes Were Watching God*, Zora Neale Hurston's creation of a character such as Janie constitutes one such act of rebellion against the discursive and material violence to which the black female body and image were subjected under white domination. In this study, I argue that Hurston's creation of Janie is an act of rebellion that constitutes a major catalyst in African-American letters: the black woman writing back to right the great wrong written (and performed) against her—a wrong that robbed her of a unitary subjectivity.[4]

Zora Neale Hurston's engagement with the character Janie Crawford—who is far from idealized, yet consciously determined to achieve spiritual, sexual, political, and emotional wholeness—provides a prototype for Hurston's literary daughters writing across the black diaspora. In *Tell My Horse*, Hurston wrote capaciously about the role of women in Haiti and Jamaica, making her, as Daphne Lamothe argues, the sole writer of her day to interrogate black female subjectivity from a broad diasporic rather than a single African-American perspective.[5] *Eroticism, Spirituality, and Resistance* takes into account the diasporic reach of Hurston's intervention by reading *Their Eyes Were Watching God* alongside (and as a precursor to) Toni Morrison's *Beloved*, the Jamaican writer Opal Palmer Adisa's *It Begins with Tears*, and the Haitian-American writer Edwidge Danticat's *The Farming of Bones*. This diverse group of writers intent on reclaiming the lost ground of black women's sexual and spiritual wholeness creates female characters who are uniformly in conversation with Hurston's Janie and with each other.

Theoretical Implications of Eroticism in African Cosmology

In *Sister Outsider*, Audre Lorde theorizes about the dangers of separating the sexual from the spiritual: "we have attempted to separate the spiritual and the erotic, thereby reducing the spiritual to a world of flattened affect, a world of the ascetic who aspires to feel nothing" (56). Lorde unsettles conventional theories about subjectivity by introducing the role of spirituality and arguing that there is a coterminous relationship among sexuality, spirituality, and personal and political empowerment for women. In the process, Lorde attempts to tear down the hierarchy between thoughts and feelings, ideas and emotions, by examining the relationship between political action (external forms) and "internal knowledge and needs" (58).

According to Lorde, the separation of spheres that are inextricably linked leads to a world of "flattened affect" that cannot support creative transformation. Scholars of African cosmology are diverse in their political and disciplinary orientations, but they all seem to share the view that the principles of interconnectedness, interrelatedness, and interdependency of everything in the known cosmos is the basic tenet of the African worldview.

For the purposes of this study, I would like to propose that Lorde's definition of the erotic contains an implicit definition of spirituality. Spirituality implies and hinges upon interiority. Spiritual people are inwardly focused, relying more upon internal acquisition of knowledge (intuition, messages from the body, insight gained from meditation or fasting, gut feelings, dreams, sensory and supersensory perceptions, prayer, praise, and rituals) than upon external directives and epistemes to guide their choices. Spirituality may center on the belief in one supreme, omnipotent being or, as in many African religions, on several divine powers.[6] However, for the purposes of this study, spirituality is only one part of the equation. Lorde's definition of the erotic hinges on the self-conscious awareness that to truly effect transformation one must be spiritually and sexually in balance. Lorde's premise is not a prerequisite for every spiritual tradition, and especially not for Christianity. To effect a crucial historical corrective, black women writers implicitly and explicitly theorize the necessity of a return to the principles of interrelatedness that reunite the spiritual with the sexual, a return to the transformative power of the erotic. Zora Neale Hurston, Toni Morrison, Opal Palmer Adisa, and Edwidge Danticat all infuse African-American and Afro-Caribbean spirituality into their narratives to underscore cultural resistance and female agency. In so doing, each of these writers affirms the social, political, and philosophical efficacy of Lorde's argument in "Uses of the Erotic: The Erotic as Power."

Although the suffering inflicted by institutionalized, state-sanctioned racial oppression and even genocide clearly cuts across gender lines, the authors I discuss highlight the specifically gendered effects of mental, emotional, sexual, and psychological trauma on their black female protagonists. Alternatively, African cosmologies are rendered as healing tropes in these texts as they are modified, creolized, understood, and practiced by New World blacks, ultimately becoming the locus around which black female characters formulate autonomous subjectivities and exercise sexual agency. Black female goddess figures with origins in African and New World cosmologies are continuously evoked and invoked throughout these works. Representations of highly sexualized female orishas, river deities, spirits, and loas, combined with a spirituality grounded in sociohistorical experiences, religious mythology, and spiritual worldview of the folk, foreground a necessary poetics of eroticism to counter the effects of historical traumas and facilitate healing, creative adaptation, recuperation, and resistance.

The purpose of this study is not to rehash theories of black identity construction, or even to challenge them, but rather to interrogate the multifaceted issue of black subject formation as it pertains to gender. Thus, my discussion foregrounds the interrelatedness of identity, autonomy, sexuality, and spirituality in black women's writings. I argue that spiritual processes are necessary for subject formation, and highlight the spiritual practices, perspectives, and theories that inform black female subjectivity, agency, and autonomy in the work of Hurston, Morrison, Adisa, and Danticat. My study corroborates the findings of other critics such as Karla Holloway who argue that a black women-centered spirituality is a recurring trope in black women's writings across the diaspora. My primary intervention is to argue for the relational ways in which culturally diverse black women writers signal the presence of an African-based spirituality in their works while highlighting the liberating quest for a mutually constitutive sexuality, a necessary corollary to a fully developed spirituality in the search for a self-directed, counterhegemonic sense of agency and wholeness representing a unitary subjectivity.

In his germinal work *The Signifying Monkey*, Henry Louis Gates Jr. writes about the need to explore the black vernacular tradition as a theoretical model for analyzing texts from the African-American literary tradition. Gates declares that his intention is "to allow the black tradition to speak for itself about its nature and various functions, rather than read it, or analyze it, in terms of literary theories borrowed whole from other traditions, appropriated from without" (i). Gates continues with the simple but radical assertion that "each literary tradition, at least implicitly, contains within it an argument for how it can be read" (i). Gates shares this position with another eminent scholar, Barbara Christian, whose adoption of a similar position in her essay "The Race for Theory" has been excoriated as "antitheory" in some camps. Christian's argument that black women writers use their texts to "creatively theorize" about the nature of identity, politics, and human relations substantiates Gates's assertion that each text "contains an argument for how it can be read." However, their shared perspective with regard to the reading of black literature has been obscured both by their differing relations to Western theoretical models, and by subtle and not so subtle gender biases that condition and inform black scholarly output and reception.

My theoretical approach, modeled on those of Audre Lorde, Henry Louis Gates Jr., Houston Baker Jr., Karla Holloway, and Barbara Christian, examines the political, cultural, spiritual, historical, and gendered particularities that inform each text. However, there are at least three significant differences between my project and the critical works of the scholars mentioned above. In the chapters that follow, I foreground the presence of New World syncretic belief systems such as Kumina or Pukumina in Jamaica and Voudoun in Haiti. Furthermore, I argue that black female writers inscribe these creolized religions within their texts to provide an epistemic grounding for the spiritual worldview and practices that inform a proposed (or imagined) unitary black female identity. Despite the fragmentation, distortion, and repression of West African spiritual practices, a unifying theoretical thread derived from these "broken" belief systems connects ideas about African spirituality to female intuition, knowledge, sexual power, spiritual agency, and psychic and spiritual redemption. Moreover, as my readings demonstrate, for black women, the relationships among sexuality, spirituality, identity, and political agency are transnationally, transculturally, and transhistorically coterminous.

This study proposes a critical reading of explicit and implicit encoding of signs, symbols, characterizations, and themes from African cosmological systems and New World syncretic religions within black women's texts to underscore an African-American or Afro-Caribbean worldview that contests and revises the discursive, theoretical, and conceptual models of Western canonical discourses. Anthropological and ethnographical investigations, such as those proffered in the works of Maya Deren and Robert Farris Thompson, bolster many of the claims I make about the extent to which African derived spirituality informs these works of literature. Audre Lorde's definition of the erotic principle—the reimagining of spirituality and sexuality as interdependent modalities—provides a connecting motif for the chapters, each of which centers on the work of one writer. Spirituality and sexuality emerge as foci around which authors formulate identities that are fully fleshed out and able to serve the external and internal needs of the individual and the community. By analyzing the works of black women writers beginning with Hurston and moving chronologically to Morrison, Adisa, and Danticat, this study traces the development of a black female theory of subjectivity that is predicated on the conviction that both sexuality and spirituality are essential to identity formation, community building, and sociopolitical agency for women.

Zora Neale Hurston's *Their Eyes Were Watching God* begins the tradition of textually foregrounding African spirituality as central to black female subject formation. Throughout the text, Hurston inscribes Janie's spirituality as a significant aspect of her personality that enables her resistance to multiple systems of repression and domination. In addition to numerous references to the Christian concept of God, Hurston evokes, through specific signs and symbols, the presence of the Haitian Voudoun goddess of love and sexuality, Erzulie, as the leitmotif that introduces and sustains the synthesis of spirituality and sexuality in the portrayal of Janie's character.[7] Hurston's connection to Haiti as an anthropologist and true citizen of the black diaspora provides the epistemological basis for claiming the centrality of Haitian folk culture in her work, the principles and beliefs of which are infused throughout the novel. Janie's eroticism represents a radical break from earlier constructions of black female sexuality in the literary tradition of New World black people. Hurston's willingness to engage with this model of female subjectivity was a political act, and one that was decidedly radical for her time. With it, she laid the groundwork for a model of black female subjectivity that would reconnect sex and God-consciousness, spirit and flesh, in the making of a nonidealized, possibly self-contradictory, assuredly self-seeking, folk-directed, black woman whose ontological motivation is a divine quest for wholeness.

Joan Dayan explains that the Haitian Voudoun goddess, or loa, Erzulie "dramatizes a specific historiography of women's experiences in Haiti and throughout the Caribbean."[8] In a close reading of *Their Eyes Were Watching God* that builds on the work of Daphne Lamothe, I demonstrate how Hurston's text extends Erzulie's historiography to the African-American context, thus making Janie both subject and sign and linking the experiences of black women in the Caribbean to the experiences of African-American women (Lamothe 165–87).

There are definitive intertextual connections between Hurston and her successor, Toni Morrison, and in chapter 2, I explore the continuities that build upon the erotic model of black female subjectivity. In *Eroticism, Spirituality, and Resistance*, I trace and substantiate Morrison's use of African and African New World religions in *Beloved* through essays written by Morrison, an interview between Morrison scholars that demonstrates Morrison's research into the ethnographic studies of Robert Farris Thompson in preparation for writing *Beloved*, and through *The Black Book*, which was edited by Morrison long before *Beloved* was written. I then analyze the sign systems of Haitian Voudoun in Morrison's text through a nexus of spiritual symbols and images that permeate the work. Beloved's unknowability and mystique highlights the fact that Hoodoo and Voudoun, like many African spiritual practices, are shrouded in mystery for the uninitiated New World black person. As mentioned above, many New World blacks possess only a fragmented knowledge of African spiritual practices. Even when they are familiar with certain symbols through everyday folk contact (such as the use of herbs), uninitiated New World blacks are generally ignorant of the intricate systems of knowledge and spiritual empowerment from which certain folk symbols emanate, and of the broader codifications and richly symbolic systems they represent.

Morrison also consolidates several important features of West African belief systems from Yoruba cosmology in *Beloved*. The figure of Amy Denver, the working-class white woman in the novel, embodies characteristics of Yoruba goddesses Yemonja and Oshun. But perhaps no other passage in *Beloved* invokes New World religious signification more profoundly than the lovemaking scene between Beloved and Paul D in which Beloved, like Janie in *Their Eyes Were Watching God*, appears to embody the characteristics of the Haitian Voudoun deity Erzulie. Beloved's true name, "Red Heart," is finally recognized and loudly proclaimed by Paul D as he approaches orgasm. Joan Dayan informs us that the symbol of a heart pierced with a dagger is the primary sign that identifies the Voudoun loa Erzulie-Dantor, "the black woman of passion identified in Catholic chromolithographs with Mater Salvatoris" ("Erzulie: A Woman's History of Haiti" 2). In the Haitian Vèvès or Voudoun flags she is also identified with a dagger pierced through a red heart.

Beloved's link to the Haitian Voudoun goddess Erzulie signals a continuation of narrative dialogue between Hurston and Morrison in this study. Hurston inscribes Janie's Erzulie-like characteristics within the purview of human interactions, thus making her character credible to an earlier twentieth-century audience whose views on African religions were informed by Western stereotypes that promoted the demonizing of African and African-derived spiritual practices. However, Morrison is able to draw upon her readers' familiarity with the tradition of magical realism in literature, as well as upon various credible ethnographic and anthropological sources of the later twentieth century to provide a model for Beloved's multiple and conflicting identities as goddess and woman, child and ghost. Sethe, Baby Suggs, Paul D, and almost every other character in *Beloved* suffer from physical, spiritual, sexual, and emotional violence that interrupts the process of subject formation. Beloved's excessive and disruptive sexuality represents a transgressive model of eroticism that enacts a counterhegemonic discourse through which to read, reinscribe, and reconstitute the healthy synthesis of sexual and spiritual energies as a necessary antidote against the vitiating effects of slavery on the African-American spirit and flesh.

Opal Palmer Adisa's first novel, *It Begins with Tears*, represents a more contemporary revision of the Janie paradigm. Set in a fictional village in rural Jamaica, Adisa's novel interrogates contesting ideologies and values vis-à-vis notions of progress and modernity in the late twentieth century. Adisa's text does not privilege tradition at the expense of progress, but neither does it oversimplify the challenge that modernity represents to a way of life that is steeped in the traditional values of communality and interdependence. Rather, Adisa's text uses a female-centered, Afro-Caribbean spirituality as the bridge between two competing ideologies (modernity and tradition) whose oppositional imperatives threaten the cohesion and stability of the community. Drawing upon the syncretic religious traditions of Jamaica, Adisa uses strong female characters modeled after West African orishas and linked with nature to demonstrate the coterminous relationship between individual female empowerment and sociopolitical viability for the community. The foregrounding of female sexual agency within Adisa's text links sexuality and spirituality as coterminous sources of female empowerment and political agency.

Adisa's codification of the erotic as both spiritual and sexual energy takes place at several levels within the text: through the singular and conflated identities of Yoruba divinities Yemonja and Oshun; through reverence for and respectful recognition of the healing properties of elements supplied by the natural world, such as trees, rivers, and herbs; through the identification of women as healers, free sexual agents, nurturers, community builders, and spiritual leaders; and through carefully constructed images that show the interconnectedness of sensuality, sexuality, spirituality, and personal and political agency.

In the final chapter, I discuss Edwidge Danticat's representation of subject formation within the Haitian migrant community in the Dominican Republic during the 1930s. The chapter explores Danticat's treatment of the concomitant destabilization of Haitian identity in the wake of the 1937 Haitian Massacre enacted under the former Dominican dictator General Rafael Trujillo. The interdependent relationship between the material and the spiritual is carefully introduced in this narrative as Danticat attempts to demonstrate that human beings need to have both realms in balance if they are to be fully functional. My discussion of *The Farming of Bones* foregrounds the efficacy of female sexuality as a trope through which interrogations about the nature of subjectivity, the meaning of historical trauma, and the relationship between spiritual health and political autonomy are filtered, examined, contested, and revised. My study proposes that Danticat purposefully downplays Voudoun as a leitmotif in this novel to force the reader to engage with the historical realities she is fictionalizing, namely the 1937 massacre of approximately thirty thousand Haitian migrant laborers in the Dominican Republic. However, in its structural organization and symbolic orientation, *Farming of Bones* exposes Voudoun as the basis for the Haitian folk philosophy, the "absent presence" that haunts Danticat's text.[9] Voudoun interpolates the narrative at crucial points in Amabelle's storytelling. These instances represent formative, life-changing moments for Amabelle, and in each of these moments Voudoun's hidden presence asserts itself in subtle symbolic glimpses that disrupt the thread of the narrative and allow Amabelle a certain *connaissance* (spiritual power and insight) she does not normally possess.[10] The imagery, metaphors, and symbols of Voudoun, while not always inscribed, are strategically encoded as narrative tropes that invoke memory, ancestry, culture, history, survival, and continuity. They mimetically recall a worldview that is specific to the Haitian folk experience, while simultaneously linking Haitians to other New World blacks.

But what do Amabelle, Janie, Monica, Arnella, Sethe, Beloved, Denver, and other fictional characters have to do with today's black woman? How are they relevant? Studies such as the one contextualized by Thulani Davis, clearly indicate that the majority of young black women whose overexposed bodies dominate popular culture are spiritually and sexually out of balance. They lack autonomy and are not in charge of their image, nor are they active agents in its appropriation and dissemination. Many of them do not even get paid for appearing in music videos, and are exploited by producers and demeaned by rap singers in lyrics and visual presentations in a manner that evokes comparisons to Sara Baartman, whose body was placed on display in nineteenth-century Paris and London.

Given the complex and problematic historiography of black women's sexual discursivity and their continued exploitation in contemporary popular arenas, *Eroticism, Spirituality, and Resistance* reads a viable corrective in the writings of black women across the diaspora. Like Audre Lorde, who worked tirelessly until her death to challenge systems of domination on behalf of all the marginalized identities to which she laid fierce claim, Zora Neale Hurston, Toni Morrison, Opal Palmer Adisa, and Edwidge Danticat have clearly established themselves as activist writers. These authors create with the intention of producing work that will have relevance to the lives of black women in particular, to women in general, and to society at large. Their writing, therefore, is a fundamentally political act as well as an act of restoration. They do it with a sense of urgency born of love and respect for black women as well as for all women. Where this study fails to clarify the deliberate integration of their political motives with their literary ambitions, the failure is my own and not theirs. Where it demonstrates the symbiosis of literary ambition with political acts of love and the integration of the sacred and the profane, it is a testament to the literary genius and political commitment of African diasporic women writers.

1

The Cult of Nineteenth-Century Black Womanhood

> The four primary criteria for judging a woman's suitability for her influential role as wife and mother were her "piety, purity, submissiveness and domesticity." Special attention was given to the ideal of purity, for perceived sexual immodesty—and any expression of overt sexuality might qualify as such—could banish one from the realm of womanhood entirely.... Such a prescription makes clear that the cult of true womanhood was never assumed to include all women.
>
> Candice Jenkins, *Private Lives, Proper Relations*

From the time of the black woman's first appearance on the New World stage, her moral character was beleaguered by vituperative stereotypes steeped in pseudoscientific myth, virulent rumor, and salacious fallacy. As a consequence, black women were conflicted regarding the issue of sexuality. How could they not be? Most sought refuge in silence and repression. Still, there were others who attempted to rehabilitate black female sexuality by displacing it onto more acceptable discursive terrains. Such varied and disparate attempts to repress and even suppress black female sexuality resulted in a disturbing lacuna in the literature produced by black writers from the nineteenth century until well into the Harlem Renaissance period. Black women, in these texts, are disallowed sexual expression.

In "Black Bodies, White Bodies: Toward an Iconography of Female Sexuality in Late Nineteenth-Century Art, Medicine, and Literature," Sander Gilman argues convincingly that by the eighteenth century, the sexuality of black men and women was already a metonym for sexual deviance (212). Gilman asserts that early travel literature, dating as far back as the twelfth century, commented on the apelike sexual appetite of black people and speculated that black women copulated with apes. When Europeans encountered the original inhabitants of South Africa (formerly misnamed Hottentots but now known as Khoisans to denote their relationship to the Bushmen or San people), they considered the Africans the lowest rung upon the great chain of being. Europeans fastened upon the physical differences between the anatomy of so-called Hottentot women and the European female to justify the difference/deviance model they had concocted. These comparisons provided more fodder for European theories of black inferiority.

Sara, or Saartjie, Baartman was born in 1789 and was working as an enslaved person in Cape Town when she was "discovered" by the British doctor William Dunlop. Dunlop convinced Sara to travel with him to London, telling her that she would be paid handsomely for her services. When Dunlop arrived in London with Sara, he placed her on exhibition as a scientific curiosity. Her buttocks and genitalia, considered abnormally large, were placed on display, causing a public scandal in London in 1810. The discourse of abolition had already permeated English society. Londoners were becoming sensitized to the dehumanizing treatment of blacks under slavery. Because of the objections raised in London, Sara was taken to Paris, and again she was displayed like a circus freak. There she remained for the next five years until she fell ill and died in 1815 at the age of twenty-five.

One famous nineteenth-century reproduction of Sara Baartman's body shows a black woman with a protruding derriere that appears excessively large in comparison to the buttocks of the white men and one white woman represented with her in the drawing.[1] However exaggerated this drawing may have been, and however "abnormal" Sara may have appeared in comparison to other Khoisan women, is anyone's guess. Gilman contends that Sara was not the only African woman to be displayed nude in public: "in 1829 a nude Hottentot woman, also called the Hottentot Venus, was the prize attraction at a ball given by the Duchess Du Barry in Paris. A contemporary print emphasized her physical difference from the observers portrayed" (213). The central proof of sexual difference/deviance that attended these stories of so-called Hottentot women rested not on the fact that their anatomical structures were abnormal when compared to those of other Africans, but that they were considered grotesque in comparison to European women. Hence, Sara, and others like her, represented proof of the fact that Africans were different and therefore subhuman. Naturally, these differences constituted inferiority to whites according to the constructions of difference that attended contemporary European discourses of the racialized "other."

Gilman's essay highlights central themes in the association of black female sexuality with sexual deviance. First and foremost, there is no doubt that Europeans in the Victorian era associated the buttocks with sexuality, and female buttocks with sexual deviance. In his famous studies of human sexuality, Sigmund Freud established the link between deviant sexuality and women: "female genitalia is more primitive than that of male, for female sexuality is more anal than that of the male" (Gilman 219). In addition, Europeans were fascinated with the black woman's body, and especially with her derriere, which was rounder and fuller than that of the average European woman. Gilman's comments on Victorians' obsession with the black female anatomy confirms this: "when the Victorians saw the female black, they saw her in terms of her buttocks and saw represented by the buttocks all the anomalies of her genitalia" (219). Another racially eroticized caricature shows a black woman being observed through a telescope by a white man. Although she is fully dressed, her ample derriere obscures his view of the rest of her body, or, put another way, her bottom is the focal point of his gaze. The rest of her body is obscured, not because it is not visible in the picture, but because he is completely preoccupied with her bottom to the exclusion of everything else. The visual narrative presented by this caricature is obfuscated: which figure is sexually deviant—the observer or the object of the gaze? To this observer, the sexual obsession lies with the European man who is actively engaged in gazing at the black woman through a telescope. Yet the black woman—the object of the gaze—is constructed as sexually deviant. Her bottom is raised in the air as if she is flaunting it in his face. Moreover, the black woman's back is turned to the man, and her head faces forward away from him. Her posture, though clearly meant to be read sexually, could also indicate bending in a posture related to work.[2] Furthermore, she is being viewed through a telescope, which suggests that she is some distance away from the observer and her awareness of his gaze is unlikely. Yet, because her anatomy is different (and of course this difference is entirely configured from the perspective of a European male observer), the stigma of sexual deviance inheres in her persona, not his (Gilman 220, fig. 8).[3]

This difference/deviance model in which black women were portrayed in Europe as both grotesque and fascinating, repulsive and yet so strangely compelling that Europeans would go to great lengths to view their bodies, is reproduced in the discourse that attended nineteenth-century American slavery. Furthermore, given the fact that white men did not stop at visual objectification, but went out of their way to secure sexual unions with black women through measures as extreme as violent rape and sexual coercion, how should a twenty-first-century reader assess this difference/deviance model in which the "other" is presented as both an extreme and a familiar? Is sexual deviance a projection of white male sexual fantasy about the "other" external to him or the "other" in himself?

In his writings, Thomas Jefferson associated the nature of blacks with unbridled and deviant sexuality, yet the evidence suggests that this did not stop him from seeking sexual liaisons with black women. Jefferson maligned black female sexuality by discursively positioning black women in sexual relations with orangutans, claiming that the orangutan male preferred the black female to its own species (Peterson 187). This example is just one of many that demonstrate how the pseudoscientific discourse of black inferiority provided the continued justification for subjugation and sexual domination of black women under slavery. White men, unable or unwilling to control their own deviant sexuality, played upon already extant ideologies of black female hypersexuality to rationalize their extramarital sexual liasions with female slaves. These pseudoscientific arguments produced and justified the perception that black female sexuality was abnormal and bestial, and that white men had no control over themselves when confronted with the voracious sexual appetites of the aberrant black females. Deborah Gray White demonstrates the insidious dialectics within which pseudoscience, rumors, and myths colluded to justify the systematic raping of black women:

> by the nineteenth century, coarse jokes about "negro wenches" were commonplace, and both Northerners and Europeans accepted the premise upon which they rested. Alexander Wilson, a European poet, wrote from Savannah that "the negro wenches are all sprightliness and gaiety." Citing circulating rumors, he continued, "if report be not a defamor," the sexual habits of black women, "render the men callous to all the finer sensations of love and female excellence." Another visitor, Johann Schoepf, wrote that "in almost every house there are negresses, slaves, who count it an honor to bring a mulatto into the world." Even the abolitionist James Redpath wrote that mulatto women were "gratified by the criminal advances of Saxons." (30)

The proliferation and wide dissemination of these myths and misrepresentations resulted in the entrenchment of sexual stereotyping and the denigration of black women in nineteenth-century public discourses. From Candice Jenkins's words in the epigraph to this chapter, one can infer the silences, distortions, and erasures of black female subjectivity that were produced by these discourses. Echoing Hazel Carby's famous study, Jenkins and other critics comment on the four cardinal virtues of the cult of true womanhood that rendered black women "non-women." For if a woman had to be pious, (sexually) pure, submissive, and domestic, where did that leave black women who were sexually coerced out of virtue and piety and then sent out to work in someone else's field or house? Black women, by the definition of the cult of true womanhood, could not be "true women." If not "true women," they had to be the opposite: fallen women.

Numerous studies on early European gender discourses foreground the now commonplace idea that the category "woman," seen as "other" to the "normative" white male, was subjected to pseudoscientific stereotyping that shaped and justified the hierarchical position white men assumed over their female counterparts. Studies such as Sander Gilman's argue cogently that European men aligned women's sexuality with sexual deviance. The emergence of the European prostitute—the ultimate "fallen" woman—epitomized and made credible extant ideas vis-à-vis female sexual deviance. However, critics also agree that the existence of this stereotype did not categorically abase all white women. After all, for the fallen woman to exist she had to have her corollary in the "good" woman. The "good" woman was the woman who fit the definition of the cult of true womanhood. Furthermore, the fallen woman could be discursively uplifted and redeemed if she were white.

In "The Rise of the Fallen Woman," Nina Auerbach discusses the potentially "transformative power" of the "fall," which enabled white female characters such as Nathaniel Hawthorne's Hester Prynne to ascend to the iconic status of "empowered and transfigured womanhood" in the critical reception of Hawthorne's novel in the nineteenth century (38). Such was not the fate of the "fallen" black woman in discourse, literature, or life. Auerbach's depiction of one fallen white woman—Hetty Sorrel in George Eliot's *Adam Bede*—as persistently linked throughout Eliot's narrative with "lower forms of life," parallels the myth of black inferiority and is consistent with the abasement of black womanhood in a discourse that posits her as immoral and promiscuous beyond redemption (45). Given that both blacks and women were viewed as lower forms of life, it is easy to see how race and gender stereotypes were conjoined to vilify black women in nineteenth-century discourses.

How did black women react to this ideology that presented them as less than pure, and less than women? In "Toward a Genealogy of Black Female Sexuality: The Problematic of Silence," Evelynn Hammonds argues trenchantly that black women reformers developed a strategy to counter the systematic denigration of their characters that made it possible for white men to justify sexually exploiting black women. The strategy, according to Hammonds, involved "the politics of silence," which included reverting to

Victorian standards of morality and repressing black female sexuality to demonstrate that the stereotypes had no basis in fact (97). In effect, the "politics of silence" delimited sexual expression for black women in both public and private spheres.

By the late nineteenth century, black women had achieved remarkable progress as physicians, dentists, lawyers, ministers, journalists, writers, artists, musicians, and schoolteachers. They had positioned themselves to take their rightful place as "race leaders" for the social, economic, and political uplift of the black community, but found their efforts thwarted by discrimination against black women in the industrial sector bolstered by a public discourse that foregrounded the moral degradation and natural inferiority of black women. One white male writer for the *Independent* wrote that he could not conceive of "such a creature as a virtuous negro woman" (Giddings 82). Black women were frustrated by the fact that there was no strong race leadership and no platform from which to defend themselves against wholesale character assassination.

It was at this historical juncture that Ida B. Wells emerged on the scene with her antilynching platform. Black women's political and social clubs, which became a prominent feature of the movement for social change in American race relations, grew out of the impetus created by Wells's political platform. Wells's forceful resistance and eloquent speeches galvanized nascent race leaders such as Victoria Earle Matthews, Susan McKinney, and Josephine St. Pierre Ruffin, the co-organizers of the first black women's clubs in New York and Boston. The historian Paula Giddings states: "between 1892 and 1894, clubs proliferated throughout the country, from Omaha to Pittsburg, Rhode Island to New Orleans, Denver to Jefferson City" (83).

The Women's Era, edited by Josephine Ruffin, created a platform from which to challenge the systematic denigration of black women and promote black women's agendas for racial advancement and women's progress. There was a downside, however. In their zeal to discredit the falsehoods that deliberately maligned the moral character of the black woman, these activist women created a climate of sexual repression and silence surrounding the subject of black female sexuality. This culture of silence and denial had a most enduring impact, and, in the long run, proved almost as damaging to black women as the most vituperative prevarications of their white male detractors.

In "*The Changing Same*," Deborah McDowell argues that black clubwomen were instrumental in the repression of black female sexual expression and that their influence was extremely effective in transforming sexual behavior among blacks nationwide. Citing a letter written by a white editor that severely attacked the moral character of all black women, McDowell underscores the slanderous atmosphere that galvanized black clubwomen into action (37). In trying to protect themselves and their community from denigration, black clubwomen insisted upon the systematic denial of black women's sexual expression.

The critic Candice Jenkins names this desire for the restoration of the black woman's reputation "the salvific wish": "a longing to protect or save black women, and black communities more generally, from narratives of sexual and familial pathology, through the embrace of conventional bourgeois propriety in the arenas of sexuality and domesticity" (14). Clubwomen were aided and abetted by their black male counterparts, who wanted to preserve an image of respectability for the race and counter the damaging stereotypes that justified the continued oppression of black people.

Hazel Carby's examination of the historiography of black female subjectivity is instructive in its depiction of the legacy of shame black women inherited as a result of these hurtful and damaging stereotypes.[4] According to the cult of true womanhood, white women were expected to "civilize" the baser instincts of their men. But, Carby argues, "in the face of what was construed as the overt sexuality of the black female, excluded as she was from the perimeters of virtuous possibilities, these baser male instincts were entirely uncontrolled" (*Reconstructing Womanhood* 27). And indeed, if the slave narratives are to be believed, the white male slave owner was in dire need of "civilizing" influences. Narrative after narrative portrays his predatory sexual behavior vis-à-vis enslaved black women.

In *Narrative of the Life of Frederick Douglass*, Douglass describes a horrible beating he witnessed as a child. His Aunt Hester, who had "very few equals, and fewer superiors, in personal appearance, among the colored or white women" of the community, had been subjected to the beating by her master, Captain Anthony (51–52). Determined to keep Aunt Hester's sexual affections for himself, Captain Anthony had forbidden her to go out at night. When he discovered that she had been out with a male slave from a neighboring plantation, he stripped her naked and whipped her until her blood dripped to the floor (52).[5]

Similarly, Harriet Jacobs's *Incidents in the Life of a Slave Girl* depicts her life as a teenage slave whose carefully sheltered innocence (guarded by her devoutly Christian grandmother) was shattered by the aggressive sexual advances of her master. Jacobs's master did not brutally rape her as many might have done, but instead used emotional blackmail, beatings, death threats, and many similar tactics akin to psychological terrorism to force her to submit to him sexually. Her refusal maddened him and provoked even more outrageous reprisals. When she was sixteen, she fell in love with a free black man, but her master berated and insulted her when she told him of her desire to be married. Heartbroken, she plunged into despair and broke off her engagement. Mr. Flint continued to pursue her relentlessly, verbally and emotionally abusing her when he could not have his way with her. Finally, in defiance, she gave herself to another white man who had befriended her. She reasoned: "it seems less degrading to give one's self, than to submit to compulsion" (385). Jacobs believed that by defying and humiliating her master she could goad him into selling her and the children she conceived by her white lover, Mr. Sands. But Mr. Flint was incensed that she had outsmarted him and became even more hardened against her. He was more determined than ever that Jacobs, and now her children too—who were rightly his property (as children born to slave women followed the condition of the mother)—would never be free.

These accounts of the predatory sexual practices to which black women were submitted clearly demonstrate that they were the ones in dire need of protection from their masters. If the slave woman was a "direct threat to the conjugal sanctity of the white mistress," it was certainly through no deliberate machinations of her own (Carby, *Reconstructing Womanhood* 27). To heartlessly blame her for the rape and abuse to which she was subjected (as she was blamed by contemporary sexual discourses) was a flagrant example of blaming the victim.[6] Jacobs's account shows that "civilizing" the slave master was no easy task. Mrs. Flint went to extreme measures to curtail her husband's pursuit of Harriet, all to no avail. In none of these accounts does the black female emerge as overtly sexual. In fact, Jacobs went to great pains to construct her relationship with Mr. Sands as a strategy of resistance against Mr. Flint. It is only after she discovers that Mr. Flint is building a house in which to install her as his mistress, far from the watchful eyes of his vigilant wife, that she begins the affair with the hope of foiling his plan and making herself less desirable to him once she is no longer "virtuous."

While attempting to define the parameters of sexual morality for women, the cult of true womanhood effectively reproduced double-vitiation for the black woman. Under the terms of this ideology, she just could not win for losing. Harriet Jacobs, in *Incidents in the Life of a Slave Girl*, employs interesting narrative strategies to convince her predominantly white female readership that she should not be judged by the same sexual standards as white women. Carby explains:

> Jacobs's letters to Amy Post, although to a friend, revealed her consciousness of their different positions in relation to conventional moral codes. Desiring a female friend who could write some prefatory remarks to her narrative, Jacobs consulted Post, but the occasion led her to indicate that the inclusion of her sexual history in her narrative made her "shrink from asking the sacrifice from one so good and pure as yourself." (*Reconstructing Womanhood* 48)

Jacobs's appeal to white women to understand why she had children out of wedlock was an appeal for them to understand why she had sex before marriage, even though she entered into that sexual relationship of her own volition. Jacobs gives the reader the impression that she chose a white male lover over her master as a way of heading off the master's advances, and to protect any likely offspring from the vicissitudes of the slave machinery. Nowhere in this appeal does she reveal sexual desire; sex is shameful, and when its evidence comes to light, apologies are necessary to restore the good name of the fallen woman or at least to garner sympathetic understanding of the predicament that led her to engage in sex outside of marriage. However, Jacobs's text stands as testament to the fact that such understanding was never guaranteed; Harriet's beloved grandmother drives her from her home when she discovers that her granddaughter's virtue has been compromised and tells her, "I would rather see you dead than to see you as you are" (Jacobs 387).

Despite their strategies to subvert and challenge the cult of true womanhood, black women found that the way they were perceived by white America, their own public expression, and even their private lives were overdetermined by this ideology. Hazel Carby documents the subversive narrative techniques employed by black women writing in the nineteenth century to counter the ideological hold of the cult of true womanhood, and demonstrates how the ideology "determined the shape of the public voice of black women writers" (*Reconstructing Womanhood* 40). Both Harriet Jacobs in *Incidents in the Life of a Slave Girl* and Mary Prince in her *Life and Travels* questioned the relevance of the ideology of the cult of true womanhood for black women and condemned the hypocrisy that undergirded notions of sexual purity and morality for women when black women were subject to rape as a matter of course.[7]

In addition to operating as the blueprint for patriarchal control of female sexual behavior, the cult of true womanhood relied on the equally dominant ideology of Christianity to ensure its institutionalization. Manipulated and appropriated to fit the needs of the slave system and white patriarchal privilege, Christianity's application in fulfilling the objectives of slave-based capitalism is well documented.[8] Black women who were raised to be "good" Christian girls (like Harriet Jacobs) were especially vulnerable to feelings of shame about their sexuality.

However, the evidence suggests that black women also used Christianity in subversive ways to counter that shame-engendering discourse. For the black woman, sexual desire was encased in such a powerful ideology of shame that the natural reaction on her part was to deny its existence. Christianity provided black women with an alternative language through which to articulate their claims to good moral character. The literary history of black women as writers demonstrates that they also appropriated the morality and language of extant Christian doctrine to provide themselves a bulwark against the oppressive ideology of the cult of true womanhood and its negation of the institutionalized rape of black women. Both Harriet Jacobs and Mary Prince, in challenging the system of slavery, assumed rhetorical positions of moral superiority not annexed to standards of sexual purity, but rather informed by humanistic principles of justice, fairness, empathy, and cofraternity with other human beings, principles that are themselves fundamental to Judeo-Christian doctrine.

Similarly, Harriet Wilson, in *Our Nig*, which Carby rightly argues is an allegory to a slave narrative and uses similar narrative conventions, clearly assumes a position of moral superiority over Mrs. Bellmont, the white woman for whom she labors as a domestic servant, and who treats her like a slave. Claudia Tate observes: "Frado's psychological liberation occurs when she claims that her Christian conversion gives her the authority to refuse to accept her mistress Mrs. Bellmont's repeated physical abuse" (82). It becomes clear that black women writers who specialized in slave narratives and related genres were able to employ the teachings of the Christian doctrine in their counternarratives to establish good moral character and a sense of self.

However, insofar as the cult of true womanhood also relied upon the teachings of Judeo-Christian doctrine to establish proper female behavior, Christianity's usefulness to black women as a tool of resistance against this ideology was severely limited. Sex, discursively constituted within the framework of Judeo-Christian morality, was already considered "sinful" outside of marriage. As a result, the cult of true womanhood found covalence in the teachings of Christianity. Black women's spiritual narratives evince this duality in Christian doctrine.

Katherine Bassard's *Spiritual Interrogations* demonstrates, in no uncertain terms, that black women's early literary productions—many of which foregrounded spirituality—were neither empirically nor epistemologically monolithic. From Phillis Wheatley's poetry (eighteenth century), to Ann Plato's essays and poems (written in the early part of the nineteenth century), to the later nineteenth-century writings of Jarena Lee (an African Methodist preacher), and Rebecca Cox Jackson (a Shaker elder committed to the doctrine and practice of celibacy), Bassard interrogates "private encounters with Spirit" that conferred subjectivity upon African-American women who were denied it in other social arenas (3). Yet despite the evidence that these writings were used strategically to empower black women as both speakers and writers, they all demonstrate the limitations placed on black women's sexual expression. Jarena Lee, Julia Foote, Maria Stewart, Rebecca Cox Jackson, and others were able to use their authority as divine messengers to subvert hegemonic imperatives that effectively barred blacks and women from full participation in the social and political arenas of American society. These women used their roles as bringers of "the Word" to insert themselves into national discourses, and in so doing claimed a space and a voice for themselves through the authority of none other than God himself. The irony of their dual missions is representative of the discursive ingenuity black women employed to insinuate their voices into national dialogue.[9]

Although they addressed spiritual issues of import to all Americans—and especially to blacks—their reflections on female sexuality were often either nonexistent or subsumed under and shaped by a discourse of sanctification and piety.[10] As a Shaker, Rebecca Cox Jackson may have been the most radical, eschewing sexual relations altogether and preaching celibacy as the way to salvation (Bassard 9). In her essay "Religion and the Pure Principles of Morality, the Sure Foundation on Which We Must Build," Maria Stewart takes a less extreme stance. Stewart suggests that the salvation of the black race rested upon the cultivation of "piety, morality and virtue" among blacks, with the burden resting more heavily on the black woman (6).[11] By virtue of their calling, their race, their sex, and their time, these spiritual warriors inherited discursive modes that mandated against sexual expressivity for black women: Judeo-Christian negation of female sexuality, and the racist and sexist narratives of carnal licentiousness that so unfairly painted black women as inherently "fallen" when subjected to the ideals of the cult of true womanhood.[12]

Jackson, Lee, Foote, Stewart, and others were not just purveyors of Christianity; they were "called" to deliver the teachings of Christ's doctrine, and their very existence as black women traveling and teaching God's word was transgressive and revolutionary.[13] However, this radicalism did not extend to a revised interpretation of standard biblical teachings with respect to female sexual behavior. Sexuality and spirituality, deemed separate and opposing modalities by the extant teachings of Christian theology, had to remain that way in black female ministry to restore the moral character of the black female from the "fallen woman" status that the slave masters and the cult of true womanhood had imposed upon her.

In her introduction to the Schomburg 1988 edition of *Spiritual Narratives*, Susan Houchins identifies the following chronological steps in the path to spiritual mysticism revealed in spiritual texts:

> First, during a period of purification, the individual recalls her past life, reviews her autobiographical data—so to speak—attains profound self-knowledge, and is overcome with remorse. Second, along the mystic way, God enlightens her, reveals to her esoteric theological truths, sometimes bestows a gift of deeply erotic visions, which symbolize the depth of their shared mystical love, and promises her eternal salvation. (xxxiv)

Images of the body and of a male Christ figure covering, overpowering, or joining with the body of female mystics also characterize the experiences of the black women who wrote spiritual narratives. Julia Foote, in "A Brand Plucked from the Fire," writes of her sanctification in sexually evocative language: "the glory of God seemed almost to prostrate me to the floor. There was, indeed, a weight of glory resting upon me" (43). Similarly, in her baptism scene, she writes: "My hand was given to Christ, who led me into the water and stripped me of my clothing, which at once vanished from sight. Christ then appeared to wash me, the water feeling quite warm" (70). Jarena Lee writes: "That instant, it appeared to me as if a garment, which had entirely enveloped my whole person, even to my fingers, split at the crown of my head, and was stripped away from me, passing like a shadow from my sight—when the glory of God seemed to cover me—Great was the ecstasy of my mind" (Houchins xxxvii). These writers' narration of spiritual passion evokes the language of sexual desire and fulfillment. Religious ecstasy, the desire to be filled with the Holy Ghost and possessed by the spirit of God, becomes the only sanctioned way for black women to speak about bodily passions. Sexual desire, since it cannot be expressed openly, must be subsumed under spiritual possession and sanctification. This is not to delegitimize the experience and meaning of sanctification for these women. Houchins insists: "the incarnation, then, is discursive like prayer, like autobiography. And one site of this discourse is woman's body—"(xxxviii). Although many of these spiritual narrators were married, all references to their bodies—and to feelings of passion—were channeled through the discourse of sanctification.

Clearly, the only safe space in which nineteenth-century black women could speak of desire was within the discourse of religious mysticism. For, as Jenkins observes, the black woman was forced to adopt bourgeois convention not just to protect her reputation, but also in order to protect herself physically from predatory white men (13).[14] If, instead of being sexually promiscuous, the black woman was, in fact, "pure and virtuous," white men could not justify sexually abusing her. In this way, black women used the ideology of true womanhood to gain the protected status that it offered to white women, knowing full well it was never meant for them (Jenkins 13). Given the severity of the violence—discursive and actual—to which black bodies were subjected (through rape, lynching, and other forms of terror endemic to the institution of slavery and extending into the post-Reconstruction era), the surrender of black female sexuality may have seemed like a small price to pay for physical safety and peace of mind.[15]

The suppression and displacement of black female sexuality in literature carried over to the early twentieth century, when it annexed to the black man's burden of proving himself worthy of equal treatment in American society. To make a case for equality, he had to earn it, and therefore had to prove that he was morally, spiritually, and intellectually the equal of the white man. There was also an indefinite moratorium placed on sexual expression in writing for blacks of both sexes. One instruction for contributions to a journal written by the Harlem Renaissance writer George Schuyler—famous for his radically assimilationist posture in the essay "The Negro Art Hokum"—clearly states: "nothing that casts the least reflection on contemporary moral or sex standards must be allowed. Keep away from the erotic! Contributions must be clean and wholesome."[16] Schuyler's views were shared by many influential black leaders and writers including W.E.B. Du Bois, Jessie Fauset, and Alain Locke. These African-American leaders hailed from highly privileged backgrounds, and they believed that the salvation of their race rested upon the abilities of the "talented tenth."[17] To them, white acceptance of black humanity—which could only be proven by black approximation to whiteness in values, education, aesthetic taste, artistic expression, and spiritual integrity—depended upon blacks presenting the best possible facade in the public sphere, and especially in their writing (through which they were already proving themselves able competitors). Writers like Claude McKay, Langston Hughes, and Zora Neale Hurston were strongly criticized for representing the seamier side of black life, and especially black working-class life.[18]

This desire on the part of black leadership for legitimization—through American standardization—resulted in popular novels from the 1920s that showed a marked reticence to render black female sexuality within the bounds of healthy sexual desire. This was especially the case with the "passing" narratives. Passing narratives exploited white anxiety over miscegenation by dramatizing the plight of so-called "tragic mulatto" characters whose loyalties were divided between both races.[19] These protagonists were trapped in a perpetual state of confusion and self-hatred, generally loathing their blackness but disallowed any legal or social claim to their white lineage. The dialectic between sexual repression and sexual desire shaped the contours of the passing narrative, operating as a subtext of the racial indeterminacy that constituted the larger framework of the tragic mulatto genre. Racial dualism, psychic anxiety, sexual inconstancy and indeterminacy, spiritual disquietude, and moral confusion were prominent features of the tragic mulatto trope.

In this chapter, I focus on Nella Larsen's *Quicksand* and *Passing*, as well as Jessie Fauset's *Plum Bun*, as examples of passing narratives written by black women in the early twentieth century that extend, complicate, but still sacrifice black female sexual expression to the mandate of social respectability. As Deborah McDowell observes, Fauset and Larsen were writing in "the Jazz Age of sexual abandon and free love," when female sexuality was acknowledged and commercialized in the advertising, beauty, and fashion industries" (McDowell, "*The Changing Same*" 80). Yet, McDowell argues, "they lacked the daring of their contemporaries, the female blues singers such as "Bessie, Mamie, 'Clara' Smith (all unrelated), Gertrude 'Ma' Rainey, and Victoria Spivey" who celebrated black female sexuality openly and with abandon in their lyrics (McDowell, 80).

However, Larsen and Fauset were restricted by their class allegiance to the same codes of respectability and fear that undergirded the "salvific wish" of the nineteenth century, and could only "hint at the idea of black women as sexual subjects" (McDowell, 80). As a result, their representations of black women seem stilted, unbalanced, unrealistic, a little neurotic, perhaps even tied to an earlier era when compared against, say, the women in Claude McKay's *Home to Harlem* or even the character Oceola Jones in Langston Hughes's short story, "The Blues I'm Playing."[20] Nella Larsen's tragic mulatta characters are beautiful, desirable, and extremely troubled. However, to be desirable is to be the object of another's gaze. In Larsen's novel *Passing*, Clare, who wants to desire as well as to be desired, has to be expunged from the text before her sexual impropriety can be actualized. Although within the narrative Clare is already inscribed as improper, her impropriety arises from her duping a white man into marrying her by passing as a white woman. Born on the wrong side of the tracks both in terms of class and race, Clare, who is light enough to pass for white, sees an opportunity when her drunken mulatto father dies and she is adopted by his white aunts. The aunts suppress Clare's black identity out of shame for their brother's indiscretion. Clare, interpreting their silence as a chance to obtain the finer things in life that are available only to white women, decides to play along with this omission. Eventually, she meets a man who knows her aunts and assumes Clare is also white. She tricks him into marrying her without her aunts' knowledge. They relocate to parts of the country where no one knows Clare's origins, and she lives a life of luxury and ease as the wife of a wealthy white man.

However, despite her rejection of her race, Clare's happiness is marred by the strange dialectics of "passing." Her husband despises black people, so she is constantly subjected to his racist comments. Moreover, although her daughter appears white, she is plagued by the fear that other children may be born dark, thus revealing her dangerous secret. Clare's sexual relationship with her husband is severely compromised by this fear, and deep inside she also misses black people. Clare's life changes when she runs into a childhood friend, Irene. Irene is also light enough to pass for white, but is married to a black doctor and lives the life of the black bourgeoisie. Irene is a socialite and well known in Harlem. They rekindle their friendship and Clare begins to frequent social gatherings in Harlem. But Irene is ambivalent about Clare. She is attracted to her beauty, and yet repelled by a ruthless streak in Clare's personality that Irene describes as "a having way."

Irene, a "race woman," cannot forgive Clare for abandoning the race in pursuit of the trappings of the white world. The critic Cheryl Wall underscores the irony of Irene's judgment since she herself moves in an elite social circle that is only concerned with keeping up appearances. Wall observes: "Each of these characters, like Clare, relies on a husband for material possessions, security, identity. Each reflects and is a reflection of her husband's class status. Clare's is merely an extreme version of a situation all share" (Wall, "Passing for What?" 107). Irene's feelings for Clare are contradictory. She finds Clare strikingly beautiful, but Irene also envies Clare and sees her as a threat to the stable life she has created for herself. Events come to a head when Irene suspects that Clare may be getting too attached to Harlem and to black people, but especially to Irene's husband, Brian. Clare, for her part, seems to have reached the conclusion that being black was not so bad after all, especially if one could be black Irene-style.

It is important to note at this juncture that while Clare may be "passing" as white, Irene is also "passing" as black. Critics such as Hazel Carby and Cheryl Wall are very critical of the elitism of Irene's social group, modeled after the "talented-tenth" society comprised of the more conservative elements of the Harlem Renaissance literati such as Alain Locke, Du Bois, and Jessie Fauset. Wall argues that "passing" is not just a reference to the social phenomenon of blacks crossing the color line. It represents, as well, the loss of racial identity and the denial of self required for women who conform to restrictive gender codes. Like the term "quicksand," "passing" is a metaphor for death and desperation, and both central metaphors are supported by images of asphyxiation, suffocation, and claustrophobia (Wall, "Passing for What?" 105).

Clare, who was raised in poverty as a child, has never known anything of the black bourgeois life. This is her first exposure to it, and for the first time she realizes that she could have married the "right" black man and thereby passed, like Irene did, without disavowing her blackness. Irene and her social group are not living the typical life of the black masses. Irene is self-serving and an unreliable narrator as many critics observe, but her belief that Clare would pose a threat to her marriage is not unfounded.[21] By her own admission, Clare will do anything to get what she wants. When Clare's husband discovers her racial background and confronts her at the party, Irene panics. The novel ends with Clare plunging to her death from an open window. Did Irene push her? Did Clare's husband? Did she fall accidentally? Larsen leaves the reader to make up his or her own mind. What is indelibly imprinted in the mind of this reader is Clare's racial indeterminacy, which registers her presence within the text as "not safe," a term she uses to describe herself.

Clare's flirtation with both Irene and Irene's husband, Brian, and the fact that she is seen keeping company with other men besides her husband, hint at sexual improprieties that are never confirmed, but are enough to reify her sexual instability and ontological (and narrative) unreliability. Her problematic and ambiguous sexuality is a marker of her transgressive racial identity, as well as her refusal to abide by conventional expectations for blacks and for women. Clare is a tragic mulatta because her identity is unstable. Uncontained and uncontainable, her presence registers excess, disturbing the sanctity of normative racial and gender codes. Her death, obfuscated by mystery just like her life, is inevitable, and further underscores her ontological instability and justifies her discursive erasure.

In Larsen's *Quicksand*, Helga Crane is a beautiful mulatta woman who seems incapable of finding a place where she truly belongs. When the text opens she is teaching at Naxos, a southern university modeled after Tuskegee. Although Helga is engaged to an eligible black man from a stable middle-class background, she is unhappy. Helga hates the repressed, unimaginative life of the middle-class black community at Naxos and abhors their conservative outlook on life and their narrow views on everything from fashion to politics. Helga abruptly resigns her teaching position and eventually ends up in Harlem, where she seems at first to enjoy the lively culture, vibrant social life, and dynamic political climate, worlds apart from the conservatism of Naxos.

But even Harlem loses its charm before long and Helga finds herself discomfited once again, feeling like she does not belong. One night at a cabaret, she gets carried away by the music, and is appalled that she has allowed herself to abandon her inhibitions. She decides she is not a "jungle creature" and resolves to leave Harlem. This time, Helga leaves America for Copenhagen and stays with white relatives of her mother. Deborah McDowell clearly links Helga's retreat from the cabaret scene and from Harlem to her attempt to escape her sexual desires: "Throughout the novel, Helga retreats from these sexual feelings. Wanting to avoid them, she leaves Harlem, the Mecca of the exotic, the primitive, and escapes to Copenhagen" ("*The Changing Same*" 84). Helga is transformed into an exotic spectacle in Europe, dressed up like a doll to be paraded on display in the fashionable social circles frequented by her aunt and uncle. McDowell further observes: "The Danes transformation of Helga into a sexual object continues the familiar pattern in the novel in which Helga is alternately defined by others (primarily men) as a "lady" or a "jezebel" ("*The Changing Same*" 84). She is even offered marriage by a renowned Danish artist, Axel Olsen, who decides that since she refuses to sleep with him, he will marry her to gain her sexual favors. Helga is, of course, insulted and tells him that the men of her race would never make such indecent proposals to respectable girls. Hortense Thornton questions whether Helga's response is not an attempt to feign racial injury "as a mask for her sexual repression" (299).

Helga grows disenchanted with Europe and the European brand of racism and returns home to Harlem after discovering that Dr. Anderson, on whom she has a crush, is engaged to be married. Upon her return to Harlem, Dr. Anderson makes a pass at her. She rebuffs him at first and is insulted by his lack of judgment. However, later she thinks better of it, and decides to approach him in order to gauge his sexual intentions. But because she is sending him mixed signals, he believes he has offended her and apologizes to her for his former indiscretion. Helga perceives Dr. Anderson's apology as a sexual rejection and flees into the cold, rainy night in embarrassment. Distraught, unhappy, wet, miserable, and disheveled, she seeks refuge in a church right at the point when sinners are being called to the altar. The church folk mistake her for a repentant prostitute and her overwrought state of mind is misconstrued as religious conversion. In a state of apathy, disillusionment, and sexual frustration, she goes along with their assumptions. Before long, Helga is married to the minister of the church, having babies, and—you guessed it—she hates it all and wants to run away again.

Like Clare, Helga Crane is also an object of desire for both white and black men, but is only able to express desire within the confines of a marriage that stunts and eventually kills her soul. For the married Helga, sexual desire is masked as submission to the sexual "duties" of a wife as sanctioned by the Christian faith. She seems to find her husband repulsive, although she clearly engages in sexual intercourse with him. Helga's sexual repression, though self-imposed, is informed by the discourse of impropriety that shapes black female sexuality. Larsen's satirizing of the domestic sphere in which Helga finds herself after marriage is a critique of the discourse inherent to the cult of true womanhood, which reifies domesticity. Any potential for female sexual gratification in *Quicksand* is eventually foreclosed by the encroachment of several unwanted pregnancies and the revulsion that Helga develops for her husband, the state of marriage, and the role of motherhood. Helga's children represent an unremitting burden to her, and she longs for escape from the imprisonment of domesticity. However, Helga never manages to escape this final ordeal. The novel ends with yet another pregnancy that drives her into an abysmal state of depression. Hazel Carby argues that this last child represents Helga's "certain death" (*Reconstructing Womanhood* 174).

Carby believes that Larsen's *Quicksand* levels a clear and unstinting critique at the proponents of racial uplift. Her comments suggest that their prodigious racial uplift activities often masked the black elite's desire to "lift" themselves away from the ordinary life and concerns of the black masses. Helga is "disdainful of the ideology of racial uplift, critical of Annie's continual preoccupation with the problems of the race, and disparaging" of the problems encountered by the emerging black middle class (Carby, *Reconstructing Womanhood* 168). This class, she felt, condemned white racism while imitating white middle-class behavior and adopting its social mores (168).

Both *Quicksand* and *Passing* bear out the critique that Wall and Carby level at this elite group within the black community. Larsen, a member of this group, was permitted a critique of the hypocrisy inherent to her own cohort because she couched her insights in a novel. The irony is that Larsen's contemporaries did not seem to see themselves reflected in her pages, and even lauded her work as if her critiques merely complimented their lifestyle and exposed their cultured ways. Perhaps they were so busy focusing on her treatment of the tragic mulatta trope that they missed some of the other tragedies she labored to expose. Or perhaps Larsen's critique lacked "bite" or "rancor" because she was one of her community's privileged few, and her denunciation amounted to little more than self-reflection.

For all her critique of their shallow, hypocritical ways, Helga is also a product of the black elitism she exposes.[22] Larsen's complicity in black elitist mores and conventions concerning female sexuality is what traps her protagonist, Helga, in a role she wishes to be free from, but from which she cannot extricate herself. Larsen seems incapable of writing Helga free of these constraints because Larsen herself cannot imagine a viable alternative. Wall argues that Helga is trapped by the need to conform to middle-class standards of propriety that dictate that she "repress her sexuality, to assume the ornamental, acquiescent role of 'lady,'" which not only Vale but the entire Naxos community expects (Wall, "Passing for What?" 99).

Hortense Thornton insists that *Quicksand* is not a tragic mulatta story.[23] Thornton argues that it is sexism rather than race that holds Helga in its tenacious "quagmire." Thornton claims that unlike the tragic mulatta characters of black fiction, Helga is not a "lost, unhappy, woebegone abstraction," but rather a sensitive woman who has repressed a most significant part of her identity: her sexuality (290). Thornton makes important connections between Helga and her creator, Nella Larsen: "She was a woman, just, like her creator, living in a male dominated society, a woman who repressed her sexuality and thus placed herself in a most vulnerable situation leading to her tragic degeneration" (289).

But despite its complexities, critics can hardly be faulted for reading *Quicksand* as another tragic mulatta text. For one thing, its epigraph features Langston Hughes's poem "Cross," which depicts the dilemma of the tragic mulatto figure. Larsen clearly intended for the novel to be read within the context of that genre. In addition, for many readers—myself included—Helga seems pretty "lost" and "unhappy" throughout the entire text. What temporary happiness she finds is so fleeting that it is gone before either reader or character can settle upon it as a defining feature. Although Helga herself never attempts to pass, it is true that she is never happy in either the white world of Denmark or the black ones of Chicago, Harlem, Naxos, and Alabama. Her isolation (even in a crowd) and radical sense of alienation—an existential angst that is part and parcel of the tragic mulatta portrayal—mark her as a tragic figure. Furthermore, Helga is tragic because she persists in adhering to the moral codes of people she seems not to like or respect, but whose opinions and values mean more to her than her own happiness.

Thornton and I agree on one point that is foundational to her thesis: Helga's greatest tragedy inheres in the fact that sexual expression is denied her, and without it she cannot find fulfillment. I would also add that Helga's misery is exacerbated by a crisis of faith. She has no spiritual grounding and nothing in her life holds or retains meaning. By the novel's end, Helga resents her children and only stays with them out of a sense of obligation. She hates her husband and cannot bear the thought of him touching her. Moreover, she hates the Christian God and is contemptuous of black people for believing in Him. But Helga has absolutely nothing of her own to believe in; her life is completely meaningless and she sees no way out of her misery. Carby's suggestion that Helga dies physically at the end is not narratively actualized, but her spiritual death is repeatedly insinuated.

Carby reads *Quicksand* as "a crisis of the representation of the period" (*Reconstructing Womanhood* 169). According to Carby, by making Helga such an alienated heroine, Larsen proffers a two-pronged critique aimed at the black middle class and at writers who saw "the people" as the rural folk: she indicts the hypocrisy of a black middle class that is preoccupied with racial uplift, yet avoids any sustained contact with the black masses and models itself after white society. Larsen refuses to participate in the romanticization of rural blacks as "the folk" like Hurston and others did, while in the process failing to acknowledge the fact that the urban poor constituted the new "folk" identity.[24] While I would argue that Hurston can hardly be accused of romanticizing the folk in *Their Eyes Were Watching God*, Carby's point that the urban black masses also constitute "the people" is a valid one.[25] However, it seems to me that rather than advocating the shift of folk identification from rural to urban blacks, more might be gained from recognizing the continuities between these two groups, both of which constitute "the people." Carby's point forces one to consider the rich layering to be found in a juxtaposition of these two visions of the folk in one narrative. Rudolf Fisher's "The City of Refuge" comes readily to mind. Quintessentially postmodern, both versions of the folk are provocatively and complexly represented in Fisher's narrative.

Sadly, despite her critique (and Carby's), Larsen's text does not succeed in providing readers with an alternative vision of folk identity. It demonizes the rural folk by making them appear ignorant and spiritually deadened by their adherence to hegemonic (and patriarchal) institutions that do little to promote female empowerment: traditional forms of Christianity and marriage, both of which demand the sacrifice of the female self for God, husband, and children.

Quicksand also vacillates between admiration for and condemnation of the black middle class, of which Larsen was a prominent member from roughly 1920 to the late 1930s when charges of plagiarism caused her to disappear from the literary scene. The biographer Thadious Davis suggests that Larsen's inability to fit comfortably into the world she had created for herself during the Harlem Renaissance stemmed from a troubled childhood: "The paternal legacy she carried out of Chicago was the emotional baggage of familial rejection and color consciousness, and her maternal legacy was emotional ambivalence towards women and African Americans" (4). Davis's description of Larsen evokes unfavorable comparisons to her character Helga who is neither transparent to herself nor to the people in her life, and who can never find happiness in any of the social roles she plays. Furthermore, Larsen's upper middle-class lifestyle (which, in many ways, mirrors Helga's life), her marriage to a physicist from one of the leading black families, and her refusal to give any literary ink to the black urban masses, belie any serious protestation either of the class-consciousness of the black middle class or of the myopic ruralization of the folk noted by Carby. Indeed, the picture Davis paints of Larsen, while psychologically complex, reveals a woman who is not only ambitious and driven, but also quite the social climber and a bit of a snob.[26]

Carby's analysis of Larsen's representation of black female sexuality in *Quicksand* is germane to my comparison of Janie with other mulatta figures of the period, and so I quote at length:

> Larsen recognized that the repression of the sensual in Afro-American fiction in response to the long history of the exploitation of black sexuality led to the repression of passion and the repression or denial of female sexuality and desire. But, of course, the representation of black female sexuality meant risking its definition as primitive and exotic within a racist society. Larsen attempted to embody but could not hope to resolve these contradictions in her representation of Helga as a sexual being, making Helga the first truly sexual black female protagonist in Afro-American fiction. (*Reconstructing Womanhood* 174)

It is true that Helga's character embodies these repressions and denials of black female sexuality. But her embodiment of them only reifies the idea that black female sexuality was inexpressible. Even in marriage, Helga does not transcend these limitations to her sexual expression. Furthermore, as Deborah McDowell observes, Larsen seems to associate female sexuality with "moral degradation": "sexuality is linked throughout the novel to imagery of descent and animalism" ("*The Changing Same*" 87). Larsen merely reproduces what Carby describes as the "displacement" of sexuality onto some "other terrain." The conversion scene in *Quicksand* mimics scenes of religious sanctification as seen in the spiritual narratives. Helga's passionate manifestation of religious conversion—her erotic contortions and heightened state of emotional expressivity—mimics scenes of spiritual sanctification in the black churches.[27] However, coming immediately after the devastating rejection by Dr. Anderson (who is only rejecting Helga because he believes he has insulted her sense of propriety with his sexual advances—hence his apology), neither Helga's conversion nor her feelings for the minister she marries are authentic. Her spiritual passion is a mask for repressed sexual passion, and her marriage is a sham. Larsen's attempt to critique black female sexual repression is hampered by the same codes that shape this repression: the inexpressibility of black female sexuality as nothing more—and nothing less—than sexual desire and its fulfillment. Helga's subsequent marriage to the minister—resulting in sex that leaves her unfulfilled and burdened with children—represents an even more problematic example of sexual displacement and denial. She cannot have the man she wants, Dr. Anderson, because she cannot admit to him that she wants him.

She therefore marries someone she does not love and appears to engage in sex as a matter of duty rather than desire.

Contrary to Carby's claim above, Helga represents Larsen's failure to accurately render a truly sexual black woman. While Helga may have occupied positions both inside and outside the black middle class, Larsen did not. Larsen went to great lengths to demonstrate that she was not a member of the masses. She carefully cultivated an air of sophistication, intrigue, and distinction from ordinary blacks: "she manifested a desire for access to power connected to wealth, to middle-class comfort, to public life, to male privilege, to white people, and to artistic communities" (Thadious Davis 6). Larsen invested too heavily in the values of her own social cohort to offer any authentic critique of its composition or conduct.[28] Carby's statement that Larsen "could not hope to resolve these contradictions" is a tacit admission of Larsen's failure to offer up an empowering model of black female sexuality. Deborah McDowell states Larsen's dilemma best: "We might say that Larsen wanted to tell the story of the black woman with sexual desires, but was constrained by a competing desire to establish the black woman as respectable in black middle class terms" (McDowell, Introduction to *"Quicksand" and "Passing"* xvi). Or, as Candice Jenkins might argue, Larsen found herself an unwitting victim of the "salvific wish," and, like the other writers before her, ultimately sacrificed black female sexual expression for respectability.

However, Larsen was not the only female writer of the Harlem Renaissance era who found it difficult to represent black woman as sexual beings. Like other women who wrote spiritual narratives, Jessie Fauset also displaced black women's sexuality onto more acceptable terrain. Fauset's *Plum Bun* includes scenes that signal a return to the representation of black female sexuality subsumed under the trope of religious ecstasy. As Kathleen Pfeiffer observes: "Religious services conjure a reaction in Virginia so intense as to evoke sexuality. Virginia experiences communal services as spiritually sensual; the description of these services resemble orgasm."[29] While Virginia is the one who experiences religious ecstasy as a stand-in for sexual fulfillment, it is Angela who embodies all the tropes of the tragic mulatta in *Plum Bun*. Angela, fair enough to pass for white, relocates from Philadelphia to New York to live the life of a white woman far from the prying eyes of Philadelphians—white and black—who could identify her racial lineage. She changes her name from Angela Murray to Angèle Mory, rejects her sister (her only close relative), and lives in Greenwich Village, an enclave for bohemian artists and intellectuals. As a credible painter enrolled in art school, Angela appears to fit in quite well with this group and begins to mimic its behavior and lifestyle.

Fauset's text differs from Nella Larsen's *Passing* in significant ways. Angela does not enjoy the life of luxury that Clare Kendry is afforded as a white woman. Despite the Victorian moral standards under which she was raised, Angela gambles her sexual favors in an attempt to secure a wealthy white suitor and loses. Her lover deserts her, and she learns a painful lesson that, whether white or black, women are not permitted the same sexual license as men, and sexual permissiveness does not guarantee marriage. Unlike the Jewish character Rachel, who enjoys sex for itself and pursues sexual relationships as an expression of her freedom from conventional mores, Angela only uses sex to gain the economic stability of marriage. Brought up under the codes of black female sexual conduct as established by the nineteenth-century clubwomen—the same codes of conduct sanctioned by the black elite—Angela was raised to believe that sex was only permissible within the sanctified bounds of the marriage bed. Consequently, Angela's enjoyment of her sexual experience is undercut by her disappointment when she discovers that her lover, Roger, was never interested in marriage. Ultimately, she regrets her sexual encounter because it does not lead to marriage.

In her introduction to *Plum Bun*, Deborah McDowell concludes that the novel is not just about racial passing, but also critiques gender inequities and the entrenchment of the fairy-tale idealization of romantic love and marriage. McDowell delineates *Plum Bun*'s feminist subtext as an iteration and reflection of "the unequal power relationships in American society," particularly as they cohere around gender relations (McDowell, Introduction to *Plum Bun* xi). Even as a "white" woman, Angela can only hope to obtain power and economic stability through marriage to a white man. But since marriage to Roger is never attained, Angela is forced to reject this fantasy. For this reason, McDowell concludes that *Plum Bun* "moves towards de-idealizing romantic love and criticizing those literary and cultural structures that reinforce and promote this idealization" (McDowell, Introduction to *Plum Bun* xxii).

However, in my reading of the novel, romantic love is de-idealized only to be later re-idealized, undermining the premise of McDowell's analysis. The fairy-tale ending of *Plum Bun* is predicated not only on the promise of happiness as a corollary to perceived economic security, but also on the triumph of romantic love. Angela's disillusionment with the *idea* of Roger, is realized the moment she admits that she was never really in love with him; just with the stability that he represented. Angela suddenly realizes that her true love is fellow artist Anthony Cross, whose advances she has rejected because he does not possess the financial wherewithal to offer her a comfortable life. With Roger no longer available, Angela decides to declare her love to Anthony (with the intention of revealing the secret of her passing), only to be blindsided by his own secrets. Anthony is also passing, and worse yet, is engaged to Angela's sister, Virginia. Just when the reader thinks all is lost, it is revealed that Virginia is in love with another man from her past, Matthew Henson, a childhood friend of the sisters. Through Angela's interference, Matthew Henson is made aware of Virginia's feelings for him and—wonder of wonders—he feels the same way! Up to this point, the reader has been led to believe that Matthew Henson was himself hopelessly in love with the almost-white Angela (who didn't know he existed), and not with her brown sister, Virginia.

The text ends with both Angela and Virginia in romantic bliss, perfectly happy with their respective soul mates. Anthony Cross is delivered to Angela in Paris on Christmas morning, a gift from her sister, Virginia, who is, once again, her closest confidante. For this reader, the ending of *Plum Bun* is not only frustratingly unrealistic but also inauthentic in that Fauset cooks up a contrived ending in order to arrive at a narrative closure that reifies romantic love, marriage, and domesticity as proper vehicles for female happiness and fulfillment.

If Larsen's writing betrays her ambivalence about race, class, and gender codes, then Fauset's novel is downright acquiescent to conventional norms for women and to black bourgeois notions of propriety. In her desire to achieve a "happy" (conventional) ending for her black female characters, Fauset undermines every political intervention she attempts. McDowell credits Fauset for not pandering to the white controlled publishing industry's demand for "sex and sensationalism" from black writers and thereby breaking the code, established among respectable writers, to present blacks in the most favorable light in order to counter negative stereotypes.[30] I agree with McDowell that Fauset included no overt sexual scenes in her novel, merely teasing readers with her title, *Plum Bun* (a "vulgar term" for sexual intercourse) (McDowell, Introduction to *Plum Bun* xx).

McDowell's comments on the "vulgarity" and "sensationalism" of writing about sex elucidate a crucial dilemma for the black writer of Larsen's era. Suppose a given writer wanted to write about sex, not to satisfy some prurient fascination of whites but to validate an aspect of black life for reasons having to do with realism, or to portray an aspect of a character's life that is important to the development of the plot. How does one write about an aspect of black life that is clearly taboo among respectable black folk for the precise reason that it is exactly what white folks want to read, and for all the wrong reasons? Furthermore, how could a writer imagine a fully developed black subject devoid of the sexual and spiritual elements that round out characters, making them recognizably and fully human? It is not difficult to imagine that these or similar questions would have vexed black writers of that era. In "The Erotics of Talk," Carla Kaplan observes that while some male writers of the Harlem Renaissance era defied convention and wrote about sexuality, "admonitions against its representation were much more rigorously applied to the works of black women" (144).

In *Spiritual Interrogations*, Katherine Bassard established important links between black women's close encounters with God or Spirit and the "conferral of personhood" such an intimate connection with the divine engendered, even in enslaved subjects (3). Bassard clearly and convincingly theorizes that spirituality was essential to black subject formation. But what of the bruised and battered flesh of the black woman, flesh she could not lay claim to as it was owned (and often abused) by someone else? Wasn't flesh as important as spirit in the reclamation of identity and in the establishment of personhood? For the victims of collective, systematic, institutional, and generational rape, as well as every conceivable form of sexual terrorism, repossessing their bodies meant laying claim to their sexuality. I argue that none of the texts examined thus far allow black women that option. And without the ability to integrate her sexual with her spiritual being, the black woman will always, like Helga Crane, be a divided subject, unable to achieve full self-possession.

This book argues that not only was it essential for black women to be allowed both spiritual *and* sexual expression, but that without that integration she could never achieve full subjectivity. Using Audre Lorde's model of the erotic as a synthesis of sexuality and spirituality that inaugurates creative agency and political transformation in women's lives, I argue for the reclamation of the erotic as a source of black female empowerment.[31] The texts analyzed in this chapter fully dramatize the sexual prohibitions—historically mandated and collectively sanctioned by blacks for purposes of self-preservation—by which black writers were constrained when they attempted to represent black women as both spiritual and sexual beings. Hurston's second novel, published in 1937, marks a dramatic departure from this unhappy state of affairs. *Their Eyes Were Watching God* laid the groundwork for examining a question that has dogged black women since their emergence into the literary arena: Given the peculiar sexual history of the black woman in the New World, how does one inscribe an autonomous, fully integrated, well-balanced, and self-possessed black female subject in fiction?

I argue that it is Hurston—and not Larsen—who took up the challenge of representing the first truly sexual black woman in the African-American literary tradition.[32] However, her character Janie was not just the first sexual black woman; she was also the first protagonist to integrate her sexuality and her spirituality in order to achieve wholeness. In chapter 2, I examine the ways in which Hurston's interventions in *Their Eyes Were Watching God* challenged and transformed the representations of black women in literary texts, thereby laying the groundwork for her legatees to continue the work of imagining the black woman as a sexually vibrant, spiritually whole, fully autonomous, perfectly imperfect subject.

2

Literary Interventions in *Their Eyes Were Watching God*

> She saw a dust-bearing bee sink into the sanctum of a bloom; the thousand sister calyxes arch to meet the love embrace and the ecstatic shiver for the tree from root to tiniest branch creaming in every blossom and frothing with delight. So this was a marriage! She had been summoned to behold a revelation. Then Janie felt a pain remorseless sweet that left her limp and languid.
>
> After a while she got up from where she was and went over the little garden field entire. She was seeking confirmation of the voice and vision, and everywhere she found and acknowledged answers. A personal answer for all other creation except herself. She felt an answer seeking her, but where? When? How? She found herself at the kitchen door and stumbled inside. In the air of the room were flies tumbling and singing, marrying and giving in marriage.
>
> Zora Neale Hurston, *Their Eyes Were Watching God*

Their Eyes Were Watching God revolutionized the depiction of black female sexuality in African-American literature. Critics of Hurston's work generally agree that in 1937, when she wrote her second novel, the damaging effects of nineteenth-century sexual ideology on black women's subjectivities and writings were fully entrenched. The black press cautioned writers to keep their submissions free from overt sexuality. Gloria Naylor points out that "black women's sexuality had been deadened to the point of invisibility" in literature written by black writers by the mid-twenties.[1] In *Wrapped in Rainbows* Valerie Boyd argues that while several of the Harlem Renaissance male writers were openly gay or bisexual, "Less is known about the sexual and affectional preferences of the Harlem Renaissance's Women" writers (128). In "The Erotics of Talk," Carla Kaplan raises the question of why Hurston would choose to begin her novel with a woman awakening to her sexuality, and answers her own question by concluding that Hurston "rewrites desire as the desire to tell one's story" (139). However, as seductive as the desire to self-actualize through speech can potentially be, it may also serve as another device with which to subsume and displace black female sexuality.

In my reading, Hurston attempts the mammoth task of revising the entire literary tradition by recalling black female sexuality into normative discursivity, thereby rescuing black women's sexual expression from the refuse heap of "vulgarity and sensationalism." To accomplish this remarkable feat, Hurston has to give her character the spiritual grounding that will ensure a proper balance, so that sex becomes naturalized in the novel as a part of human development rather than sensationalized to demonstrate black aberration. In order to achieve this balance, Hurston could not rely on Christianity as a spiritual foundation since, as I argue above, it clearly separated sexuality from spirituality, subversively canonizing the Christ-figure as the appropriate object of female passion.

The central premise of any spiritual ethos is the individual's belief that he or she is part and parcel of a cosmological order, and that every relationship, action, and thought should ultimately propel one toward the fulfillment of the highest good—the ontological mandate, which is one's divine purpose for being. The question Janie poses to her unseen interlocutor early in the text ("why am I here?") is the central question of the novel, and it signals her highly developed spirituality, even at her tender age. The fact that Hurston ties Janie's quest for divine purpose to her emerging sexuality is what catalyzes my interrogation of eroticism (by Lorde's definition) as the agent of transformation responsible for the paradigmatic shift in black female literary representation.

Daphne Lamothe's germinal study of the presence of the Voudoun loa Erzulie in *Their Eyes Were Watching God* is foundational to my critique of the way black female spirituality is depicted in Hurston's text.[2] Lamothe's analysis of Janie as an Erzulie character is central to my theory that Janie is the first literary representation of an autonomous and fully integrated African-American woman whose struggle to maintain the crucial balance between her sexuality and spirituality is what defines and catalyzes her subjectivity. Hurston's body of work reveals that her interest in anthropology led her into contact with African diasporic cultures in Haiti, Jamaica, Honduras, and elsewhere, and it is inevitable that the scope of her epistemic framework would be broadened and deepened by such contact. Lamothe argues that Hurston draws upon Voudoun beliefs and practices and that it is this alternative mode of spirituality that undergirds *Their Eyes Were Watching God* and enables Hurston to explore issues of cultural and political transformation, female empowerment, and African-American cultural identity (157).

Their Eyes Were Watching God is charged with eroticism, and in the narrative it is this ineffable something, this ability to blend a mature spirituality with a natural and womanly sexuality, that makes Janie's character so memorable. Janie is a spiritual being who is neither under nor oversexed, but who recognizes sexuality as a crucial factor in her yearning for autonomous selfhood. This fusion of the secular and the sacred has been noted by Audre Lorde, who explicates the erotic as the synthesis of sexual and spiritual energies in women, which—when properly in balance—cohere in political agency, personal development, and autonomous subjectivity. Lorde theorizes that the erotic is a source of agency and transformation, and that by tapping into this source women are able to effect lasting transformation in their personal lives, as well as powerful social changes in the world. Lorde theorizes that it is when women are in touch with the erotic that they do their best work. The merger between the sexual and the spiritual is also a political act, an act of recovery that can potentially restore the black woman's sense of wholeness, making her fully capable of acting in her own best interest and in the interest of the collective black community. Barbara Christian theorizes in *Black Women Novelists* that African women must have found themselves totally dumfounded and psychically disturbed by the separation of the sexual and the spiritual that would have been de rigueur in their socialization to the New World order of slavery. Christian argues that for Africans, sexuality was expressed through dances and religion, and that black slave women must have been confounded by the ambivalent responses of white society to expressions of sexuality, and to the separation of the sexual from every other realm of human behavior. Yet our literary history makes clear that, out of moral necessity, black women did adapt to this strict separation between the sexual and every other sphere of human life. Janie, in my reading, finds her source of empowerment in the erotic, and she does so by tapping into her sexual and spiritual energies and keeping both in proper balance.

Their Eyes Were Watching God restores the balance between black female sexuality and spirituality. It represents the first successful literary model to consciously reinscribe the erotic as a source of agency and transformation for black women. Lamothe argues that *Their Eyes* uses female sexuality as a source of empowerment through the Voudoun loa Erzulie. Although Erzulie is not explicitly present in Hurston's work, Lamothe explains that she is, nevertheless, integral to the development of Janie's character in terms of her physical characteristics, her narrative motivations, and her constantly evolving relational circumstances. Each of these factors signifies a particular stage of growth, transformation, and empowerment for Janie. Lamothe writes: "For Hurston, representing a woman's sexuality in full bloom is not just affirmative, it is revolutionary" (163).

Hurston's second novel and most successful work opens with its central character, Janie, raising important questions about her place in the universe. Hurston inscribes Janie's sexuality and spirituality as coterminous elements in her developing subjectivity, and allows the text to play out the scenario of what happens when either of these elements is repressed. *Their Eyes Were Watching God* is the first African-American text to unabashedly proclaim the black woman's freedom to simultaneously express her sexuality and spirituality within the confines of a society that insists black women can be either spiritual or sexual, but never both. Given the baggage of the cult of true womanhood against which the integrity of African-American womanhood was habitually weighed, Hurston had to turn to a different paradigm to articulate Janie's desire to integrate her sexual and spiritual life into a coherent and autonomous whole.

Written toward the end of the Harlem Renaissance, Hurston's novel presents a strong counternarrative to extant ideologies that carried over from slavery, ideologies that mandated against and made untenable the free and unfettered expression of black female sexuality. *Their Eyes Were Watching God* depicts a black woman attempting to redefine black womanhood within a cultural context that does not recognize the existence of such a category.[3] To do so, Janie must reclaim her sexuality from hegemonic forces both black and white, male and female, that denied the free expression of black female sexuality.[4] To do so she must also reclaim God in her own image, a black female conception of God not contravened by whiteness and maleness. Janie must also experience life for herself in all its complexities, and learn her own lessons that will take her to the place where she is at peace with herself, where it matters not whether she will die after being bitten by her rabid husband, Tea Cake because she has already lived fully and completely.[5] Twice Hurston alerts us to the fact that Janie believes there are fates worse than death: "She was in the courthouse fighting something and it wasn't death. It was worse than that. It was lying thoughts" (187). And again: "It was not death she feared. It was misunderstanding "(188). The apparent conflation of authorial anxiety with the character's is not to be missed here. One cannot help but discern Hurston's own anxiety about the legacy she would leave to the world as a writer, knowing that death was inevitable, but wondering if future generations would understand and appreciate the body of work she left behind. In her own time, Hurston received mixed reviews for her critical output. Her ethnographic collection of black folklore from the southern United States, *Mules and Men*, was fairly well received. However, *Tell My Horse*, Hurston's ethnographic collection on Haiti and Jamaica, was harshly criticized. Some of the textual failings cited were Hurston's "naïve" attempt to offer a political analysis of Haitian society and her incorporation of national or local gossip into what was supposed to be a strictly ethnographic work.[6] Hurston's biographer, Robert Hemenway, argues that *Tell My Horse* is "Hurston's poorest book, chiefly because of its form" (248). Hurston clearly had reason to be concerned about her legacy. The poor reception of *Their Eyes Were Watching God* by black critics such as Richard Wright and Alain Locke must have confirmed her worst fear that she would be misunderstood, and that her legacy would be compromised as result (Hemenway, *Zora Neale Hurston* 241).

It is ironic that *Their Eyes Were Watching God*—the book Richard Wright dismissed as having "no theme and no message"—is Hurston's most enduring legacy to black women in the African diaspora, and to women in general, and arguably one of the most canonical texts written by a black person. In creating Janie, Hurston left her literary daughters a blueprint for writing about an independent black female character who is not afraid to express sexual desire. This creative synthesis engendered a bold new model of black womanhood that rechoreographed paradigms and relocated the geography of black female consciousness. Janie is a black woman of mixed race who is neither tragically conflicted nor "tragically colored," a combination of traits that both validates and subverts the confines of heterosexual relations and the institution of marriage, asserting the right to sexual, spiritual, and emotional fulfillment as paramount to marital happiness. Finally, Janie's character affirms the necessity of material self-sufficiency, even as she manifests signs of entrapment in economic dependency.

Their Eyes Were Watching God bears the imprint of the syncretization of rural southern and Caribbean cultural modalities and influences, problematizing and transgressing the borders of cultural specificity, and revolutionizing the discursive terrain of gender convention, sexual expression, and spiritual ideology. What emerges in the text is a syncretic model of spirituality that does not jettison Christianity, but reproduces transformative theoretical principles and spiritual significations of African and New World syncretic religions, especially as they pertain to notions of female empowerment.

Subverting the Tragic Mulatta Archetype

Still, when [the southern white writers] did present this image, the mulatta is tragic. Often she is shown as caught between two worlds, and since she is obviously the result of an illicit relationship, she suffers from a melancholy of the blood that inevitably leads to tragedy. In contrast to the Southern lady, whose beauty, refinement, and charm bring her admiration, love, and happiness, the fruit of miscegenation is Tragedy, regardless of what other positive characteristics the mulatta might possess. The word mulatto itself etymologically is derived from the word mule and echoes the debate Americans engaged in about whether blacks were the same species as whites. If they were not, the result would be similar to a mule, a cross between the donkey and the horse and a being that itself was incapable of producing life.

Barbara Christian, Black Women Novelists

Judith Berzon's *Neither Black nor White: The Mulatto Character in American Fiction* was written in 1978 at the beginning of critical reengagement with *Their Eyes Were Watching God*. Berzon describes Janie as "a beautiful mulatto who had lived among whites [and] did not recognize the difference between herself and them until she was six years old" (75). Some Hurston critics seem to take Janie's mulatta identity as a given, although Hurston's text never conclusively identifies her father as white. Janie's mother, Leafy, is the offspring of Janie's grandmother, Nanny, and Nanny's former slave master. Janie is Leafy's child, the product of Leafy's rape by her teacher. Janie barely knows her mother and does not know her father at all. She is raised by her grandmother, Nanny, who has told her about the circumstances of her birth, but never indicates whether her father is black or white. Hurston gives us one clue that the father is more than likely a black man. The children at school tease Janie about being the product of rape, and the narrator explains that they never bother to tell Janie that her father came back later to marry Leafy, but was run out of town by the Washburns (the white family that employed Nanny as a domestic servant). *Their Eyes Were Watching God* was written in 1937 and set in the early 1900s. Miscegenation laws outlasted almost every other Jim Crow law, and were dismantled late in the civil rights movement. Laws against interracial marriage existed from 1664 to as recently as 1967 when the U.S. Supreme Court finally declared them unconstitutional in the *Loving v. Virginia* case. Although this historical information might lead one to speculate that Janie's father is black, it does not offer conclusive proof.

Widespread critical acceptance of Janie as a mulatta figure cannot be dismissed as a misreading of the text, despite the racial ambiguity surrounding Janie's paternity. A cursory survey of the literature of that period demonstrates that the term "mulatta" referred to individuals who had both black and white ancestry, and not strictly to someone who was the product of one white and one black parent.[7] Janie's physical characteristics afford Hurston the opportunity to critique and subvert not one but two literary conventions: the tragic mulatta archetype and the beautiful mixed-race heroine.[8]

Barbara Christian explains why phenotypically black (not mixed-race) women were not generally represented as literary heroines:

> The literary conventions of the novel at that time also legislated that the heroine of a story be beautiful, since physical beauty, at least for a woman, was an indication of her spiritual excellence—but not just any kind of physical beauty. The nineteenth-century novel promoted a rather fragile beauty as the norm; qualities of helplessness, chastity, and refinement rather than, say, strength, endurance and intelligence were touted as the essential characteristics of femininity. The nineteenth century heroine not only had to be beautiful physically; she had to be fragile and well bred as well. (*Black Women Novelists* 22)

Extant standards of female beauty made it impossible for the average black women to be considered beautiful, and her low socioeconomic status made it inconceivable that the term "well bred" could be applied to her. The only credible black heroine, then, was the mulatta. She could approximate white standards of beauty, and by virtue of her father's wealth, could also attain the proper breeding that characterized a female heroine. Christian comments on the overdetermined relationship between social and literary conventions: "The social philosophy that denied the beauty of black women and the economic policy of slavery that relegated black people to the bottom of the economic ladder made it very difficult for anyone to write a novel in which a credible black woman could be the major focus of attention" (*Black Women Novelists* 22).

Hurston inscribes Janie's ambivalence about some of the features conscripted upon the female heroine, such as helplessness and fragility. Hurston's inscription simultaneously recognizes Janie's engagement with—and transgression of—such symbols of the feminine. Indeed, Janie is a product of her time and of Nanny's teachings even as she struggles to subvert their tenacious ideological hold. At times, Janie attempts to subvert definitions of herself as fragile, while at other times she plays into expectations of her fragility to get her own way. When she is married to Logan, she refuses to chop firewood or work in the field, and insists that her place is in the domestic realm doing "womanly" chores. However, when she is married to Jody, she resents his assumption that because she is a woman she is not capable of engaging in traditional male activities, such as cutting tobacco properly or participating in the storytelling or games they play on the store's porch. Finally, when Janie is married to Tea Cake she seems to forget her determination not to do fieldwork and is happiest when she is by his side working in the muck. Nanny's often-quoted warning that the black woman is "the mule of the world," and that Janie should do everything to avoid being consigned to this archetypal role, seems to be what drives Janie to subvert her appropriation as workhorse on Logan's farm. However, when she is on the muck, she is responding to a different directive, one that counters everything Nanny taught her, and one that, in Nanny's view, can potentially reduce her to the status of a mule: romantic love and its attendant fatuity.

In accordance with Christian's interpretation, Janie's beauty is portrayed through some of the signs of mulatta beauty, which were long hair and a good figure: "the men noticed her firm buttocks like she had grapefruits in her hip pockets; the great rope of black hair swinging to her waist and unraveling in the wind like a plume; then her pugnacious breasts trying to bore holes in her shirt" (2). Early in the text, however, Hurston makes us aware that Janie is not light enough to pass for white. She darkens so much in the Florida sun that she cannot recognize her photographed self as the little colored girl who stands out from the white Washburn children. Some critics have used this example to highlight the fact that as a child, Janie has no real black identity and lacks a racial fixity that is consistent with the tragic mulatta formula. However, Janie's darkening also represents her recognition of herself as a racial "other" only in comparison to the white children. Janie's exclamation, "Ah, I'm colored," is consistent with theories of identity that constitute race as a social construction. The black subject as the racial "other" can only be understood in relation to the "white" subject who is constituted as the possessor of the normative body.[9]

Recent scholarship has commented on the Rhinelander case, a 1924 annulment proceeding in New York in which a white man from a wealthy family sued his mulatta wife for passing herself off as white, thereby deceiving him into marrying her.[10] The case was mentioned in Nella Larsen's *Passing* and would have been familiar to all Harlem Renaissance writers, including Hurston. Miriam Thaggert argues that "what escalated the trial to the point of drama was the role played by the nonwhite body" of Alice Rhinelander (2). Alice had to disrobe in court in order to prove to the judge, lawyers, and all-white, all-male jury that she could not have deceived her husband because her color would have been evident to any man who had been intimate with her (2). The fact that Alice had to disrobe highlights the eroticization of the mulatta figure, as well as the sexual exploitation to which all black women have been historically subjected in both the public and the private sectors of American society. Miriam Thaggert also argues that "Alice's disrobing situates her in a long line of women of color who have had their bodies, literally and figuratively, placed on trial" (5). Furthermore, this public disrobing points to the fact that Alice's body was darker than her face and that the jury could not discern her race by the parts of her body visible to them. This complex discursive and visual template surrounding the figure of the mulatta represents what Cherene Sherrard-Johnson refers to as "moments of racial recognition and misrecognition that created the sustained motif of a muddled color line and dispel the notion that whiteness is physiologically impossible to penetrate" (852).[11] Set in the 1920s, Hurston's *Their Eyes* pointedly mimics this racial ambiguity early in the text, but abandons it quickly. Early in her life, Janie is unaware of her blackness until she sees a photograph of herself with the white Washburn children. Apparently the Washburns do not treat her as though she is inferior so Janie is not made conscious of her difference, and of this difference as a negative marker. Like Alice, Janie's dark body is what reveals her racial origins. Ironically, Janie is passing socially, but only to herself: she is the one unconscious of her nonwhite body. Although Mr. Rhinelander accused his wife of deceiving him, the facts in the case demonstrated that he was complicit in Alice's passing; when she did pass, she did so with his knowledge and help in order to avoid awkward situations for both of them.[12] Nanny and the Washburns are all complicit in Janie's unconscious passing since no one bothered to inform the young Janie of her racial status.

Yet the text reveals that there are significant differences between Janie's consciousness vis-à-vis her racial identity, her sexual politics, her class affiliation, and the role of the tragic mulatta figures who appeared in the fiction and film of that period.[13] As a child, Janie is indeed unaware of her racial identity, but she is not hostile to her racialized body once she is identified as black . Janie, as an adult character, is conscripted by the narrator to critique the trope of the tragic mulatta figure with whom she shares some physical characteristics. Janie is presented as a mixed-race character who chooses not to pass. She defies the tragic mulatta prototype and invents herself as a self-assured woman of mixed racial heritage who chooses to identify politically and culturally with the black race. I argue that Hurston makes use of this popular iconographic archetype in *Their Eyes* in order to rewrite and revise the formulaic racial indeterminacy and spiritual fragmentation that makes this figure so tragic. By the end of the novel, Janie develops into a character who is spiritually whole, and who fully accepts her blackness as a cultural, historical, and political reality.

The figure of the tragic mulatto served as a useful symbol to examine America's anxieties concerning racial miscegenation. It highlighted the absurdity of the "one-drop rule" (a person with any trace of African ancestry was considered legally black in the United States) and white America's fear of racial corruption, while foregrounding the psychological and emotional trauma of living in a society so divided by racialism. When Hurston wrote *Their Eyes,* the tragic mulatta figure was very much in vogue. Fannie Hurst's 1933 novel was made into the popular movie *Imitation of Life* in 1934, three years before *Their Eyes* was published. The story revolves around a young girl of mixed race named Peola. She fits the prototype of the tragic mulatta figure that refuses to be black but cannot be white, and therefore lives a life of utter frustration and self-alienation as a result of her racial indeterminacy.

In her essay "A Plea for Color: Nella Larsen's Iconography of the Mulatta," Cherene Sherrard-Johnson examines the iconography of the mulatta figure in photography and art of the Harlem Renaissance period, focusing particularly on Archibald Motley's paintings depicting octoroons and mulattas. Sherrard-Johnson argues that "a preponderance of photography, visual art, and narrative texts produced during the Harlem Renaissance featured the mulatta as either heroine or primary subject, reinforcing her role as the representative New Negro woman" (835). Sherrard-Johnson explains that these representations of the New Negro woman ran counter to the modernizing impulse of the era because she was invariably cast in service roles such as those of teacher, nurse, and librarian. Moreover, her behavior, appearance, and vocation had to be genteel and modest (835).

While Janie is dark enough to stand out from the Washburn children in the photograph, she is nevertheless light enough to play the part of the mulatta heroine, a factor that becomes obvious when Mrs. Turner suggests that Janie (and herself) rightly belong to a race between black and white: "You'se different from me. Ah can't stand black niggers. Ah don't blame the white folks from hatin' 'em 'cause Ah can't stand 'em mahself. 'Nother thing, Ah hates to see folks lak me and you mixed up wid 'em. Us oughta class off" (141). But although she is meant to be "read" as a representation of the mulatta archetype, Janie represents a radical break from such characterizations of the tragic mulatta figure.[14] She identifies not only with blacks but also with the black working class (which is not genteel), and exhibits racial pride and a fondness for dark-skinned people (such as her third husband, Tea Cake). Hurston makes it clear that once Janie makes her declaration ("Ah, I'm colored"), she does not dwell on it. Unlike Fauset's character Angela Murray and Larsen's characters Clare Kendry and Helga Crane, Janie does not live in a state of perpetual anxiety over race and racial identity. In fact, Janie spends most of the novel trying to figure out how to negotiate her place in the world as a woman, while devoting very little time to agonizing over what it means to be black or mulatta. This represents a significant way in which Hurston deliberately overturns one of the central tropes of the tragic mulatta. In "Crayon Enlargements of Life," Nellie McKay discusses the difference between Janie, who achieves "positive identification with the black community," and the mulatto character from James Weldon Johnson's *Autobiography of an Ex-Colored Man*, who "lives with ambivalence toward his racial self" from the moment he discovers that he has black blood. Johnson's character is so anguished about his "tainted" blood that he eventually decides to pass for white and rejects any further identification with his black community. McKay concludes that Janie, "when confronted with this information, accepts herself fully" (64).

Although all the men in the text are obsessed with Janie's long, straight hair—a symbol of her mulatta approximation—her racial identification is only questioned at one other point in the text, this time by the obnoxious Mrs. Turner (quoted above). In her suggestion that she and Janie ought to "class-off," Mrs. Turner's concerns about mulattas as a separate class mimic Jody's concern that Janie, as the mayor's wife, occupies a separate class from the other women in the town and should not associate with them. This integration of contemporary ideas about class, color, and money as categories of division and social hierarchy in the black community demonstrates Hurston's critical engagement with the extant discourses of the period. Leading figures of the Harlem Renaissance's elite, such as Alain Locke, W.E.B. Du Bois, George Schuyler, and Jessie Fauset wanted blacks in public life and in writing to conform to standards of respectability in order to demonstrate that black people were just as moral, just as intelligent, and just as well bred as whites, and therefore qualified for equal rights in America. Hurston, McKay, Hughes, and others rejected this mandate and wrote whatever they wanted to write. Mrs. Turner's statements embody the absurdities of the mandate of the "race leaders." In the character Mrs. Turner, Hurston accentuates the fallacies of elitist assumptions and ill-conceived prejudices against the disadvantaged majority of black people that were masked by the language of racial uplift, upper-class gentility, social mobility, and American standardization employed in essays like George Schuyler's "The Negro Art Hokum" and Jessie Fauset's novel *Plum Bun*.[15] Janie seems embarrassed and bewildered by Mrs. Turner's racist remarks. She explains to Mrs. Turner that blacks come in all shades and that it would be impossible to draw a strict line between light- and dark-skinned blacks: "Us can't do it. We'se uh mingled people and all of us got black kinfolks as well as yaller kinfolks. How come you so against black?" (141). The voice of the character is conflated with the authorial voice as Hurston uses Janie to articulate her commitment to the folk, her total identification with blackness, and her complete renunciation of internalized racism.

Hurston uses Janie's complete lack of identification with Mrs. Turner—the real tragic mulatta figure in Hurston's text—and her insistence that they both belong to the black race to signal that Janie rejects both the bourgeois values of the black elite and the premise shared by both black and white integrationists of that era: that blacks must adapt to white cultural norms to achieve equality in America. For example, in "The Negro Art Hokum" George Schuyler suggests that there really were no social or cultural differences between blacks and whites in America and that "the Aframerican is merely a lampblacked Anglo-Saxon" (1172). Unlike the tragic mulattas of Fauset's and Larsen's texts, Janie is not vacillating between identifications; she likes being culturally black. She is as secure in her black identity as Hurston, who declared herself not "tragically colored" in her autobiographical essay "How it Feels to Be Colored Me" (Hurston 152). Sherrard-Johnson insists that Nella Larsen's "fiction is anchored in a critique of the visual images of African American women then circulating throughout the culture and limiting the mobility of the New Negro woman in the intellectual and artistic communities of the 'talented tenth'" (836). Yet she admits that Larsen's critique is at best "equivocating," in turn admiring and disdaining the New Negro woman (840). I submit that Hurston does not equivocate in her condemnation of the elitism, repressiveness, and antimodernism of this figure. Janie represents the first truly "transgressive, transcendent heroine" of Hurston's period.[16] Janie's insistence that she loves Tea Cake and married him for his ability to have fun and make her happy runs counter to the values of the black elite, represented in Hurton's text by the figures of Jody Starks and Mrs. Turner. Her declaration of love for Tea Cake is a double-voiced counternarrative to Jody's belief in the supremacy of money and status, and Mrs. Turner's belief in the supremacy of white skin.

Although Mrs. Turner intends to infect Janie with her language of self-hatred, Janie is able to deflect the attack simply by asserting a counterdiscourse to the ideology of white and mulatta superiority. Tea Cake, on the other hand, begins to have serious self-doubts when he overhears Mrs. Turner's critique of him. His internalization of Mrs. Turner's theories of black inferiority leads to violent aggression against Janie's body and spirit. Tea Cake beats Janie because he feels helpless in the face of something larger than himself that he believes to be true: the pervasive and persistent ideology maintaining that his black skin makes him inferior to his wife and, therefore, undeserving of her.

Ultimately, Tea Cake's death can be attributed to his internalization of the ideology of white supremacy and black subordination. He refuses to leave the muck even though the Native American population has left before the onset of the storm. Tea Cake relies on the white man's wisdom to guide him in making decisions regarding his own life and Janie's: "Indians don't know much ah nothing, tuh tell de truth. Else dey'd own dis country still. De white folks ain't going nowhere. Dey oughta know if it's dangerous" (156). Despite his hatred of Mrs. Turner, Tea Cake is clearly aligned with her views about the inferiority of nonwhite peoples. His death after the hurricane symbolizes Hurston's rejection of these views and her impatience with black self-hatred. Tea Cake is killed by Janie after he is driven mad by the bite of a rabid dog, which in context represents the ideology of white supremacy and its virulent manifestation in American society. Tea Cake is a stand-in for the millions of people, both black and white, who are infected with this racist ideology. Mrs. Turner is literally and symbolically the carrier of this ideology in the text. The rabid dog that bites Tea Cake is carried across the Okeechobee on the back of a cow, an animal associated in the text with Mrs. Turner. Tea Cake himself alerts the reader to Mrs. Turner's resemblance to a cow: "Tea Cake made a lot of fun about Mrs. Turner's shape behind her back. He claimed that she had been shaped up by a cow kicking her from behind. She was an ironing board with things throwed at it. Then that same cow took and stepped in her mouth when she was a baby and left it wide and flat with her chin and nose almost meeting" (140). Twice, Tea Cake associates Mrs. Turner with the image of a cow. Then, like a rabid dog, he does something entirely out of character when Mrs. Turner's brother poses a threat to his hold on Janie: he beats Janie just to show that he is boss. During the hurricane, Tea Cake comes face to face with the cow and the terror of the rabid dog—a metonym for racial hatred—that it carries "like a great weight" on its back: "He saw a cow swimming slowly towards the fill in an oblique line. A massive built dog was sitting on her shoulders and shivering and growling. The cow was approaching Janie. A few strokes would bring her there" (165). The burden of self-hatred and internalized racist ideology is the rabid dog that the cow (Mrs. Turner) metaphorically carries on her back. The killing bite is meant for Janie, just as Mrs. Turner's comments are meant to persuade Janie to leave Tea Cake. However, it is not Janie who succumbs to the racist ideology (or the dog bite), but rather Tea Cake who is bitten and eventually dies. Tea Cake puts up a valiant fight and kills the dog, but not before he has been bitten and infected. Eventually, it is this bite that drives Tea Cake insane, forcing Janie to kill him in self-defense. Interestingly, once the virus takes hold, Tea Cake attempts to repeat what he had done when the effects of Mrs. Turner's racist language made him insecure in his identity and manhood: he attempts to harm Janie, but this time she does not sit and endure the abuse in silent submission. Janie fights back—as she did discursively when Mrs. Turner tried to infect her with racism and self-hatred—and again, she overcomes. Janie loses Tea Cake but preserves her life and her self-respect. She also regains the ground she lost in her self-development when she allowed herself to be beaten earlier and did nothing in her own defense.

Janie's act of self-defense and self-empowerment marks her separation from female mulatta characters who are diffident and submissive in moments that call for self-confident, resolute action. The instability of their identities is reflected in their inability to make sound decisions at crucial moments. Fauset's character Angela Murray, when faced with choosing between keeping her racial identity secret from her white lover and alienating her only sister, chooses to do nothing, thereby forcing her sister to assess the situation and choose for her. Angela almost loses Virginia as a result of deliberate inaction and is forced to suffer loneliness and depression until Virginia relents and decides to forgive her passive rejection. Similarly, Clare, in Nella Larsen's *Passing*, cannot stick with her decision to join the white race. She constantly vacillates between her world and Irene's until her racist white husband catches up with her. Her inconstancy is also reflected in the ambiguity surrounding her sexual preference and possible extramarital affairs. Clare falls to her death or is pushed by Irene as she is on the brink of leaving her husband to rejoin the black race. However, her death forecloses the possibility of resolute action and, unlike Janie, Clare is not allowed to savor the empowerment that the difficult but necessary choice of leaving her husband would bring.

Janie's ability to grow from her experience marks yet another way in which Hurston inscribes her departure from the tragic mulatta paradigm. Faced with a difficult decision, Janie is not conflicted like the tragic mulatta heroine. She makes a choice between her life and Tea Cake's that demonstrates her self-love and personal growth. The novel ends with Janie fully aware of how much she has grown and entirely prepared to live out the rest of her life alone but fulfilled, having known love and lived a life of her own choosing.

Despite Jody's attempt to elevate Janie and himself above the folk, both of them remain rooted in folk culture. This signals another way in which Janie departs from the tragic mulatta figure. Those readers that critic VèVè Clark would consider "diasporically literate" fully understand that the people of Eatonville believe that Janie has used Hoodoo to "fix" her husband. It is Phoeby who alerts Janie to this information: "Janie, Ah thought maybe de thing would die down and you would know nothin' bout it, but its been singing round here ever since de big fuss in de store dat Joe was 'fixed' and you wuz de one dat did it" (82).

Jody's belief in Janie's culpability is symbolized by his refusal to eat food she has prepared: "She was worried about his not eating his meals, till she found out he was having old lady Davis to cook for him" (82). Janie is hurt and humiliated that Jody would think her capable of using black magic to hurt him. She laments: "Tuh think Ah been wid Jody twenty yeahs and Ah just now got to bear de name uh poisonin' him! It's bout to kill me, Phoeby. Sorrow dogged by sorrow is in mah heart" (83). Robert Hemenway explains that "Hoodoo and conjure are collective terms for all the traditional beliefs in black culture centering around a votary's confidence in the power of a conjure, a root, a two-headed, or hoodoo doctor to alter with magical powers a situation that seems rationally irremediable" (118).

Here, Hurston's belief in the efficacy of folk wisdom is both undercut by Janie's characterization of the "two headed" root-doctor as "a faker from around Altamonte Springs" and validated by her acknowledgment of the scientific basis of root-work as it applies to herbal poisons in food. As I will explore later in this chapter, this is not the only incident in which Janie reveals ambivalence about the legitimacy of Hoodoo.

Janie's disappointment and regret concerning the rumors of her practicing conjuring to harm her husband are sincere. Her strategies of resistance, when she chooses to employ them, are far more direct. She does not want anyone to think her capable of manipulating spiritual knowledge to gain the upper hand. When she chooses to fight back, Janie uses the power of her voice, which Jody had suppressed for years. Hurston is unequivocal about asserting the transformative potential of Janie as an empowered speaker. Twice Janie speaks back to Jody in her own defense. The first time she confronts Jody is in the store when he accuses her of being old and assures her that no one is looking to make a wife out of her. Janie responds: "Naw, Ah ain't no young gal no mo' but den Ah ain't no old woman neither. Ah reckon ah looks mah age too. But Ah'm a woman every inch of me, and Ah know it. Dat's a whole lot more'n you kin say. You big-bellies round here and put out a lot of brag, but 'taint nothing to it but yo' big voice. Humph! Talking 'bout me looking old! When you pull down yo' britches, you look lak de change uh life" (79). Janie invokes the African principle of Nommo, the power of the word, and it overturns Jody's "illusion of irresistible maleness" (79). The concept of Nommo suggests that the "word" is a living, active agent with the power to make things happen and effect transformation.[17] In calling Jody an old woman, Janie effectively emasculates him. He begins to look like what he accuses Janie of being, an old woman past the prime of life, wasting away in bed and waiting for death. The power of Janie's words rests as much in her intimate knowledge of her husband's sexuality as in her command of "the dozens," the African-American vernacular dialogue in which one wields words to destabilize his or her opponent. Who besides Janie would be able to speak with authority about her husband's virility or lack thereof? Frustrated by his continual verbal put-downs and challenges to her sexuality, Janie decides to fight fire with fire by challenging Jody's own sexuality in public.

However, according to extant sexual ideology, female sexual prowess is not a determinant of femininity. In fact, female sexual empowerment is even perceived as antithetical to femininity. Nevertheless, male sexual prowess is a major and traditional component of masculinity. Hence, Jody's words do not have the same power as Janie's. Her arsenal is effective because she is his wife and in the "know." Her words bear the imprint of truth, and it is his inability to deny them or prove them wrong that forces Jody to surrender his power and eventually his life. The doctor says that Jody died from kidney failure. The community, however, knows that Joe died because Janie decided to take her power back.

Janie's command of the power of Nommo and manipulation of it in service of her own empowered speech signal her nascent command of the black vernacular to which she had been denied access by Jody. Jody's refusal to allow Janie to participate in the storytelling sessions on the porch curtailed her ability to associate with the folk and to meet them on equal terms. Hurston eschews the notion of the well-bred mulatta who speaks in rarefied English and tries to live above the fray of ordinary black folk. Unlike the tragic mulattas in the novels of her contemporaries, Janie is a character who cares nothing about refinement. Janie resists the attempts of others to refine her, preferring the values, lifestyle, and speech of the common folk. This is evidenced most in her speech, which is approximate to that of Phoeby, her lower-class best friend. Most tragic mulattas are highly educated (for instance, Helga in *Quicksand* and Angela in *Plum Bun*), and, apart from other differences such as color, they are distinguishable from lower-class blacks through speech patterns that reflect an elite education in institutions of higher learning. Significantly, in *Their Eyes Were Watching God*, the reader cannot use speech patterns to distinguish between Janie and her best friend. This is significant in a novel that foregrounds both class and gender, and provides even more fertile ground for reading the novel as a departure from the tragic mulatta formula.

Janie is clearly not tragic. Although the text ends in tragedy with her being forced to kill the love of her life, Janie is happy in the Everglades until Tea Cake becomes infected by the "mad dog" of internalized racism and first beats, then tries to kill her. For the first time since she left Nanny's house at the age of sixteen, Janie is able to be herself. She participates in the storytelling in her front yard, goes hunting with Tea Cake, works beside him in the fields, and loves him with a reckless abandon born of freedom from the constraints of conventional gender expectations and class pretensions. The one time that Janie has occasion to be jealous of Tea Cake's attention to another woman, she responds, in her insecurity, by hitting Tea Cake. Her response replicates the behavior of the tough working-class women that Hurston had encountered in her ethnographic studies, women such as the memorable character Big Sweet from *Mules and Men*, who can cuss and fight better than most men. Janie is not as tough as Big Sweet, but her response to Tea Cake's presumed infidelity was modeled on the actions of women who were antithetical to the tragic mulatta heroines of Hurston's contemporaries. As with her later rendering of Tea Cake's beating of Janie, Hurston's depiction of this fight is dismissive of its more serious implications of domestic violence. bell hooks argues that physical abuse is represented as commonplace in the black community because women like Janie are used to being hit by authority figures since childhood and are, therefore, more likely to accept physical abuse from their lovers (*Talking Back* 86–88). Nanny also slaps Janie on one occasion (14). I would argue that Hurston's intention is to present fighting between men and women as a normal and regular feature of life on the muck. In this particular example, Hurston seems bent on demonstrating the love between Janie and Tea Cake, as well as the playfulness in his character that allows him to respond without rancor to her assault. Their fighting turns to lovemaking because he decides to make a sport of it:

> They fought on. "You done hurt mah heart, now yuh come wid a lie to bruise mah ears! Turn go mah hands!" Janie seethed. But Tea Cake never let go. They wrestled on until they were doped with their own fumes and emanations; till their clothes had been torn away; till he hurled her to the floor and held her there melting her resistance with the heat of his body, doing things with their bodies to express the inexpressible; kissed her until she arched her body to meet him and they fell asleep in sweet exhaustion. (138)

Hurston uses this scene of domestic conflict to show the level of erotic bliss that Janie enjoys in her relationship with a younger man. Unlike in the spiritual narratives where clothes are torn from black women's bodies so that the Holy Ghost or Christ can overshadow them, Janie's clothes are torn from her body for sexual union with another human being. Unlike Angela Murray in *Plum Bun*, Janie has no reason to regret her free sexual expression. Unlike Helga Crane in *Quicksand*, marital sex for Janie does not lead to unwanted pregnancies and domestic entrapment. Janie gives her body freely and without angst, and her "sweet exhaustion" denotes her sexual satisfaction.

Critics observe that the frame story structure of *Their Eyes Were Watching God* is a narrative device that allows Hurston to have her text narrated alternately by Janie and the omniscient narrator. Janie's story of her life (which she tells to her best friend Phoeby) is framed by the opening story told through an omniscient narrator in which Janie returns to Eatonville after burying Tea Cake in the Everglades. The final pages of Hurston's novel are also narrated by the omniscient narrator, thus closing the frame. Storytelling is another device that often interrupts the flow of the primary narrative. Henry Louis Gates observes that storytelling's main function in *Their Eyes Were Watching God* is "to demonstrate forms of traditional oral narration."[18] However, Hurston's use of storytelling also allows for ideational interventions and innovations that revise and invert stereotypical race ideology. These interventions pave the way for Janie's emergence as the quintessential modern black woman. One such strategically interventionist revision coheres around the mule stories in Hurston's novel. In *Black Women Novelists*, Barbara Christian mentions the metonymic relationship between mules and the term "mulatto," highlighting the discursive fallacy of nineteenth-century pseudoscience that intimated that the mulatta, like the mule, was incapable of reproducing. Hurston makes use of this stereotype, devoting important narrative moments to the trope of the mule and highlighting Janie's metonymic association with this much-maligned animal.[19] However, in a curious reversal, Hurston reinscribes and recuperates the stereotype, refurbishing it with positive associations for Janie.

There are several different narrative interventions that feature the mule trope, beginning with Nanny's declaration that the black woman is "the mule of the world" (14). Nanny's statement is two-pronged: she is referring to the black woman's role in slavery as a laborer and beast of burden. But she also implies that the black woman occupies a social position beneath that of white people and also beneath black men. Throughout the narrative, Janie alternately embodies and subverts this stereotype. She resists muledom in her marriage to Logan by running off with Jody.[20] In Eatonville, however, she occupies a subordinate position to Jody, working as his underling in the store and enduring his hegemonizing "big-voice" authority in the town of Eatonville while he suppresses her voice, sexuality, and subjectivity. Susan Willis's trenchant critique underscores this point: "Like Matt Bonner's starved and abused yellow mule, which her husband turns into the town mascot, Janie was freed from brutal labor and turned into an object" (48). In the muck, Janie embraces physical labor. However, because she freely chooses to work side by side in the fields in partnership with Tea Cake, her labor here is a sign of agency rather than muledom. She does not find it oppressive. In fact, she seems to relish the physicality and freedom of outdoor labor (in contrast to being cooped up in the store) and the opportunity to spend time with her lover. Hurston's refusal to annex burdensome associations to Janie's work in the muck represents an innovation in the trope of muledom as defined by Nanny. Choice, a luxury for black women, is the prerogative of the new black woman Janie is becoming.[21] She can perform hard labor by her own choice without assuming the function of a mule or servant.

The central intervention in the mule trope surrounds Janie's apparent barrenness and Hurston's refusal to make it a point of narrative conflict or conversation. Janie has three marriages but no children, and the reader can only speculate that she is indeed incapable of reproducing. However, Janie's state of barrenness is an "unspoken" issue in the text and is therefore not presented as a point of contention. But in choosing to make her character a wife but not a mother, Hurston allows Janie the freedom to invent herself.[22] Janie's inability to have children frees her to explore her inner consciousness. In the absence of maternal responsibilities, Janie is allowed to develop her interiority, a central step in her spiritual maturity. Here, Hurston offers another corrective to the tragic mulatta trope. Helga Crane—whose sexual expression leads to unwanted pregnancies—is spiritually dead by the close of Larsen's narrative after giving birth to her fifth child. Critics such as Carby who read her as "physically" dead are responding to her spiritual inertia—a condition that forecloses the possibility of Helga's recovery of her self.

Spirituality hinges on interiority and self-knowledge. Janie's admission that she had "an inside and an outside and knew not to mix them," speaks to her developing inner consciousness and spiritual awareness.[23] Janie's heightened spirituality allows her to survive her marriage to Jody while "saving up feelings for some man she had never seen" (72). This quotation suggests that Janie anticipates Tea Cake before she has even met him. How would she know this? Her deep knowing, her clairvoyance, is not externally derived but rather a by-product of her highly developed inner consciousness: "in a way it was good because it reconciled her to things" (77). Janie's spirituality is what allows her to survive what, for most women, would have been a soul-killing twenty years of married hell.

Deborah McDowell observes that Larsen closes *Quicksand* with a pointed critique "of the dual price—marriage and pregnancy/childbearing—that women pay for sexual expression" (86). In contrast to Helga Crane, Janie's barrenness facilitates free and unfettered sexual expression. Liberated from annexation to the conventional role of motherhood and the threat of unwanted pregnancy, Janie's sexuality renders her freer and happier, mimicking her state of orgasmic bliss under the pear tree in Nanny's yard when she was only sixteen. Again, Janie's sexual completion stands in direct contrast to all the other mulatta characters: Helga Crane, who appears to sink further into an abyss with each pregnancy; Clare Kendry, who stops sleeping with her husband out of fear that another pregnancy may reveal her racial identity; and Irene Redfield, who does not even sleep in the same bedroom as her husband for reasons never revealed to the reader. What readers do know is that because he is not allowed to have sexual relations with his wife, Irene's husband, Bryan, thinks "sex is a big joke." Sexual displacement, sexual ambiguity, sexual repression, and sexual denial marked the literary representation of the black woman until the emergence of Janie. Hurston allows her character to spend two marriages—spanning over twenty odd years—suffering the same sexual frustrations as her literary sisters. With Tea Cake, Janie finds deliverance. Her relationship with Tea Cake provides Janie with the spiritual and sexual balance she has sought since the day under the pear tree when she witnesses the whole of nature participating in the sex act and wonders aloud about her place in the scheme of things. Indeed, Hurston's departure from the tragic mulatta paradigm and the distorted representation of black female sexuality enable the emergence of Janie as the modern black woman.

Inspiriting God(s) and Goddesses

> Because of the experience of diaspora, the fragments that contain the traces of a coherent system of order must be reassembled. These fragments embody aspects of a theory of critical principles around which the discrete texts of the tradition configure, in the critic's reading of the textual past. To reassemble fragments, of course, is to engage in an act of speculation, to attempt to weave a fiction of origins and subgeneration. It is to render the implicit as explicit, and at times to imagine the whole from the part.
>
> Henry Louis Gates Jr., *The Signifying Monkey*

Henry Louis Gates's formulation of the "Talking Book," the text that talks to other texts, is an appropriate metaphor to describe the way *Their Eyes Were Watching God* talks to nineteenth-century black women's narratives that self-consciously inscribe the ideology of the trope of true womanhood, and the early twentieth-century narratives of passing that reinscribe, revise, and ultimately reify this formulation and its attendant shame-making discursive strategies. But if, as Gates states, "Signifyin' is the figure of the double-voiced as epitomized by Esu's rendering in sculpture as possessing two mouths,"[24] then Hurston must have found it necessary to use not one, but two Yoruba avatars to help her cut through the dense ideological underbrush that was choking off the creative expression of black female writers of her time. For indeed, Esu is present in his double-voiced signification, but so too is Shango, the Yoruba warrior god of thunder and lightning with his double axe cutting both ways, clearing one path for the emergence of Janie's voice and another for the literary daughters that would come to build upon the project of revoicing black women's sexual discursivity.

Carole Boyce Davies and VèVè Clark both write separately about the necessity of critically engaging with the shared diasporic connections and symbolic systems of meaning evidenced in the works of black writers from different geographical and cultural landscapes.[25] We have another black female critic, the late Barbara Christian, to thank for gifting us with the language through which to recognize that Hurston had already been doing precisely what Davies and Clark suggest is a critical necessity.[26] In *Their Eyes Were Watching God*, Hurston creatively theorizes about diasporic connections, building upon her black folklore collection started in the American South and continued in diasporic points of interest such as Haiti, Jamaica, and Honduras. While other writers of her generation traveled to Paris, England, and even the Soviet Union, Hurston was a citizen of the black *diaspora* before the term was invented. Lamothe correctly argues in reference to *Their Eyes Were Watching God* that "the elements of the text which [Hazel] Carby identifies as displacements to the South and the Caribbean actually allow Hurston to explore through metaphor and symbolism the social and political concerns of African-Americans in the North, South and throughout the Caribbean" (172). Because she was an avid and expert collector of black folklore, it stands to reason that Hurston would come into contact with forms of African spirituality, both in fragmented forms such as Gates describes in the above quote, and in more coherent systems such as she discovered in New Orleans and in Haiti. These, she of course expounded upon in her two ethnographic studies *Mules and Men* and *Tell My Horse*.[27]

Zora Neale Hurston's novel *Their Eyes Were Watching God* encodes spiritual symbolism that engenders liberating stances and transformative action in Janie's life and in those of the black communities she inhabits. Through Janie's search for fulfillment, the text dramatizes an interdependent relationship between social and political empowerment and sexual autonomy for black women. Janie is the first "respectable" black female protagonist in the history of black women's writing in America to transparently express sexual desire and the need for sexual fulfillment. Through Janie's search for personal empowerment, sexual expression, and political agency, Zora Neale Hurston advances the theory that sexuality and spirituality are coterminous elements that facilitate the process of self-revelation and self-knowledge, and that both are integral to the development of black female consciousness.

Hurston wrote *Their Eyes Were Watching God* in seven weeks while in Haiti conducting research for *Tell My Horse*. Hurston's previous ethnographic work in the South and *Their Eyes Were Watching God* contain references to Hoodoo, the African-American version of African spirituality that has nominally survived in the southern United States, although more coherently in New Orleans than elsewhere. While in Haiti, Hurston became immersed in Voudoun, a fully cohesive Haitian folk religion with roots in Africa. Haitian Voudoun—replete with complex philosophies, legends, creation myths, spiritual ideographs, liturgies, patakis (stories), textured theoretical abstractions, and intricate iconographies—must have provided fertile ground for Hurston's imagining of an alternative spirituality for black people. Lamothe argues that images of Voudoun are not transparently displayed in *Their Eyes*. However, Lamothe also suggests that Hurston employed strategies of cultural metissage and disciplinary cross-fertilization to inscribe a syncretic blending of Voudoun philosophical and ethical principles into *Their Eyes*, the book she wrote while fully immersed as both student and initiate in the Voudoun world (160).[28]

Karla Holloway's study on the relationship between the goddess-figures in West African women's writing and the ancestral figure in African-American women's writing provides a useful model for interpreting Hurston's encoding of Voudoun principles and symbols within *Their Eyes Were Watching God*. In *Moorings and Metaphors*, Holloway writes: "I believe that far from being a coincidental selection of metaphors, the ancestral presence in contemporary African-American women's writing reconstructs an imaginative, cultural (re)membrance of a dimension of West African spirituality, and that the spiritual place of this subjective figuration is fixed into structures of the text's language" (3). The synchronicity of ancestral continuity between the Hoodoo she had studied in the United States and the metaspiritual dimensions of Voudoun she experienced in Haiti provided a wealth of figurative material for Hurston's imagining of her heroine as a modern black woman in *Their Eyes Were Watching God*. Janie's complexly orchestrated subjectivity constituted by her mother's and grandmother's painful history—which Janie must somehow transcend—and Janie's independent urge toward a very different future from the one Nanny imagines for her underscore the complexly polyvalent historiography of the figure of the black woman "across the boundaries of culture and countries" (Holloway 3).

Critics of Hurston's work generally agree that by the time she wrote *Their Eyes Were Watching God*, the damaging effects of racist and sexist ideology on black female subjectivity and writing were fully entrenched. However, Janie's desire for autonomy—sexual and otherwise—is expressed in the saying, "Ah wants to utilize mahself all over." (169). What would that look like for a woman of Hurston's time? How could she imagine an uncompromised black female subjectivity, one that would allow a black woman to "utilize" herself all over? How would a black woman like Janie come by the material, spiritual, and emotional means to self-realize so completely? To be satisfied with herself sexually, materially, experientially? Does she do it independently of men or in relationship with them? Upon whom could she model herself?

Janie's desire to be fully self-actualized—to know her divine purpose and to live actively in pursuit of it—is a revision of Nanny's desire for a pulpit from which to preach a great sermon. To remodel herself in a new image, Janie must incorporate the ancestral presence without reifying the historical past. Nanny and Leafy are insufficient models for Janie's stated desire to be fully actualized and completely empowered as an agent of her own transformation. A new genealogy must be configured for Janie, one that constructs ancestry through spiritual rather than blood lineage. In Haiti, Hurston discovered the route to the spiritual lineage of the modern black woman in Voudoun, the New World religion of Haiti that unambiguously foregrounds positive figurations of the black female ancestral presence.

It could be argued that Hurston need never have gone to Haiti to discover the figurative dimensions of the new black woman. Some critics may say that Hurston could have found what she was looking for in Hoodoo. But outside of New Orleans, where did Hoodoo exist in the United States as a cohesive tradition similar to the Haitian folk religion of Voudoun? There is no question that *Mules and Men* establishes the coherent presence of Hoodoo as a tool of African spiritual continuity and African-American cultural adaptability in New Orleans. However, Hoodoo's liminal existence in the American cultural landscape is mirrored in its marginal and fragmented discursivity. Hoodoo's liminality is narratively reproduced and reinscripted in both critical and creative texts.[29] Charles Joyner writes of conjuring, or Hoodoo, in terms that reveal the discursive and practical subalternity of African-American spiritual practices in the dominant culture: "African cosmology maintained a subterranean existence outside of and inimical to African-American Christianity. This element of slave religions continues to be largely unknown and unknowable. Documentation of voodoo, or hoodoo, (as African conjuration was called in the New World) is inevitably scanty, as such magical shamanism was practiced clandestinely" (324).[30] While Hurston argues in *Mules and Men* that "Hoodoo, or Voodoo, as it is pronounced by Whites, is burning with a flame in America, with all the intensity of a suppressed religion," her admission that "nobody knows how it started" signals the peripheral existence of a claimed African spirituality in American culture and also confirms Joyner's argument for its marginal status as an underground religion that is shrouded in mystery and thus subject to unflattering speculation (193). Joyner's dismissal of Hoodoo as "magical shamanism" reflects the historical denigration of African religions in the New World. However, in Haiti, Hurston found a religion that was neither underground nor peripheral to the dominant black culture. In *Tell My Horse,* Hurston states: "As someone in America says of whiskey, Voodoo has more enemies in public and more friends in private than anything else in Haiti. None of the Sons of Voodoo who sit in high places have yet had the courage to defend it publicly, though they know quite well and acknowledge privately that Voodoo is a harmless pagan cult that sacrifices domestic animals at its worst" (92).

Hurston's findings on Haitian Voudoun reveal that she knew it was more than just "a harmless cult." Her in-depth knowledge of the complex cosmology and rituals of the religion as well as her intimacy with various priests and priestesses who constituted the vast network of Voudoun society is recorded in *Tell My Horse*, and many of her assertions about Voudoun are confirmed by ethnographers such as Alfred Métraux, Michel Laguerre, Maya Deren, and others. Hurston's access to privileged information and inner sanctuaries reflected both Hurston's professional and personal audacity as well as the openness of Voudoun in Haitian society.

Hurston was both overwhelmed and excited by the vastness of Voudoun's presence, and while collecting her research in Haiti in the winter of 1936, she requested a formal renewal of her Guggenheim Fellowship on the grounds that "the task is so huge, so huge and complicated that it flings out into space more fragments than would form the whole of any other area except Africa" (Hemenway, *Zora Neale Hurston: A Literary Biography* 246). Hurston respected Voudoun as a complex religion "as formal as the catholic church anywhere" (Hemenway 246). In an unfavorable comparison with the fragmented African spiritual practices in the United States, she makes the following claim for Haitian Voudoun: "It is more than the sympathetic magic that is practiced by the hoodoo doctors in the United States" (Hemenway 246). Hurston clearly established a hierarchical relationship between the Hoodoo she was familiar with in the American context (outside of New Orleans) and the evidence of a more formalized religion that had retained its African potency.

Voudoun provided the framework for Hurston's answer to the question of how to create an autonomous, spiritually grounded black woman who was not afraid of her sexuality. In the Voudoun religion, Hurston found a form of spirituality in which women were neither peripheral nor subjugated. Women functioned centrally as priestesses or as adepts with varying degrees of responsibilities in the hounfour, or temple. In comparison with the sexual subjugation of Caribbean women and the denigration of darker-skinned Jamaican women that Hurston observed with distaste in the first section of *Tell My Horse*, women clearly enjoyed a position of respect in the Voudoun community.[31] Hurston's definition of Voudoun in *Tell My Horse*, which stands in stark contrast to her statement in *Mules and Men* that nobody knows the origins of Hoodoo, affirms the centrality of the woman's role in the cosmology of the religion:

> Thus the uplifted forefinger in greeting in Voodoo is really phallic and that means the male attributes of the Creator. The handclasp that ends in the fingers of one hand encircling the thumb of the other signifies the vulva encircling the penis, denoting the female aspect of deity. "What is the truth?" Dr. Holly asked me, and knowing that I could not answer him he answered himself through a Voodoo ceremony in which the Mambo, the priestess, richly dressed is asked this question ritualistically. She replies by throwing back her veil and revealing her sex organs. (113)

Voudoun clearly recognizes the centrality of sexuality, giving it a place of prominence in creation mythology. In the Voudoun worldview, human history owes its origins to divine copulation and female sexuality is the locus of "the ultimate truth." In response to this revelation from her source, Hurston declares, "There is no mystery beyond the mysterious source of life" (113).

In Voudoun, the goddess Erzulie ritually embodies the principles of human sexuality and sexual autonomy for women. In "Erzulie: A Women's History of Haiti," Joan Dayan focuses on three aspects of this goddess: the elegant mulatta Erzulie-Freda; the cold-hearted and "savage" Erzulie-ge-rouge; and the passionate black woman Erzulie-Dantor. Dayan argues that Erzulie dramatizes a specific historiography of women's experiences in Haiti and throughout the Caribbean" (Dayan 41). Hurston's novel extends Erzulie's historiography to the African-American context, thus linking the experiences of black women in the Caribbean to the experiences of African-American women.

Early in *Their Eyes Were Watching God*, Hurston draws attention to the fact that neither Nanny's Christianity nor the fragmented remains of African spirituality are enough to sustain the new woman Janie is becoming. Hurston gestures to Hoodoo several times in *Their Eyes* and each mention is a representation that signals negation. As previously noted, when Jody accuses Janie of working Hoodoo on him, Janie is both appalled by this suggestion and dismissive of Hoodoo. Hurston's belief in the efficacy of folk wisdom is undercut by her characterization of the root-doctor as "a faker." Similarly, in the opening passages of the text, the narrator's description of Nanny is double-voiced: "Nanny's head and face looked like the standing roots of some old tree that had been torn away by storm. Foundation of ancient power that no longer mattered. The cooling Palma Christi leaves that Janie had bound about her grandma's head with a white rag had wilted down and become part and parcel of the woman. Her eyes didn't bore and pierce. They diffused and melted Janie, the room and the world into one comprehension" (12). I perceive a metonymic relationship between Nanny and Hoodoo, this unnamed (and perhaps unknowable) remnant of an "ancient power" that no longer held relevance for Janie. Maligned as devil worship, dismissed as baseless superstition, disparaged as evil, stripped of its legends, liturgies, intricate rites and symbolic configurations, mythologies, and values, and relegated primarily to herbal cures (represented by the Palma Christi leaves) and spells and potions of dubious effect, Hoodoo had not proven effective as a source of political transformation for blacks in America. Similarly, Nanny, an elder expected to be the repository of wisdom in African culture, is incapable of envisioning or assisting the new black woman, Janie. In reference to Janie and Hurston's reliance on Voudoun symbols to shape Janie's developing consciousness, Lamothe writes: "Voudoun is a religion that expressed black people's capacity for self-determination" (158). Exploited for her labor, sexually seduced, and bred against her will—and therefore suspicious of all sexual activity not delimited by capitalist patriarchal structures—Nanny is ill-equipped to shape or sanction the revolutionary ideals of self-determined womanhood and liberated sexuality to which her granddaughter aspires.

Hoodoo—instead of sustaining community and augmenting black selfhood as Voudoun is reputed to have done during the Haitian revolution—becomes, in *Their Eyes*, another means of "othering" Janie, creating division and fostering black-on-black antagonism.[32] Janie is accused of using Hoodoo to harm Jody, and this accusation sets the community even more against her than before. But why would Hurston, herself initiated into Hoodoo at the time she wrote the novel, implicate it in Janie's alienation from the community? In his germinal text *Workings of the Spirit*, Houston Baker explicates Hurston's successful entrance into Hoodoo society in New Orleans as both insider and outsider, ethnographer and adept:

> We come, therefore, to the successful initiations that Hurston undergoes before becoming a friend, apprentice, and co-worker to Kitty Brown. Behind her and behind the reader of *Mules and Men* is a vision of a ruptured, but productive, vernacular community, a world whose undoing seems the result of competition for narrative authority, an absence of female bonding, and a philandering propensity of axe-twirling, prolifically articulate males. What type of initiation into

what manner of poetic or spiritual space enables Zora to occupy a world in conjure? (88)

Baker's description of the "ruptured" vernacular space in the first half of *Mules and Men*, where contestations over narrative authority and over men engender female-to-female alienation and disruption of communal bonding in the Everglades cypress camp seem to echo Janie's sense of alienation from the community of Eatonville. Janie is set apart, "classed-off" by Jody. Phoeby seems to be her only close friend. Janie's inability to participate in the speech-life of the community signifies both her outsider status and the repression of her voice. In this community that takes pride in its oral tradition, Janie lacks narrative authority because Joe forbids her to speak. Narrative authority is the prerogative of Jody and his male comrades.[33] Class is not an arbiter of male acceptance in storytelling, but both class and gender effectively prevent Janie's participation in these narrative transactions that have the power to facilitate her acceptance by the group. But even when she is invited to speak by the men who wield this power, Jody prevents her from doing so. He is the "Big Voice," the ultimate power to whom the others yield.

Baker's analysis of the second half of *Mules and Men* shows the empowering potential of African spirituality in its full coherence in New Orleans, the historical stronghold of Hoodoo power in the African-American context. Hoodoo acts as a bearer of folk traditions that cohere in rituals of community bonding and cultural resistance. Baker argues cogently that, "The wisdom [Hurston] is able to transmit, in fact, is that of an entire vernacular community and its conditions of both harmony and possible cure. That such a community has faith in the conjure wisdom, the hoodoo power, the Spirit work that she carries is attested by the attention devoted to an audience in *Mules and Men*'s penultimate chapter" (*Workings* 91).

Conjuring, like storytelling, is a communal activity that necessitates a relationship of trust between spiritual leaders and followers. But in *Their Eyes*, no such relationship exists for Janie when she is married to Joe. She cannot have faith in a spiritual and communal network from which she is excluded. Although she longs to participate and be part of a community, Janie is silenced, alienated, and therefore unable to trust the spiritual superstructure of her community. Community and faith become metonyms for Janie's displacement. This is a faith-based community to which she cannot belong.

Janie's alienation from the folk begins not with Jody but in the Washburn yard where she grows up wearing the cast-off clothing of white children. Jealous of her cast-offs, which are still better-looking than their own clothing, black children tease Janie about the circumstances of her birth as a product of rape and warn her not to "take on about her looks." Other than her brief interaction with Johnny Taylor, Janie has no black friends, male or female, and seems to share more positive memories of growing up with the Washburn children than with the black children in the community, who antagonize her mercilessly at school. However, Janie's inability to find community does not stem from a lack of desire or identification, but rather from a certain disdain within which she is held in what Baker might describe as a "ruptured" vernacular space that cannot sustain communal bonding. Janie's alienation from the community, then, stems from the fact that other blacks view her as being "different" and "set apart" from them. Wrongfully inferring that Janie believes she is superior to them, they react by treating her with disdain or suspicion. The community of Eatonville's suspicion of Janie is confirmed when they accuse her of "conjuring" to make Jody ill.

Baker's analysis of *Mules and Men* also demonstrates the potential for misuse when "conjure falls into the wrong hands" (*Workings* 91). And, indeed, in *Their Eyes*, the "two-headed faker" from Altamonte Springs reveals himself to be just that, a fake, whose lies only help to entrench Janie's status as an outsider. Janie's state of alienation in Eatonville mirrors the fragmented and ineffectual folk wisdom extant in the ruptured vernacular space of her community.

Similarly, Nanny's faith in Christianity is inefficacious against the forces with which Janie will be compelled to contend for the rights to her sexual and spiritual wholeness. Early in the text, Janie wonders if marriage ended "the cosmic loneliness of the unmated?" Already Janie imagines a different kind of cosmology than that available to Nanny and a kind of marriage that is shaped not by the demands of the marketplace, but instead by the values of intersubjective relations and spiritual connection. Janie states, "But Nanny, ah wants to want him sometime. Ah don't want him to do all the wanting" (23). Janie is speaking of sexual desire that she wants to feel for her husband. But Nanny responds in economic terms: "If you don't want him yuh sure oughta. Heah you is wid de onliest organ in town" (Hurston 23). Raised as her master's sexual property and having absolutely no control over her sexuality, Nanny cannot imagine a sexual union that is not already delimited by economics. Nevertheless, Nanny feels remorse for forcing Janie into an unhappy marriage and turns to her God to find solace: "She stays on her knees so long she forgot she was there." All night long Nanny wrestles with her decision and "towards morning she muttered, 'Lawd, yuh know mah heart. Ah done de best Ah could do. De rest is left to you'" (24). Nanny's religion teaches her to surrender to a higher power, but it also teaches her nothing about sexual agency for women, and, ultimately, although she feels remorse, she is incapable of relieving Janie's suffering.

But Janie is not acquiescent to her fate, and her resistance to forces over which she has no control demonstrates an alternative spiritual consciousness from the one available to Nanny and her community. Neither Nanny's Christianity nor the fragments of African spirituality that are part and parcel of folk wisdom are enough to sustain Janie's complex spiritual needs. Janie invents a new spirituality that is charged with erotic energy. Janie's syncretic spirituality is crystallized in the image of the pear tree that stands for Janie's emerging sexuality. The reader is first made aware of Janie's syncretic spirituality in the following passage:

> She was stretched on her back beneath the pear tree soaking in the alto chant of the visiting bees, the gold off the sun and the panting breath of the breeze when the inaudible voice of it all came to her. She saw a dust-beating bee sink into the sanctum of a bloom; the thousand sister calyxes arch to meet the love embrace and the ecstatic shiver of the tree from root to tiniest branch creaming in every blossom and frothing with delight. So this was a marriage! She had been summoned to behold a revelation. Then Janie felt a pain remorseless sweet that left her limp and languid. (11)

Janie's orgasmic connection with nature in this passage is augmented by a deep sense of spirituality as well as a natural curiosity that recognizes the centrality of nature as an expression of divine creativity and purpose. Janie seeks "confirmation of the voice and vision, and everywhere she found and acknowledged answers" (11). Janie is actively seeking God and asking questions about the nature of being and her purpose in the divine plan. The natural world responds ubiquitously to Janie's questions. Her orgasmic experience confirms the nexus between Janie's search for spiritual purpose and her heightened awareness of nature and sexuality.

Hurston's syncretizing of sexuality and spirituality as dual components of female development anticipates Audre Lorde's essay written several decades later. In "The Uses of the Erotic: The Erotic as Power," Lorde advances the theory that women are most effective as agents of political and social transformation (on the individual and collective levels) when they recognize and use their erotic power to its full potential. Lorde describes the erotic as a synthesis between sexuality and spirituality: "The dichotomy between the spiritual and the political is also false, resulting from an incomplete attention to our erotic knowledge. For the bridge which connects them is formed by the erotic—the sensual—those physical, emotional, and psychic expressions of what is deepest and strongest and richest within each of us, being shared; the passions of love, in its deepest meanings" (56).

Lorde suggests that through the confluence of spiritual and sexual energy, women are empowered to act politically and effect social transformation within their lives and communities. Hurston's inscription of a similar syncretic model for Janie's developing consciousness is a political act. Its purpose is to restore black female subjectivity through the synthesis of sexuality and spirituality. Hurston blends these disparate spheres seamlessly in her embodiment of Janie as consciously sexual and spiritually mature while achieving both states coterminously.

In a cogent critique of Hurston's politicizing of Janie as a figure of transformation, Daphne Lamothe explores the link between Janie and two distinct manifestations of the Haitian Voudoun goddess Erzulie.[34] Lamothe concludes that Janie represents both Erzulie-Freda, the mulatto goddess of love, as well as Erzulie-Dantor, the black working-class goddess who is associated with maternal rage (170). Unlike the Judeo-Christian God, the Voudoun goddess Erzulie is characterized by her very human needs and desires. Sexual passion is not only ritualistically necessary for Erzulie, but practically useful as well in achieving material objectives. In the case of this goddess, sex is both the means and the end. By inscribing Erzulie-Freda and overlaying Janie's character with this Voudoun goddess of love, Hurston is able to use the construction of Erzulie—the powerful sex goddess—to highlight Janie's sexuality. Multiple marriages, a prominent aspect of Erzulie Freda's personality, become a way for Janie to express sexual desire within the legitimacy of marriage.[35]

Given the absence of community and communal folk wisdom as sources of sustenance for Janie—both in Eatonville and in West Florida, where she grew up with Nanny—Hurston conjures up an alternative route to actualize Janie's transformation. In an act that parallels Karla Holloway's description of textual "recursion and revision,"[36] Hurston displaces Hoodoo and replaces it with Voudoun in the text. The folk religion of Haiti does not just serve to enable community, but also fosters Janie's liberation from all structures of patriarchal dominance. The muck represents the primordial mud of creation and the origination of human community, therefore providing the perfect locus for Janie's rebirth into a communally nurturing space. As such it has a certain innocence that borders on idealization, but this seems to be a deliberate textual ploy because the communal values of the muck stand in opposition to the rupture of Eatonville. The muck is the place where Janie's hunger for community is sated. According to Lamothe's reading, it is also in the muck that Janie is reborn as Erzulie-Dantor, the working- class black goddess:

> The similarities between Janie and [Erzulie] Freda go only so far because, ultimately, Janie rejects the aristocratic ideal that Freda embodies (represented by her love of jewelry, brushes and combs, the valorization of her light skin and long hair and her preference for French over Creole, the language of the lower classes in Haiti). She laments to Phoeby the fact that "Jody classed me off"; and rejoices when she finds in Tea Cake not only romantic love, but also the connection with the folk from which she has so often been discouraged. (163)

Janie tells Phoeby that as a child she was called Alphabet "cause so many folks done named me different names." Janie's multiple identities serve to reinforce her connection to Erzulie, who is said to have over fifteen different emanations and to possess multiple and conflicting attributes. Janie combines the physical attributes of Erzulie-Freda—the mulatta goddess—with the down-to-earth, unpretentious attributes of the working-class peasant loa, Erzulie-Dantor (Lamothe 164).

Through the symbolic inscription of Erzulie-Dantor, Hurston reintroduces African spirituality as a tool of transformation and agency after Janie has had an opportunity to experience the workings of a tight-knit community, an extended family headed by herself and Tea Cake, and to occupy a space in which her voice finds full expression. Narrative authority, physical labor, love, cards, fishing, shooting—all are shared by both sexes in the muck. Janie is happiest in this rough-and-tumble egalitarian space, this primordial mud that breeds some level of equality and gives birth to women as divine expressions of spiritual and sexual synergy. Lamothe's reading of Janie as Erzulie highlights Hurston's reinscription of conjuring and folk wisdom, not through Hoodoo, but through Voudoun: a system of folk resistance that is even more coherently structured in Haiti than in New Orleans, and has a reputation for effecting political transformation against mammoth odds.[37] Houston Baker reminds us that "the bearer of the spiritual legacy in 'modern' African-American—indeed, one might say, modern African diasporic—life was not a king like Solomon, but a queen, priestess, or mambo like Marie Laveau" (*Workings* 91). Hurston's inscription of the Voudoun goddess Erzulie recognizes the passing down of this legacy to Janie, not through the historical line of a priestess—even one as powerful as Marie Laveau—but through the spiritual and ancestral lineage of the goddess Erzulie, the symbolic figuration of female sexual power and the avatar of women's erotic potential. The transference of power from a male "two-headed faker" to a legitimate female progenitor (Janie) accomplishes for Hurston's heroine what Baker explains is the purpose of conjure: "retribution, redress, reward and renewal" (90).

Janie's transformation from skeptic to conjure woman—with the audacious Erzulie-Dantor seated in her head—represents the culmination of a long spiritual and sexual journey.[38] Although Tea Cake is described as the "bee to her blossom," and therefore necessary to Janie's sexual development, it is Janie who imagines and invokes Tea Cake into her space. Tea Cake's precursor, Johnny Taylor, is a "shiftless" individual who Janie idealizes as "sun-up and pollen" in order to achieve a sexual connection with another human being. However, Johnnie Taylor is not responsible for Janie's sexual awakening, and neither is he the agent of her first orgasm. Janie achieves her first orgasm while lying on her back in the grass observing nature, contemplating the meaning of her existence, and envisioning the role of sexuality in her life. Similarly, Tea Cake—although he teaches Janie to fish, play cards, and relate with the folk—merely facilitates Janie's transformation. She calls him up from her soul, because she needs a man like Tea Cake, not to help her experience sexual passion, but to share it with her, in the same way she needs a friend like Phoeby to listen to her story. Nellie McKay writes and I quote:

> Janie's meeting with Tea Cake, who fulfills the role of the bee to her blossom, opens the way for her to construct a language of liberation . . . With Tea Cake, she tells Phoeby, 'new thoughts had tuh be thought and new words said. . . . He done taught me the *maiden language* all over.' The new language she appropriates not only facilitates her relationship with Tea Cake, but also permits her to join the communities from which she was previously excluded, first on the muck and then in Eatonville. (68, my emphasis)

Sexuality and language are rendered coterminous in this passage. What is revealing about McKay's reference to this "maiden language" is that Janie is not taught it for the first time by Tea Cake, but rather taught "over," suggesting that she knew this maiden language at one point, but lost it. "Maiden" traditionally connotes sexual innocence. The "maiden" or "virgin" language is related to Janie's sexual education before she has ever been with a man. Through the conflation of sexuality and language, Hurston encodes a double-voiced discursivity that allows Janie to speak as a sexual subject and come to subjectivity through her sexuality. We see how she first achieves this language as she brings herself to orgasm under the pear tree. But what does it mean that Tea Cake teaches it to her again? When and where does she lose it? And how is Tea Cake able to execute what Logan and Jody both failed to accomplish?

Janie's voice and her sexuality are interdependent, and her spirituality is an expression of her political consciousness. Janie's spirituality, which reached maturity as she communicated with God and nature, was suppressed by Nanny when Janie was forced to marry Logan. Janie has a voice (and always had one), and it is Nanny who begins the process of suppressing that voice.[39] Nanny tells Janie that the black woman is "the mule of the world" and encourages Janie to marry as a way of avoiding the kind of subjugation that has historically been the lot of the black woman. However, Janie's marriage to Logan is another form of muledom. When Logan attempts to buy her a mule to help him plow the fields, Janie decides to leave him. When Janie says she hates Nanny, she repudiates the values of an older generation still beholden to the recent slave past, its repression of black and female subjectivity, its silencing of female voices, and its insistence that black women remain tied to a different kind of victimhood through secure but emotionally stagnant relationships.

Marriage for security clearly replaces slave labor as the new paradigm for muledom, a transition that Nanny, having only known slavery, domestic labor, and unmarried motherhood, is unaware of or unable to articulate. Janie's spiritual expression, so intimately tied to her sexuality, is submerged in the marriage to Logan when she can no longer express herself sexually. Janie's abandonment of her marriage to Logan and subsequent escape with Jody signals her desire to escape the psychological violence of this stagnant marriage. After seven years of marriage to the power-driven misogynist Jody, Janie realizes that she is trapped in the workings of the same paradigm: both her voice and sexuality are driven further underground by the psychological violence of her marriage to Jody. Janie develops a spiritual strategy to preserve her sexuality and her sense of self until she meets the right partner. When Jody slaps her for ruining his dinner, Janie understands that her love life with him is over and immediately puts her strategy into play:

> She had no more blossomy openings dusting pollen over her man, neither any glistening young fruit where the petals used to be. She found she had a host of thoughts she had never expressed to him, and numerous emotions she had never let Jody know about. Things packed up and put away in parts of her heart where he could never find them. *She was saving up feelings for some man she had never seen.* She had an *inside and an outside now* and suddenly she knew not to mix them. (72, my emphasis)

Hurston allows Janie to imagine Tea Cake long before she has met him. By investing her with the power to define the terms of the relationship she wants, the kind of lover she would choose when life finally allows her a real choice, Hurston creates in Janie a character who is self-determined and spiritually and politically conscious, with both an "inside" and an "outside" that she knows not to mix. Interiority is a necessary component of spirituality because it inaugurates self-reflection, meditation, and communion with the divine. Interiority facilitates the interrogative dialectic between humanity and the divine that we see when Janie is lying on her back in the grass questioning an unseen interlocutor about the meaning of life. Her spiritual maturity is what allows Janie to wait, knowing intuitively that she will outlive Jody. Her *inside and outside*—twin metonyms for her spiritual awareness—allow Janie the space in which to cultivate the economic independence she will need to facilitate the kind of relationship she imagines.

Without an education, Janie has few economic options outside of marriage, and no other viable option of attaining financial security. She works as hard as Jody in the store and is also expected to be a perfect housewife (as evidenced by his beating of her when she spoils a meal). Janie deserves a fair share of the store's profits, but will likely receive nothing if she walks away. Her abandonment of Logan testifies to the fact that leaving yet another marriage without benefit of a settlement, while heroic, would be neither economically sound nor sustainable in the long term. Her spiritual maturity (her inside and outside) allows her to bide her time and wait for what is rightfully hers. Upon Jody's death, Janie is finally equipped to finance her own dreams of happiness and security. She no longer needs a man for financial security and can finally choose a sexual partner to whom she can relate as an equal. Hurston makes it clear that Janie can only achieve subjectivity through sexual and spiritual synthesis. With Tea Cake, Janie learns to love herself and another flawed human being, accepting his flaws as well as her own. The fact that Janie first attacks Tea Cake over jealousy signals Hurston's inscription of the interpolation of human imperfection into this otherwise wholesome spiritual union. Similarly, Tea Cake's beating of Janie reflects his interpolation by racist and patriarchal discourses, as discussed previously. When the marriage begins to do violence to Janie's body and her sense of self, Hurston chooses to end it in the most dramatic way possible. To retain her subjectivity, Janie has to choose her life over Tea Cake's, and the fact that she makes this difficult choice is a testament to Janie's spiritual maturity.

Through Janie, Hurston theorizes that true spiritual maturity requires both individuation and collective identification. Janie achieves this synthesis in the muck and returns to Eatonville as an authoritative vernacular subject who can "talk back" to the folk on equal terms. Through the development of Janie's character from an alienated but independent individual to one who maintains her individuality but identifies with the collective, Hurston eschews displacement and alienation as sustaining models for subjectivity. This may well represent a conflation of authorial values with that of her heroine. Hurston herself, though very much an individual, had an amazing propensity for fitting into any group into which she inserted herself. The ease with which she became incorporated (however temporarily) in the folk communities in which she did ethnographic research attests to Hurston's own desire for folk acceptance and validation.[40]

The text ends with Janie happy and fulfilled, although she clearly regrets having been forced to kill her beloved. Her return to Eatonville signals the healing of the communal rupture and her readiness to return to this vernacular community in full possession of the narrative authority she gained in the muck. As though struck dumb in the presence of a deity, the folk are speechless as Janie makes her entrance, confirming that Janie indeed has the upper hand: "Nobody moved, nobody spoke, no body even thought to swallow spit until after her gate slammed behind her" (193). As is typical of Erzulie-Freda—the goddess whose claim to her male devotees precludes any sexual contact between them and human females, often for extended periods of time—Janie's relationship with most women is oppositional (Desmangles 133). Janie is jealous of Tea Cake's attention to other women while the female porch-sitters are envious of her beauty and power over men. Like Erzulie, Janie has few female devotees, but those she has are loyal. Phoeby, Janie's "kissing friend," is one such devotee who defends Janie against the group of gossipers and immediately leaves their company to bring her friend an offering of mulatto rice.

The conversation that ensues between Janie and Phoeby also reveals discursive connections between Hurston's protagonist and Erzulie-Dantor.

Janie's speech is down to earth and laced with working-class humor in perfect synergy with Phoeby, who has no middle-class pretensions. This from Phoeby: "'Gal, you sho looks good. You looks like yo' own daughter.' They both laughed. 'Even wid dem overhalls on, you shows yo' womanhood.'" To which Janie replies, "'G'wan! Gwan! You must think Ah brought yuh something. When Ah ain't brought home a thing but mahself'" (4).

The word "kissing" is repeatedly used to describe the relationship between Janie and Phoeby, Janie and the community, and Janie and nature.[41] Kissing symbolizes love and devotion, and Janie herself suggests that true knowledge and spiritual insight can only come through devotion and loyalty. In response to the unasked questions of the folk gossiping on the porch, Janie says: "If they wants to see and know, why don't they come kiss and be kissed? Ah could sit down and tell em things. Ah been a delegate to de big 'ssociation of life. Yessuh! De Grand Lodge, de big convention of living is jus where ah been dis year and a half y'all ain't seen me" (18). Janie's knowledge, gained through the experience of love, loss, pain, and passion can only be shared if the folk are willing to submit themselves to her teachings, and to love and honor her in all of her complexity. Here, she is both human woman and female deity; at one with the folk in her experience of hardship and pain common to all, and yet surpassing them with her growth, development, and wisdom garnered from a very full life.

The noted anthropologist Alfred Métraux takes the position that the relationship between humans and the spirits in Voudoun is a symbiotic one (134). Through possession, the loas come to earth in human flesh. Similarly, the devotees, while they are possessed by the loa, become the loa and thereby experience divinity. Janie's sentiment that the folk should "come kiss and be kissed" and her elevation of living to an art form that leads to true wisdom and self-knowledge, affirm the theories of Métraux and others regarding the importance of spirit possession and other forms of ritual worship to the spiritual efficacy and continuation of Voudoun religious processes.

Similarly, Janie's statement to Phoeby, "You can tell 'em what ah say if yuh wants to. Dat's just de same as me 'cause mah tongue is in mah friend's mouf" (6), also recalls possession in Voudoun rituals. Métraux states: "Intercourse between the visible and the invisible world is easy and constant. The loa communicate with the faithful either by incarnating themselves in one of them, who then becomes his mouthpiece, or by appearing to them in dreams, or in human form" (120). The god or loa mounts the initiate (the horse) and gets to speak through him/her. Gods usually remain under the water in mythical Guineè, until called forth ritually, at which point they are made corporeal as they "mount" their "horse" or take possession of the devotee.[42] Gods need "horses" to express their personalities on earth and to communicate their wishes to the faithful.

In giving Phoeby permission to speak for her, Janie is able to communicate the wisdom of all her experiential knowledge in much the same way that the gods or loas are able to pass on instruction to the *houngans*, or priests, through the "horses," dispensing advice and spiritual information to the Voudoun community and generally facilitating the dynamic relationship so central to the serving of the loas. In giving Phoeby permission to speak for her, Janie as Erzulie-Dantor does not abdicate responsibility for her words and their possible impact. One could say that during possession, the god's tongue is literally "in the mouth" of the possessed in the sense that the possessed "becomes" the god. The horse, or cheval, is not held accountable for what he or she may say or do during possession because all in attendance understand that it is the god who is speaking (Métraux 132). In allowing Phoeby to speak her words, Janie is able to communicate to the folk who may otherwise not be so receptive to hearing her. The wisdom of her experience, if properly communicated, has transformative potential for the collective. Phoeby confirms the value of Janie's experience: "'Lawd!' Phoeby breathed out heavily, 'Ah done growed ten feet higher jus' listenin' tuh yuh Janie. Ah ain'yt satisfied wid mahself no 'mo. Ah means to make Sam take me fishin' wid him after this. Nobody better not criticize yuh in mah hearin'" (192).

Significantly, after Janie completes her story, in the silence that follows "Phoeby's hungry listening," Janie's thoughts turn to her bedroom where she shared many erotic moments with Tea Cake. She turns to go upstairs with lamp in hand: "The light in her hand was like a spark of sun-stuff washing her face in fire" (192). Janie is ready to reflect upon her experience with Tea Cake and to contemplate the meaning of her life. The questions she asked God at the beginning of the text are all answered for Janie, and she is well satisfied with the life she has lived: "here was peace. She pulled in her horizon like a great fish-net. Pulled it from around the waist of the world and draped it over her shoulder. So much of life in its meshes! She called in her soul to come and see" (193). Michael Awkward's interpretation of this passage is instructive: "Janie's pulling in to herself of the horizon suggests her achievement of indivisibility, the reconciliation of formerly disparate dimensions (56)." Spiritual and sexual synergy is reflected in the symbolism of the bedroom, her thoughts of Tea Cake, and the light that signals Janie's illumination and the clarity of her vision. The fishnet full of life is also symbolic of the richness and fullness of her experience, and she calls in the world to bear witness, and her soul to observe.

Lorde's theory that women live their best lives when in touch with the erotic, and are able to engender positive transformation within their communities only when this union is realized, is borne out in Hurston's final words. Janie's erotic energy catalyzes transformation for herself, Phoeby, and the community. Through Janie, Hurston provides us with a radical model of female empowerment that rejects binaries in favor of multiple perspectives, marries the sacred to the secular, and privileges both individuation and communality as agents of liberation. Janie's search for empowerment is both personal and political.

In "I Found God in Myself and I Loved Her, I Loved Her Fiercely," Michelle Cliff observes that her essay's title comes from the final line in Ntozake Shange's play "for colored girls who have considered suicide when the rainbow is enuf." Cliff states: "I return again to Shange's statement: do her words startle or thrill because a black woman recognizes herself as divine, claims God lives in herself, rather than observing the divine as something 'out there,' which will grant favors or redemption according to its own will, as the result of righteous (by whose definition) behavior or passive acceptance of one's fate? If a black woman is able to recognize God in herself, by herself, and is able to love this God, then she can love herself also. She will love herself, believe in her worth, hold on to her dignity, no matter how many forces on the outside are causing her to consider suicide—the death of the body, but also the death of her self, her spirit, her voice" (11).

Janie is one such black woman who found God in herself and loved her so "fiercely" that she was willing to kill the man she loved to protect her self and nurture the goddess inside her. Janie knew her worth because she had grown through trials, tribulations, and life experiences to love herself deeply, and in learning to love herself she learned to love other women like her and to value black womanhood and black community. Through Janie women are able to reclaim their erotic power and transform their lives. After reading her tale, many women will lose their complacency and perhaps echo Phoeby's sentiments: "Ah ain't satisfied with mahself no mo'" (192). Self-knowledge is the precursor to change. *Their Eyes Were Watching God* proposes radical self-knowledge for the black female psyche, thus allowing for liberating stances and transformative action in black women's lives.

Subsequent generations have built upon Hurston's legacy, demonstrating the sincerest form of flattery by writing Janie-like characters who will try (in some instances successfully) to "out-Janie" Janie. Hurston's literary daughters, from Alice Walker to Toni Morrison, Audre Lorde to Sonia Sanchez, Opal Palmer Adisa to Edwidge Danticat, have all followed in Hurston's footsteps, creating black female characters whose autonomy and agency depend upon the full integration of their sexual and spiritual selves, reclaiming the agency and transformative power of their African and New World spiritual legacies. The fact that black writers imitate each other is nothing new. As Henry Louis Gates points out in *The Signifying Monkey*, "by 1941, it was apparent to these seminal scholars that black writers read, repeated, imitated, and revised each other's texts to a remarkable extent" (xxii). Similarly, Cheryl Wall's observation about the relationship between contemporary black women writers and the women writers of the Harlem Renaissance further supports this contention: "these legatees critique, revise, and extend the themes, forms and metaphors that they employed in their poetry and fiction" (*Women of the Harlem Renaissance* 204).

Consciously or unconsciously, black women writers have imitated, revised, and reformulated Janie since Alice Walker rediscovered the novel and returned it to circulation in the 1970s. Thanks to Walker, more than seventy years after it was written, *Their Eyes Were Watching God* still has women of all races and socioeconomic backgrounds in colleges around the world saying, like Phoeby, "Ah ain't satisfied with mahself no mo.'" To say that Hurston, "the genius of the South," was a woman way ahead of her time is an understatement, and to ensure that her legacy is perpetuated as long as the word is written and spoken is a most worthy cause—one that literary daughters such as Toni Morrison, Opal Palmer Adisa, and Edwidge Danticat have pursued in their own texts explored in this study.

3

Contradictory Directives and the Erotics of Re-membering

New World Spiritual Practices and Black Female Subjectivity in *Beloved*

Reclaiming and Renaming Spiritual Practices

The African cultural referents in *Beloved* have indeed been ignored by most critics, probably because of the dearth of knowledge in the West about the actual religious practices and philosophical traditions of African peoples. Despite a growing body of literary, historical, anthropological and theological work produced in the past thirty to forty years, Africa still remains a "dark continent" to many, if not most, Western readers; few expect to find respectful evocations of African philosophy and spirituality in a book that is being touted as the new classic in American literature. Too often, slaves are still seen as Western subjects manqué, whose sense of themselves are constructed primarily in terms of Eurocentric or Anglocentric concepts of self. Morrison's inclusion of African characters, belief systems, and practices in *Beloved* illuminates the hidden lives of the slaves, the mental attitudes and rituals that allowed slaves to survive and to resist their bondage.

Arlene Keizer, *Black Subjects: Identity Formation in the Contemporary Narrative of Slavery*

In "Rootedness: The Ancestor as Spiritual Foundation," Toni Morrison suggests that what we call a "black aesthetic" is largely informed by an African-centered epistemology. The black writer is invested with an authoritative control that derives from the worldview of her real-world community and is recoded into the mimetic—but imaginary—community in the text. The notion of an African-centered epistemology is important to the concept of what VèVè Clark dubs "diaspora literacy"—"the ability to read and comprehend the discourses of Africa, Afro-America, and the Caribbean from an informed, indigenous perspective"—for two reasons.[1] First, it privileges folk knowledge, beliefs, and practices by forcing the writer to return to the folk for textual material with which to enrich the narrative and make sense of the worldview of the characters who belong to the community about which he or she writes. Second, the act of situating knowledge within the realm of the folk suggests a flipping of the script governing who teaches what to whom, because the concept of a folk-informed epistemology suggests that blacks with formal education and not enough folk-knowledge may find themselves in the position of "student," instead of in the privileged position of "teacher" or "leader," normally assigned to intellectuals in the black community. Toni Morrison's *Beloved* captures the privileged knowledge of the folk and forces the reader to confront the critical apparatuses and hermeneutical processes that provide the narrative structure and interpretive logic of the text.

Like Zora Neale Hurston and many others before her, Toni Morrison consciously employs a black aesthetic that is informed by folkways of knowing and being. I have already discussed at length, in chapter 1, Zora Neale Hurston's use of a particular folk cosmology to portray Janie as the modern black woman. The use of African cosmology in African-American literature dates back to the works of nineteenth-century African-American writers. Frances Harper's text *Iola Leroy* is particularly instructive in its privileging of folk knowledge, while Frederick Douglass's narrative reflects his ambivalence about it. In the figure of Aunt Linda, Harper presents us with an African-centered epistemology that privileges gesture, oral tradition, and experience as folkways of reading. In *Narrative of the Life of Frederick Douglass*, Douglass mentions a mysterious root that Sandy, another slave, advised him to carry for protection against beatings. Douglass carries the root and is able to overpower his master. He never has to submit to another beating, but he expresses uncertainty about the magical properties of the root, thereby demonstrating his ambivalence about whether the African belief system is merely superstition or whether it has validity. Douglass neither confirms nor denies the efficacy of African spiritual practices, but instead allows the reader to consider the possibility that his newfound power could have come from the root. Charles Chestnutt's *The Gophered Grapevine and Other Folk Tales* affirms the centrality of the African worldview in African-American culture and in the oral tradition adapted for literature.

The Black Book (1974) is a compilation of newspaper clippings, family portraits, photographs of lynchings, letters, slave bills of sale, folk tales, interpretations of dreams, advertisements depicting racial stereotypes, and a wide assortment of early Americana chronicling over three hundred years of the African presence in America. *The Black Book* cites the use of witchcraft (Gullah Jack, an African conjurer) in the slave rebellion staged by Denmark Vesey in 1822, Marie Laveau's reign as High Priestess of Vodoo in New Orleans from 1827 to 1869, and various spells, potions, artifacts, and stories highlighting the fragmented but historically abiding presence of an African belief system throughout the African-American community. Contemporary texts like Gloria Naylor's *Mama Day*, Morrison's *Sula and Song of Solomon*, Audre Lorde's poetic evocation of the orishas and the damballah myth of origin in several of her poems, John Edgar Wideman's *Damballah*, and many past and contemporary Caribbean texts continue this tradition of negotiating the relationship between the African past and its own systems of meanings and the complexly creolized present of blacks in the diaspora.

The Black Book also chronicles the Margaret Garner story, the historical account of a slave woman who killed her child rather than have her return to slavery, and also the narrative from which *Beloved* was fictionalized. Morrison admits (in articles and interviews) that she learned the story of Margaret Garner while working on *The Black Book* as an editor at Random House. What particularly interests me is the degree to which significant imprints from African cosmology that are depicted in *The Black Book* also permeate *Beloved*'s narratological structure. Even when they are not thematized within *Beloved*, these spiritual elements are a "haunting" presence in the narrative, enacting a double-voiced discourse that speaks to the resiliency of African spirituality and its efficacy not only as an enabler of the "site of memory" for a people who have had their culture stolen from them, but also as a polyvalent signifier, fully capable of being pressed into service as a literary device that allows for both narrative complexity and open-endedness.[2] These elements of the African cosmology afford the narrative an uneasy but necessary (and partial) closure, a concept that, while problematized by literary criticism, is essential to the African worldview with which Morrison tries to keep faith in her writing.[3] These narrative interventions allow the narrative to encode radical resistance strategies even when the characters themselves are too mired in the historical exigencies of the period to set themselves free. As the character Beloved haunts the text, making her restlessness known to the inhabitants of 124 Blue Stone Road (the setting of the novel) before she is manifested in the flesh, likewise the symbols and icons of African cosmology haunt Morrison's narrative, disrupting the already circuitous path of this polyphonous text.

There is a beautiful and unusual design of a heart in *The Black Book*, depicting the Haitian Voudoun goddess Erzulie Freda. Erzulie's symbol is a red heart, and although *The Black Book* is not depicted in color, there can be no doubt that this is the symbol for Erzulie, not only because her name is inscribed under the drawing, but because of other elements like the knife through the heart, an image distinctive to Erzulie and one that distinguishes this symbol from the Catholic symbol of the sacred heart of the Virgin Mary. Erzulie's symbol, the red heart, appears in *Beloved* in connection with Paul D, Mister—the intrepid rooster—and Beloved. I return later in this chapter to Morrison's use of this symbol as a narrative device, but suffice it to say for now that there is no doubt that Morrison would have come across the Erzulie symbol while editing the book.

Further evidence that Morrison consciously employs these symbols is revealed in the following conversation between the critics Barbara Christian, Nellie McKay, and Deborah McDowell: "A professor from SUNY-Albany where Morrison used to teach, told me that she (Morrison) did a lot of research in Brazil, particularly looking at the work of the scholar who wrote *Flash of the Spirit,*" states Christian (Andrews and McKay 205). *Flash of the Spirit* (published in 1983, four years before *Beloved*) traces the continuous links between five distinct African civilizations: Yoruba, Kongo, Ejagham, Mande, and Cross River, as well as the spiritual traditions and culture of New World blacks in the United States, Brazil, Cuba, Haiti, Trinidad, and other New World spaces. It was written by Robert Farris Thompson, an art historian at Yale University who is widely acknowledged as one of the leading specialists in African and New World religions. If the information Christian was given from a secondhand source is to be believed, Morrison would have had one of the most credible and comprehensive sources of African and New World sign systems from which to create the framework for the spirituality that permeates and enriches *Beloved*. Almost every Morrison critic comments on the Margaret Garner story as a source for *Beloved*, and most also comment on Morrison's indebtedness to the slave narratives, particularly those written by women.

However, as Keizer argues in the epigraph above, few Morrison experts attempt to interrogate African belief systems as foundational to the creation of *Beloved* or significant to their own critical apparatuses. In my own research, I have not encountered any mention of the information Christian spoke of in her conversation with McDowell and McKay. Morrison stated that she wrote *Beloved* so it could stand as a monument to slavery since no other monument to this human tragedy existed (Andrews and McKay 3). It stands to reason that the worldview of the people Morrison wrote the book to commemorate should have a place of authority and legitimacy in the interpretation of *Beloved*. If, as Caroline Rody asserts, having opened up a space for themselves in the American canon, "black writers began to speak with the tongue of the ancestor, claiming their place in American culture and letters upon the same ground,"[4] then I argue that the tongue of the ancestor re-memories its own lost and dismembered spiritual trajectory, and its own mythological system through images of African spirituality encoded in *Beloved*. Their reemergence in *Beloved*'s narrative structure represents a reclamation in much the same way that *Beloved* pays homage to and reclaims those 60 million or more in Morrison's dedication.[5]

When I teach *Beloved*, I always tell my students that while there are many ways to approach this difficult text, there are three interpretive models that are central for me as both critic and teacher: the historical, the psychoanalytic, and the African cosmological. I also tell them to layer these interpretive strategies one on top of the other, rather than choosing from among them. Like Naomi Mandel, I don't buy into the idea that *Beloved* is too oblique or that certain groups cannot legitimately interpret this text.[6] I believe that this view is a cop-out, much too simplistic, a disservice to this brilliant masterpiece, and counterproductive to Morrison's attempt to reclaim a piece of history for those who have no monument to their suffering.

Christian's conviction that Morrison deliberately employs features of African cosmology is borne out repeatedly in *Beloved*. Their thematic prevalence and narratological function within *Beloved* draw attention to the encoding of African spiritual practices as a system of meaning that is applicable not just ethnologically, but also as a literary tool.[7] They are neither intrusive nor forced, and so, like the character Beloved, they are ghostly, appearing to haunt the text in their insistent amorphousness. But the haunting effect of African cosmology provides both closure and open-endedness in the reading of *Beloved*. True, the narrative refuses to surrender to easy readings; no one knows where Beloved has disappeared to at the end of the book, and there is evidence that she might still exist as a ghost. But in African cosmology, this ability to exist in the spirit world is perfectly natural, while Beloved's embodiment in the flesh is unnatural and throws the cosmological order out of balance. This interpretation is supported by the fact that Beloved can be physically exorcised at the end, but still remain textually present.

Beloved is indeed a multilayered text, and, as stated above, it lends itself to multiple readings that can accommodate various interpretive models. However, the potential of a creolized cosmology—based on African diasporic images and signs—for unearthing some of its mysteries has only been partially interrogated. The fact that Morrison admits to employing African cosmology (in "Rootedness" and allegedly to Christian's informant) is significant and certainly lends credibility to any attempt to read her work through the particular lens of an African diasporic worldview. Morrison's argument in "Rootedness" recognizes slavery as a dominant superstructure employing various interpellative strategies to deny black subjectivity, not the least of which was the systematic undermining of black spiritual processes and hermeneutics as authenticating discursive and interpretative frameworks. Morrison's admission that she consciously writes these "discredited knowledge" systems back into the literature represents a deliberate reconstitution of discursive and theoretical structures—a counterinterpellative strategy, if you will—based on African and New World spiritual practices and beliefs.

In *Beloved*, Morrison's preoccupation with death, ghostly presences, and the need to re-member the past, can be made more transparent if interpreted within the complex framework of African and New World cosmologies. The peoples of the African continent evolved complex cosmologies that functioned to enable much more than myths of origin and existential ruminations regarding the ontological viability of a divine order and man's relationship to it. West and Central African cosmologies provide philosophies predicated on the belief that everything in the universe is interconnected. There is no separation between the spiritual, emotional, psychological, physical, and metaphysical realms of human existence. Animate and inanimate objects, supreme beings and humans, are all located on an invisible cyclical registrar. Time itself is perceived as cyclical, not linear, so that birth, death, and rebirth all operate in a cyclical continuum.[8] In African cosmologies, the world is divinely ordered by spiritual principles that enable man's relationships with the Creator, the lesser deities, the animals, and the entire natural world. These cosmologies recognize a hierarchical ordering system that posits a supreme creator as an all powerful—albeit distant—being who delegates responsibilities to lesser deities who are more accessible and possess humanlike characteristics. These lesser deities manifest and symbolically abide in forces of nature, in special inanimate objects, and in important man-made phenomena. For example, in Yoruba cosmology, Shango is the orisha who represents thunder and lightning, while Ogun is the god of war who is represented by iron, tools, and weapons fashioned out of iron.[9] Both are warrior orishas and as such share certain common characteristics. However, unlike Ogun, Shango was a mortal king who ascended to the status of a deity.

Na'im Akbar is just one among a number of African-centered scholars who propose that interdependence and interconnectedness are central to the worldview of African peoples.[10] In "Rhythmic Patterns in African Personality" Akbar explains:

> African people throughout the world have a worldview that is conceived as a universal oneness. There is an interconnection of all things that compose the Universe. . . . This interconnectedness is conceived as a kind of vitalism or life force which pervades all of nature: rocks, trees, lower animals, the heavens, the earth, the rivers, and particularly man, who is a vessel for this oneness which permeates and infuses all that is. (Akbar 123)

African people's belief in the interconnectedness of animate and inanimate aspects of nature is maintained through ritual practices that are often misinterpreted by Westerners. Ancestor veneration is one such practice. Africans do not worship their ancestors, as some Westerners believe, but they do maintain the interconnectedness between the living and the dead through rituals that may resemble worship when observed through a Western lens. Because time is cyclical in West African cosmology, the ancestor is revered as the spiritual and physical head of the family, and this relationship does not terminate after death. Death, in some respects, offers more mobility because it allows movement across corporeal and metaphysical boundaries, shape-shifting, and rebirth into other life forms including newborn babies. Slavery represented a violent disruption of the ritual practices that sustained kinship ties, and the psychic disruption and personal and collective fragmentation of the characters in *Beloved* is, in part, a testament to this rupture.

In *Spirituality as Ideology in Black Women's Film and Literature*, Judylyn Ryan examines the centrality of kinship ties in *Beloved* and in West African cosmologies. Ryan provides an interpretation of the way West Africans understand and mediate the relationship between the living and the dead (55). Through the figure of Baby Suggs, Ryan makes a case for the syncretization of West African religions with Christianity in the development of what we know as African-American spirituality. However, this kind of scholarship, which employs African cosmology as an interpretive tool for *Beloved*, was indeed rare when that book first made its explosive entrance onto the literary stage. Many feminist scholars utilized a Freudian or Lacanian model in their interpretation of *Beloved* without recognizing the centrality of kinship in the African cosmology and the irreconcilable dysfunction that slavery's violence wrought on the "collective" African mind.[11]

I have no quarrel with the use of historicist criticism, psychoanalytic theory, Jungian metaphysics, theories from European goddess traditions, and others to navigate the complex landscape of Morrison's writing. I certainly find Jungian metaphysics and psychoanalytic theory useful in understanding the textually layered rendering of Beloved's description of the place she inhabited before coming to 124 Bluestone Road, and her narration of the relationship to the mother she describes as her "woman" in this section of the book. But, while it is true that the mother that Beloved sees from the bridge is at once Sethe and not Sethe (she appears to be the primordial mother-figure in whose image the child sees her own reflection and from whom the child believes herself to be inseparable), Morrison complicates this reading by layering the Middle Passage experience upon the pre-oedipal one, making Beloved's consciousness a repository for the experiences of the millions of Africans who made that journey or died in the attempt. In allowing us to "re-memory" the Middle Passage, it is the character Beloved who best renders the "unspeakableness" of the spiritual holocaust that made a mockery of the interconnectedness on which African cosmology is predicated. In other words, the kinship dyad is not fully discernible without the "African diaspora literacy" within which to ground its entire meaning. Similarly, Beloved as a character will remain shrouded in mystery (is she human, ghost, or the return of Sethe's repressed pain and guilt?) if one does not make use of the theoretical and interpretive tools extant in the worldview Toni Morrison self-consciously inscribes.

In fact, it was the deluge of articles that interpreted *Beloved* purely from a psychoanalytic perspective that prompted certain well-known critics of African-American literature, such as Barbara Christian, to proffer an alternative reading of *Beloved* that centered the African cosmology as an additional interpretive model. Barbara Christian's essay "Fixing Methodologies" was first presented at a conference entitled "Psychoanalysis in African American Contexts," at U.C. Santa Cruz in 1992. In this essay, Christian alerts critics to the presence of African cosmology in Morrison's *Beloved* and urges us to examine its potential as a theoretical perspective from which to approach this complexly layered narrative. Christian draws parallels between the ghostly presence of Morrison's character, Beloved, and the prevalence of ghost narratives and ghostly sightings in Caribbean societies ("Fixing Methodologies" 366). Christian connects the relationship between living and dead family members that is negotiated through ritual in West African religions with the pouring of libation in Caribbean and African-American contexts (366). She recognizes in *Beloved* the popular Caribbean myth that individuals who die through violence cannot rest in the spirit world and return periodically to haunt the living.

In a similar vein, in the essay "Mobility, Embodiment and Resistance," Carol Boyce Davies examines the relationship between Beloved's ghostly presence and the abiku children of Yoruba religious narratives as well as the ogbanje children in Igbo culture. Davies describes these troublesome spirits as:

> children who die and are reborn repeatedly to plague their mothers and are marked so they can be identified when they return. The marks of the saw on Beloved's neck become the one visible sign to Denver and subsequently to Sethe that this is the physical manifestation of the dead child. (139)

Undoubtedly, these early critiques prompted later Morrison scholars (such as Keizer and Ryan) to read *Beloved* using the formerly elided African cosmology as a theoretical framework. However, none of these readings have fully interrogated the complex array of spiritual symbols in *Beloved* that allude to an alternate interpretation fully grounded in "diasporic literacy."

As mentioned above, Morrison consciously incorporates aspects of the "discredited knowledge" of African people's cosmology into her body of work, and publicly acknowledges that she intends this to be part of her literary legacy. Even a cursory survey of Morrison's other books will reveal the deliberate use of African and New World spiritual signs and symbols. The emphasis on dream interpretation as symbolic rather than psychoanalytic is one prominent example of the use of African and New World cosmology in *Sula*. The "plague of robins" that accompanies Sula when she returns to Medallion is another "sign" of Morrison's use of African cosmology in that text. In African cosmology, nature (like dreams) furnishes symbolic significations that, if interpreted properly, can provide correctives or issue warnings to humans. In *Song of Solomon*, Morrison's portrayal of Pilate, the conjure woman born without a navel, has its roots in the African cosmology.[12] The emphasis on kinship ties, the importance of the theme of orality, and the myth of the flying Africans are other obvious symbols of an Africanist presence in *Song of Solomon*. If Morrison says that she inscribes African cosmology, and if its presence is foregrounded in her other texts, it stands to reason that the same would be true of *Beloved*, a text that obviously interrogates otherworldly phenomena such as spirits and haunted houses.

In *Beloved*, Morrison employs African cosmology self-consciously, but never transparently. Sign systems that derive from African and New World spiritual practices are emblematized through both formal and narratological structures. Part 1 of this chapter explores the connections between African-American spiritual forms and those in the Caribbean and other areas of the African diaspora. I explicate and interpret *Beloved*'s deliberate encoding of spiritual signs and symbols that derive from the beliefs and practices of the folk as they are extant in the narratological apparatuses governing the text, and as they are dramatized thematically.

Spirituality in the African-American context is informed as much by Christianity as by the enduring retention of African spiritual practices and beliefs found in West African cosmologies.[13] Thus, African-American spirituality is, indeed, as much a creolized form as Afro-Caribbean spirituality. African-American spirituality incorporates aspects of the old (African) and the new (American) to produce a dynamic spiritual form equal to the task of resisting America's systematic assault on the African-American spirit.[14] Forms of worship from the black church such as shouting, getting in the spirit, and dancing are all adaptations of African religious practices creolized to conform to Christianity's norms, values, and sacred teachings, while still retaining the flavor of their African origins. Juju, root-work, Hoodoo, haints, charms, amulets, and the significance given to dreams—far beyond the Freudian interpretive model—all belong to a knowledge system that is considered incomprehensible to most mainstream Westerners and is therefore either dismissed as superstition or demonized as devil worship in American popular cultural and discursive arenas.[15] The fact that these beliefs and practices survived slavery and live on in African-American and Caribbean cultures to be reproduced in folktales, poetry, fiction, nonfictional narratives, music, everyday folk discourses, and spiritual practices offers a testament not only to their resilience, but to their incredible adaptability.

In Morrison's *Beloved*, African-American spirituality is a complexly orchestrated organ of resistance that is not based in religious modalities easily identifiable by the Western worldview or easily interpreted from a Western theoretical framework. African-American spirituality is an effective tool in the war of resistance waged in *Beloved* precisely because it is decentered, dispersed, and emblematic of the interconnectedness between matter and spirit, secular and religious orders, and personal and private spaces. *Beloved* demonstrates—more effectively than any critical text to date—that African-American spirituality cannot be contained. It can be suppressed, fragmented, even driven underground, but not contained. From deep in the darkness of the blackest black, beneath the refuse heap of history, it will send up roots and infiltrate our psyches with the seeds of resistance as it does throughout *Beloved*. African cosmology in Beloved operates not just thematically, but as a narrative device that mediates the relationships between language and action, between action and meaning, between the characters' implicit and explicit intentions, and between the narrator's various interventions.

Structurally, Morrison inscribes a metonymic relationship between key characters in *Beloved* (such as Amy Denver, Paul D, Beloved, Sethe, and Baby Suggs) and New World religious symbols and principles to dramatize the socioreligious functionality of specific divinities (orishas/loas/gods), and specific spiritual principles, concepts, and ritual practices inherent to New World and African religions. For example, the character Beloved represents the embodiment of the Haitian loa Erzulie, the Voudoun goddess of love and sexuality. There are narrative moments in which Beloved's hypersexuality is overtly dramatized. These narrative interventions represent the contiguity of Voudoun parlance with Morrison's reclamation strategies mentioned in the essay "Rootedness": Beloved is the "horse," or "cheval," who is mounted by the spirit of Erzulie for the purpose of textually dramatizing the principles and spiritual functions of the loa. In Voudoun, a synergistic and symbiotic relationship inheres between horse and rider, human devotee and loa. The loa comes to earth, is made corporeal, and is actualized through possession of the Voudounist, or practitioner of Voudoun. During possession, the consciousness of the devotee is obliterated entirely, and he or she becomes the god, manifesting the personality, whims, behavior, dietary preferences, dress, and functions of the spirit by whom he or she is possessed.[16] Beloved is not always sexually driven, but when aroused she is insatiable, like Erzulie. Her sexual behavior serves a spiritual purpose (individual and collective healing) that, though thematically problematized, is narratologically necessary.

The purpose of this chapter is twofold. First, I argue that, in Toni Morrison's *Beloved*, what enables the survival of the African-American subjects who people the text and what informs their subjectivities is a creolized form of spirituality forged by the experiences of the slave past, and nourished by an often unreliable, unforgiving, sometimes unrelenting, broken, strained, fragmented, but nevertheless sustaining memory of ancestry, ritual worship, and cultural practices. Second, I contend that sexuality is a primary component of these spiritual practices, rituals, and remembrances, and that until they fully integrate their spiritual and sexual selves, the characters in

Beloved can never achieve full subjectivity. The manner in which this necessary integration occurs in the text is neither seamless nor linear because the repressive conditions of slavery either rendered ancient African rituals obsolete or drove them so far underground that they could only be retrieved in bits and pieces. In addition, Christianity, as an ideological framework for expressions of American spirituality crucially altered the seamless relationship between sexuality and spirituality and in most cases effectively rendered them as separate, even opposing modalities.[17] This is not to suggest that subjectivities are ever stabilized in *Beloved*. Characters in *Beloved* are forced to improvise, adapt, and invent their own rituals, and it is only when they have arrived at a model that fully integrates sexual and spiritual energies that they are able to resist the soul-killing legacy of the slave past and move forward toward a more autonomous subjectivity.

Such resistance is made possible through improvisation, which is itself a defining feature of African-American culture, vested as it is with the power to enact social transformation. In *Black Subjects*, Keizer explores the improvisational nature of African-American culture and notes the ways in which improvisation inaugurates resistance strategies in *Beloved* (37–39). Keizer's analysis signals the parallels between African-American and Afro-Caribbean cultural expressions as critical modes of resistance and adaptation to New World experiences. In the process of creolization, various models of resistance are put into place by the subordinate culture, including improvisation, integration, reinterpretation, adaptation, diversion, revision, and accommodation.[18] In African-American and Caribbean culture, the forms of cultural expression reflect a determination to resist interpellation, erasure, and cooptation by the dominant culture's hegemonizing and homogenizing imperatives.

The prevalence of images in *Beloved* that mimic symbols from African cosmology is a fascinating iteration of ethnography and literature. This mimetic and recursive interplay of literary and spiritual symbols bear further interrogation precisely because it choreographs an alternative model for reconstituting black female subjectivity in *Beloved*, a text that itself foregrounds the problematic nature of African-American identity at a historical juncture. Recurring images of cloth, color, quilts, trees, the bridge, the clearing, the red heart, and many others are merely signposts along the road alerting us to ancient and newly refurbished myths that inform Morrison's craft. Although the ghostly presence of the character Beloved is the most obvious example of how Morrison uses African cosmology to inscribe a black aesthetic, all of the characters in *Beloved* are forced to confront, contain, enact, and embody a worldview that is decidedly alternative, atypical, and subversive. Besides Beloved, characters such as Baby Suggs, holy, and Amy Denver represent very specific aspects of West African cosmology, and their function in the text is disruptive, figurative, transgressive, and ultimately redemptive. Morrison is able to marry spiritual hermeneutics, African religious practices, and sociopolitical critique in the relationships between Amy and Sethe, Sethe and Baby Suggs, holy. Thus, these figures embody the interconnectedness of the political and the spiritual in African and African-American worldviews.

Judylyn Ryan identifies Baby Suggs as a spiritual leader in the tradition of Maria Stewart, Jarena Lee, and other slavery-era and postslavery-era black preachers. Ryan insists that Baby Suggs's "multiple liberating roles are jointly shaped by African and Afro-Christian theological elements" (*Spirituality as Ideology in Black Women's Film and Literature* 53). Ryan cites certain "christological" elements in Morrison's construction of Baby Suggs's character, such as her invitation to the parents to let the children come to her first, echoing (according to Ryan) Christ's call to "suffer the little children to come unto me and forbid them not" (53). Ryan underscores the complexity of Baby Suggs's representation, however, by suggesting that Suggs both embodies and rejects the theology of Christendom. Suggs's doctrine also rejects Christendom's "explanation of black people's enslavement and oppression as either retributive or salvific" (53), and eschews black self-hatred in favor of self-love. Suggs's intervention proposes what Ryan calls a "self-conscious agency that is contiguous with the parameters of an African cosmology"(53).

Ryan situates Baby Suggs within a syncretized tradition of spiritual leaders in the diaspora, many of whom blend Christianity with African spiritual practices and beliefs. Like Baby Suggs, these women have gifts of discernment, prophecy, and healing. Many belong to the Shango Baptist, Revivalist, Kumina, Zionist, or Pukumina churches: New World religions in the Anglophone Caribbean that derive from the synthesis of African religions and Christianity.[19] Others have no church affiliation but are identified (whether explicitly or not) as spiritual leaders in the community. In Jamaica, these women are called "Seeyah women," a Jamaican creole term for "seer." Sometimes they are also called "warner women" or "Maddas," as in church mothers in Afro-Christian or New World religious congregations.[20] These spiritual leaders frequently have visions that they believe are given to them by God as a warning to the community of impending danger or an evil that must be purged from the community. It is not unusual for these "mothers" to wake up before dawn to "warn": literally marching the length of the town or village "exhorting" the community against danger or evil. Ryan reads Baby Suggs as a fictional representative of this New World figure—a female spiritual leader with the authority to preach the Word and command respect in her community.

However, Morrison's narrative also highlights the limitations of a spiritual gift. Spiritual leaders are often able to "read," or discern, a person's future or past. Morrison's narrative suggests that Baby Suggs's power to "read" is hampered by the meanness that hangs in the air after the feast she gives for Sethe. The community misreads her extravagance as pride and resents her ability to have so much and to give of herself and her material goods so freely when they themselves have so little to give. Morrison's view of the community's reaction to Baby Suggs's generosity is very much in keeping with New World and African beliefs about the dangers of pride and extravagance. For example, this Jamaican Creole parable (made famous by singer Bob Marley) admonishes against pride and social climbing: "the higher the monkey climb the more him will expose." It is also considered foolish to brag about your achievements, to comment on the beauty of your child, or to live too extravagantly, as these demonstrations will bring about resentment and negative reactions from the community as well as from the spirits: "Everything depends on knowing how much. And good is knowing when to stop" (Morrison, *Beloved* 87). In his article "Circularity in Toni Morrison's *Beloved*," Philip Page affirms, "the community circle is thus two-edged: supportive and necessary, yet divisive and petty" (32).

However, it is Baby Suggs's inability to "read" the sign of those "high topped shoes" that she discerns that really prevents her from alerting her family to the imminent horror that approaches with the arrival of schoolteacher. Baby Suggs's power as a Seeyah woman is limited, curtailed by her extravagance and by the community's ill will. She can see the danger, but cannot interpret it: "Now she stood in the garden smelling disapproval, feeling a dark and coming thing, and seeing high-topped shoes that she didn't like the look of at all. At all" (147).[21] In being unable to "read" the signs correctly, Baby Suggs is unable to save her kin.

It is no accident that divination in the Yoruba and Santeria cosmologies is often referred to as a "reading."[22] The high priest ("Babalawo" in Yoruba tradition), priestess ("Madrina" in Santeria religion), or "Mother" in Kumina and Pukumina churches, usually officiates over rituals in these New World religions. The African cosmologies that inform these religions are extremely complex systems, and the high priest or priestess has to either be born with the gift or undergo years of intensive training before he or she is ready to divine, read, or heal through ritual. The training may include knowledge of numerology, an in-depth understanding of the sacred legends of the religion (called "patakis" in the Santeria/Lukumi tradition of Cuba), the names and functions of all the gods, loas, and deities, and the complex relationships between them, and an in-depth knowledge of herbs and potions and their uses. It also includes knowledge of mysticism and magic, and a working knowledge of all the rituals that encompass every aspect of human development from birth to death and everything in between. People who have no understanding of these religions often assume that the religious leaders are psychics. However, the word "psychic" cannot be usefully applied to Babalawos and Madrinas as these religions require a systematic epistemological framework that can be obtained only through intense training, divination, ritual practice, and experience.[23]

The ability to "read" signs and symbols that denote African cosmology is an important component of "diasporic literacy" because the reader has to be able to tell, for example, whether the emphasis on color in Morrison's *Beloved* means anything outside of the conventional symbols (racial or otherwise) we might attach to it. Similarly, when he or she encounters colored bottles hanging from a tree in the work of a Caribbean writer, or in the contemporary movie *Ray* portraying the extraordinary life of the late Ray Charles, the reader should know that the image is not merely gaudy yard decoration, but a Kongo-derived practice: "trees garlanded with bottles, vessels, and other objects for protecting the household through invocation of the dead" (Thompson, *Flash of the Spirit* 142). The iteration of this image in the movie demonstrates the survival—albeit sometimes in syncretized manifestations—of rituals and practices that foreground spiritual protection, guidance, and empowerment in the seemingly impoverished black southern community in which Ray Charles was born. As a literate diasporic reader, the moviegoer is able to understand the source of Ray Charles's strength and resilience after observing the "flash of the spirit" in the movie (as represented by the bottle trees).[24] While apparently impoverished and disempowered, the community that is able to produce a Ray Charles is, in actuality, spiritually empowered. The community's agency is linked to ancestral and kinship ties, and to tenacious rituals and practices that, while connected to the past, are constantly revised, refashioned, and reinvested to fit the needs of the present.

Many critics observe that, as in Morrison's other works such as *Sula, The Bluest Eye,* and *Song of Solomon, Beloved* also centralizes and problematizes the role of the black community. However, *Beloved* also engages with a broader notion of the American community and its constitutive elements in relation to class and race, and to notions of freedom and slavery. Historically, as well as in contemporary times, political discourses in America have tended to privilege racialized discourses over class discourses, rather than juxtaposing the two in a relational and operational model. However, Morrison's text disrupts this false dichotomizing by introducing the complex figure of Amy Denver, who, while physically "white," is figuratively "not white" because her class position exempts her from the associative signs of white womanhood. Amy is on a journey to Boston in search of velvet, an item that connotes the life of luxury, ease, and sensuality associated with nineteenth- century southern (plantation) white womanhood. However, the fact that Amy is making this journey on foot, and has no money with which to buy food to sustain her on her journey (Amy stumbles over Sethe in the grass when she is looking for huckleberries to assuage her hunger), suggests that Amy's quest is merely wishful thinking fueled by her desperation to attain white womanhood, or at least possess the associative signs of it.

However, Amy's experiences as an indentured servant mark her as someone who is intimately familiar with many of the hardships and privations that were common to the slave experience. She is accustomed to working hard and being beaten over trifles. She has no money of her own because, as an indentured servant, she is not allowed to earn money. In addition, she has never known her own biological father and suspects that the man to whom she is indentured is her father. Amy's ambiguous paternity alone is enough to exempt her (and her mother) from the status of true womanhood. Under the codes of the cult of true womanhood, Amy is the bastard child of a fallen woman. Amy's life, then, mirrors that of a slave, and in truth she has more in common with Sethe than with any of the few white women we encounter in *Beloved*.

In juxtaposing Sethe's condition (pregnant runaway slave woman with near-fatal injuries sustained from a beating) to that of a white woman who is herself running away, hungry, and intimately familiar with the lash of a master, Morrison provides an instructive comparison between the harshness of indentured servitude and the inhumanity of slavery. In a society driven by racialized discourses, particularly regarding anything to do with the sociopolitical arena in nineteenth-century America, class is often elided in our discursive practices. Morrison's articulation of class issues through the figure of Amy Denver forces readers to confront the fact that despite our discursive lacunae, class and race are often imbricated with each other in ideology and in praxis.

In the appendix to *American Voudou: Journey into a Hidden World*, Rod Davis comments on the revolutionary potential of an imagined black and poor white alliance, an alliance that was unfortunately foreclosed in America and is aborted in *Beloved*: "Had African slaves joined ranks with white workers, many of them "white trash" descendants of the once thriving European indentured servant (i.e. slave) trade, Dixie might have become the paradigmatic revolutionary model for race/class alliance in the Western Hemisphere, if not the world" (351).

However, the alliance between Sethe and Amy cannot outlast Amy's usefulness as a midwife and healer. Amy, as a representative of poor "white trash," uses racist language to distance herself from Sethe. As Judylyn Ryan observes: "working class whites will consent to economic and social policies that are harmful to themselves because they see those policies as having restricted application—to blacks only" (*Spirituality as Ideology in Black Women's Film and Literature* 59). Ultimately, Amy's objective is to find common ground with other white women as signaled through her pursuit of velvet, the sign of luxury associated with white womanhood. Creating alliances with black women who, by virtue of skin color and slave status, are truly and irremediably exempt from white womanhood, is counterproductive and dangerous for a disenfranchised white woman like Amy.

However, Morrison allows the reader a glimpse into the imaginary by allowing us a taste of what such an alliance might possibly yield. The social, political, and spiritual benefits of such an alliance represent revolutionary potential. Thus, Amy and Sethe share an exchange of spirit that enables their survival and cements a spiritual union between two unlikely allies.[25] Although she appears to be politically and socially at the mercy of the system that disenfranchises both blacks and poor whites, Amy Denver is the possessor of knowledge and experience that enable her to act as savior, healer, and midwife to Sethe and the baby she is carrying. The narrative invests this white female character with secrets of folk medicine and healing, knowledge common to—though not exclusive to—practitioners of African and syncretic New World religions. For example, Amy Denver applies spider webs to the open sore on Sethe's back. She seems to know exactly what to do and how to do it, and although she is a young white woman, she cares for her patient with the same unflinching sureness of self that is displayed by Baby Suggs when she confronts the injuries on Sethe's back and feet.

Through the interpretive aegis of the African cosmology, the reader can understand Amy Denver's role as a spiritual figure within the text, even after her figurative usefulness for the purpose of political commentary has reached its limit. The orisha Yemonja is the quintessential mother-figure, nurturer, healer, and midwife in the Yoruba religion. She protects children and officiates at their births. An ocean deity in Yoruba cosmology, Yemonja is characterized by the colors of the ocean, blue and silver. In New World religions her colors are either crystalline or blue and white. In the Caribbean, Yemonja is sometimes conflated with the river deity, Oshun. Oshun's characteristics include creativity, sexuality, fertility, and sensuality. She loves sweet things and is usually given honey, sweet cakes, and gold or yellow fruits in ritual offerings. In Jamaica, these two water deities become conflated into River Mumma, a mermaid who is dressed in Yemonja's colors of blue and white but carries a comb and mirror, symbolizing Oshun's vanity and sensuality.[26] Like River Mumma in Opal Adisa's text, Amy Denver embodies essential characteristics of both Oshun and Yemonja. Like Yemonja, Amy Denver is a healer and a midwife. Like Oshun, she appears to be a sensual creature who craves luxurious feminine things, such as the velvet. The combination of maternal and sensual energy that is combined in Amy Denver signifies Morrison's conflation of these two deities in *Beloved*:

> On a riverbank in the cool summer evening two women struggle under a shower of silvery blue. They never expected to see each other again in this world and at the moment couldn't care less. But there on a summer night surrounded by the blue fern they did something together appropriately and well. A pateroller passing would have sniggered to see two throw-away people, two lawless outlaws—a slave and a barefoot white woman with unpinned hair—wrapping a ten minute old baby in the rags they wore. (84–85)

The river is decidedly a feature of Oshun (a sweet water deity who is of primary importance in both Santeria and Yoruba religions), the spirit of love and beauty, sex and sensuality, owner of rivers in Santeria, and the deity who lives in streams and fresh waters in the Yoruba religion. The blue fern, particularly the silvery blue, represents Yemonja or Yemeya, spirit of the ocean, whose colors are blue and white or crystalline (silvery blue) like the blue of the ocean. Oshun is the deity who governs fertility, the spirit who has to be propitiated if a woman is having trouble conceiving, while Yemeya is the protector of children, the midwife and nurturer, the quintessential mother-figure represented by her long breasts in Yoruba art and by "spores of blue fern" in which "the whole generation sleeps confident of a future" in Morrison's *Beloved* (84). Both of these spirits are said to protect pregnant women, and both are therefore present at childbirth. Amy's long, unpinned hair is a very prominent and defining feature that Sethe remembers and continuously refers to when she narrates the story of Denver's birth. Oshun is similarly defined by her preoccupation with her hair—a sign of female beauty—and by her charm and sensuality in New World religions like Santeria and Condomble.[27]

Paralleling the characters Amy and Sethe, Oshun and Yemeya were "throw-aways" in the United States, lost to the African-American mythological, critical, and oral knowledge systems because in the United States, African religion was discredited, forced underground, and relegated to the pejorative "superstition" or, worse, "demonism." Joseph Murphy, in his essay "Black Religion and Black Magic: Prejudice and Projection in Images of African-Derived Religions," states that "Beginning in the 1790s, crystallized in the 1880s, flowering in the 1920s, and seemingly resurgent in the 1980s, images of 'black religion' as violent and licentious 'black magic' have dominated all popular discourse on African derived religions" (8). Morrison's stated attempt (in "Rootedness") to recover black religious iconography from the realm of the demonic and the terrifying, thereby recentering their a priori status as symbols of cultural and spiritual/religious tenacity, is evidenced throughout *Beloved*. I contend that through fictional figures such as Amy, Sethe, and Beloved, Morrison attempts a radical reinscription of African and New World spiritual figures and principles to demonstrate the ways in which blacks in the diaspora resist interpellation by the dominant culture.

Carolyn Mitchell, in her article "'I Love to Tell the Story': Biblical Revisions in *Beloved*," writes that Amy Denver's quest for velvet appears frivolous until one places it in the context of a spirit that prompts her to action, which is not normal for a white woman of her time. Mitchell reads Amy Denver as a Christ-figure. However, while Christ is known as a miracle-worker in the Christian tradition, Yemonja is considered the quintessential midwife and mother in Condomble, Yoruba, and Santeria. Her sister Oshun is the giver of children. Amy Denver's role as a midwife to Sethe secures her approximation to these figures from African and New World religions. In addition, the seemingly innocent but pervasive presence of cloth in Morrison's narrative is anything but arbitrary when contextualized within the framework of African cosmology. Cloth figures prominently on altars to African and New World religious deities. For example, altars to Oshun, Oya, Yemonja, and Shango are quite spectacular. Bedecked in elaborately patterned gold, blue, red, or multicolored cloth, depending on which deity is being ritually represented, and trimmed with plates of food, cakes, mirrors, jewelry, fruits, animals, or whatever offering the deity accepts, such altars represent a sensually gratifying portion of the religious festivities.[28] The texture of the velvet that Denver describes also engages with sensual aspects of Oshun's personality. Denver, though clearly not a great beauty or a woman of means, emanates sensual potential that is characteristic of Oshun's devotees. Most of the literature on Oshun is quick to point out that while her children are not all beautiful, they all possess an unmistakable sensuality and charm.

Cloth also figures into *Beloved* in forms that represent healing. It is cloth that Clara uses to bind Sethe's bloody feet. Baby Suggs also enlists the aid of cloth when she ministers to the "chokecherry tree" on Sethe's bloody back. In the following passage from *Beloved*, Sethe invokes the importance of cloth:

> There was this piece of goods Mrs. Garner gave me. Calico. Stripes it had with little flowers in between. 'Bout a yard—not enough for more n' a head tie. But I been wanting to make a shift with it. Had the prettiest colors. I don't even know what you call that color: a rose but with yellow in it. For the longest time I been meaning to make it for her [Beloved, the crawling already baby] and do you know like a fool I left it behind? (163)

Of course, there are multiple ways of reading Morrison's foregrounding of velvet, calico, and other cloths. However, a consciously engaged reading that deliberately employs African "diasporic literacy" renders it transparent as a symbol of African and New World cosmologies that may shed light on previously unexamined aspects of Morrison's text. The persistent textual references to cloth and the significance with which these references seem invested narratologically, forces this reader to confront and incorporate them as part and parcel of normative hermeneutical strategy.

Piecing Together the Critical Quilt

Place also plays a central role in Morrison's signifying of the African cosmology in *Beloved*. The clearing in which Baby Suggs, holy, conducts her sermons is a sacred space; the house at 124 Bluestone Road is haunted; streams, rivers, and oceans represent the Middle Passage and the mythical home of ancestral spirits; the keeping room is both a refuge for the women and a place in which ritual is enacted and memory is stored; and the cold house is where Paul D releases his past and discovers Beloved's true identity as the New World goddess Erzulie.

Place is important in each of Morrison's novels. In *Sula*, Morrison's description of "The Bottom"—from the way its name was obtained (from a joke played on "niggers") to the tragic collapse of the tunnel—marks the African-American characteristics of the place. The Bottom is marked by the history of racism, the experiences of segregation and racial prejudices of the people who live in it. It is a "black place," and it has a character that expresses the joys and sorrows of the black experience. The tragedy of Chicken Little's ritual death; Nel's joyous wedding celebration; Plum's sacrificial burning; Sula's ominous return; Hannah's abundant sexuality; Shadrach's singular sanity disguised as madness; Sula's deep-seated passions, joyful sexual abandon, and frustrated creative energies; Nel's spitefulness—all give The Bottom its distinct character. It is a fictional place, but when some readers enter the world of The Bottom, they feel as if they are living in it. After each reading of Sula, I miss The Bottom, and the feeling that remains with me is like the feeling of exile: an anguished yearning to return to an impossible place.

There are also similarities between the naming of The Bottom in *Sula* and Macon Dead's name in *Song of Solomon*. In the latter novel, a drunken white clerk gets the senior Macon's (Milkman's grandfather) information mixed up when he goes to the "Freedmen's Bureau" to register after the Civil War. So instead of recording the fact that Macon Senior is a free black, and that his father is dead, the clerk writes "Dunfrie" for the place name (a corruption, perhaps, of "done free") and "Dead" in the place for Macon's surname. Milkman's obsession with finding an original identity to replace the troubled one he associates with "the Deads" (Macon, Pilate, Hagar, himself, and his sisters) leads him to the place that holds the secret to his identity and freedom. Morrison makes it clear that the place Milkman needs to get to is both physical and spiritual. Milkman comes to Shalimar with all the trappings of an "outsider": new car, the wrong attitude, asking the wrong questions, and ignorant of the linguistic codes of orality. It is imperative that he learn quickly how to become an "insider," so he can internalize the lessons that will save him from annihilation. Before Milkman can learn the secret of his family's history—the secret of what makes the Deads different from any other family—he must acquaint himself with the rhythm, the worldview, and the language of Shalimar. It is in Shalimar, the home of his flying ancestor Solomon, that Milkman discovers the secret he carries in his blood: that he comes from an ancestral line of vast empowerment, a people who could fly. The fact that the secret Milkman seeks is encoded in a child's ring game is Morrison's way of signaling the importance and complexity of the oral tradition.

Milkman first hears a version of the song from Pilate who sings of "Sugarman" flying away home. When Milkman hears the song again in Shalimar, it is "Solomon" who flies away home. In making the connections between these narratives, Milkman has to intuit some of the basic principles of orality. For example, he learns that specifics such as names may be changed in each retelling of the tale, but the essence of the story remains intact. Each time he hears the song, Milkman discerns a different name or detail that helps him put the pieces together. When Milkman finally hears the song in its entirety, he attempts to write it down on his airline ticket, but finds that he has no pen. He decides that "he would just have to listen and memorize it" (306). Part of what Milkman learns is the importance and power of the oral tradition. Just as Solomon does not need an airline ticket to fly, Milkman does not need a pen and paper to remember the legend that sustains his kinfolk in Shalimar.

It is through memory—in the remembering and in the retelling of this story—that the people of Shalimar find the strength to survive and overcome racism, poverty, and every other evil that threatens their existence. Once he understands these principles, Milkman is on his way to understanding Shalimar, the ancestor Solomon, and Solomon's descendants (Pilate, Reba, Hagar, Macon, and Milkman himself), and the tools he needs to ensure his own survival. It is not incidental that the legend of Solomon is passed down through the children's ring games. The years of childhood are not only our most impressionable, but the games, stories, and songs we learn in these years leave the most indelible markings on our subconscious. Through the ritual repetition of Solomon's legend, the community of Shalimar is able to sustain itself and pass down important lessons of transcendence and survival to each generation. The memory of Solomon's incredible act of resistance and agency lives on in Shalimar and in his descendants. What Milkman learns of resistance he must learn through the legends and lessons left behind by his Solomon kinfolk, as well as through Pilate's New World adaptations, which weave together elements of the old with the new: her name dangling from a box in her ear, the site of orality.

Solomon and his descendants leave lessons in escape, transcendence, and transformation for Milkman and the generations yet to come. Once Milkman learns these lessons, he can begin to make sense of the ties of kinship, survival, and history that he shares with Pilate, Hagar, and Reba. *Song of Solomon* ends ambiguously: Milkman either dies, takes flight, or does both simultaneously. If he dies, Milkman does so with the knowledge of self and ancestral connection that will allow him to take his rightful place among his ancestors, a position from which he will, like Solomon and Pilate, be able to effect lasting transformations in the lives of his descendants. Since kinship ties do not end with death, and since the power to effect transformation is not only the province of the living, the ambiguity at the end of *Song of Solomon* only underscores the efficacy of African and New World hermeneutical strategies vis-à-vis Toni Morrison's oeuvre.

In *Beloved*, Morrison makes place a venue for personal, social, and cultural contestation where ancestral and archival memory, personal and political trauma, and spiritual exigencies jostle for position in the divided subjectivities of black Americans. In the first pages of *Beloved*, Sethe explains that memory lives in places as surely as it does in people. Unlike The Bottom, 124 Bluestone Road is not a place of nostalgic daydreams; it is a place of nightmares. Like the terrifying nightmare from which the sleeper desperately wishes to be awakened, but is not, 124 holds the reader in bone-chilling thrall. From the very opening of *Beloved*, Morrison signals the belief, common to the black diaspora, that baby ghosts are both vengeful and powerful:[29]

> 124 was spiteful. Full of a baby's venom. The women in the house knew it and so did the children. For years each one put up with the spite in his own way, but by 1873 Sethe and her daughter Denver were its only victims. The grandmother, Baby Suggs, was dead, and the sons, Howard and Buglar, had run away by the time they were thirteen years old—as soon as merely looking into a mirror shattered it (that was the signal for Buglar); as soon as two tiny hand prints appeared in the cake (that was it for Howard). Neither boy waited to see more. (3)

Clearly, 124 is an empowered speaker. It articulates its haunting in polyphonic resonances.[30]

Baby Suggs also articulates the significance of place in her sermons on healing and empowerment. Baby Suggs, holy, ministers to her congregation in a place that is itself sacred and mysterious: "a wide-open place cut deep in the woods nobody knew for what at the end of a path known only to deer and whoever cleared the land in the first place" (87). The clearing is described as though it were hallowed ground, and it is certainly treated as such when Sethe visits it with Beloved and Denver: "Yet it was to the clearing that Sethe was determined to go—to pay tribute to Halle. Before the light changed, while it was still the green blessed place she remembered: Misty with plant steam and the decay of berries" (89).

Robert Farris Thompson credits the Bakongo, or Kongo, people of Central Africa, whose ancestors also arrived in the New World as slaves, for having transported the importance of trees in African-American culture. In *Face of the Gods*, he writes: "The Bakongo consider trees sentinels of the spirit. An offshoot of this belief diffused through the Black United States, constellating around New World trees, where in Central Africa it had involved the fig and other species" (81). In Jamaica, the cotton tree, a relative of the baobab tree that is revered in West Africa, is said to be the dwelling place of spirits.[31] It is bad luck to chop down a silk cotton tree because the spirits of the tree become so angry at this affront that they allow the tree to fall in the direction of the cutters and crush them to death. Only ritual sacrifice can appease the silk cotton tree's spirits: an animal must be killed, its blood spilled at the base of the tree, and rum poured liberally over the trunk. Rum plays a central role in most New World religions; it is often offered to both orishas and ancestors. Blood sacrifices are also a favorite offering for several of the orishas, including the orisha Egungun who represents the spirits of the dead.

Thompson cites an ex-slave's recollection of trees as sacred spaces:

> "I usually prayed behind a big birch tree, a little distance from the house, and often during the night when I would feel to pray, I would get out of bed and go to this tree." . . . Little did the planters know: right on their property Africans had covertly transformed trees into sites of religion. (*Face of the Gods* 81)

The clearing in Morrison's description echoes the description of the grove in Thompson's depiction of New World religious spaces. But if the clearing is a church when Baby Suggs is alive and still preaching, it becomes an altar—along with the keeping room—after her death. Sethe goes to the clearing to honor Halle, whom she believes is dead. She also goes to consult with Baby Suggs: "at the most to get a clue from her husband's dead mother as to what she should do with her sword and shield now, dear Jesus" (89). Although Sethe is not related to Baby Suggs by blood—and perhaps because she is not—Morrison stresses the ancestral connection that marriage creates between the two women. By underscoring that Suggs is Sethe's husband's dead mother, Morrison signals to the reader the importance of kinship ties, the continued interconnectedness between living and dead kin, and the relationship between the spirit world and the physical realm. The language of the narrative also draws attention to the fusion of African and Christian belief systems in the African-American worldview. In *Their Eyes Were Watching God*, Janie begins her narrative (lying outside under the trees) with ontological questions to an unseen interlocutor who could be the Christian God or any of a number of African or New World deities who are embodied in aspects of nature. Here, Sethe's is also a creolized spirituality: she is questioning the dead ancestor Baby Suggs, as well as the living but "unbodied" Jesus.

There are also intertextual connections between Gloria Naylor's *Mama Day* and *Beloved* that cohere around the image of the bridge in both texts. The bridge is symbolic of the crossroads in African and New World cosmologies, the gateway between the world of the living and the world of the dead. In Naylor's text, the bridge is a metaphor for the unincorporated area known as Willow Springs, that space that is in neither South Carolina nor Georgia: "But Georgia and South Carolina ain't seeing the shine off a penny for our land, our homes, our roads, or our bridge" (6). The bridge is the only thing that connects the inhabitants of Sweetwater with the mainland. It represents a crossing over into another sphere, a sphere in which characters such as Mama Day and Abigail are legitimized along with their gifts of prophecy, conjuring, and healing, a family tradition passed down from the mysterious ancestor Saphira Wade, through whose sorcery and mysterious sexual powers the land has been wrested from its white owner and deeded to the black inhabitants of Willow Springs. But the bridge does not simply separate; it also links the physical plane with the spiritual plane.

The image of the bridge resurfaces in *Beloved*. The bridge that Beloved claims to have lived on is a metaphor for the space between the physical and the spiritual world. In the African and New World cosmologies, if Beloved is indeed a ghost, then she exists in suspension between the world of the living and the world of the dead and is tormented because of her lack of grounding in either. This undefined space that Beloved occupies within the text, along with her ability to defy easy categorization, gives rise to a certain "discursive liminality" rendering her even more potent because of her unknowability.[32]

I would like to suggest that the bridge also symbolizes the connection between the past and the present, the living and the dead, and links the enslaved Africans who made the Middle Passage journey across the Atlantic with their New World descendants. Legba, the Yoruba, Santeria, and Voudoun spirit of the crossroads, is the orisha who links past and present, spiritual and physical. He is the avatar of communication between the spirit world of the ancestors (the dead) and the world of the living, and is the god who has to be propitiated first before the commencement of any ritualistic or ceremonial events. Legba, also known as Eshu/Ellegua, represents duality, and is often performed as either a wise old man or a young and mischievous child. He is said to be the personal messenger of destiny and the chief linguist. Legba is a trickster figure whose presence in events is often emblematized by indeterminacy, caprice, chaos, unpredictability, and absurdity. However, his ritualistic function is to bring about positive change. Beloved, while not a Legba figure in my reading, inscribes the Legba principle through the metonymic relationship between the bridge—which links blacks on the Middle Passage with the characters in the text—and the crossroads, also a transitional space. The chaos that reigns at 124 when the text first opens emblematizes and deploys Legba's trickster principle, and in that sense, Morrison's narratological apparatus mimics New World religious propitiation rites by first inscribing the Legba principle before introducing any other orisha precepts.

As discussed above, Ryan's positioning of Baby Suggs as a spiritual leader in the African New World tradition is crucial to my reading of the narrative encoding (or haunting) of African and New World sign systems in *Beloved*. As a spiritual leader, Baby Suggs's role in *Beloved* is similar to those of Mama Day and Abigail in Gloria Naylor's *Mama Day*. These female characters challenge the patriarchal power structure's relegation of women to positions of subservience. They offer alternate models of power and agency as well as alternative discourses that resist the metanarratives of Western knowledge systems. Ryan argues that by positioning themselves as spiritual leaders who spoke by leave of the ultimate authority figure—God himself—nineteenth-century black women preachers were able to transgress the barriers to public articulation placed on both women and blacks. They used their spiritual authority to challenge both the institution of slavery and the patriarchal power structure of the Christian church (Ryan, "Spirituality and/as Ideology in Black Women's Writing" 275). The spiritual and social vision that Baby Suggs espouses and tries to impart to her congregation differs from Christianity both in terms of its doctrine of self-love and in terms of its revalorization of the flesh that was abused and appropriated by slavery. Baby Suggs tells her congregation to love their bodies, and honor all of its parts, while Christian doctrine dictates a transcendence of the body and its pleasures for the richer rewards of the soul and spirit.

In *Let the Circle Be Unbroken: The Implications of African Spirituality in the Diaspora,* Marimba Ani (also known as Dona Marimba Richards) explains how rituals survived in African-American religious practices:

> The ultimate expression of the African world-view is the experience or phenomenon of ritual. It is only through ritual that death can be understood as rebirth. It is only through ritual that new life was given to the African spirit. We performed and experienced ritual drama in North America. The modality of ritual drama was foreign to the Euro-American ethos, and, therefore, could not have come from that source. We performed the "ring" shout in the "hush harbors," the "night sings," and the prayer meetin's. (24)

Ani's analysis is intended to demonstrate the seamless transmission of African retentions into African-American cultural life. But instead of an essentialist notion of purity, what her example effectively highlights are the similarities between African-American spirituality and other creolized spiritual traditions in Haiti, Jamaica, Brazil, and elsewhere in the New World. Baby Suggs's sermon both mirrors and departs from Christian sermons in significant ways, hence its syncretic, creolized character. Unlike Jarena Lee, Maria Stewart, and other early black preachers from the Christian tradition, Baby Suggs does not feel the need to assert any authority other than her own. Furthermore, Baby Suggs's gospel does not evoke the Christian theological precept of salvation through the figure of Jesus Christ. Her gospel is informed by the slave experience, and she preaches salvation through the enactment of ritual modes of healing, transformation, and transcendence. These include ritualized acts of self-love, crying, and ritual dancing. In Yoruba, Santeria, Voudoun, Pukumina, Kumina, Condomble, and other diasporic religions, dancing serves a dual purpose: it connects the individual with ancestral spirits and allows him or her to invoke the presence of the loas and orishas.[33] The memory of her mother that Sethe finds most sustaining is the one of her engaged with other Africans in a ritual dance: "And oh they danced and sometimes they danced the antelope. The men as well as the ma'ams, one of whom was certainly her own. They shifted shapes and became something other" (31).[34]

Baby Suggs's gospel acts as a counternarrative to that of schoolteacher and the institution of slavery that he represents. While schoolteacher trains his white pupils in a discourse of mastery that names and catalogs the animal and human characteristics of his slaves, Baby Suggs's sermon is a ritualized renaming, a revaluing of the African body and a reaffirmation of the parts whose health and well-being are essential to the physical, emotional, psychological, and spiritual wellness of the whole.

As Ryan argues, Baby Suggs is not just a preacher; she is a spiritual leader whose stewardship of her community is based on a profound sense of intersubjectivity between the individual, the community, and the entire cosmos. Baby Suggs's doctrine is not exclusive to African or black New World cosmologies. In fact, her theological discourse and its practical applications are, in many respects, aligned with both New Age and neo-Confucian thought.[35] Ryan also links Baby Suggs doctrine of self-love to the black Christian tradition. However, to many fundamentalist Christians, Baby Suggs and her congregation dancing in the woods may seem to be enacting a pagan ritual. Her emphasis on the importance of being in touch with one's emotions (crying, laughing) could certainly lead to comparisons with New Age "touchy-feely" indoctrination. In this sense, Baby Suggs's doctrine is very much in keeping with beliefs derived from ancient spiritual practices that maintain that the healing of the individual depends upon the full integration of sensory, bodily, spiritual, and cognitive planes, and furthermore, is inextricably linked to the well-being of the community.

But most significantly, Baby Suggs's doctrine is directly informed by experiential knowledge gained in the trenches of slavery. She knows and tries to impart two essentials: first, the only way the black body and spirit can heal from the brutality of slavery is through acts of self-love and self-validation; second, the survival of the individual is inextricably linked to that of the community and vice-versa. Sadly, despite her best efforts, Baby Suggs fails to teach her community the value of intersubjectivity, as signaled by their abandonment of Sethe and Baby Suggs at two crucial points in the narrative: when they spot schoolteacher coming to retrieve his slaves and after Sethe murders her baby. Hence, Baby Suggs is forced to retreat to the spirit world to continue her lesson.

The Colors of Life and Baby Suggs's Fixing Ceremony

Like the image of the bridge or the motif of dancing, color and cloth are central and significant in Morrison's text. This is demonstrated most complexly in Baby Suggs's contemplation of color on her deathbed. Robert Farris Thompson affirms that the African-American quilt originates in African textiles that were woven for spiritual purposes. He points out that among the Mande people, African textiles are woven with breaks in the pattern to confuse evil spirits. This sentiment is echoed in Jamaican folklore: any individual who wears a profusion of bright colors may be asked if he or she is trying to "run duppy," which may be translated as "chase away evil spirits."[36] In *Beloved*, Morrison refers to the plans of escape made by the Sweet Home slaves as follows: "night gives them more time and the protection of color." The character Beloved frequently refers to schoolteacher and to the white slave owners on the Middle Passage journey as "ghosts" and "men without skin." Color, the single-most important marker of racial difference, as well as the biblically sanctioned excuse for racist practices, is inverted in Morrison's text. Color, especially the color black of nighttime, becomes a protection against the evil spirits that slavery and slave owners represent. Marimba Ani explains the spiritual and practical importance of night to the resistance strategies of the slaves in the African-American context: "We would gather slowly, a few at a time, at night—a special time for us. Night was special not only because the day's work was over and because it helped to hide us, but also because that is when spiritual energies are more potent" (24). Morrison's comment on the night as protective coloring parallels the two claims made in Ani's quote: that the night helped to hide the resistance practices of the slaves, and that there are spiritual energies to be drawn from the color and essence of the night.

Therefore, Baby Suggs's insistence that she wants to retire to her bed "to fix on something harmless in this world" (meaning color) is ambiguous, if not downright misleading (179). For it is Baby Suggs who begins the fixing ceremony that leads to Beloved's eventual expulsion from the house at 124 Bluestone Road, a house haunted by a baby ghost and named after the color blue, Erzulie's color.[37] Baby Suggs's retirement to her room to contemplate color can be interpreted as a ritual exercise meant to banish Beloved's vengeful ghost and the evil system that precipitated her untimely death. "Morrison uses ritual as a model for the healing process," writes Linda Krumholz.[38] She continues, "Rituals function as formal events in which symbolic representations—such as dance, song, story, and other activities are spiritually and communally endowed with the power to shape real relations in the world" (108). Baby Suggs's seemingly benign contemplation of color is one such ritual that has the "power to shape real world relations" by exorcising vengeful spirits, and teaching those she leaves behind how to wage the necessary spiritual warfare (ritualistically) that will engender their recuperation from personal and historical tragedy. Sethe observes: "it took Baby Suggs a long time to finish with blue, then yellow, then green. She was well into pink when she died. I don't believe she wanted to get to red, but

I understood why because me and Beloved outdid ourselves with it" (201). Blue—Erzulie's color—is Baby Suggs's first choice to begin her ritual work. It is little wonder, then, that Erzulie will later reincarnate in Beloved to assist in the spiritual labor begun by Baby Suggs. But the other colors also have ritualistic significance in African spiritual practices.

Lydia Gonzàlez Huget, in a study of orisha worship in Cuba, reports: "if the owner of the house is a devotee of Oya, or the person has learned of an accidental death, creating the danger of spirits haunting the house or attracting death, one sets up a banner made of pieces of cloth in nine different colors, dedicated to Oya, begging her to make death, or Iku, depart" (Lydia Gonzàlez Huget as quoted in Thompson, *Face of the Gods* 201). Nine is the number of Oya's favorite child, Egungun, and the colorful patterns represent the colors in his gown (201). One Yoruba legend explains that once upon a time, Shango was deathly ill as a result of evil spirits who were plotting his demise. He dressed himself in the costume of the Egungun and the spirits who had created his illness scattered when they saw him coming dressed like the dead (201).

Baby Suggs's inability to complete the ritual is evidenced in the fact that although she spends a considerable portion of her last days on earth contemplating color, the quilt that she leaves behind has only one bright spot of orange. There are creolized links between Baby Suggs's quilt and those made by the Mande people mentioned previously. In the African-American context, quilting replaces weaving and the intricate textiles fashioned by the Mande become beautiful quilts in African-American folk artistry. African-American quilting also maintains the spiritual connections with Mande weaving. Orange is often used to represent Oshun in some New World religions, including Condomble. Like Yemonja, Oshun is an orisha who is associated with life and healing. Morrison's use of orange signals Baby Suggs's invocation of the healing power of Oshun, another force of female creativity who is expressed through quilt making (in chapter 4 I briefly discuss how Adisa's character Arnella, a seamstress and artist, expresses Oshun's energy in her craftwork). But the multiple ghosts in Morrison's narrative will not be scared off by the efforts of one individual or even one orisha. A true exorcism requires a ritual that invokes the power of the entire community, and the combined ashé of all of the spiritual forces to expel the evil of slavery and the monstrosity of Sethe's act of resistance against it.

Jane Hindman examines the communal nature of quilting in her article "African American Quilt Making as Metaphor in Morrison's *Beloved*": "Another essential aspect of the context of slave quilters' creative responses to functional necessity is the opportunity that quilt-making afforded women, men and children to gather together and share stories, gossip about plantation events and news of escaped or captured slaves" (107). Hindman cites Gladys-Marie Fry's book *Stitched from the Soul* for its emphasis on the community building aspects of quilt making in slave society. However, at the point at which Baby Suggs begins the quilt, the community has already abandoned her and her household, and so she begins a solitary ritual that she cannot complete because the paradigm of individualism is alien to the process and function of quilting and to African spiritual praxis.

Baby Suggs's inability to finish the quilt opens up the possibility for community effort in this project of ritual resistance at 124 Bluestone Road. Toward the end of the novel, we find Beloved and Sethe working on the quilt that Baby Suggs started, each participating in an unnamed ritual, the culmination of which will result in the restoration of balance and harmony to 124. In addition, the ritual will facilitate the recovery of intersubjective relations in a community desperately in need of healing. Beloved and Sethe finish the quilt that Baby Suggs started. Their combined efforts cause them to join forces in a ritual meant to remove the overbearing presence of evil, as embodied by Beloved, fed by the memory of the horrors of the slave past and of Sethe's act of mercy and desperation against it, and reinforced by the community's rejection of the inhabitants of Sethe's household.

The centrality of quilt making as an African diasporic artifact and conveyor of African "diasporic literacy" is explored by several critical works. For instance, Michelle Cliff's article "I Found God in Myself and I Loved Her/I Loved her Fiercely: More Thoughts on the Works of Black Women Artists" comments on the levels of meaning and African spiritual sources encoded in the quilt work of black women seamstresses: "The idea of levels of meaning, the deeper levels of meaning known only by initiates, the decoration of seemingly ordinary objects with images of power, are things which [Harriet Powers's] quilt holds in common with the *mbufari* [symbolic appliquéd cloths] of Ejagham women" (27).

Jacqueline Tobin and Raymond Dobard's text *Hidden in Plain View* provides a detailed account of the importance of African-American quilt making and theorizes that these quilts may have played a central role in the Underground Railroad. More recent scholarship has challenged these conclusions.[39] However, what cannot be refuted are the similarities between many of the images found in African-American quilts and symbols found in

African textiles. For example, the image of a monkey wrench stitched into many African-American quilts also appears in the Nigerian Ukara cloth as a symbol of honor and status for the blacksmiths in Nigerian society (Tobin and Dobard 85). In American slave society, the blacksmith was the most highly skilled craftsman and enjoyed a place of honor among the slaves. In addition, Ogun, the Yoruba warrior orisha of iron and other metals, is also the patron saint of the blacksmiths in Yoruba culture. As a warrior orisha, Ogun is the one to whom a devotee would go when he required a will of steel and superhuman courage; and indeed the long and treacherous journey north—beset with slave-catchers, dogs, and other evils—would be just the kind of situation in which Ogun's energy would be invoked.

Hidden in Plain View also references other noteworthy symbols used in African-American quilt making to encode symbolic messages of resistance and transformation:

> The *nsibidi* and the *vai* syllabaries are symbolic ideographs, which, like words, depend on context for meaning. According to Dr. Maude Wahlman, one of the foremost authorities on African writing systems, there are 690 known *nsibidi* symbols. One example of the *nsibidi* is the cross or X design that stands for "word" or "speech." It is a symbol that looks like the Kongo cosmogram depicting the "four moments of the sun," a reference to the cycles of life. The X appears on many objects as well as textiles. The *nsibidi, vai,* and other African writing systems constituted a visual encoded language system evident in many African textiles. (44–45)

In Morrison's *Beloved*, Sethe's mother is marked with the symbol of the Kongo cosmogram by the master's branding iron: "Right on the rib was a circle and a cross burnt right into the skin" (61). In *Flash of the Spirit*, Robert Farris Thompson explains the significance of the Kongo cosmogram:

> This Kongo "sign of the cross" has nothing to do with the crucifixion of the son of God, yet its meaning overlaps the Christian vision. Traditional Bakongo believe in a supreme deity, Nzambi Mpungu, and they had their own notions of the indestructibility of the soul. Bakongo believe and hold it true that man's life has no end, that it constitutes a cycle. The sun, its rising has no end and setting, is a sign of this cycle, and, death is merely a transition in the process of change. The Kongo Yowa cross does not signify the crucifixion of Jesus for the salvation of man kind; it signifies the equality compelling vision of the circular

motion of human souls about the circumference of its intersecting lines. The Kongo cross refers . . . to the everlasting continuity of all righteous men and women. (108)

Sethe's mother reacts to her daughter's insistence that she "mark" her too, by slapping her face. The Kongo cosmogram, symbol of the cycle of life, becomes inverted into a symbol of death and oppression under the slave system. When it is appropriated by the master to be used in the branding of his slaves, it becomes a symbol of interpellation, subjugation, and spiritual death for the African woman. Sethe's mother makes the link between the Kongo symbol and death very clear. She alludes to the fact that "something" may "happen" to her, and informs Sethe that all the others who bore that symbol are "gone now." The reference Sethe's mother makes to her daughter's inability to recognize her face in death suggests the horrific brutalization and torture—often resulting in permanent disfigurement—to which the slave women were often subjected. Although the cosmogram has been transformed into a symbol of death and erasure, it may ultimately be the only marker of identification between mother and daughter. This double inscription of the violence of slave beatings on top of the psychological violence of having her group's symbol of life turned against her, is the point that Morrison so painstakingly makes in this poignant scene. The black woman's ability to nurture life within her body is used against her as a mechanism for fueling the slave machinery. Hence, the black woman's body becomes the site upon which all the horrors and trauma of slavery are inscribed. Naomi Mandel writes, "Baby Suggs who 'speaks' by dancing with her twisted hip, presents a vision of community that is irrevocably marked by the bodily violation that is its history" (595). Sethe's mother slaps her daughter because she refuses to accept that the only point of recognition between them is a scar they both bear, the sign of the denial of their subjectivity under the oppressive system of slavery.

Sethe's mother's violent reaction is an act of resistance against this interpellation, and a warning to her daughter against complicity in the dominant culture's misappropriation of the symbol as something evil.[40] The Kongo cosmogram, branded beneath her breast as a sign of her master's ownership, cannot possibly maintain its original Ki-Kongo meaning. It has been transformed by the brutality of slavery into a sign of slavery's interpellation of African subjectivity. Sethe's mother's reaction displays a creolized sensibility, one that fosters resistance: the recognition that a new symbol is needed to replace the one that has been irrevocably corrupted and transformed. In place of the Kongo cosmogram, she gives her daughter a memory, a story for Sethe to pass on to her own daughter.[41] Through the telling of this story, Sethe is able to ascribe her vivid memory of the symbol, and the context within which her mother passed down this lesson about the importance of kinship ties, familial remembrance, and spiritual resistance.

Another fascinating link between Morrison's use of the Kongo cosmogram and the way this symbol is analyzed in Tobin and Dobard's book has to do with the Ohio connection that is so clearly made in both texts. The action in *Beloved* takes place primarily in Cincinnati, Ohio. Clearly, the historical association of Ohio with the closest link to freedom on the Underground Railroad is being evoked in Morrison's novel. Tobin and Dobard's text shows the link made in quilt making between concepts of freedom linked to a specific geographical point—in this case Cleveland, Ohio—that was marked by the symbol of the Kongo cosmogram:

> Symbolically the Kongo crossroads is represented by a cross, made in the shape of what we know as a Greek cross, with vertical and horizontal intersecting lines of equal length. This cross, according to Kongo scholar Wyatt MacGaffey, is often marked on the ground to indicate the point where a person taking an oath would stand. In Kongo symbology, this person is standing at the intersection between the Ancestors and the living, the horizontal line being the division between the two (Thompson, p. 109). What would be a more accurate representation of arrival in Cleveland, the axis of many roads leading to freedom, the concept of the African crossroad, the point at which a final decision affecting the rest of one's life must be made? (98–99)

Seen in this context, it is clear that Sethe's mother anticipates her own death as the only freedom she will ever know, and in this sense her "mark" symbolizes her position: standing in the space between the ancestors and the living. However, this is no place for the young girl Sethe to occupy, hence another reason that she must not bear the mark as her mother does.

Like these quilts of the Underground Railroad that embody codes that may take researchers many years to decipher completely, the quilt that Baby Suggs starts in the keeping room may also convey levels of meaning not easily observed or interpreted. For indeed, the keeping room in which Baby Suggs spends her last days contemplating color represents the space between "the ancestors and the living" in Morrison's *Beloved*. In that room Baby Suggs is "Suspended between the nastiness of life and the meanness of the dead" (4). It is from within this liminal space that Baby Suggs conjures up a protective ritual, a fixing ceremony for Beloved's ghostly presence that involves the use of bright colors and draws upon the African-American tradition of quilt making.

Morrison draws upon the African cosmology—the meaning of the Egungun and the bright colors of their garments—to demonstrate Baby Suggs's spiritual intentions in creating a quilt that calls attention to itself in its drabness and in the spots of orange that only serve to draw the viewers' attention to the need for more color in the quilt:

> Kneeling in the keeping room where she usually went to talk-think, it was clear why Baby Suggs was so starved for color. There wasn't any except for two orange squares in a quilt that made the absence shout. The walls of the room were slate-colored, the floor, earth-brown, the wooden dresser the color of itself, curtains white, and the dominating feature, the quilt over an iron cot, was made up of blue serge, black, brown, and gray wool—the full range of the dark and the muted that thrift and modesty allowed. In that sober field, two patches of orange looked wild-like life in the raw. (38)

According to the myth of the Egungun, color represents life and its presence serves to ward off death and evil. The drabness of the quilt belies Baby Suggs's intention to retreat to her room to contemplate color. Except for orange, none of the colors in Sethe's quilt represent the Egungun, the spirit of the dead. Yet the bright colors she contemplates in her room—even the red that she could not get herself to focus on—are Egungun colors. Although Baby Suggs is unwilling or unable to finish the Egungun quilt, she leaves the encoding of Egungun colors in her room for Sethe.

Both Sethe and Denver (at different times) develop the habit of retreating to Baby Suggs's old room with all its encoded messages of spiritual resistance. Sethe goes to the room to "kneel" and "think-talk," activities that connote prayer and meditation. In African religious houses, there is usually one room set aside for the orishas and ancestors. In it are colorful altars representing each orisha. Devotees "talk" or "pray" to a particular orisha in front of his or her respective altar, bedecked with the orisha's colors and other special adornments. Baby Suggs's room is a pared-down, bare-bones version of this sacred space while she is alive. When she dies, it becomes a place of worship, retreat, refuge, deep reflection, and spiritual renewal, and is called "the keeping room" (perhaps because this is where the spiritual codes of resistance are kept). It is the only place in the house where Sethe and Denver feel safe and unhaunted by the horrors of the past.

At the point in the narrative when Sethe becomes convinced that Beloved is her daughter returned to her, she is prompted to continue Baby Suggs's ritual of healing and spiritual resistance. She too begins to contemplate color. For Sethe, this is a joyous breakthrough since the last color she remembers seeing was the pink on her daughter's headstone. She says, "think what spring will be for us! I'll plant carrots just to see them" (201). Sethe's decision to begin observing color progresses to the point where she is "tacking scraps of cloth onto Baby Suggs old quilt, it was difficult for Denver to tell *who was who*" (241, my emphasis). The ambiguity in the pronoun referent is intriguing. Can Denver not tell Beloved from Sethe or Sethe from Baby Suggs? Sethe's dresses, made of carnival colors, mirror the costumes of the Egungun, who represent the ancestral spirits honored and embodied by masked dancers in both Africa and the Caribbean. These masked dancers appear in carnival parades as well as in orisha ritual events.[42]

Sethe's decision to begin the ritual of spiritual resistance represents an important narrative shift that facilitates her healing and Beloved's return to her proper sphere (the spirit world). There is a forward movement in the narrative that seems to propel Sethe away from her own recuperative efforts while giving in to every demand Beloved makes. Sethe's guilt seems to be what drives her, but the narrative enacts a recursion that is a necessary part of this healing ritual. Thematically, Sethe appears to give in to Beloved's demand for attention as well as to satisfy her own newly acquired taste for color. But it is at this point in the narrative that Sethe's initiation into the art of spiritual resistance begins to pay off. Sethe's sense of vindication, her pleasure at having her daughter returned to her in the flesh, runs contiguously with the narrative strategy to finalize the serious business of Beloved's exorcism. Linda Krumholz explains the three stages of Sethe's healing process:

> In part one the arrival first of Paul D then of Beloved forces Sethe to confront her past in her incompatible roles as a slave and as a mother. Moving from the fall of 1873 to the winter, the second part begins Sethe's period of atonement, during which she is enveloped by the past, isolated in her house by Beloved, who forces her to suffer over and over again the shame of the past. Finally, part three is Sethe's ritual "clearing," in which the women of the community aid her in casting out the voracious Beloved, and Sethe experiences a repetition of her scene of trauma with a difference—this time she aims her murderous hand at the white man who threatens her child. (109)

When the business of waging spiritual warfare becomes too much for her to handle, Sethe receives help from "the other side." It is at this point in the narrative that readers are made aware that Beloved is not the only spirit in the house on Bluestone Road. Baby Suggs's spirit, though not vengeful, is an abiding and active presence in the house. Baby Suggs is a conjure woman; she can talk to Denver although she is no longer in the world of the living. It is Baby Suggs who urges Denver to leave the yard and go out into the community to find help after Sethe's breakdown:

> Denver stood on the porch and couldn't leave it. Her throat itched, her heart kicked and then Baby Suggs laughed, clear as anything. "You mean I never told you nothing about Carolina? About your daddy? You don't remember nothing about how come I walk the way I do and about your mother's feet, not to speak of her back? I never told you that? Is that why you can't walk down the steps. My Jesus my." (244)

Baby Suggs's intervention propels her granddaughter to action. So Denver goes out into the community, dressed in the carnival colors of the Egungun that were inspired by her grandmother's quilt and made by her mother, warding off evil and drawing the positive energy of the community (ashé) to assist her in reclaiming her family from the brink of spiritual death.

Despite the fact that she no longer inhabits the physical realm, Baby Suggs's spiritual intervention in the final stages of the healing ceremony is undeniable: through the quilt she leaves behind, through her prompting of Denver to remember the past and to use its lessons to recuperate a future for herself and her mother, and through her insistence upon the recognition of the community as a source of healing and transformation. Though she might have grown tired in life, the narrative suggests that even in death, Baby Suggs never gives up on the community.

Morrison's narrative interventions posit Baby Suggs as a good ancestral spirit who died easy (in bed), and is at rest (unlike Beloved). She can therefore occupy her proper place as spirit guide for her lineage. Susan Comfort explains the presence of conjure women: "As transitional liminal figures in symbolic systems, sorceresses, hysterics and conjure women possess a 'symbolic mobility' that threatens to disrupt and deconstruct that system" (123). This is an appropriate assessment of Beloved's narratological function in the text, but it also applies to Baby Suggs. Although she may appear to characters like Stamp Paid to have given up after the community's betrayal, the centrality of Baby Suggs's presence in the text is consistent. Whether it is ministering to the physical and spiritual needs of her community, feeding them extravagantly, or helping her granddaughter and Sethe to exorcise the demons of slavery haunting 124 Bluestone Road, Baby Suggs's actions and intentions are disruptive (to the slave system), sustaining, and transformative, even after she becomes a liminal character in death.

Baby Suggs is a spiritual leader whose interrupted vision forecloses the possibility of her preventing Beloved's murder. However, her spiritual protection of her household and community does not end with her death, just as it did not end when she retired to the keeping room to contemplate color. Color represents life in *Beloved*, as it does in New World religions. Color also represents spiritual agency, as all of the orishas or Yoruba deities are represented by a color. Baby Suggs's encoded spiritual resistance stands in opposition to the discourse of slavery that rendered black people as passive objects, devoid of agency. African and New World cosmologies—oppositional, disruptive, subversive, and transgressive within New World spaces, particularly within a context in which they are juxtaposed in a binary oppositional relationship to Christianity—are nevertheless conduits of agency and black subjectivity. By carving out a space for resistance and transformation in her keeping room, Baby Suggs is able to continue teaching black self-love from beyond the grave. Despite Baby Suggs's best efforts and those of Sethe and Denver, it is ultimately the community's participation in the ritual that compels Beloved's retreat into the spirit world. The community's return to the values of intersubjectivity is what enables the completion of the fixing ceremony that is necessary before the restoration of balance can be effected. Because the individual and the community are intrinsically interconnected, Sethe's healing is also the community's healing. The community's recuperation in *Beloved* depends upon a model of creolization that syncretizes principles of the African cosmology with New World acculturations. The spiritual resources that the community employs as weapons against the evil of 124 Bluestone are elements of a creolized spirituality, a combination of Christianity and African cosmology:

> Some brought *what they could and what they believed would work*. Others brought Christian faith as shield and sword. For Sethe it was as though the clearing had come to her with all its heat and simmering leaves, where the voices of women searched for the right combination, the key, the code, the sound that broke the back of words. Building voice upon voice until they found it, and when they did it was a wave of sound wide enough to sound deep water and knock the pods off

chestnut trees. It broke over Sethe and she trembled like the baptized in its wash. (Morrison 261, my emphasis)

Sethe's ritual baptism (which is also Beloved's exorcism) is a source of healing and transformation for her and her family, enacted through the combined (ashé) energy of the community. It is connected in Sethe's mind with Baby Suggs's sermons in the clearing because it is indeed a ritual act meant to facilitate the healing of the body, soul, and spirit of the community. Torn asunder by the brutality of slavery, divided by insecurity and distrust, and marked by Sethe's sacrifice of her child for the sake of freedom, the community in *Beloved* represents what Houston Baker would call a "ruptured vernacular community" badly in need of spiritual healing (*Workings of the Spirit*).

Thus, as she does in *Song of Solomon*, Morrison returns to community as the site of spiritual and psychological healing in *Beloved*.[43] The fact that the individual's recuperation and wholeness is inextricably linked to the community's sense of harmony and unity is a continuation of Morrison's examination of the theme of intersubjectivity in the African cosmology. Ultimately, Morrison's texts support the view that the creolized forms and strategies of resistance that black people developed in the New World to deal with the forces of oppression that threatened their survival were only sustained through the combined efforts of the community. Although the individual's sense of autonomy and individuation is important, the needs of the individual should not eclipse those of the community. Because of the constant threats to black survival, the maxim that there is strength in numbers is real for black people on a fundamental spiritual, emotional, and psychological level. Audre Lorde insists that "we cannot live without our lives." Morrison's anthem seems to be, "we cannot live our lives without each other."[44]

In keeping with the ethos of interconnectedness that undergirds African cosmology, I have tried to demonstrate the intertextual, intercultural, and interdisciplinary links that connect *Beloved* to other black New World texts (both creative and ethnographic), as well as to less formal epistemological sources in part one of this chapter. I have explored an array of signs and symbols that have specific meaning in African and black New World spiritual practices in order to demonstrate Morrison's pervasive use of African cosmology in *Beloved*. I do so with the belief that Morrison intends to make use of African cosmology in the same way Western writers make use of

Greek mythology. In addition, Morrison introduces her readers to a rich and complex mythological and philosophical epistemology that has its roots in the most sophisticated African and black New World thought.

In part 2 of this chapter, I demonstrate the nexus of sexuality and spirituality that connects *Beloved* with *Their Eyes Were Watching God* and other texts in this study. I explore *Beloved*'s incarnation as Erzulie, the Haitian Voudoun goddess of sexuality, showing that it is through Beloved that the characters in the text—most of whom have suffered from sexual trauma of one kind or another—are able to find healing. Part 2 continues the work of restoring black subjectivity, creating a balance between sexuality and spirituality through a reintegration of the sacred and the secular. I will expand my exploration of black female subjectivity to include Paul D, who must learn to reject the slave masters' model of masculinity if he is to find his own humanity. In rejecting certain patriarchal codes of behavior, Paul D adopts ethical principles and social behaviors usually associated with the feminine. It is through this integration of male and female attributes that Paul D finds a workable model of manhood, one that will restore his own fragmented subjectivity and augment his role as an agent of creative transformation within the text. Through the aegis of Erzulie, the avatar of female sexuality and divine agency, Morrison's characters are empowered to transcend the trauma of the slave past and begin the journey toward a unitary subjectivity.

Sexual Encounters in Spiritual Dimensions

> Your vagina looks like what a god would look like if there was a god.
>
> Ted Jonas, "Cuntinent," *Erotique Noir*

Strict transcendence means that God is God and does not depend on the world for anything at all, though the world is believed to depend perfectly for its very existence on the gracious creation and support of God.

> John Berthrong, *Buddhist-Christian Studies*

Erzulie herself, though the embodiment of every feminine sweetness, has her whims and does not give herself until her will is done. For a man to succumb to her, or to a real woman, upon the instant is to fail her, and to treat her as though she were nothing but mere impulse. But the loa are not impulses or objects of desire. They are persons and principles of action. It is perhaps only when an impulse meets with a desire for order, that the loas are born, and they lead their imperious existence in a space which man creates in himself, but can hardly enter.

Francis Huxley, *The Invisibles*

The three quotations above represent contesting views of the divine. The first provides a concept of the divine from the perspective of an atheist. He expresses the belief that should a supreme being exist, and should S/he choose to manifest existence in the flesh, the divine would assume the appearance of the poet's idea of perfection: his lover's vagina. Indeed, as I discuss in chapter 1, the Voudoun religion gives the vagina prominence as the locus of the ultimate mystery: the mystery of human origin. The second quotation represents the conventional Judeo-Christian perspective of God as a transcendent being whose existence and perfection is totally independent of humanity, while humans, conversely, are completely dependent upon God's benevolence. The third quotation presents a Voudoun perspective of God as both human and divine, a principle as well as a person. Erzulie, the Voudoun goddess of sexuality, represents the erotic principle that drives human sexuality. She is both metaphor and metonym, the principle itself made flesh, embodied as it were to perform, project, manifest, and activate human desire, sexual and spiritual agency, and creation itself.

In *Passage of Darkness: The Ethnobiology of the Haitian Zombie*, Wade Davis weighs in on the Haitian religion, noting that

> Vodoun itself is not an animistic religion. The believers do not endow natural objects with souls; they serve the loa, the spirits, which by definition are the multiple expressions of God. There is Agwe, the spiritual sovereign of the sea; and there is Ogoun, the spirit of fire and the metallurgical elements. But there is also Erzulie, the goddess of love; Ghede, the spirit of the dead; Legba, the spirit of communication between all spheres. Vodounists, in fact, honor hundreds of loa because they so sincerely recognize all life, all material objects, and even abstract processes as the sacred expression of God. Though God (Bon Dieu) is the supreme force at the apex of the pantheon, He is distant, and it is with the loa that the Haitian interacts on a daily basis. (Deren 1953; Maximilien 1982: Rigaud 1946, 1953; Simpson 1980; Courlander 1960)[45]

In this section, I would like to take a closer look at the Haitian loa Erzulie, the goddess of love and sexuality. Perhaps no other single passage in *Beloved* invokes such provocative comparisons to New World religious symbols as the lovemaking scene between Beloved and Paul D. In her article "Erzulie: A Women's History of Haiti,"[46] Joan Dayan notes that most ethnographers, Haitian or foreign, present Erzulie in three emanations: as Erzulie-Freda, the lady of luxury and love; as Erzulie-Dantor, the black woman of passion identified in catholic chromolithographs with Mather Salvatoris, her heart pierced with a dagger; and as Erzuli-ge-rouge, the red-eyed militant of fury and vengeance (Dayan 42). When Beloved enters the shed in which Paul D sleeps after she has mysteriously removed him from Sethe's bed, she immediately demands sex. She tells Paul D: "You have to touch me. On the inside part. And you have to call me my name" (117). When Paul D refuses, Beloved offers a bribe, "Please call it. I'll go if you call it." So Paul D repeats the name he knows, "Beloved," but she does not go. With no power to control his own will, Paul D reluctantly makes love to Beloved. "What he knew was that when he reached the inside part he was saying, 'Red Heart.' 'Red Heart.'" over and over again (117)." The recurring image of a rusted tobacco tin that resides in the place where Paul D's "red heart" should be is prevalent in *Beloved*. But this is the only place in the narrative where the words "red heart" are repeated consecutively, capitalized, and inscribed like a proper noun, like a name. The narrative positioning of Paul D's exclamation of the phrase "Red Heart" at his sexual climax, and the simultaneity of the release of emotions he has kept bottled up inside him, leads this reader to view Beloved's sexual aggression as a positive intervention. Here again a prominent and recognizable icon from the African New World cosmology haunts Morrison's narration. Joan Dayan carefully deconstructs the various misreadings that accompany many interpretations of the Erzulie figure:

> whereas Western religions depend on dualisms such as matter and spirit, body and soul, for their perpetuation and power, Vodoun unsettles and subverts such apparent oppositions. Although a woman, Erzulie vaccilates between the attraction for the two sexes. She holds her servitors in between two irreconcilables. What Frantz Fanon in *The Wretched of the Earth* has called "the zone of occult instability" becomes in the practices of Erzulie, a suspension between the supposedly antithetical constructions of masculinity and femininity. Erzulie is not androgynous, for she deliberately encases herself in the trappings of what has been constituted as femininity in the social world. Erzulie thus goes beyond false dichotomizing, as she prescribes and responds to multiple and apparently incoherent directives. (42)

Paul D's confusion about the object of Beloved's sexual "shining" represents and mimics the misreadings, misinterpretations, and contradictions that abound concerning Erzulie. Similarly, Stamp Paid, Ella, and other members of the community are curious about Beloved, but nobody really knows who she is or from whence she appears at 124 Bluestone Road. Her very first appearance (in the flesh) at Sethe's home is shrouded in mystery, none of which gets resolved, even at the close of the narrative. Beloved's sexual attentions to Sethe, Paul D, and, at times, Denver, also signal Erzulie's attraction to both sexes and to multiple partners. Like Janie in *Their Eyes Were Watching God*, who, according to Lamothe's reading, can shift between Erzulie-Freda and Erzulie-Dantor, Beloved seems to embody all of the Erzulies, including Erzulie-ge-rouge, the red-eyed woman of fury. Beloved's articulation of this vengeful spirit makes Denver afraid of her at times, but she can quickly shift back to Erzulie-Freda, object of feminine desire and mystique, or to the black working-class Erzulie-Dantor.

Caroline Rody's reading of the character Beloved is instructive for theorizing the Erzulie-like energy of this female spirit/child/woman:

> the ghost Beloved is an eruption of powerful, physical female desire that radically threatens the distinction between past and present as well as the household and the throats of the living. The disruptive sexuality of a murdered girl returned from the dead is a funky nightmare, an agony of limitless sexual desire expressive of the lot of disremembered in time. (92)

That the relationship between sexuality and spirituality is crucial to the restoration of a healthy black female subjectivity hinges upon the concept of Erzulie as a restorative, regenerative model for black sexuality in *Beloved*. As a character, Beloved is the ultimate polyvalent signifier, and this fact is institutionalized in her embodiment of the principles associated with the Haitian loa Erzulie. Beloved, like Erzulie, proposes diverse models for black sexuality; her sexuality runs on a continuum between men and women, between Paul D, Sethe, and Denver. In its application to the character Beloved, sexual difference is not inscribed as sexual deviance, but is itself a recuperative trope for the deviance model that warps black sexuality—and by extension black subjectivity—in the text. The difference/deviance model of black sexuality is proposed in *Beloved* through the references to the men of Sweet Home being forced to engage in sexual acts with cows.[47] In "naming" his "niggers" men, Garner invests them with normative male sexuality, fully anticipating that, like all other men, his slaves will possess sexual desire and the concomitant urge to satisfy those desires. However, although all of his slaves appear to be heterosexual, Garner does not provide them with suitable female counterparts. Until Sethe arrives many years later, the only women on the plantation are Mrs. Garner and Baby Suggs, the lame and elderly slave woman who is old enough to have mothered all of the Sweet Home men. Both Mrs. Garner and Baby Suggs are off limits to the Sweet Home men, leaving them only calves as a sexual option. Under the aegis of the goddess Erzulie, Beloved provides the corrective to this bestializing of black male sexuality.

As Mary Carden astutely observes, Garner's assertion of his slaves's manhood institutionalizes and confirms his own hypermasculinity.[48] Garner's slaves would never dare to challenge his superior manhood by making advances on his wife. Hence he taunts other white men with insinuations about the sexual frustrations of their own wives, resulting in their wives turning to slave men for sexual gratification:

> "But if you're a man yourself, you'll want your niggers to be men too."
> "I wouldn't have no nigger men round my wife."
> It was the reaction Garner loved and waited for. "Neither would I," he said. "Neither would I," and there was always a pause before the neighbor, or stranger, or peddler, or brother-in-law or whoever it was got the meaning. Then a fierce argument, sometimes a fight, and Garner came home bruised and pleased, having demonstrated one more time what a real Kentuckian was: one tough enough and smart enough to make and call his own niggers men. (13)

While Garner's sexual potency confers inviolable, unquestioned manhood upon him, it does not, by extension, bestow any credible criterion of manhood upon his sexually frustrated slaves. Mary Carden argues: "the benefits of Sweet Home manhood accrue [only] to Garner, who brags while other farmers [shake] their heads in warning." If manhood, by Garner's clever inference, is defined by the ability to keep one's woman sexually satisfied, then by Garner's own definition, Paul D, Halle, and the other Pauls are not, in fact, men. They do not have any women to keep sexually satisfied. Only Sixo has a woman, but he has to travel thirty miles to see her. Because of the distance, and the fact that he has to sneak away from Sweet Home to spend time with her, the possibility of Sixo keeping his woman sexually satisfied is foreclosed, and with it, his manhood: "he left on a Saturday morning when the moon was in the place he wanted it to be, arrived at her cabin before church on Sunday and had just enough time to say good morning before he had to start back again to make the final call on time Monday morning" (26). The hastiness and infrequency of his sexual contact with the thirty-mile woman mark, abbreviate, and distort Sixo's sexuality as defined by Garner.

The distortion of black male sexuality is engendered through acts of bestiality that Paul D cannot erase from his mind. The memory of bestiality as a sexual model informs, distorts, and corrupts his sense of himself as a man, and as a whole human being: "they were young and so sick with the absence of women they had taken to calves" (12). Yet they decide to "let Sethe be" when she arrives. This decision is not taken lightly, and does not result from Garner's training in principles of masculinity. In fact, had they been living up to Garner's model, they "would have beaten each other to a pulp for her" just to have a woman to gratify their sexual urges and prove their masculine prowess.

The narrative juxtaposition of bestiality on the one hand, and "courtly" manliness on the other, is a curious counterinterpellative strategy that disrupts Garner's self-serving discourse of masculinity. Despite being forced to bed calves, these slaves who cannot be men by Garner's definition are, in fact, "gentlemen" by their own sexual discipline. Morrison presents this model of courtly masculinity to counter the image of bestiality. In allowing Sethe to choose, they assert self-discipline, brotherhood, and respect for women as their own version of manhood. The image of bestiality is replaced with that of sexual sacrifice, black male bonding, and respect for women. This representation of black masculinity also honors the sense of intersubjective relations between these slaves who are willing to sacrifice the group for the ultimate good of one individual: the man Sethe chooses.

This representation of black masculinity, as an expression of noncompetition between black men and respect for black women as autonomous sexual beings, is a narrative intervention that demonstrates resistance to the bestial associations and stereotypes of black men as rapists that pervade images of black masculinity at the turn of the nineteenth-century, popularized in films such as *Birth of a Nation*. Halle's sacrifice of his Sundays to buy his mother out of slavery, and the sacrifice of all the Sweet Home men who allow Sethe to choose, confirms a version of black masculinity that belies the discourse of inhumanity and sexual savagery that denigrated black men.

This positive inscription of black masculinity also inaugurates black female autonomy in *Beloved*. Baby Suggs is freed before slavery is abolished because her son is both a good black man and a good son. Until she is "milked," Sethe is the most empowered of the slaves on Sweet Home plantation. By having the power to decide whom she sleeps with, Sethe is able to exercise sexual agency. Audre Lorde's definition of sexual agency as a precursor to political empowerment holds true for Sethe. She is able to make the difficult choices that others around her find so incomprehensible. Although she is fully nine months pregnant, she escapes Sweet Home and makes it to Ohio while Sixo and Paul D are caught and Halle is left behind in a state of mental anguish. Sethe makes the choice of death, rather than slavery, for her child because she thinks she has a right to choose. She claims ownership of her sexuality and the products of that sexuality. Sethe's control over her sexuality is what animates and catalyzes her subjectivity, rendering her capable of making that unenviable political choice (see Cliff, "I Found God in Myself" 19).

The character Paul D seems to vacillate between these two very different representations of manhood: virility and hardness on the one hand, and empathy and courtliness on the other. The narrative dramatizes the distortions that attend sexual coercion and rape, and their implications for the deformation and corruption of black masculinity. While in a Georgia prison camp, Paul D performs sexual acts for the white prison guards. The first time he witnesses black men engaging in fellatio at gunpoint, he vomits. But the narrative suggests that he has no choice but to participate in this act on subsequent mornings. Paul D's subjectivity is so distorted by his sexual, physical, and psychological trauma that he is incapable of understanding either Sethe's choice to protect her child at all cost, or his own motivations for sleeping with Beloved and for abandoning Sethe. As one of the Sweet Home men who had the discipline to allow Sethe to choose Halle, Paul D is confused by how easily he is sexually manipulated by Beloved. His questions about manhood demonstrate his inability to choose even a working definition of manhood that serves his own needs: "Was that it? Is that where the manhood lay? In the naming done by a whiteman who was supposed to know? Who gave them the privilege not of working but of deciding how to?" (147).

Is manhood the prerogative of those with the authority to define? Despite previous exposure to two competing definitions of manhood, Paul D cannot pick one because he is still unsure of himself, and his aborted subjectivity renders it difficult to make life-affirming choices. The narrative proposes that any defining that is not internally driven by one's own spiritual motivations and needs, but serves an external agenda, invalidates and circumvents an autonomous subject position. Incapable of taking his reasoning to its logical conclusion, Paul D backs down from this interrogative stance: "No. In their relationship to Garner was true metal: they were believed and trusted, but most of all they were listened to" (Morrison 147).

Paul D's alignment of his relationship to Garner with "metal" highlights the metonymic relationship between metal and one brand of masculinity in *Beloved*. This metal/masculinity dialectic represents another textual moment in which a prominent symbol from African cosmology shadows or haunts the narrative. Ogun, the Yoruba avatar of war, iron and maleness is evoked and deconstructed in a contiguous and metonymic relationship that positions Garner's brand of masculinity as a failed model for Paul D. Garner is described as a tough Kentuckian who can fight and make love better than any other man, white or black, and whose virility is so unchallenged he has no need to fear making men of his slaves. His slave "men"—though virile and tough—are forced to abuse cows as an outlet for their "natural" sexual aggression.

Garner's double-edged relationship with his slaves and inability to allow them to be slaves by conventional mores, or men in accordance with his own definition of manhood, inform Paul D's own conflicted relationship with his sexuality and sense of self. Much of Paul D's internal self-dialogue and narrative posturing as someone with decidedly male characteristics in a given moment (as in the moment he literally beats the ghost out of the house) and unambiguously female characteristics in another (for example, when he becomes the confidant of sexually hungry women) is reflective of this dualism. However, because he has been taught by Garner to respect hardness and virility as the preferred traits of manhood, he cannot comfortably assimilate his dualism, and therefore cannot resolve his internal conflict and integrate his subjectivity to find wholeness.

Throughout much of the narrative, Paul D's personality is activated through Morrison's coded inscription of the Yoruba god Ogun, who is himself represented by iron, virility, physical strength, and masculine prowess in the arts of war and love. In *Flash of the Spirit*, Robert Farris Thompson highlights Ogun's nature: "The art of Ogun reflects his nature as a 'hard god,' a deity of war and iron. He lives in the flames of the blacksmith's forge, on the battlefield and more particularly on the cutting edge of iron" (52). Praise-chants for Ogun collected in ancient towns like Ire, Ketu, and Ilesha illustrate his ambivalent nature: his power to destroy (like Garner) as well as to construct:

> (from the towns of Aramoko and Ilesha)
> Ogun, master of the world, support of the newborn child
> Ogun is virile
> Ogun, master of the yam I cut
> Ogun, with the coronet of blood
> *Burns the forest, burns the bush*
> *Leaves the forest screaming in the sound of flames.* (52, my emphasis)

However, Ogun's potency and agency is severely compromised by the apparatus of slavery, rendering him an ineffective model of masculinity for black male figures in the text. Thus, Paul D becomes shackled by the very iron that undergirds his personality. In a shocking inversion, he is unmanned by the very symbols of manhood with which he identifies and through which his virility and power is repeatedly contested:

> When he turned his head, aiming for a last look at Brother, turned it as much as the rope that connected his neck to the axle of a buckboard allowed, and, later on, when they fastened the iron around his ankles, and clamped the wrists as well, there was no outward sign of trembling at all. Nor eighteen days after that when he saw the ditches; the one thousand feet of earth five feet deep, five feet wide, into which wooden boxes had been fitted. A door of bars that you could lift on hinges like a cage opened into three walls and a roof of scrap lumber and red dirt. Two feet of it over his head; three feet of open trench in front of him with anything that crawled or scurried welcome to share that grave calling itself quarters. And there were forty-five more. He was sent there after trying to kill Brandywine, the man schoolteacher sold him to. Brandywine was leading him, in a coffle with ten others, through Kentucky into Virginia. He didn't know exactly what prompted him to try—other than Halle, Sixo, Paul A, Paul F and Mister. But the trembling was fixed by the time he knew it was there. (125)

The iron shackles on his ankles and hands, the hinges on the door that entraps him, the chains on the coffle and the chain gang, and the tobacco tin that has rusted shut in the place where his heart should be, all represent the associative signs of Paul D's connection with the Yoruba avatar of iron and brute force. However, in a cruel inversion, none of these iron implements represent freedom or empowerment for Paul D. Conversely, they all signify his complete and utter subjugation to the will and whim of external directives from the white power structure—the actual seat of power and masculine prowess in antebellum society—and his inability to exercise real choice over his own destiny. The Yoruba sign of masculine prowess holds no positive meaning for Paul D, a black slave who is reduced to copulating with animals, and whose sense of himself as a man and human being is contested and undermined nearly to the point of complete effacement:

> He would keep the rest where it belonged: in that tobacco tin buried in his chest where a red heart used to be. Its lid rusted shut. He would not pry it loose now in front of this sweet sturdy woman, for if she got a whiff of the contents it would shame him. And it would hurt her to know that there was no red heart bright as Mister's comb beating in him. (86)

In an even crueler irony, Mister, the rooster and potential "ebbo," or direct sacrifice to the Yoruba deity Ogun, mocks Paul D as he stands in abjection with the iron bit in his mouth. Paul D becomes the human sacrifice to a god greater than Ogun, a god who has the power to mastermind and execute Ogun's deformation and make a mockery of his potentiality, a god called slavery that can reduce the Ogun-like character to such abjection that he becomes lower than the sacrificial rooster that would be placed upon Ogun's altar:[49]

> Mister was allowed to be and stay what he was. But I wasn't allowed to be and stay what I was. Even if you cooked him you'd be cooking a rooster named Mister. But wasn't no way I'd ever be Paul D again, living or dead. Schoolteacher changed me. I was something else and that something was less than a chicken sitting in the sun on a tub. (86)

Schoolteacher, as a representative of the true ideal of American slavery, symbolizes the consolidation of might and right that was a trademark of the institution of slavery. Garner's nobler but conflicted brand of slavery has no institutional sanction, and therefore no power to protect Paul D and the Sweet Home slaves after Garner's death. There were only two logical (not necessarily morally right, but logical nevertheless) discursive positions vis-à-vis slavery: abolish it or execute it according to convention. Each was held, respectively, by slave owners and abolitionists. Garner's "kinder," "gentler" brand of slavery is a cruel joke that is dramatized by the suffering of the Sweet Home slaves after his death, and by the distorted sexuality of his male slaves while he is still alive.

Contiguous with the inscription of total effacement of power and agency that renders Ogun's principles powerless to activate Paul D's subjectivity is Morrison's recognition of the necessity of a new God-principle, a new paradigm in the form of a creolized version of masculinity, forged in the New World to respond more effectively to the needs of the newly freed black male subject. Morrison's narrative underscores the need for a revised definition of black masculinity, one that is informed by principles associated with both sexes. Although these are not the traits that he valorizes (because they do not conform to the definition of manhood he has learned from Garner), Paul D possesses the sensitivity, empathy, contemplativeness, and intuition commonly associated with the female gender.

Buffeted about by the double-edged character of a masculine identification that does not reflect his true circumstances, and therefore cannot serve his needs, Paul D is opportunely situated for a radical repositioning of black male subjectivity. And indeed, the text represents him as a special kind of man: the kind who can comfortably integrate both male and female traits, prompting critic Karen Fields to dub him "embodied kindness" (Fields 161). His sexuality is tempered by a deep spirituality that provokes and evokes a cathartic emotional release in others, but at the point when he enters the text he is too disturbed to activate these feelings in and for himself. Nevertheless, Paul D is the kind of man to whom women confide sexual secrets:

> Strong women and wise women saw him and told him things they only told each other: that way past the change of life desire in them had suddenly become enormous, greedy, more savage than when they were fifteen, and that it embarrassed them and made them sad; that secretly they longed to die—to be quit of it—that sleep was more precious to them than any waking day. (20)

For a black woman to admit to having untamed sexual desire, the voracious appetite for sexual release, would only further entrench the stereotype that damned black women in the nineteenth century, effectively excluding them from the category of "true womanhood."[50] Sexual desire was shameful, something no "wise," "strong," black woman would admit to. Why then would any black woman confess uninhibited sexual desire to Paul D? The answer is that Paul D is no ordinary man. Although he is incapable of dealing with his own painful past, he understands that it is a necessary exercise. He is not afraid to feel for others or to make them open up in his presence. He encourages Sethe to come to grips with her past, and promises to help her with the trauma he knows can occur with such dangerous introspection: "Go as far inside as you need to, I'll hold your ankles. Make sure you get back out" (55).

Paul D's deep spirituality aligns his sensibilities with those of the strong women in the text. Paul D is able to learn Sethe's sorrow by connecting with her physically: "He rubbed his cheek on her back and learned that way her sorrow, the roots of it; its wide trunk and intricate branches" (21). It is through his own physical laying on of hands—which mimics both Amy Denver's physical ministrations upon Sethe and Baby Suggs's healing touches—that Paul D is able to connect with Sethe on a level at which no other man has been able to do. Although Sethe has chosen Halle, Paul D is really her rightful soul mate: "Halle was more like a brother than a husband. His care suggested a family relationship rather than a man's laying claim" (31). When Paul D rounds the corner of her house and finds her washing chamomile sap off her legs, Sethe is as easy with him as if she had only seen him yesterday. She is totally uninhibited in his presence, as though she has been waiting for him for the past eighteen years.

Despite Paul D's ability to harness his spirituality in aid of others at key narrative moments, he lacks the ability to heal himself. His sexual history distorts his sexual worldview. However, through his sexual encounters with Sethe and Beloved, the narrative offers him a corrective. When Paul D first encounters Sethe at 124 Bluestone, the sap on her bare leg reawakens dormant sexual desire he has been holding on to since Sweet Home. Paul D cannot contain his feelings for Sethe. He cannot wait until they climb the stairs to her bedroom. He grabs hold of her breasts the minute he is alone with her, and continues to embrace her by the stove right there downstairs, with Denver in the next room and the undead baby ghost also close by. Consumed with passion, Sethe and Paul D stumble up the stairs and fall into bed. It is only after their passion has been sated that either can think clearly.

His passion spent, Paul D no longer sees Sethe's beauty, but only notices her imperfections: "Out of the corner of his eye, Paul D saw the float of her breasts and disliked it, the spread-away flat roundness of them that he could definitely live without, never mind that downstairs he had held them as if they were the most expensive part of himself" (25). Here again is a narrative moment in *Beloved* that mirrors Hurston's *Their Eyes Were Watching God*. It is not Sethe that Paul D finds disgusting; it is himself. But just as Joe Starks insults Janie's sexuality to detract attention from his own diminishing virility, Paul D finds fault with Sethe's body to avoid examining his discomfort about sex. Sex with Sethe releases the memories of an unexamined sexual history that enslaves Paul D and binds him unnaturally to a painful past that he keeps locked in the tin box that has replaced his red heart. Through making love to Sethe, the box is pried just a little bit loose, but Sethe, on her own strength, cannot penetrate the iron barriers Paul D has erected.

Paul D needs Sethe to help him find himself both sexually and spiritually, and it is the sexual energy between Paul D and Sethe that acts as the catalyst for Erzulie's manifestation through the character Beloved. Francis Huxley, quoted above, states that "it is perhaps only when an impulse meets with a desire for order, that the loas are born" (202). Erzulie is born of the need for order, normalcy, and healing of male/female relations in postslavery America. Paul D's sexuality has been perverted by the slave experience. Forced to bed calves on Sweet Home and perform fellatio on white prison guards, Paul D suffers from cognitive dissonance, sexual distortion, and the trauma of sexual abuse.[51] This distortion is dramatized by the fact that Paul D is turned off by Sethe's very normal-looking, mature, but by all accounts attractive, female body. Paul D is a cracked vessel, with a tin can in the place where his heart should be. What is broken in him is not only his sense of self, but his sense of himself as a sexual being, a human male whose sexuality should be freely negotiated in consensual relations with other human beings, instead of with farm animals or at gunpoint with white prison guards.

Sexual distortion and sexual coercion marked the lives of black slaves, both male and female, and it is partially this disorder, this deeply ingrained sexual dysfunction permeating black psyches, that effectively forecloses healthy subject formation in *Beloved*. However, this disturbing lacuna is also the impetus for a new principle of sexuality, one that confers sexual agency and personal autonomy. It is this urgent need for restorative sexuality that gives rise to Erzulie's sexually healing presence in the narrative. Both Paul D's and Sethe's sexual histories are permeated with images of death, bestiality, perversion, and rape. Sethe is haunted by the sexual trauma of being held down and milked by the mossy-toothed nephews of schoolteacher. The sight of this perversion drives Halle mad, and sends him into oblivion, effectively erasing his presence in the text. Paul D's sexual history forces him to deny the existence of his own red heart, his ability to feel and to love deeply. Sethe sells her body to the engraver in exchange for Beloved's name on the headstone with the engraver's young son looking on. This experience makes Sethe feel dirty, corrupts the young boy, and taints the memory of Beloved's death with even more disgraceful connotations. Sex, corruption, and death are clearly linked in Beloved in a chilling revision that recalls twentieth- and twenty-first-century sexual discourses in which sex is associated with the AIDS pandemic.

However, when Beloved enters the text, her sexual exploits return life-affirming normalcy to human sexual relations. Summoned by the passion between Sethe and Paul D, Erzulie comes to restore order to the physical, spiritual, and sexual planes. Her embodiment as Beloved will first disrupt, subvert, and displace all of the relationships in the text. But ultimately, Erzulie's purpose is to restore intersubjective relations and a sense of order to the raw impulses and chaos that permeate and disrupt the narrative. Beloved's pregnancy—presumably with Paul D's seed—reaffirms the relationship between sex and life. Healthy sexual expression is restorative.

Although the house at 124 Bluestone Road has been haunted all along, it is significant that Beloved becomes embodied only after Paul D arrives. Marshalling Garner's brand of manhood, Paul D beats and subdues the haunting spirit before ascending the stairs to make love to Sethe for the first time. The ghost disappears, and the next day, upon their return from the carnival, they find Beloved sitting on a tree stump in the yard. As a polyvalent character, Beloved is Sethe's daughter and jealous of Paul D's claim on her mother, but she is also Erzulie, and therefore must possess him sexually to restore balance and order.[52]

Beloved's entrance into Paul D's life, while unwelcome, is necessary for his spiritual development and growth, and for the healing of his relationship with his past and with Sethe. As the sexual principle governing human sexuality, Erzulie is summoned by the unbridled and mutual sexual passion between Sethe and Paul D. As Erzulie, Beloved is a divine being who moves Paul D in ways that Sethe, as a human, cannot. She moves him physically, sexually, and spiritually. She moves him to do what he would never have done of his own accord: examine the places within himself that need healing. Paul D does not understand how he can be sexually attracted to a woman he despises. He makes love to her against his will and better judgment and is angry with himself for "Fucking her when he was convinced he didn't want to. Whenever she turned her behind up, the calves of his youth (was that it?) cracked his resolve" (Morrison 148). Erzulie is a sexually aggressive spirit who will not take no for an answer, but she is also the principle of human sexuality, a necessary precursor to healthy subject formation. Interestingly, the narrative invocation of the calves at this particular moment is a reminder of why Paul D needs healing and underscores Erzulie's recuperative sexual agency.

As an Erzulie figure, Beloved embodies contradictory characteristics. She loves Sethe, but she also hates her. She overwhelms Sethe with affection, but she chokes her in the clearing. In addition, Beloved articulates her desire to merge with Sethe in language that is both sexual and pre-oedipal, the language of a grownup lover and infant offspring: "I am Beloved and she is mine. I am not separate from her" (210). And later, "She is my face smiling at me doing it at last a hot thing now we can join a hot thing" (213). Like Erzulie, Beloved defies dualisms: she is both matter and spirit, the ghost returned and a live being, a child who craves sweets and her mother's attention, and a woman who offers her body up to Paul D with no inhibitions. Like the figure of Erzulie, whose different manifestations contribute to the misconceptions about her, Beloved means something different to each character in the book. She is Paul D's lover and antagonist, Denver's long-lost sister and only friend, and Sethe's second chance to set things right with her Beloved. Beloved also touches Sethe both sexually and maternally. By consuming Sethe's time and emotional energy, Beloved feeds off her like a child feeds from her mother's breasts. In contemporary colloquial expression, one can say Beloved is "milking" this relationship for all its worth. Beloved's milking of Sethe is reminiscent of the scene in which Sethe is milked by Garner's nephews. In remembering that scene of rape, Sethe laments that they took the milk that belonged to her "crawling already" baby. Disturbing as Beloved's "milking" of her mother may be, it reconstructs Sethe's nurturing of this child she was prevented from mothering. However, the connection between them is both maternal and sexual, and Beloved becomes pregnant both with the sexual attention she receives from Paul D, and the devotion she drains from Sethe. In many ways, Beloved serves the same function for Sethe that Tea Cake serves for Janie in Hurston's text. With Beloved, Sethe learns to play and to enjoy the time spent with her children. Beloved propels Sethe to go outside and plant carrots, pick flowers, make pretty dresses in carnival colors, and even learn to roller-skate. Carol Rody argues for a lesbian moment in the text in which the historical tensions are resolved or held at bay:

> In this fantasy of fulfilled female desire, the text seems to find its heart. When Beloved's "lesbian" desire first disrupts Sethe's household, it is one with the volcanic return of the repressed past she brings with her, out of the closet, as it were, and into the house of the present. But when Sethe locks her house against the world—in particular the male world of Stamp paid and Paul D—lesbian desire is no longer disturbing; rather, the jouissant communion that ensues seems a momentary utopian resolution of the war between present and past. (111)

Rody's reading runs contiguous to my argument that Beloved, at certain moments, embodies the spirit of Erzulie in much the same way a devotee would if possessed by Erzulie in a Voudoun ceremony. In these sacred moments, past and present, myth and reality, loa and human, metonym and metaphor merge and remain conjoined until the possession is over. The ethnographic research makes it clear that most Erzulie devotees are men, but there are some women, and the dialectic between Erzulie's female devotees and this loa is decidedly and overtly sexual. Erzulie, bisexual, is also said to be the protector of lesbian women and female victims of domestic violence.

As in the loa-devotee dialectic in which the devotee is able to suspend human worries and vulnerabilities during the possession ceremony, Sethe's relationship with Beloved represents an emptying out of her painful past. As she "lays it down" finally, in the telling and retelling of the story to the only one she thinks has a right to demand it of her, Sethe becomes empty, drained. She appears to be wasting away, while Beloved gets larger and larger, as if the story Sethe tells nourishes her. She is a succubus figure, but what, in fact, is she sucking from Sethe? Is it life, or is it the horror of the past that Sethe cannot relinquish? Beloved has already participated in the fixing ceremony by helping Sethe to gather the colors from life and nature with which to adorn the house. She has already assisted Sethe in completing the quilt that Baby Suggs started in the keeping room. Sethe has to experience her own catharsis if she is to find healing and forgiveness for her past. Her wasting away in bed represents a spiritual and mental break, a final and long-awaited catharsis, and a moment of clarity when she actually confronts the fact that she has murdered her "best thing," her beloved daughter.[53] Paul D's reassurance to her that she is her own "best thing" is a revision of the African worldview in which the needs of the individual are sometimes sublimated to those of the community, and the needs of the children are often privileged above those of the mother. His response, "you your own best thing," represents the substitution of a creolized ethos, a recognition that the needs of the individual are also important to the healthy development of the community, and that the well-being of the mother is as important as that of the child.

Beloved is seeking a similar kind of resolution. Her relationship with Baby Suggs signifies her connection to the spiritual plane and underscores her participation in the fixing ceremony that Baby Suggs began on her deathbed. Beloved retires to the keeping room to rest shortly after her arrival at 124. She is immediately preoccupied with Baby Suggs's Egungun quilt: "She seems totally taken with those faded scraps of orange, even made the effort to lean on her elbow and stroke them" (Morrison 165). Later, Beloved helps Sethe to finish the quilt and helps her decorate the house with plants, flowers, and Egungun colors, creating charms to exorcise evil and ward off death. What might appear to be contradictory directives make perfect sense if Beloved is an Erzulie character because her purpose in the text is to restore balance and normative (healthy) sexual, spiritual, and emotional relations to 124. According to the African worldview, because she died a violent death, Beloved can never be at peace in the spirit world. She is a wandering spirit, floating between the world of the living and the world of the dead. Although she seems determined to stay in 124 Bluestone, Beloved's vengeful ghost is also seeking peace and rest, and ultimately that is her motive for haunting the characters. It therefore makes sense that Beloved, once manifested in the flesh, would participate in the fixing ceremony to restore balance and order to 124.

Such ambiguities as are endemic to Erzulie are also reflected in Beloved's relationship to Denver. This relationship is described in language that recalls sibling rivalry as well as sexual intimacy: "Denver nursing Beloved's interest like a lover whose pleasure was to overfeed the Beloved" (92). Lonely to her core, Denver's sense of self has also been distorted because of the community's rejection of her family. Beloved's appearance in Denver's life helps restore subjectivity to Denver as well. With Denver, as with the others, Beloved's presence is not without conflict. Beloved is argumentative, controlling, selfish, self-absorbed, often cruel in her insensitivity toward Denver and in her desire to consume all of Sethe's attention and love—all attributes of Erzulie. But ultimately, it is precisely because Beloved poses such a serious threat to her mother's life that Denver is mobilized, catapulted into the community to seek help, with Baby Suggs's encouragement from the spirit world.

In addition to the pain of sexual trauma experienced at Sweet Home and the trauma of losing Halle, Sethe's brokenness is exacerbated by her overwhelming feelings of guilt over killing the "crawling already baby." Her subsequent loss of Baby Suggs, Howard, and Buglar, as well as the love and support of her community, only serve to highlight and dramatize her sense of alienation. Tough as Sethe appears, she cannot be whole. There are too many broken pieces in her life, and she cannot repair them because she cannot take back the actions that precipitated them. Sethe's most significant act of agency—that of a mother trying to protect her child from the ravages of slavery—is magnified and transformed into monstrous associations because her choices are so limited. Agency for her leads to death, not life. In other words, she has so few viable choices that she literally has to choose between two extremes: living and allowing her children to live in slavery, or dying and taking them with her.

Sethe's act magnifies the plight of the black woman in antebellum society who had no control over her sexuality, her sexual reproduction, her physical labor, the fruits of such labor, or the fruits of her womb. In killing Beloved, Sethe acts out of desperation born of too few choices. Had Sethe any life-affirming choices at her disposal, she might have used them, but none were available. Slavery was not a life-affirming institution, even the kind of slavery that purportedly made men and women out of chattel, but in fact reduced them to animal status at the whim of the master. How can one, then, recoup one's humanity in the face of such a tortured past?

Audre Lorde argues that women who are in touch with the erotic can become fully actualized by utilizing the creativity and agency that it engenders.[54] The latter parts of Morrison's novel confirm Sethe's realignment with her sexuality as she develops a healthier relationship to sex:

> Tucked into the well of his arm, Sethe recalled Paul D's face in the street when he asked her to have a baby for him. Although she laughed and took his hand, it had frightened her. She thought quickly of how good the sex would be if that is what he wanted, but mostly she was frightened by the thought of having a baby once more. (154)

Although she is dangerously overidentified with her maternal role in the moment that she kills her daughter, it is later made clear that Sethe has very strong feelings about sexuality, feelings that have been dormant for eighteen years. It is not the thought of having another baby that engages her interest in the lovemaking. She revels in the thought of good sex, sex for the pleasure of sex itself. With her sexuality restored, Sethe's confidence returns. She believes she can take on the world again: "There was no question but that she could do it. Just like the day she arrived at 124—sure enough, she had milk enough for all" (118). No longer interested in biological reproduction, Sethe becomes the quintessential mother-figure whose role is much larger than that of a biological mother.[55] Her milk, then, is no longer tied to her maternity, but becomes a sign of her largesse, creativity, abundance, ability to dispense life-giving sustenance and, ultimately, to regain control of her power and agency.

In fact, one could say that Beloved replaces Sethe as the figure of biological maternity in the latter part of the novel.[56] Most critics read the final pages of *Beloved* as depicting the self-negation and erasure of Sethe as she becomes subjected to Beloved's voracious appetite. It is indeed true that Beloved appears to be sucking the very life out of Sethe. Sethe appears to dwindle away as Beloved grows rounder and bigger. But Beloved's pregnancy has multiple significations. As Erzulie, she symbolizes fertility and creativity as well as healthy sexuality. Before Paul D, the last man who Sethe had sex with was the man who carved the headstone. She sold him her sex in the cemetery among the gravestones in exchange for the word "beloved" on her daughter's headstone, "her knees wide open as the grave." Before Paul D, Sethe's last sexual encounter is associated with death, not life. She has killed her child and must use sex not to generate life, but to purchase a fitting burial for the life she was forced to take. After that dehumanizing experience, sex between a man and woman leads to and reproduces symbols of death for Sethe. Every time she remembers the word carved on her daughter's headstone, she remembers what she had to do to get it done. The memory of her last sexual encounter only reproduces the metonymic relationship between sex and death.

Beloved's pregnancy restores the relationship between sex and life. Sethe has sex with Paul D, and although it shakes things up, it does not reproduce death. It leads to a series of events that restore balance and order, continuing the fixing ceremony that Baby Suggs began before she died. Paul D, Beloved, and Sethe are able to finish what Baby Suggs could not. What was missing from Baby Suggs's life was also missing from her healing formula: the spiritually revivifying impetus of raw, human sexual desire and its fulfillment. Baby Suggs knew this; hence she cautioned Denver not to suppress her sexuality (Morrison 247). Beloved's purpose as Erzulie is to normalize sexual desire and make sexual fulfillment an acceptable, reachable, life-affirming human goal with no disastrous consequences. In the Voudoun religion, converts who are possessed by Erzulie are freed up sexually and can act out the range of human sexual desires and fantasies. The level of sexuality displayed by the devotee is directly correlated to the believability of the possession: the more sexual the personification, the more plausible the possession. Thus, Erzulie creates a sexual escape valve, a way to channel human sexuality into an acceptable paradigm. Convention does not allow women to act out sexually without being sanctioned, but goddesses can do whatever they please, and Erzulie, by definition, represents sexual abandon and freedom from sexual repression.

Paul D's sexuality is chained to the memory of the cows and the forced homosexual encounters of the chain gang. Sethe's sexuality is chained to her rape and the prostituting of her body in exchange for a proper word on her daughter's headstone. As a character, Beloved has no sexual history. She learns the mechanics of sex from watching the turtles mate under the bridge. But Erzulie has "sexpertise"—if I may coin a phrase—and she is the avatar of human sexuality, the essence as well as the totality of sexual desire and its fulfillment. As a principle she is the sexual urge that drives pleasure and reproduction, fulfillment and creation. She is sexual urge as well as sexual orgasm. When she moves Paul D, she teaches him how to use what he already has inside of him, the ability to connect emotionally and spiritually, in his own redemption. Although he does not know that he is making love to a goddess, Paul D grudgingly admits the deep satisfaction he receives from his sexual encounters with Beloved. There is a spiritual connection that he does not understand, but senses on a deep level: "and afterward, beached and gobbling air, in the midst of repulsion and personal shame, he was thankful too for having been escorted to some ocean-deep place he once belonged to" (Morrison 311).

Michel Laguerre explains that Erzulie is the mistress of both Ogou, the god of fire and metals in the Voudoun religion, and Agouétaroio, the Voudoun spirit known as the protector of the sea (72). And, in her foreword to Laguerre's text, Vera Rubin explains that the majority of the Haitian loas live in Guineè, "a mythical Garden of Eden beneath the sea" from which they traverse between Haiti and Africa quite frequently (Laguerre 14). What Paul D experiences as he makes love to Beloved is spiritual possession by the goddess Erzulie, and in this possession he discovers the ancestral links to the world of the spirits that he carries in his DNA. I have already explored in detail Paul D's connection to the Yoruba deity Ogun, who becomes Ogou (Erzulie's lover) in Haiti. As Erzulie's lover, Paul D is also linked with Agouétaroio, hence the reference to "the ocean-deep place" that used to be his home, a place he has forgotten, but that Beloved is intimately connected to through her memories of the middle passage. The phrase "Red Heart" that he screams again and again as he reaches orgasm with Beloved is at once his recognition of her as the Haitian loa Erzulie, and his acknowledgment of the emotional baggage responsible for his alienation from himself. The tobacco tin in his chest that has been guarding his emotions is forced to give way to the blood-red heart that has been locked away until Erzulie moves him sexually, spiritually, and emotionally, releasing a floodgate of emotions that force him away from Sethe, and into his own journey into wholeness.

Paul D is resentful of Beloved because he suspects that there is more to her than meets the eye, but he can neither place her nor properly categorize her sexuality. Paul D's lack of familiarity with Erzulie mimics the fragmentation of African spiritual practices in the New World. The following quotation highlights Paul D's confusion as to who the object of Beloved's sexual attraction might be since she appears to have nothing but hostility for him:

> But if her shining was not for him, who then? He had never known a woman to light up for nobody in particular, who just did it as a general announcement. Always, in his experience, the light appeared when there was focus. Like the Thirty-Mile Woman, dulled to smoke while he waited with her in the ditch, and starlight when Sixo got there. He never knew himself to mistake it. It was there the instant he looked at Sethe's wet legs, otherwise he would never have been bold enough to enclose her in his arms that day and whisper into her back. (78)

Paul D clearly knows when a woman is sexually attracted to a man. He can sense Sethe's attraction for him when they meet again, and he also senses Beloved's highly charged sexual energy. Much of the ethnographic literature on Erzulie confirms that she is very jealous and often forbids her servitors to have sexual intercourse with their human partners for extended periods of time, thus saving themselves exclusively for her. It is this heightened sexuality of Erzulie's that Paul D senses in Beloved but cannot properly situate, and his discomfort with Beloved mirrors society's uneasiness with overt displays of sexuality in women. Linda Krumholz dubs Beloved "both the pain and the cure," referring to her role as a catalyst for healing and recovery, as well as the thing from which the characters need to recover (114). Krumholz continues, "countering traumatic repression, she makes the characters accept their past, their squelched memories, and their own hearts, as beloved" (114).[57]

In addition, that Sethe's "wet legs" are a sign of her heightened sexual desire is reconfirmed in the lyrics of Paul D's song: "Bare feet and chamomile sap" (310). His identification and celebration of Sethe as a sexual being is reflected in his reference to her legs wet with sap, and to the light that illuminates her sexuality when they meet again after eighteen years. Here again there are intertextual links with Hurston's Janie. When Janie finally meets Tea Cake, she has been saving up her sexual feelings for a special man for years. Morrison, like Hurston, clearly theorizes that women who are spiritually centered (even highly sexual women) will choose prolonged celibacy rather than throw themselves away on some unworthy male. The relationship between Sethe's sexuality and her spirituality is clearly marked in Paul D's song where the chamomile sap on her bare legs evokes the love juices he anticipates sharing with her. Chamomile, a herb used for healing and soothing, is linked in Santeria with the Yoruba goddess Oshun, the goddess of love, sexuality, creativity, and fertility.[58] Later, when Sethe and Beloved tie packets of herbs and flowers on the stairs and all over the house, this narrative intervention recalls a ritualistic purging closely tied to African and New World religious belief systems. In his discussion of herbal uses in Santeria, Paul Canizares explains that in addition to their medicinal uses, herbs are also used for spiritual cleansing and for conferring positive ashé:

> Aside from the uses we have so far discussed, plants are also used in Santeria in what are called despojos. In a despojo, a person or place is spiritually cleansed by having the right herbs or plants passed over his or her body or, in the case of a place, by striking the walls of the place with a bunch of the right plants. Despojos are said to work on two levels: by frightening away evil spirits and by conferring on the person positive energy. . . . The plants are said to attract all negative vibrations, leaving only positive ones.[59]

Sethe and Beloved, both clearly linked to New World religious deities, carry on Baby Suggs's spiritual legacy in an attempt to restore normalcy to the house at 124 Bluestone Road. Like Janie in *Their Eyes Were Watching God*, Sethe is forced to destroy her beloved in order to save herself. Also like Janie, Sethe suffers a period of remorse (and in Sethe's case, depression) afterward. However, Sethe's ability to choose herself over her beloved signals the restoration of her self.

After the final fixing ceremony in which the entire community participates in a ritual of exorcism, Beloved disappears. But like a goddess, she remains the object of fascination and mystique. Mr. Bodwin is so mesmerized by Beloved's naked beauty that he isn't even aware that Sethe is chasing him with an ice pick. One could say that Beloved herself saves Sethe from serving another term in jail: "Jenny say all he wants to know is who was the naked blackwoman standing on the porch. He was looking at her so hard he didn't notice what Sethe was up to" (Morrison 312). Erzulie is the object of everyone's gaze. But when she possesses a servitor, she becomes more than a mere object. She consumes the devotee and fills all the spaces in his or her imagination with erotic energy. The community exorcises but does not forget Beloved: "Later, a little boy put it out how he had been looking for bait back of 124, down by the stream, and saw, cutting through the woods, a naked woman with fish for hair" (267). Michel Laguerre informs us that Erzulie (spelled "Ezili" in Laguerre's text) is closely identified with the ocean, giving credibility to the fish imagery in the above quotation: "Ezili likes fresh air and water; she is a sea spirit" (Laguerre 75). But, in ethnography, as in literature, Erzulie cannot be spatially contained. One popular song to Erzulie recorded in Laguerre's text describes her as the female protector of the temple who lives in the woods, and indeed, this seems to be the place she inhabits after the fixing ceremony that brings Baby Suggs's congregation and community to 124 Bluestone Road (323–24).

The symbiotic interdependence of spirituality and sexuality is boldly outlined in Toni Morrison's *Beloved*, but to find it, one has to have the tools to unlock the codes of the African cosmology that permeate this richly evocative text. It is true that most characters in Beloved never find wholeness. But it is also true that no character in *Beloved* can hope to find wholeness without confronting and assimilating the twin tropes of sexuality and spirituality. As she attempts to do in *Sula*, Morrison drives home the point that true subjectivity is dependent upon spiritual and sexual symbiosis. *Beloved* theorizes a radical repositioning of sexual discourse vis-à-vis black folk in general, and black women in particular. No interrogation of slavery and its impact upon black subject formation can be complete without a sustained analysis of sexual politics between black men and women, and between white society and black. Erzulie, the Haitian goddess of sexuality, is the invisible character whose disruptive presence haunts the complexly layered landscape of *Beloved* with African and black New World signs and symbols that dramatically express the sacred and the sexual, the spoken and the unspeakable, giving rise to multiple metaphoric and metonymic significations of the erotic in Morrison's brilliant novel.

4

The Erotics of Change

Female Sexuality, Afro-Caribbean Spirituality, and a "Postmodern" Caribbean Identity in *It Begins with Tears*

New World Cosmologies and Postmodern Innovations

> Well it all not too strange if you can read de signs, you know. Change is always nasty. De life we know is changing, dat's all. Some for de good, and oder, well now, dat's a horse of a different colour. You got to be prepared for change, Milford, or it will come and run you ova'.
>
> Opal Palmer Adisa, *It Begins with Tears*

As someone who was born and raised in Jamaica but spent most of her adult life in the United States, Opal Palmer Adisa writes with a full recognition of the interrelatedness of African diasporic cultures and the foundational aspect of West African cosmology for the worldview of these cultures. Inherent in her oeuvre is the seamless interweaving of philosophical, religious, mythical, cultural, and psychological elements that define the syncretic worldview of Caribbean peoples. In *African Beliefs in the New World*, Lucie Pradel argues for the continuity of African belief systems in the Caribbean and their adaptability to secular usages such as those employed in Adisa's fiction: "Caribbean popular and literary traditions turned to the sacred African sources to pollenize and to enrich their métissage and creolization processes and to diversify the literary and artistic forms" (287). As is the case in West African societies, the sacred is expressed in the Caribbean through art, craft, dance, folktales, rituals of birth, death, and healing, worship, proverbs, music, myth, and what some Westerners might dismiss as superstition, and of course, through literature and orature. Adisa makes use of multiple expressions of African and New World cosmologies to add depth and texture to the mythological structure of her writing.

As a consequence of Adisa's diasporic literacy, we find in her short-story collection *Bake-Face* (written several years before Toni Morrison's *Beloved*) one character who is intermittently haunted by the ghosts of her grandparents. The initial event that occasions these dead grandparents' emergence from the spirit world into the physical plane of human existence is the imminent arrival of their great-grandchild. Although dead, the grandparents are vested with the ancestral power to shape the destinies of their living relatives, much like Baby Suggs, holy, in *Beloved*. The ancestral spirits in *Bake-Face* run interference to prevent their granddaughter, Lily, from giving birth to her child far away from her people and their ancestral land.[1] The same grandparents resurface again to prevent Lily from marrying the wrong man, although he happens to be the baby's father. Clearly, Adisa is cognizant of the importance of ancestors in African cosmology and expertly negotiates the theory of unbreakable kinship ties between living and dead relatives, and the primacy of elders in the worldview of the descendants of West Africans living in Jamaica.

In this same collection, Adisa employs mythology from the Yoruba people of Nigeria. "Widow's Walk" is a story about a missing fisherman whose wife awaits his return from sea with a mixture of fear and hope. The orisha Yemonja[2] is evoked as the supreme mistress of the ocean who has the power to seduce and lay claim to the men who venture into her mysterious domain. Adisa's use of these mythologies is both inventive and experimental. She attempts to give a coherent form and authentic source of origin to elements of West African belief systems that have helped to shape Jamaican culture and yet remain fragmented, misnamed, denigrated, or historically unaccounted for.

This chapter is primarily concerned, however, with Adisa's interweaving of signs, symbols, fragments of mythologies, rites of passage, ways of being, living and loving, and sacred rituals from West African, New World, and invented "mythical" cosmologies into her first novel. In *It Begins with Tears*, Adisa thoroughly interrogates contesting ideologies and values vis-à-vis notions of progress and modernity in late twentieth-century rural Jamaica. Adisa's text does not privilege tradition at the expense of progress, but neither does it oversimplify the challenges that modernity represents to a way of life that is steeped in the traditional values of communality and interdependence. Rather, her text uses a female-centered Afro-Caribbean spirituality as the bridge between two conflicting ideologies (modernity and tradition) whose oppositional imperatives threaten the cohesion and stability of a traditional peasant community. Drawing upon fragments of

West African religions, as well as upon the syncretized religious traditions of Jamaica, Adisa's text uses strong female characters modeled after Yoruba deities and linked with nature to demonstrate the coterminous relationship between individual female empowerment and sociopolitical viability for the community. The foregrounding of female sexual agency within this text links sexuality and spirituality as coterminous sites of empowerment and political agency for women.

Structurally, the novel consists of a prologue and five distinct components that weave the different threads of the narrative together. Each part is separated into individual descriptive sections that define one of the main characters or events that will become central to the plot. For example, part 1 is divided into seven subsections: "Cloth" denotes the character Arnella, the free-spirited artist and priestess-in-training who is clearly modeled on the Yoruba deity Oshun. "Clay and Indigo" follows, encoding both overt and subtle differences of skin tone, culture, and identity between Angel and her husband, Rupert. "Midday "describes both the time of Monica's arrival in the village and her preference for engaging in sexual activity in the middle of the day. "Left-over" reveals the emptiness of Beryl's present, wracked with the misery and sense of irremediable loss that is a "left-over" from her painful past. "The Elements" references Mrs. Cotton, the sage, elder priestess, and "Seeyah"[3] woman who is aligned with the ancient African cosmos and connected to the natural world and the world of the spirits. "Wood" describes Godfree, who was born to be a carpenter and a sculptor and is also defined by his sexual virility ("wood" is a Jamaican Creole term for penis), which joins him in a love triangle—one that is both unconventional and unexploitative in the sense that it is informed not by his choice, but by the women's—with Arnella and her inseparable "twin," Valrie. Finally, "Water" is dedicated to the transformative element marking Rupert's childhood memories: his parents holding hands in the river, shedding their "old skins," and dancing, leaving him with one positive memory of them as happy, carefree, and able to transcend the mundane routine of their existence.

The other four parts of the novel maintain the same structure, leaving the reader with the impression that the narratological and formal apparatus governing the text is self-consciously democratic as there is no clear-cut protagonist in the novel. The novel makes a clear break with traditional form at this juncture by refusing to claim a main character. Each character is important, and although the climax of the novel revolves around Monica, there are several key characters who are central to the plot. What emerges is a polyphonic Bakhtinian model[4] of the novel, with some characters clearly central to the structure of traditional communal life in Kristoff Village, and others symbolizing the inevitability of change. The one-stanza verse "How it Began" at the beginning of part 1 clearly defines Adisa's narrative structure, and foreshadows her self-conscious and unmistakably ideological innovations:

> Several strands of thread
> held in a hand
> then woven
> into a pattern
> each strand
> remains distinguishable
> separate
> from the others.

Together, all the characters make up a seamless whole. Separately, they maintain their own individuality, but the many voices in the text delineate the structure of village life: a community made up of distinct individuals who need each other in order to survive as individuals and as a group. Like Morrison, Adisa posits a theoretical framework that is founded upon intersubjectivity, while highlighting the significance of the individual's personal, political, and social development.

Nevertheless, the profusion of characters in this novel can appear confusing at first. The unconventional structure of the text, coupled with the verse quoted above, leads one to suspect that Adisa intends to force the reader to grapple with the contrast between expectations of homogeneity in the "traditional" village culture, and the multiple and conflicting subject positions one actually encounters in the text. *It Begins with Tears* resists easy binary interpretation even as it foregrounds issues that are themselves easily catalogued in opposition to each other. Good versus evil, tradition versus modernity, wives versus whores, spiritual healers versus spirit-thieves, and community versus individual—all are themes in Adisa's novel that lend themselves to binary interpretation. However, with her remarkable aptitude for inversion, complexity, and revision, Adisa manages to subvert the reader's inclination toward binarization. She does so by presenting a community struggling to hold on to its way of life while expanding to accommodate the interventions of modernity and globalization.

We first encounter Adisa's contestation of binary opposition in the prologue of the novel, where she easily blends Judeo-Christian mythology with her own invented mythology that is derived from a Jamaican folk saying.

The Creole saying, "Rain ah fall, sun a shine, Devil a beat him wife" used to explain the phenomenon of the sun shining while the rain is coming down, is evoked in the prologue to explain the sense of unrest and agitation that pervades the village as the novel opens:

> The people of Kristoff Village didn't know what to make of the eerie gloominess that hung over their community. The clouds were puffy and the sky was a strange purple-grey and grey-pink. The people's eyes were drawn to the sky, and sometimes, while they were searching for answers, raindrops would spill down, first from the grey-pinkish side, then from the other. The rain would begin, then stop, as though someone had opened up part of the sky, poured water out, then closed it just as quickly. (6)

Adisa creates a parallel universe called "Eternal Valley" in which Devil and She-Devil actually do exist in symbiosis with the inhabitants of Kristoff Village. Devil and She-Devil do not control the actions of the villagers. Nevertheless, whatever occurs in the household of She-Devil and her husband has direct implications for the climatic conditions in Kristoff Village, the emotional temperament of the villagers, and the day-to-day routine of village life: "The adults pretended they weren't caught off guard by the raining sun as they ran back and forth first spreading clothes to dry, then rushing to gather them" (1). Similarly, when Devil and She-Devil make love in Eternal Valley, "The earth shook, the wind rose, flowers swayed and birds chirped" in Kristoff Village (7).

In addition to making use of African and New World cosmologies as architectonic frameworks for the sign systems and a priori value systems within this text, Adisa also inscribes her own mythological innovations. Devil and She-Devil appear as godlike entities that have the power to influence human relations. However, it is clear that they themselves have very human characteristics. In fact, Devil and She-Devil are clearly rural working-class Jamaicans like the inhabitants of Kristoff Village. They speak the same Creole as the Kristoff villagers, eat Jamaican cuisine, and display a Jamaican cultural frame of reference. Adisa draws upon organic Jamaican feminism to contextualize the reaction of the village women to the violent confrontation between Devil and his wife: "The women were outraged that in these times Devil still felt he could up and beat his wife. . . . 'If it was me ah would pour hot oil in him ears'" (1). In fact, although Adisa draws on a language of female victimization in her explanation of the villagers' reaction to the weather, the actual interaction between Devil and his wife does not present She-Devil as a victim, but rather as an antagonist and aggressor.[5] The climax of the confrontation occurs after Devil makes a sexist comment about how women ought to behave. Although Devil's comment is clearly out of line, it is She-Devil who throws the first blow:

> She had risen early to prepare a breakfast to Devil's liking. And this was how he thanked her, by saying that her value was only in pleasing him. She-Devil got hot. Steaming, sweating, hot. She hauled the cast-iron pot off the stove and knocked Devil on his head. (5)

Clearly, this couple is like any other couple in a dysfunctional relationship. However, Adisa seems to model the specifics of She-Devil's behavior—her excessive aggressiveness, her use of Jamaican Creole, and her weapon of choice—on extant stereotypes of working-class Jamaican women. As is the case with most stereotypes, there is some truth to this one. In working-class Jamaican society, when men and women disagree to the point where they "come to blows," any party is likely to throw the first blow, regardless of gender.[6] Adisa deliberately makes use of this stereotype to advance her own theories about the meeting of Western feminism with organic Jamaican feminism. As the following quote demonstrates, Adisa's feminist agenda is anything but subtle:

> She-Devil was a loner, and not into the sentiments of the day, but Tegreg, her daughter, had been telling her about this Woman's Thing. 'What's de word Tegreg used now?' She-Devil paused with one hand on her hip, her right side thrusting. Femi, femi-something. But whatever Tegreg called it, she had her husband Man-Stick helping her wid all de housework. (5)

Together with the homegrown feminism that is already part and parcel of Jamaican female subjectivity, Adisa introduces elements from Western feminism: its objection to the traditionally gendered division of labor that unfairly burdens women within the domestic realm, as well as its emphasis on a self-consciously oppositional self-definition that calls attention to itself both as a movement and as a theoretical position.

Introduced as it is in the prologue of the novel, the world inhabited by Devil and She-Devil instructs us as to the worldview we are about to enter in the text. As in Devil and She-Devil's world, passions will run high—both sexually and otherwise—in Kristoff Village. The parallel world inhabited by the Devils alerts us to the fact that women will play a dominant role within the text. Like She-Devil's son-in-law Man-Stick, the men in Kristoff Village will not be the main actors, but rather supporters of the dominant female figures.

There is also something distinctly subversive in Adisa's corruption/revision of Christian theology. The role that these two demigods (Devil and She-Devil) play in the text does not end with the resolution of their conflict in the prologue. In addition to providing the Devil with a partner—one who is his equal in every way—Adisa further revises the Judeo-Christian concept of the Devil by portraying him as a flawed Jamaican man instead of a demon. There are references to "God," his wife, "Sabbath," and "the Angel Boys" in Eternal Valley, but their roles are subordinate to that of Devil and She-Devil. They are summoned once, when She-Devil needs help with her son's wedding, but only to assist in the preparations. The Judeo-Christian concept of an omnipotent and transcendent God does not exist in this text, and neither does heaven or hell. Instead, the sociomoral framework normally occupied by Judeo-Christian sign systems is shared by Yoruba and New World cosmologies and by the Devil and She-Devil mythology. In effect, this decenters the a priori status of Judeo-Christian morality and forces the reader to strain against the dictum of Western hermeneutical processes and discursive formations. The Yoruba deities Oshun and Yemonja (as represented by River-mumma, Mrs. Cotton, and Arnella) serve the physical, spiritual, and emotional needs of the women. However, it is to She-Devil that Miss Madge goes immediately after her death. Monica also turns to She-Devil (looking for vengeance on her enemies and wishing for her own death) after she has been peppered[7] by Marva, Grace, and Peggy. She-Devil's home seems to represent a way station, a kind of purgatory where divine justice is meted out. She-Devil herself plays the dual roles of divine judge and consoler. Adisa alludes to the Judeo-Christian God in another section of the text, but immediately exposes him as a capricious tyrant and denounces him. Hence Miss Dahlia names her grandson "Godfree" to free him "from the tyranny of God" (41–43).

Adisa manipulates old mythological sources and invents new ones in this novel to create a worldview that syncretizes magical and mythical elements within the harsh quotidian realities of rural Jamaican life. Difference is rendered as a complexly variegated phenomenon that resists easy definitions or romanticized constructions. There is nothing romantic about outhouses, flying cockroaches, greedy mosquitoes, or the backbreaking field labor and other necessary work (butchering animals, etc.) that Beryl does to keep life and limb, head and heart together daily. Conversely, Rupert's parents' ritual dance in the river is as enigmatic as it is uncharacteristic for this stern, humorless couple. The fact that even characters as seemingly dull as these people can be endowed with a mystical power, the source of which is entirely inexplicable, helps to instill a sense of magical realism in the novel. It is not a stretch, however, to identify at least one of the sources of Adisa's myth making as West African. Characters like Mrs. Cotton and Arnella are modeled on priestess figures from the Yoruba or Congo traditions who have their counterparts in the Afro-religions of Jamaica, be they syncretized or fragments of the original: Pukumina, Kumina, Zionist, Revival, and Myal.[8] The frequent recurrence of river imagery—tied as it is to rituals of healing, sexuality, and nurturing—further helps to situate this novel's mythological source in West African and New World belief systems in which rivers are the abode of powerful female deities (Pradel, "African Sacredness and Caribbean Cultural Forms" 146).

The narrative trajectory of *It Begins with Tears* is informed by a series of interruptions and digressions that propel the forward movement of the narrative in a mazelike pattern. Consequently, Adisa's narrative resists both circularity and linear movement, but this is not a failure of Adisa's ideological or literary goals. The disjointed nature of the narrative forces the reader to surrender conditioned expectations and enter the text prepared to deal with the radically unsettling potential of difference. Like Angel, many readers will be entering a village like Kristoff for the very first time. Also like Angel, they will carry into the text their own culturally acquired stereotypes and preconceptions. The narrative's self-conscious refusal to be either linear or cyclical draws attention to itself as an artificial construct, thereby enabling readers to imagine the impact of political, social, and cultural interventions in traditional spaces.

One example of an obvious political intervention is the name "Godfree," given to the lover of Arnella and Valrie by his grandmother. Godfree's grandmother, one of the insiders in Kristoff Village, represents the consciousness of the community. The community's desire to be free of Judeo-Christian hegemony occasions Adisa's creation of a parallel spiritual universe known as Eternal Valley that has a life of its own within the text. The story of how Godfree got his name is told long after we have been introduced to Devil and She-Devil, but it helps to explain why the Judeo-Christian God has been jettisoned in this mythical construct.

At times, the narration of events in Eternal Valley breaks the pattern of the text's primary narrative, seemingly without rhyme or reason. For example, in the first section of part 2, titled "Push," Arnella goes into labor alone in the woods. Arnella has been portrayed as a priestess-in-training and is, arguably, the most unconventional and independent woman in the village. Modern female readers may identify with her and be vested in her well-being and that of her baby. But the section in which Arnella is in labor is only a page long, and it ends with her defecating on herself, slumped on the ground, panting. The narrative leaves readers alone in the outdoors with Arnella. Readers do not know why she is outdoors, and have no sense of whether the outcome of her labor will be good. This section is immediately followed by "Ring-ring," set in Eternal Valley. It seems disruptive and pointless because it does not help to answer any of the reader's questions about the main narrative and what happens to Arnella. As the title suggests, She-Devil is happy to finally have the modern convenience of a phone and is ecstatic when her daughter calls to say she will be coming for a visit. The rest of the section narrates her seduction of Devil as she attempts to sexually bribe him into helping her with the work necessary to get their house in order for their daughter's visit. The section ends with She-Devil and Devil making love, much to the consternation of their prudish talking parrot, Cheek. There does not appear to be any relationship between Arnella's labor and She-Devil's desire for sex, assistance from her husband, and modern conveniences. The only narrative continuity between these two sections is the imminent arrival of both Arnella's daughter and She-Devil's.

In the final section of part 2, after several different narratives featuring several different characters, readers return to the scene where Arnella is giving birth to Baby-Girl. In the penultimate subsection of part 2 titled "One Version," there is a legend that explains why Arnella is having her labor outdoors. Arnella is following a tradition that was begun by an enslaved ancestor who gave birth under a breadfruit tree and willed herself to have a stillbirth rather than bear a child into slavery. The final section, titled "Possibilities," shows that the community of women has arrived to assist in the birth, and Arnella and her baby receive the full benefit of the interdependence and intersubjectivity that orders the worldview of the polity. It is only at this point that one is able to observe the differences between the parallel worlds of Kristoff Village and Eternal Valley. She-Devil's newly acquired telephone is a modern convenience that is being juxtaposed to Arnella's traditional outdoor birthing. If Arnella had owned a phone, perhaps she would not have had to begin the labor outdoors on her own. On the other hand, while Arnella is assisted by the women in the village, She-Devil (who is aligned with modernity via the phone) has to seduce Devil into helping her. The connections between modernity and tradition and between intersubjectivity and individuality are very clear, but Adisa takes her readers on a circular path to these connections.

There are other narrative moments that underscore the relational disparities between Eternal Valley and Kristoff Village. For example, when Miss Madge dies in Kristoff, She-Devil is preparing for her son Brimstone's wedding to the beautiful Tallawah. An occasion for mourning and separation in Kristoff becomes a celebration of marital union in Eternal Valley.

At times, the relationship between Kristoff and Eternal Valley is neither conflicted nor contiguous, and Eternal Valley operates as a purgatory of sorts—a place where souls from Kristoff Valley go immediately after death. Miss Madge goes to Eternal Valley after death and is welcomed by She-Devil. However, when Monica nearly dies after she has been assaulted, she is not welcomed in Eternal Valley. She-Devil turns her away impatiently, telling her it is not yet her time to die. This moment represents a confluence between Adisa's ideological and narrative logic. In the community of Kristoff Village and in the economy of the text, Monica has not yet served her purpose. Her attack will provide the pretense for the final clash between modernity and tradition that will lead to a necessary reckoning between these two competing ideologies. As a result of the community uniting to save her, Monica will reassess her actions, her relationship to the community, and her role within Kristoff Village. Monica's reform represents a compromise between radically subversive individualism and the insistent demand for intersubjectivity and interdependence in the Kristoff Villages of the world. The inconsistencies, interruptions, and innovations that characterize the narrative's trajectory allow Adisa to proffer an alternative relationship between modernity and tradition. Adisa imagines a tradition that is not metonymic with stasis, lack of innovation, or intolerance, and that accepts differences with the result of a radical restructuring of social relations, lifestyles, and ideologies.

Myth is also deployed to highlight the conflict between tradition and modernity in Adisa's text. Materialistic Western value systems are juxtaposed against traditional customs and beliefs. Here again, there is no easy binary to negotiate and transcend. Milford, Peggy, Marva, and Grace seem to be the representatives of a Westernized, citified, "modern" worldview that is in conflict with the communal, old-fashioned values of Kristoff village. Angel, an outsider (in her own world as in this one), seems to represent a return to tradition, kinship ties, and community: she is a prodigal daughter coming home. Monica, on the other hand, is like Sula in Toni Morrison's text,[9] the scapegoat who mirrors everything positive and negative in the divided community. She represents modernity as well as tradition,[10] and her presence in Kristoff Village acts as a catalyst compelling the community to resolve some of its internal issues and possibly redefine itself. Like it or not, modernity is already present in Kristoff Village. Will the community be able to choose which aspects of modernity it is willing to absorb and which should be avoided at all costs? Or will the inhabitants of Kristoff Village allow modernity to destroy the fundamental spiritual values that define the community? And, significantly, what role does female sexuality play in the contestation between modernity and tradition, and how can female spirituality help to mediate this conflict?

Modernity vs. Tradition in Kristoff Village

> As used in classical theory, the concept of modernity has its roots in the attempt to come to grips with the meaning and significance of the social changes occurring in Europe in the latter half of the nineteenth century, namely, industrialization, urbanization, and political democracy on essentially rural and autocratic societies. The term "modernity" was coined to capture these changes in progress by contrasting the "modern" with the "traditional." The theme, if not the concept, of modernity pervades sociology and the work of its founding fathers, Marx, Weber, and Durkheim. In their work modernity was meant to be more than a heuristic concept. It carried connotations of a new experience of the world. Modernity referred to a world constructed anew through the active and conscious intervention of actors and the new sense of self that such active intervention and responsibility entailed. In modern society the world is experienced as a human construction, an experience that gives rise both to an exhilarating sense of freedom and possibility and to a basic anxiety about the openness of the future.
>
> Ron Eyerman, "Modernity and Social Movements"

There are competing definitions of modernity, but in this chapter, I use the definition proposed above by Ron Eyerman that places modernity within its original sociological context. Adisa's novel foregrounds the clash between modernity and tradition, as well as the cultural instability that is precipitated by the inevitable advancement of Western "progress" into even the most distant reaches of Jamaican society. Adisa's work does not preach against modernity, but is, to use Homi Bhabha's phrase, "in contention" with it. Her narratological apparatus clearly critiques how this fictional community deals with the dialectics generated by modernity and hybridity.

It Begins with Tears demonstrates that "modernity" and "tradition" are not value-free terms, but are in fact rife with political implications that situate them in a hierarchical relationship to each other. Modern means technologically advanced, bigger, more opulent, urban, belonging to the wealthy and better educated. Traditional is viewed as harsher, rural, belonging to the poor and uneducated, smaller, less desirable, inferior.

It Begins with Tears addresses issues of cultural resistance that are of particular significance in contemporary times. Although set in a village in the backwoods of Jamaica, Adisa's work manages to cross geographical and ideological lines that illuminate the political and cultural connections extant among literature of the African diaspora. Most significantly, Adisa's novel foregrounds issues of cultural and spiritual resistance to the denuding of traditional folk values and ways of being in certain segments of rural Jamaican society. These forms of resistance have their foundation in the historical and cultural adaptation of the Jamaican people.[11]

In *The Location of Culture*, Homi Bhabha argues that postcolonial critique bears witness to these countries and communities that are not considered "modern." He argues, "Such cultures of a postcolonial contra-modernity may be contingent to modernity, discontinuous or in contention with it, resistant to its oppressive assimilationist technologies, but they also deploy the cultural hybridity of their borderline conditions to translate and therefore re-inscribe, the social imaginary of both metropolis and modernity" (6).

Through a creolized spirituality already rooted in various forms of slave resistance,[12] difference—even the kind of difference that threatens certain customs and traditions—becomes assimilated into the social fabric of Adisa's fictional Jamaican community. For Jamaicans, the ability to "pick sense out of none-sense," or to extract what is useful from even the most potentially harmful circumstance, is a familiar cultural trope. This adaptability is a survivalist sensibility (also a prominent feature of hybridity), strategically deployed both thematically and structurally in *It Begins with Tears*. The rural folk in Adisa's novel are able to transcend modernity's all-consuming "assimilationist" appetite through their Anancy-like, Legba-like, ability to outsmart, transform, and transcend various hegemonic imperatives.[13] The narrative structure employs the dialectics of outsider and insider to inscribe "the social imaginary of modernity," and to articulate strategies of resistance and adaptation.

Critics of modernity have argued that it is discursively hegemonic and potentially totalizing.[14] Modernity's relationship to tradition is governed by a hierarchical ideational structure that posits the European modern as both technologically and epistemologically superior and, therefore, entitled to its position of ideological and political dominance over non-European nation-states. Saurabh Dube considers the interrelatedness of colonialism, power, and epistemology:

> Against the grain of these dominant orientations, an important body of critical thought on Latin America today focuses on the subterranean schemes and the overwrought apparitions of the modern and the colonial—in the past and the present. In other words this corpus critically considers the spectral place and tangible presence of colonial stipulations of knowledge/power within modern provisions of knowledge/power. Consequently, such moves, acutely represented in this issue, have also held up a mirror to modernity as a deeply ideological project, a ruse of history, a primary apparatus of domination, here now and there tomorrow.[15]

In the face of modernity's hegemonizing apparatus, any non-Western tradition that is worth keeping is seriously contested. To survive modernity's onslaught, traditional cultures have to wage a war of ideological resistance that can be fought on multiple planes. In Adisa's text, this resistance takes place on a spiritual plane. In this chapter, I illuminate several forms of resistance in the fictional Jamaican society of Kristoff Village. Spiritual resistance takes many forms in this narrative: loyalty to traditional values, including respect for the land; recognizing oneness with the earth and with each other; taking responsibility for each other's well-being; and acknowledging and respecting the spiritual traditions and ways of the ancestors that have enabled the survival of the community.

In Adisa's text, the drive toward modernity is mapped out along spatial and class lines. The community's efforts to subvert the negative influences of modernity—its overvaluing of accumulation and devaluing of people, its territorial and individualistic tendencies, and its discursive privileging of city living over rural—take place at a spiritual level that demonstrates the confluence of the political with the spiritual. In addition, Adisa's narrative points the reader's attention to the links between spiritual and sexual empowerment for women. In this text, spirituality and sexuality are interdependent upon each other. Unlike some Caribbean women writers, Adisa does not shy away from dealing with adult female sexuality.[16] Adisa's rendering of female eroticism in her novel serves as a creative iteration of Lorde's challenge to women to put the erotic to work in the service of their personal and political empowerment. *It Begins with Tears* combines traditional Jamaican spirituality, West African religious mythology, and Christian theology with Adisa's own spiritual and mythological inventions in a subversive, syncretic model of inversion, revision, and transcendence that effectively undercuts the moral and religious hegemony of Judeo-Christian values and mores.

In *Making Men: Gender, Literary Authority and Women's Writing in Caribbean Narrative*, Belinda Edmondson makes clear the relationship between the black middle class and colonial English value systems in the nineteenth century. She says that the black middle class, who did not own land to "produce (a) nation in its own image, had to acquire the manners, habits and positioning of the English gentleman class through the acquisition of Victorian models of intellectual authority and knowledge" (23). Edmondson suggests that with so much mimicking of English values and cultural pastimes (such as cricket), it was difficult to locate any authentic Caribbean cultural forms in the black middle class. Edmondson argues that early Caribbean writers such as C.L.R. James, George Lamming, V. S. Naipaul, Claude McKay, and Una Marson turned to the rural working-class peasants for a more authentic and indigenous representation of Caribbean culture. She cites Claude McKay's novel *Banana Bottom* as a text that exemplifies the black middle class's alienation from its peasant origins.

Furthermore, Edmondson argues convincingly that the first crop of Caribbean male writers wrote from the historicized position of "their inherited interpellated meanings of manhood and cultural identity," as defined by Victorian ideations of masculinity and authorship (5). She compares the prominent Caribbean male writers from the colonial era—who wrote from the particularity of their positions as West Indian exiles in Britain—to the later crop of Caribbean women writers who write from the position of immigrants in America. Edmondson insists that the "exiled" status of Caribbean male writers is constituted through intellectual ideation, while the "immigrant" status of female writers is founded on economic exigencies and issues of survival. Nevertheless, she observes, it would be wrongheaded to assume that female writers are writing exclusively outside the tradition already established by the male writers: "what I wish to point out is that the one has inherited the concerns of the other and must write within and against that prior tradition in order to be engaged in the process of national definition" (14).

Adisa's first novel both complicates and affirms Edmondson's theory about the differences between male and female Caribbean writers. *It Begins with Tears* is set in the peasant society of Jamaica, and Adisa clearly links the moral high ground within the text to the cultural authenticity of the peasant folk who still observe traditional values of communality and intersubjectivity. In this way, her text links authentic Caribbean culture to the folk, as Edmondson observes above. In Adisa's novel, characters migrate in search of better economic opportunities, while the spatial and temporal boundaries remain fluid but contested. Unlike the exiles in Samuel Selvon's novels, Adisa's characters traverse between diasporas somewhat seamlessly. Angel leaves as Beryl's baby born from rape and returns as Rupert's mulatta wife who initially feels her outsider status but quickly learns to fit in. Even the ex-prostitute Monica is able to reintegrate into the community. However, her refusal to abide by Judeo-Christian morality remains a bone of contention that threatens her insider status. Unlike other Caribbean women writers, Adisa does not consistently foreground the nexus between economic viability and issues of survival, a choice that perhaps constitutes one of the failings of the novel. Neither Monica nor Rupert is independently wealthy, and the reader is not made aware of how either character intends to make a living.[17] In fact, no mention is made of any business that could provide gainful employment.[18] Instead of the economic concerns that undergird the novels of immigrant women, the survival of the way of life that sustains this traditional community is what gets contested against the totalizing potential of modernity in *It Begins with Tears*.

As in the works of McKay, Lamming, and Naipaul, authentic Caribbean culture is located within and constituted by the folk in Adisa's work. Colonial value systems become metonymic with notions of progress and modernity as emblematized through certain characters and events in the text. As Kwame Dawes points out in *Natural Mysticism*, "while Africa has always been a part of the Jamaican consciousness, it was frequently a carefully submerged element" (116). It is clear that Adisa is writing within (and critiquing) a certain tradition that associates Western culture with modernism, as defined by the technological advancements of the industrial age.[19] Similarly, she is aligning tradition with the African culture of the preindustrial age, thereby creating a metonymic relationship between folk culture in Jamaica and African identity. In Jamaica, as elsewhere, whenever European value systems hold hegemonic sway, African modes of being and thinking are often denigrated as uncivilized and primitive. However, Adisa's text destabilizes notions of modernity and progress and forces the reader to positively evaluate the worldview of the folk—a worldview that is intrinsically tied to the much-denigrated but irrepressible African consciousness and African continuity—and to respect the healing, transformative, and transcendental potential that inheres in the folk who practice and preserve these traditions.

Angel as Bridge between Modernity and Tradition

In another example of traditional culture problematically and reductively rendered vis-à-vis notions of modernity, Jean Rahier critiques the Esmeraldian racial/spatial order responsible for the stereotyping of rural folk in Ecuador:

> The "blue blacks" or Northerners are considered by the urban population of Esmeraldas as people without "culture," people untouched by modernity, who maintain traditions from another age, do not mind living amidst the dense rain forest, with no electricity or running water, with mosquitoes and wild animals, and who—when they come to town—have no manners and can sometimes behave as social predators.[20]

Adisa's novel does not reproduce the stereotypical view of the folk that Rahier critiques. *It Begins with Tears* presents a counterdiscourse to modernity's negative imaging of rural environments without romanticizing the harsher realities of rural working-class life. The character Angel—the only true "outsider" in the sense that she comes from another culture altogether—first comes to Kristoff Village at night. Angel is repelled by the overwhelming presence of blackness in the landscape of the Jamaican country night. Her fear seems primal and overpowering, although there is nothing tangible of which she should be afraid. For Angel, the physical darkness of the nighttime rural landscape represents a frightening, unknown, and possibly evil thing. Images of fear, death, and erasure mark Angel's first impression of the Jamaican rural world to which she has chosen to relocate with her husband, Rupert, a native of this "terrifying" place. As the only foreigner in the text, Angel embodies the Western world's perceptions of places that are still relatively untouched by modernity as primitive, backward, and uninhabitable. Angel's initial perceptions seem to echo Rahier's description of the racial/spatial order of Esmeraldian society mentioned above:

> For the first time she understood the term pitch darkness. She respected it now.... Something was wrong. Wrong.... If she had not been immobilized by her fear of the darkness she would have sprung out of the car, into the night. But no! Not into that darkness. It would devour her. Her body would probably never be found. "We almost dere." Angel jumped. Rupert's voice coming towards her out of the blackness was a sudden shock. She glanced to her side but could not see him. He had become the night. She wanted to scream run.... Was

he crazy? New home! What home? . . . All Angel saw was darkness, in front, behind and beside her. Rupert had also become a part of darkness; she was the only light. She held up her palms to her face for confirmation, but even these she could not make out. Darkness was taking her too. It was going to swallow her whole. (21)

Angel's husband, Rupert, a familiar and loving partner who saved her from loneliness and a sense of disconnectedness in modern New York, becomes as frightening to her as the night that he embodies in his skin and in his familiarity with this territory. Because Rupert is one with the darkness, his presence gives her no protection against her fear of it. Blackness here is presented as both a total absence of physical light and as spiritual unconsciousness. The physical darkness stands in stark contrast to the bright electric light of Angel's native New York, even as its presence reinscribes the almost totalizing sense of hopelessness that defines Angel's fragmented consciousness before she meets Rupert. Angel cannot comprehend a place before modernity, before electricity. The absence of light that is the norm for moonless nights in the natural world brings her to a state of panic. Hence, what is natural and normal becomes inverted in Angel's response to the new landscape: darkness is rendered as an unnatural, abnormal, evil entity threatening to cancel Angel out.

In paralleling Angel's fear of the darkness with her newly developed fear of her dark-skinned husband, Adisa manages to convey a Conradian element to this passage that conflates fear of the "primitive" with fear of racial otherness. Angel's construction of the darkness as inscrutable and fearsome and her conflation of physical darkness with racial difference, seem to mimic the ideational construction of racial and cultural difference between Englishmen and Africans in Joseph Conrad's *Heart of Darkness*. Conrad's protagonist, Marlow, has anxieties about the "darkness of an impenetrable night" (62) that are echoed in Angel's fear that the darkness will "devour her" (21). The fact that Angel is not white, but rather a very light-skinned biracial woman, further complicates the integration of Conrad's racial difference paradigm. Nevertheless, as with Marlow, Angel's fear of the darkness encompasses both the landscape and the dark-skinned people who are native to it.

Angel's fear of blackness emblematizes her association with the tragic mulatta trope. It also forces comparisons with middle-class, fair-skinned Jamaicans who are "fixated on the principles of lightness of skin as a sign of quality and darkness of skin as a sign of abjection" (Dawes 116). Adisa's text suggests that as a biracial woman who is the possessor of both whiteness and blackness, Angel's fear of the darkness resides within herself. If one assumed, however, that this is yet another novel that foregrounds the much-touted subject of the tragic mulatta in the literature of the African diaspora, he or she would be in error. Angel is no tragic mulatta. She ultimately confronts the darkness, befriends it, and learns to accept it, and in so doing learns to accept herself in all of her complexity. More importantly, she learns to invest darkness with a meaning derived from its own context, instead of one that is oppositional and negative:

> In that instant she hated Rupert. How could he leave her there all by herself? Angry and hurt, she said to herself: "He doesn't love me." She folded in on herself. Courage came to her though, when the mosquitoes began feasting on her flesh. She stomped her feet, clapped at her face and slapped at her arms. Then she got up and started to pace, gradually getting the feel of the ground beneath her feet, gradually making out the shape of bushes and trees, gradually seeing the little match-box that was Rupert's parents' home come into focus. The house in which he was born, where he had his first meal, was now to be her home. She began to relax a little. (21)

By employing the heuristic model that later earns her a place of acceptance in Kristoff Village, Angel is able to confront the realities of her new world, and thus make peace with the traditional values of her adopted environment. Unlike her fear of the darkness that is manufactured by her own imagination and fostered by an initial fear of difference and blackness, the mosquitoes are tangible evidence of the difference between the world Angel comes from and the world of Kristoff Village. Angel's imagined horrors are quickly displaced by the realization that to survive in this environment she has to take action. Such action must necessarily be preceded by the acquisition of real knowledge about the environment. Angel develops the ability to "see" in the darkness, and with this new sight she is able to release her fears and gain perspective and balance.

Angel's ability to see in the darkness becomes a metaphor for her role within Kristoff Village. Although she is the outsider, she is taken in by the community of women who are visionaries and healers—"Seeyah" women who have the ability to discern through the spirit that they cannot see with the physical eye—and whose role it is to keep the community in balance. Angel's first meeting with one of these women, the elder Miss Beryl, reflects both fear and recognition of a mysterious consubstantiating force that links their destinies. Miss Beryl is an elder in the community and part of a select group of matriarchs who emerge as spiritual leaders within Kristoff Village. It is Miss Beryl who prepares Rupert's home for his arrival with his new wife, including preparing a meal for them on their first night home. Miss Beryl initiates Angel into the lifestyle of Kristoff Village and teaches her how to live within her new environment. On her first encounter with Miss Beryl, Angel senses a connection that frightens her: "For some reason this woman seemed familiar, yet she was as frightening as the night" (24).

Miss Beryl "adopts" this newcomer, names her "daughter," and initiates her into a process of "seeing" that will enable Angel to discover, for the very first time, a sense of identity and belonging that has eluded her all her life. The darkness Angel fears in the beginning comes to represent the unknown of her own identity, and the mysteries of the African worldview of the folk. Adopted by a white family when she was a baby, Angel grows up with no knowledge of her true identity and no sense of belonging. After the death of her father, her adopted mother rejects her and Angel is traumatized by a tragic sense of ambivalence about her racial identity. In rebellion against her mother's racist attitudes, Angel decides to live as "a nigger." However, although she chooses to attend a black college and spends time in the home of her Jamaican maid, Angel never loses this sense of alienation until she comes to Kristoff Village and makes her peace with the darkness within.

In "The Beauty of Valuing Black Cultures," Alrick Cambridge comments on the reasons why an individual conforms to the expectations of his or her social grouping:

> Thus action, in the social identity model, is a process, a patterned movement in which individuals communicate to each other that they are particular kinds of people, by the collective use of norms. One of the theory's most powerful conclusions in this regard is that individuals conform to norms when and because the norms specify how to obtain recognition and validation of significant identity, not because the actor incorporates the norms and identity into the self, as John Rex and others advocate. Thus a change in identity or role may produce an immediate and major change in the norms that are relevant to an individual. (170)

Having been without a specific place and identity for so long, Angel is ripe and open for the sense of security and place Kristoff Village has to offer. She immediately adapts to the norms of rural village life, "performing" the identity of an insider even though her initial reaction to the place was absolute terror. To fulfill her own need for a daughter, Miss Beryl helps Angel to acculturate to her new life. With characteristic lack of ceremony, Miss Beryl declares Angel part of the community immediately upon meeting her—"you fava one a we except you skin light"—and proceeds to pull her new "daughter" into the inner circle of Kristoff Village. Before long, Angel is tying her head with a scarf in the traditional way of the village women, attending a birth, and participating in a healing ritual when Monica—the ex-prostitute—is violently assaulted for sleeping with the husband of one of the villagers. Angel finds a home, a "mother," a community, and a purpose for the first time in her life.

Angel represents a second chance for Miss Beryl to find her lost child who calls out to her in the text (35). She is haunted by the loss of the child that she gave up for adoption to its white American father, who raped her on one of his visits to Jamaica. Beryl's inability to fend off the sexual advances of this wealthy American tourist reveals the class, race, and gender imbalances in this exchange. Beryl is a bright young girl from the country, saving money to attend teachers' college by working as a chambermaid in the hotel in Montego Bay. Beryl lacks the power to defend herself against her wealthy, white attacker. When she becomes pregnant, Beryl is too ashamed to return home to her parents, who sent her to town expecting her to make something of the natural intelligence she demonstrated in elementary school. After she gives the child up for adoption to her rapist and his wife, she returns home, spiritually, sexually, and emotionally dead.

Beryl's almost complete vitiation represents the confrontation between modernity—with its progress measured in terms of advanced technology, wealth, and power—and traditional values and ways of life. Beryl's decision to pursue an education in town forces her to exchange the security and safety of her village life for the modern trappings of city living with all its attendant pitfalls. Montego Bay is a favorite tourist destination, and next to Kingston, is considered the most developed and urbane city in Jamaica. Music, fashion, food, and lifestyle imported from America gets to Montego Bay first by way of the tourist industry. The tourist industry generates thousands of new jobs, drawing many country folks to the city in search of social progress and economic opportunity. Consequently, Montego Bay is generally considered more progressive and wealthy (modern), but also more perverse. The traditional values that order and define village life have no place in a modern city, where progress is measured in terms of wealth, acquisition, and approximation to Western modes of existence. Not only is one defined by one's material possessions, but, in addition, identity becomes synonymous with what one possesses. Newcomers from traditional village environments either conform or become subsumed under the pressure of trying to retain a sense of self in an environment that contests the worth of anything traditional by associating it with backwardness and primitivism.

Adisa gradually makes it clear to the reader that Angel is the daughter Beryl had given up, the product of the rape that had shamed her, ruined her prospects, and twisted her personality. As the by-product of this disturbing encounter between modernity and tradition, Angel's presence in the text has multiple significations. On the one hand, she symbolizes the violent confrontation between these disparate worlds; on the other, she emblematizes hopeful possibilities for coexistence based upon mutual respect and understanding. Although she is raised in a modern metropolitan city, Angel is able to transcend her fear of difference and embrace the spiritual and emotional sustenance that the folkways offer. In positing Angel as the bridge between the two worlds, Adisa offers a challenging theory about the possibility of modernity coexisting with tradition without the former subsuming the latter under a discourse of superiority and domination masquerading as progress and advancement. Angel comments on the differences between Kristoff Village and Montego Bay:

> Two completely different worlds, thought Angel, glancing back to see if she could still see the road that led to Kristoff Village. The village was cool, serene and lush, a place that could be compared to paradise, a place where everyone knew everyone else, where people still left their doors open, greeted each other daily, looked out and cared for one another. What happened to Monica was an aberration, something gone bad. Or was it? Angel didn't allow her thoughts to dwell on this. Kristoff Village was a world of its own, and somehow, although many of its inhabitants traveled daily or weekly to Montego Bay, they left the disease that was eating that city and the rest of Jamaica at the junction. Their values and ways were ancient and, Angel suspected, could be found duplicated in many small villages throughout West Africa, where colonization had not laid its infected hand. (172)

This is an interesting narrative intervention since Angel has not, thus far, been presented as someone who knows or cares about West African village life. This is the same Angel who was terrified when she first came to Kristoff Village. Her transformation from a naïve, fearful outsider to someone who can occupy both subject positions (outsider-insider) strains the reader's credulity. Although Angel rebels against her racist stepmother by attending a historically black college, there is nothing in the preceding text to suggest either that she knows anything about West African village life, or that colonialism is a concern of Angel's. Here, as in the passage where She-Devil tries to remember the term "feminism," the narrative intervention is polemic: characters are invested with a theoretical language to speak their newfound political awareness. It is through these textual cracks that one becomes aware of an overtly political agenda in a text whose folksy, pictorial (almost pastoral) elements make it subject to potential charges of quaintness or exoticism. It is the political thrust of the novel and the attempt to theorize modernity's confrontation with tradition that liberates Adisa's text from the threat of romanticism that its pervasive use of myth, magical realism, invention, and creolized spirituality inscribes. Thus, Adisa's text renders an authoritative representation of rural Jamaican life, even though the "authenticity" of some of the village rituals in the novel may be called into question.[21]

Angel's openness and her acceptance by the wise women of the village stand in stark contrast to the alienation of the three outsiders whose complete rejection of the folkways signals their alignment with modernity. Grace, Peggy, and Marva—although born in Jamaica of working-class origins—remain outsiders within Kristoff Village because they refuse to accept the ways of the folk. They value material possessions, position, and status over family, community, and spiritual well-being, and are depicted as ugly, mean-spirited, spiteful, and disagreeable.[22] This threesome represents what Kwame Dawes describes as "sections of the working class who are seeking upward mobility and 'respectability' and who, as a consequence, join middle-class Jamaicans in denigrating the African customs of the folk" (116).

Unlike in Rahier's rendering of Ecuadorian society, Adisa's novel recognizes class distinctions above racial ones in this modern/urban, tradition/rural dichotomy. Characters such as Grace, Marva, and Peggy are seen as having newly acquired middle-class status, and their misplaced reverence for all things foreign extends to the newcomer Angel, who does not return their attempts to befriend her:

> Marva and Grace were sitting with Peggy on her verandah, gossiping, crocheting and darning clothes when they saw Beryl and Angel with lanterns headed in the direction of the river. Peggy saluted them, "Night Sister Beryl. Night, Miss American Lady." She had tried to befriend Angel, especially since she was from America. Angel had not taken up her invitation to come and visit, yet here she was with night

approaching walking beside Beryl, who was a loner and crazy at best. (82)

The above quotation marks the outsider status of the trio discussed previously in no uncertain terms. Miss Beryl and Angel are on their way to participate—with other significant female characters including the ex-prostitute Monica and the spiritual leader Mrs. Cotton—in Arnella's birthing of Baby-Girl. Although they live in the community of Kristoff Village, Peggy, Marva, and Grace are clearly set apart. They are not invited to important events, and neither are they informed of them. When Grace shouts the following questions after the retreating backs of Beryl and Angel: "Is Arnella you all going by? She tek in?," Miss Beryl merely "kissed her teeth and said under her breath, but loud enough for Angel to hear, 'Dem worse dan fowl dat have yaws'" (82). The quote evokes an unflattering image of these women as chickens mindlessly scratching away at their own sores.[23]

Indeed, the negative characterization of these women in Adisa's text is rendered highly problematic in a novel whose subtext reveals a deliberate black feminist agenda.[24] However, further examination reveals that the narrative voice is alternately sympathetic and harsh:

> Marva, for all her dirty red hair, used to be a striking woman, but with five boys, and a sixth child on the way, she now looked like a bullfrog about to burst into flames. Her skin was all blotchy and discolored, her nose swollen to twice its normal size. In fact, you could barely see the face for the nose. Varicose veins had ruined whatever attractiveness men once admired in her calves and legs. (60)

Grace does not fare much better:

> Grace was afraid of lizards, afraid of rolling-calf, afraid of not being liked, afraid that some woman was about to steal her husband, afraid of aging. In general, she was afraid of most things. (61)

However, it is Peggy's description that most effectively demonstrates the link between their overt manifestations of and concern with materialism and modernization, and the "ugliness" with which these values are associated:

> Peggy was tight and mean-spirited. Grudged bread out of a baby's mouth. Everyone always had more than she, and to hear her talk they didn't work for or deserve it. She was a hard worker who prided herself on having one of the nicest houses in Kristoff Village. Her family

wasn't from the district, but they had land and a store in Montego Bay where she used to work, before Trevor won her heart. Hers was the first complete brick house built in the village.... Rumor also had it she bought her furniture in Kingston.... And although Peggy rarely went out, she was always dressed, right arm covered in gold bracelets, left in silver, and her earlobes hanging low under the weight of twenty-two carat gold hoops. (59)

These women are indeed outsiders, undesired by their husbands and by their community, not because of their physical attributes or lack thereof, but because of their ugly ways. We discover that it is not Marva's hair or her size that is responsible for her unhappiness, but her dissatisfaction with the rural pace and lifestyle: "Truth was, it was Kristoff Village that vexed Marva. She wanted to live in Montego Bay and go to movie shows every Friday evening. But Ainsworth was a man of simple desires" (60). As a college-educated Jamaican with a good job, Ainsworth can clearly afford to live in the city. But he chooses to reject the expense, "the corruption," and "the pace" of city living for the simplicity of village life. Ainsworth is deeply connected to the land of his ancestors and cannot see any value in moving to the city. Marva has no such connection to the land, and sees nothing of value in the traditions of Kristoff Village. But Marva is a housewife and clearly dependent on her husband. She cannot follow her heart's desire to relocate to the city, much as she dislikes country living. Although she does not present Marva as a very sympathetic character, by foregrounding Ainsworth as the decision-maker, Adisa offers an implicit critique of the traditional gender roles that force Marva to live in a place that is not of her choosing.

Yet, it is clear that Adisa's primary objective is not to critique the unfairness of Marva's situation, but rather to highlight her outsider status. Of the three women, Marva is the only one who is actually from the village. Peggy is from Montego Bay, and Grace is from Savana-la-mar. Yet Marva seems aligned with the others in their disdain for Kristoff Village and its inhabitants. The three women are characterized as shallow, petty, gossip hounds who leave their dinners on the stove to burn while they congregate at each other's houses to chew on the affairs of others. In choosing to remain "outsiders" rather than trying to fit in as Angel does, these three set themselves up in antagonism against the rest of the villagers. It is not simply their material possessions that set them apart: Peggy is described as being next in wealth to the schoolteacher, the minister, and Mr. and Mrs. Cotton. However, Peggy's wealth does not translate into personal satisfaction and generosity of spirit. She remains self-centered, contentious, and evil. When Monica arrives in the village, Peggy cannot help but compare her body to Monica's youthful-looking one. When she finds herself wanting, she launches into a harsh verbal condemnation of a woman who has done her no harm:

> Peggy was deeply disturbed. She had two boys, and had been thinking about a third child lately. Monica didn't have any children. Her body hadn't gone through any wear and tear. She was barren. All she did was fuck men, other women's men. Bitch. Whore. Curse her womb and her pussy. (63)

Peggy's vitriolic outburst serves several narratological purposes. It highlights serious thematic issues such as the alignment of aggressive materialism and lack of respect for the land with spiritual and emotional death, and foreshadows the breakdown of communal support—a crucial component of village life—that is underscored by Monica's return. It also foreshadows the evil that lies in wait for Monica, whose full possession and manipulation of her sexual powers pose a threat to women who have exchanged personal power for personal possessions.

Peggy's outburst further underscores the relationship between modernization and spiritual emptiness, notions of progress, and gratuitous materialism. For it is not only Monica's sexuality that represents a threat to these women, but her possession of the physical trappings of the modern, worldly woman. Her bright red nail polish, tight polka-dot dress, pressed and styled hair, and high-heeled shoes are representations of the world these women wish to inhabit but cannot. Having lived in the city for decades, Monica has presumably seen and done it all, while these women's marriages confine them to a life that offers little in the way of the kind of progress they deem important. In this way, Adisa's text offers up a critique of the structures of marriage that keep these women confined in lives they do not choose. Their dissatisfaction with their marriages and with the ways of the folk becomes channeled into near-murderous impulses that further entrench the rift between their modern values and the traditional values of the Kristoff Villagers. For unlike these women, Monica has chosen to reject the modern values of city living for the simple routine of ordinary village life. She has indeed seen and done it all, and her return to the village is a paradigmatic return to tradition, a rejection of the glamour and sophistication of Montego Bay, and of the emptiness of her former life as a well-kept prostitute.

Because the three outsiders are not represented sympathetically, Adisa's critique of traditional marriage becomes subsumed under her critique of modernity. Adisa's unflattering depiction of the three women sets the reader up for the ugliness of the act they will commit against Monica, and indeed against all women and against the community. In this sense, the women are emblematic of the dangers of Western notions of progress and their attendant evils if left unchecked. Their difference from village newcomers and returnees such as Monica and Angel, and their difference from the insiders such as Arnella, Beryl, and Mrs. Cotton, underscore the singularity of their outsider status. Not only will they never fit in, their difference is indeed paradigmatic of the (potentially) totalizing shift from traditional village values to the values of modernity—a shift that is deadly enough to rupture this community from the inside out.

Transgressive Sexuality: The Dialectics of Difference

Monica and Angel jockey for the position of outsider-insider. However, it is Monica and not Angel who lends the narrative its intransigence and forces the villagers to deal with the dialectics of difference. Angel's transformation from alienated foreigner to beloved village daughter is almost seamless. Angel is already constituted as an alienated individual who does not have to surrender much (not much that she likes anyway) to assimilate into Kristoff Village. Therefore, she does not afford readers a fair opportunity to observe the true dialectics of a privileged American mulatta woman married to a working-class Jamaican man in a traditional space such as Kristoff Village.

In "Resisting the Heat," Doris Sommer writes about books that resist easy interpretations:

> The strategically demure posture allows us to imagine, I want to speculate, a politics of coalition among differently constituted positionalities, rather than the identity or interchangeability of subjects as the basis for equality. And a political vision adventurous enough to imagine differences, yet modest enough to respect them, may be the most significant challenge posed by learning to read resistance. (421)

Angel's difference does not disrupt the ethos of communality, intersubjectivity, or interconnectedness that is foundational to the ontological viability of the community. As she learns to assimilate her blackness and whiteness, she also learns to integrate her two subject positions into a viable whole. But Angel does not change the village; the village changes her. Because she does not shake things up, her difference barely registers in the village. It neither disrupts nor challenges the status quo. The folk do not have to stretch themselves to accommodate Angel, and she willingly and easily gives up her metropolitan identity to become one with the folk.

Monica, on the other hand, disrupts and challenges the status quo. Although Monica is from the village, she has been away for some time. She returns a prostitute, marking her status not just as an outsider but as someone who is aligned with the shifting values of modernity. Her sharing of Desmond with his wife is different from the arrangement among Godfree, Valrie, and Arnella; she does not have the wife's permission to do so. And the open way in which Monica and Desmond carry on their affair "in the middle of the day" is also a breach of tradition. While extramarital affairs occur even in traditional Jamaican culture, the players are usually not as bold as Monica and Desmond. Although these affairs are often "open-secrets," for the sake of propriety they are carried out surreptitiously at night, giving at least the appearance of secrecy.

Monica's sexuality is indeed transgressive, and the elder Mrs. Cotton warns her that she needs to take responsibility for her actions. However, Monica's actions, while not endorsed by everyone, are not considered threatening to the way of life of the community. But the response of the three women (Peggy, Marva, and Grace) to Monica's sexual impropriety is considered egregious and threatening to the values that sustain Kristoff Village. Indeed, juxtaposed against Arnella and Valrie's consensual love triangle with Godfree, the violence directed against Monica seems especially barbarous and unconscionable.

In "Speaking in Tongues: Dialogics, Dialectics, and the Black Woman Writer's Literary Tradition," Mae Gwendolyn Henderson defines black women's writing in terms that seem applicable to the way difference is dealt with within Adisa's text:

> One discovers in these writings a kind of internal dialogue reflecting an *intersubjective* engagement with the intersubjective aspects of self, a dialectic neither repressing difference nor, for that matter, privileging identity, but rather expressing engagement with the social aspects of self ("the other(s) in ourselves"). It is this subjective plurality (rather than the notion of cohesive or fractured subject) that, finally, allows the black woman to become an expressive site for a dialectics/dialogics of identity and difference. (137)

In Henderson's formulation, black women are able to occupy several subject positions simultaneously. The women in Adisa's novel seem to model Henderson's theory in their conception of difference and social interaction.

It is not because consensual love triangles are commonplace in Kristoff Village that the community accepts the one mentioned previously, and neither is it because the community of Kristoff Village is exceptionally open that Monica and Angel are able to occupy outsider/insider status immediately. It is because the village women identify with each other as women, accepting rather than condemning difference and making room to accommodate new behavior until it becomes absorbed into the normative value system of the group. The act of violence perpetrated by the three women named above is a violent departure from this cultural model of intersubjective social relations between women. The threesome's ability to participate in such an act demonstrates a complete and unnatural lack of identification with Monica as a woman. Their objectification of her as the "other" is so totalizing that they cannot locate themselves in her.

It is against this breakdown of identification that Adisa addresses her attack on modernism's disruption of traditional systems of meanings and social relations. The "me" syndrome replaces the concept of "I and I"[25] which recognizes the interdependent relationship between the individual and the collective. This disruption of identification becomes symptomatic of these women's refusal to acknowledge community, and their dedication to establishing ownership, not just over property but over husbands and children. The villager's acceptance of the triangular relationship between Arnella, Valrie, and Godfree suggests not just an acceptance of unconventional sexual expression, but also recognition that human beings voluntarily share themselves with each other sexually and cannot belong to each other as sexual property.

The character Monica is a revision of Janie in Hurston's *Their Eyes Were Watching God* and Sula in Toni Morrison's novel *Sula*.[26] Monica's dramatic return to the village has resounding echoes of both Janie's return to Eatonville and Sula's return to Medallion. As discussed in chapter 1, critic Daphne Lamothe associates Janie with the Haitian loa Erzulie and points out Erzulie's love for the color blue. In Adisa's text, Monica is attracted to Desmond, who wears the color blue. In a situation similar to that of Janie and Sula, all eyes are on Monica, and the women of the community are envious of her blue polka dot dress and bearing. As in Eatonville, the gossips of Kristoff Village perform a running commentary as Monica emerges from the bus and weaves her way through the village to her home. But unlike Janie,

Monica is not spiritually grounded upon her return. Her sexual expression is irresponsible and inconsiderate. Instead of Janie's maturity, Monica exhibits a childlike naiveté and complete disregard for the feelings of the woman whose husband she lures into her bed.

The fact that Monica chooses Desmond as her new lover over Samuel—the wealthy married man who kept her while she was in the city—represents a significant shift in her thinking vis-à-vis her sexuality. Samuel is responsible for Monica's newly remodeled home. It is also Samuel who is responsible for Monica's return to Kristoff Village in the style that makes her the envy of Peggy, Marva, and Grace. In rejecting Samuel and choosing Desmond—who offers nothing but his blue-shirted sensuality and voracious sexual appetite—Monica replaces her obsession with material things for a more spiritually rewarding sexual exchange. As a prostitute, Monica was accustomed to commodifying her sexuality in exchange for material gratification. As Desmond's lover, she uses her sexuality to tap into her deepest erotic plane.

Monica's close relationship with the elder Mrs. Cotton—the spiritual leader of the village who can "see" into things before they occur and "read" events and people—mirrors the relationship between Baby Suggs and Sethe in *Beloved*. Monica exemplifies the corruption of the erotic when it is misused in service to the sex industry; she returns to Kristoff Village in a state of spiritual and psychological imbalance. She has an overdeveloped sexual nature, but a dormant spirituality that is reawakened in her relationship to the deeply spiritual Mrs. Cotton. Monica is frequently observed visiting with the elder priestess figure, and it is clear that Mrs. Cotton's influence is meant to restore the loss of spiritual and sexual equilibrium that marks Monica's transgressive textual presence. Monica's relationship with the blue-shirted (Erzulie devotee) Desmond and the priestess Mrs. Cotton signals the beginning of Monica's recuperation of her fragmented subjectivity. However, it takes a desperate act of jealousy to coordinate the efforts of the entire community in the full restoration of healing for Monica and for all the women. As Morrison does in *Beloved*, Adisa creatively theorizes about the necessity of collective intersubjective relations for the well being of the individual and the group.

Women as Spiritual Vanguards and Sexual Subjects

Adisa's codification of the erotic as both spiritual and sexual energy takes place at several levels within the text. Through the singular and conflated identities of Yoruba divinities Yemonja and Oshun, the spiritual roles of Arnella, Mrs. Cotton, and River-mumma are efficaciously deployed in service to the principles of balance and cosmic order that shape Adisa's utopic vision. Through reverence for and respectful recognition of the healing properties of elements supplied by the natural world, such as trees, rivers, and herbs; through the identification of women as healers, free sexual agents, nurturers, community builders, and spiritual leaders; and through carefully constructed images that show the interconnectedness of sensuality, sexuality, passion, nurturing, and spirituality, Adisa invites readers to critically engage with the concept of alternative spiritual modalities operating as corrective forces in a world beset by human-generated chaos.

When teaching Adisa's text to a college writing course at Berkeley, I was often told that the book was pornographic or too sexually detailed.[27] However, the same students who expressed that opinion also commented on the deeply spiritual nature of the book; they did not seem to know what to do with the comingling of elements they ascribed to separate schismatic orders. When I tried to demonstrate that these were not schisms, but related pieces of a whole, my students were baffled: "sexuality and spirituality are separate and conflicting modalities," they assured me. "And from the standpoint of Christianity, it is absolutely necessary that they remain separated." "Ah ha!" I would then respond, "but the moral order in this text—if there is one— is not Christian at all." I would then go on to explain that Adisa employs a creolized spirituality—that is not necessarily structured as a religion— inclusive of elements of Yoruba cosmology,[28] other West African sources, and her own invented mythological systems, to order the worldview of the folk in Kristoff Village. This creolized spirituality recognizes the centrality of the erotic as both spiritual and physical power and possibility.

From the very beginning of the text, Adisa introduces Arnella, a priestess-in-training, as a devotee of the female Yoruba divinity Oshun (also called Osun, Ochún, or Ochun). Oshun is the orisha of sweet waters, fertility, creativity, sensuality, and sexuality.[29] Like the orisha to whom she is devoted, Arnella is much more complex than the above categories would suggest. Although it is common for people who write about the Yoruba religion to focus on the sexual and sensual nature of Oshun, it is in the combined synthesis of all of her principal characteristics that the true essence of this orisha must be located. To understand her only as a sexual figure is to exoticize and reduce her to a very small portion of her potential, and to dismiss and ultimately miss the dynamic energy that this orisha embodies and can impart. In *The Way of the Orisha*, Philip John Neimark explains Oshun's energy as follows: "The sensuality of Osun also offers us an opportunity for transcendence, a chance to be open to the world of spiritual energy through orgasm. During orgasm we experience pure feeling, and afterwards we are better able to cope with our routine responsibilities. That, in great measure, is what the world of spiritual energy is all about—it replenishes our energy (140)."

The text opens with the pregnant Arnella surrounded by things from the natural world as well as things she has created with her own hands. Arnella is stamped with her own particular brand of sensual and creative energy to fully reflect her free-spirited personality:

> At the far end, a large window looked out at sunflowers and a mango tree with gerba growing around the roots. The tree was encircled by water-washed white stones, each of which she had lovingly hauled more than a mile from the river. The yellow curtains with frilly lace along the border that were now blowing softly in the morning breeze, she had sewn. Examining them gave her a deep satisfied feeling, as did the sight of the three wall hangings made partly from the same piece of yellow cloth. (12)

All of the Yoruba orishas are represented by a color, and in most New World religions, Oshun's color is a vibrant yellow, gold, or in some cases orange. Similarly, the sunflowers are the special flowers of this female divinity.[30] The yellow curtains and the three yellow wall hangings that Arnella has made all reflect the creative energy with which this deity is represented. Arnella also paints her favorite chair yellow on impulse. In addition, the references to water-washed white stones and the river are representative of elements that express Oshun's essence. As the deity who governs sweet waters, rivers, streams, and tributaries, all offerings made to this deity are presented to her in fresh water. Arnella's close relationship with the river is one way in which Adisa signals the presence of Oshun's energy in this character. Another is Arnella's pregnancy, an obvious symbol of her fertility, which further establishes this character as an Omo-Oshun (a child of the orisha Oshun).

Significantly, Adisa establishes Arnella as both "dress-maker" and "priestess-in-training" in the description of characters that appears before the prologue. This description of Arnella's occupations establishes the character both in relation to her spiritual work and her creativity, and not just to her relationships. Later in the text, however, we find that Arnella's relationship to her "twin" niece Valrie is central to the plot and to her identity as community-builder, priestess, artist, and sexual agent. It is through her relationship to Valrie that Arnella is able to establish an identity that allows her the freedom to do the work of a mother, lover, healer, and artist without the restrictive structures within which traditionally gendered roles entrap women, making them unable to fulfill their true potential.

Arnella and Valrie enjoy a close union in which they share every aspect of each other's lives including innermost secrets, child-care responsibilities, a common lover and father to their children, and a bond that is unparalleled by any other relationship in the text. Part of Oshun's power and energy is emitted through an irresistible sensuality and charm. She seduces those that she wants to seduce with very little effort. This aspect of Oshun's energy is often misinterpreted as purely sexual, but nothing could be further from the truth. Arnella's connection with her "sister" Valrie demonstrates a sensual and spiritual depth that is charged with erotic power. The bond between these two is deeper than friendship and closer than a family bond, yet they are separate and distinct individuals. As Godfree's grandmother Miss Dahlia observes: "They were very close, and would willingly die for each other, she was certain, but they were two very different women" (110). Although both women are involved in a sexual relationship with Godfree, their primary affection is for each other. When Godfree gives in to convention and decides to get married, he is first rejected by Arnella, who gives Valrie—the more conventional of the two—permission to marry him. Arnella helps to organize the wedding, makes all the wedding attire, and then tries to convince her father-figure, Milford, to pay for a hotel room for all three of them. When the outraged Milford disagrees with this arrangement, Arnella deceives him into paying for the room just for the married couple. Then she secretly "met them in town and the three spent a glorious day surrounded by each other's love" (112). As I argue elsewhere, the above quote suggests an open interpretation; the closeness between the two women indicates a wide range of intimacies that admits almost no forbidden areas of interpretation.[31] The blood ties between these two women complicate an overtly sexual reading. Nevertheless, it would not be much of a stretch to locate their relationship on what Adrienne Rich dubs "a lesbian continuum," in her article "Compulsory Heterosexuality and Lesbian Existence." Incest taboos notwithstanding, Adisa deliberately constructs a deep and provocative relationship between these two women that clearly authenticates the intersubjectivity being proposed as the antidote to female competition and to the breakdown of communal values.

As one explores the text in more depth, it becomes clear that Arnella's role as a priestess-figure is not just to transform traditional notions of sexuality and female relationships, but also to broaden the definition of community and counter attempts to restrict notions of family to Western and patriarchal models. In "Reputation and Respectability Reconsidered: A New Perspective on Afro-Caribbean Peasant Women," Jean Besson does an ethnographical study of one peasant community in the village of Martha Brae in Trelawny, Jamaica:

> Household structures in Martha Brae therefore manifest features common to Afro-Caribbean households: varying conjugal statuses, a range of household forms, foster children, "outside" children and a high incidence of half-sibling ship and so-called illegitimacy. This household structure has traditionally been regarded as evidence of a "disorganized" family system and has received much anthropological attention explaining it as a deviation from Eurocentric norms (cf. Besson 1974 (I): 36–107; Mintz 1975: 484). These explanations do not however, elucidate family structure in Martha Brae, where domestic groups and conjugal relations are generated, dissolved and integrated by an ordered family system rooted in Afro-Caribbean culture building. This family system comprises three interrelated themes: a dynamic conjugal complex, bilateral kinship networks and cognatic family lines. Each is a continuance of proto-peasant cultural resistance. (21)

Traditional social systems, including family structures, are threatened by the Eurocentric value system that invariably attends notions of modernism and progress in developing nations. After years of living among the inhabitants of Kristoff Village, Milford, who hails from the city of Montego Bay, still finds it difficult to become one of them. He cannot get used to their ways (such as barging into the bathroom to carry on a conversation when he is seated on the toilet), especially their insistence on constructing family relations in ways that defy everything he was taught in the city. When he discovers—after years of raising Arnella like his own child and the twin sister to his daughter Valrie—that she is really the blood daughter of Velma (the mother of his wife, Olive) he finally puts his foot down and demands that Arnella return to her birth mother. However, by switching places, Valrie and Arnella thwart his every move to recover his "respectable" nuclear family unit:

> "you finish you dinner daddy?" came Arnella's voice, startling him. He was mad, but he couldn't help but smile. Every evening, if he came

home after they ate, Arnella and Valrie would be waiting for him. When he sat down to eat, they sat with him. . . . They said his dinner was always sweeter. Now here was this daughter, who was not really his daughter, while his real daughter was not in his house where she should be, begging for food, like she was still a little girl. Long-legged, with breasts and hips. His hand went to his balding head, and he wiped at invisible sweat. He looked at the ceiling, then at his feet, then at Arnella.
"Don't ah tell you ah not yuh Daddy?"
"Yes, Daddy."
"Den mek you keep calling me Daddy, mek?"
She smiled at him. What was he to do? (73–74)

Although Arnella's Oshun-like powers of seduction are clearly being evoked here, her intention is not to induce sexual intimacy, but to seduce Milford into her way of seeing family and into the worldview of the "insiders" of Kristoff Village. Clearly, part of Arnella's purpose is to continue the tradition of female cultural resistance that began in slave societies, and which has allowed peasant communities to survive and transcend various ideological attempts to discredit and erase them.[32]

Such resistance is located in Arnella's fully actualized erotic power, which is accessed via the aegis of the goddess Oshun and enacted in the water ritual between Arnella and Godfree after the birth of their child, Baby-Girl. The central motif that ties Oshun's elements together is the motif of constantly flowing energy, which enacts a symbiosis between the spiritual and the sexual aspects of Oshun's eroticism. The water in a river flows in search of the ocean. The flow of blood and milk in a woman's body makes her fertile and able to sustain and nurture her offspring. Semen from a man's body flows into a woman to make new life. These three aspects of the "flow" motif are all present in the following scene where Arnella and Godfree make love on the banks of the river:

Arnella decided it was time to take Baby-Girl to the river. . . . Arnella looked around for a place to sit and nurse her. As she nursed her daughter, cooing to her, she became lost in the singular beauty of the place, closing her eyes to imprint the moment in her mind, she drifted. Then she felt the wood on her breast . . . the wood pulsed, pressing slightly on her full breast, and the milk dripped down to her waist. . . . She felt Baby-Girl pull free from her breast, asleep. She could hear the river like a flute tune, and she wanted to suck on the wood. . . . Finally their lips met and she sucked greedily, before his tongue found her tongue and her fingers joined his, sliding up and down, up and down, in and out, in and out. . . . Then she stepped into the warm, milky river. (189–91)

All of Oshun's energy flows freely in the above passage. Arnella's capacity to nurture and sustain the life of her child arouses her sensual nature; the musical rhythm of the river combined with the familiar and provocative sensation of "wood" pressing on her breast evokes her passion,[33] which in turn elicits a sexual expression. The flow of the bodily liquids—semen and breast milk—mimics the flow of the river; and the flow of the river is described as warm and milky like the bodily fluids that sustain the child and nurture the erotic connection between Godfree and Arnella. The repetition of the words "up and down" and "in and out" simulates the act of sexual intercourse that produces the life-giving semen that brought Baby-Girl into the circle.

Arnella's decision to introduce Baby-Girl to the river is a spiritual act meant to cement the child's earthly and spiritual connections through the life-sustaining force of Oshun's energy. After they make love, Godfree and Arnella dip the baby in the water in a ritualistic action that evokes a baptism, a symbolic affirmation of Baby-Girl's interconnectedness with God, her extended family, her ancestors, and her community. Significantly, this ritual act binds Baby-Girl to the community of women on several levels. In rural communities in Jamaica, the river is where one goes for spiritual healing and baptisms.[34] However, for women (and children) the river is often also a site of strenuous physical labor. In the dry season, it is the place that supplies water to traditional communities (some of which do not yet benefit from indoor plumbing) for washing, cooking, and cleaning. For the most part, women and children are responsible for hauling the water—sometimes over great distances—to fill the empty water drums. Traditionally, it is the women who travel to the river to hand-wash the clothing, towels, and bedspreads for the entire household on wash day. The river, then, is also associated with the harshness of women's domestic lives in premodern societies.

But the river can be transformed into a site of therapeutic recreation on these occasions, as well as a place for the exchanging of news, gossip, and storytelling. While they wait for the clothing (which would be too heavy to carry home wet) to dry after being placed strategically on surrounding rock surfaces and bushes, the women and children cook, eat, talk, laugh, enjoy a swim, and engage in freshwater fishing together (coaxing crawfish from beneath the river rocks).³⁵ Thus the harshness of physical labor is transcended through the sense of community, playfulness, and female bonding that the village women introduce to these domestic events on the banks of the river.³⁶

The river, then, has a specific significance in women's culture in traditional peasant communities of the Caribbean where domestic labor is still divided along gender lines. Connected as it is to sexuality, spirituality, healing, sustenance, life-giving water, and cleansing of the body and garments, the river serves multiple roles in the daily lives of these communities.

Perhaps the centrality of the river in rural Jamaican culture is responsible for the survival (albeit in syncretized form) of one West African female deity in Jamaican mythology. In her novel, Adisa evokes the presence of "River-mumma" (also called Mama Water) by titling one vignette after this figure. In Jamaican peasant folklore, River-mumma is a mermaid represented with a comb and mirror (symbolizing Oshun) and dressed in Yemaya's colors of blue and white.³⁷ She is said to bring good luck in the form of buried treasure to the man or woman who locates her comb, which she loses from time to time.³⁸ According to Lucie Pradel in "African Sacredness and Caribbean Cultural Forms,"

> the realm of water, Yemaya domain, offers water related creatures in the form of the fairymaid and the mermaid. River Muma (Tanna), Manna Dlo or Fairmaid, all embody a generous creature, giving and possessing fertility and wealth. She appears during the night or at dawn from her sea or river habitat, in close proximity to a gold mine. Some think of her as the guardian of such a treasure and point out that the comb she uses to smooth out her long hair was cast from the precious metal. (140)

In *It Begins with Tears*, River-mumma is represented as both the spirit of the river as well as the physical river itself, doubling as healing/cleansing waters and a woman/elder/leader of great spiritual power. It is to River-mumma that Mr. Cotton advises the women to take Grace to heal her from insanity. After "peppering" Monica and almost killing her own daughter with her bare hands, Grace descended into madness:

> The river was a woman and when the village women took Grace to wash off her madness the river rose up, wetting the banks that had long

been dry in this drought season, rumbling and roaring and frothing at the one moaning, "Peppa! Peppa! Peppa!". The older women, with a wisdom born of experience, feared neither Grace nor the river. They knew they had to help cool the wickedness giddy-upping in Grace's head, for they had time and time again put aside their own desires for revenge and gone on with living, gone on with forgiving. (160–61)

River-mumma's identification with Monica and the women who represent traditional values is almost total, and she has no desire to help Grace. But in the face of the determination of the elder women not to redress one wrong with another, River-mumma perfectly models the intersubjectivity on which the survival of the community is predicated: "The river frothed at Grace, and it cooled the fire storming in her head"(161). Grace is not absolved of blame, but as is her duty and purpose, the river heals even those that come to her burdened with the guilt of their wrongdoing.

In yet another scene that combines the sexual with the spiritual nature of the river's erotic power, the women gather at the river to ritually heal the fabric of the community that was almost destroyed by Monica's attackers. Significantly, it is Arnella (Oshun-figure) who first suggests a visit to the river to Monica while she is still smarting from her wounds. As Monica ponders Arnella's wise words, she makes a mental observation of how much Arnella sounds like the elder priestess and village "Mother," Mrs. Cotton (Yemonja figure) (201). The ritual healing that takes place on the riverbank mimics the ritual "laying on of hands" done in the black churches of Jamaica. Although the attack on Monica is the ostensible occasion for the ritual meeting, River-mumma will facilitate a healing of the community of women in Kristoff Village for their past and present unresolved pain:[39]

> Monica, who now stood naked, went and helped Althea off with her dress, then went and walked her over to Miss Cotton, who immediately began to anoint her body. The women all cupped their hands, taking a little of the lotion that Miss Cotton poured into their palms, rubbing it over each other's bodies. Then in single file they waded into the river.
> The water was warm and milky. The air was still, and the rays of the sun cast golden sheaths on the river. Arnella cupped a handful of water to her mouth and drank. Each woman found her own space and splashed around. Angel and Althea, the youngest and both shy, if for different reasons, stayed close together. After a while Arnella told the

women to hush. "Each of oonuh must search out oonuh own place in de river. Let her, de river, talk to you so she can soothe oonuh worries." (213–14)

As High Priestess, it is Mrs. Cotton—in conjunction with River-mumma—who does the actual laying on of hands (214–15). As priestess-in-training, this is Arnella's final initiation into her role as spiritual leader. It is Arnella who will inherit the responsibility of female affirmation, protection, and healing in this community after Mrs. Cotton's death. There is no separation of the spiritual and the sexual in this ritual healing ceremony. Vivid descriptions of "the warm water that was like expert hands massaging their bodies" and "the sweet breast milk that was the river water," coupled with scenes of Mrs. Cotton anointing the women's bodies, and the ritual bathing of Monica meant to cleanse her finally from the damage done by the pepper, fully foreground the complexly erotic nature of true female bonding:

> Velma and Dahlia stepped forward. They laid their hand on Monica's left shoulder. With a forceful, downward sweep, they pulled off the burden Monica had been hauling around; they rinsed their hands before doing the same thing to Monica's right shoulder. They ended with a sound so powerful it thrusts their chests forward. Then Dahlia stepped round and positioned herself behind Monica. She pressed her thumbs to the base of Monica's waist, just above her buttocks, and Velma cupped the flesh that cushioned Monica's stomach to her pelvic bone. Together they massaged and pressed. Monica's moans were a circle that enclosed the women, forcing each of them to release their internal frustrations and bottled anger. Monica began to throw up bile and the stench caused the other women to hold their breaths and widen the circle. (216)

The intimate spiritual and sexual experience described in the scene above is all the more powerful because of its communal nature. The ritual corresponds with another healing ritual in the text in which Desmond uses his tongue to massage the sting of the pepper on Monica's swollen clitoris and vulva, his salty tears mingling with the burning anguish emanating from the intimate depths of her body. The language of the text clearly underscores the fact that, for Desmond, this is a spiritual act meant to assist in Monica's healing process. By licking the pepper from her body, Desmond helps to absorb, and thus share, in the pain that is a result of their transgressive lovemaking. Similarly, the healing ritual that the women enact has both spiritual and sexual overtones that foreground the power and possibility of the erotic.

In "Uses of the Erotic: The Erotic as Power," Audre Lorde asserts that it is when we are in touch with the power of the erotic that we do our best work. Lorde makes it clear that the erotic is an enabling source of personal and political power. By aligning the purpose of the erotic with work, as well as pleasure, Lorde is able to do two things: to shift the definition of the erotic away from the purely sexual and sensual, and to make it clear that we dismiss the erotic only at the expense of our own fulfillment, productivity, and spiritual and emotional well-being. Lorde implies that our "work" is our divine purpose for being on this earth, not just what we do to keep life and limb together. To truly fulfill their destinies, Lorde suggests, women must recognize and nurture the power of the erotic within themselves. It is through the recognition of this power and the evoking of its presence that the women of Kristoff Village are able to heal each other and protect the community from the threat of annihilation and anarchy sneaking into their midst under the disguise of progress and modernism.

The erotic, then, becomes an enabling source of female resistance against the spiritual and physical death that inevitably accompanies absolute notions of ownership and possessiveness that lead to the kind of excessive jealousy and murderous rage that precipitate heinous acts of violence such as the one visited upon Monica. In tapping into the power of the erotic, the women of Kristoff Village are able to restore balance, equilibrium, and good old-fashioned common sense to the social relations of their group. In other words, the women may be justified in being angry at Monica for abandoning the code of sisterhood by sleeping with Desmond without regard for his wife's feelings, but they may not retaliate by attempting to destroy her. To do so is to hurt all women and to damage the social relations and life-affirming intersubjectivity on which the survival of the community is predicated. In "Reflections on the Black Woman's Role in the Community of Slaves," Angela Davis warns against the divisive reification of the black slave woman as a matriarchal figure. Davis argues that to do so is to negate the historical realities of a system that denied all agency to black people of either sex. Nevertheless, she insists, it was the very harshness of her circumstances that propelled the black woman to employ strategies of resistance to counter the self-erasing effects of slavery:

> Even the broadest construction of the matriarch concept would not render it applicable to the black slave woman. But it should not be inferred that she therefore played no significant role in the community of slaves. Her indispensable efforts to ensure the survival of her people can hardly be contested. Even if she had done no more, her deeds

would still be laudable. But her concern and struggles for physical survival, while clearly important, did not constitute her most outstanding contributions. It will be submitted that by virtue of the brutal force of circumstances, the black woman was assigned the mission of promoting the consciousness and practice of resistance. (202)

Clearly, the impetus toward resistance and survival, honed in the consciousness of the black woman under slavery, has survived in black communities throughout the diaspora. This consciousness undergirds the epistemic framework of Adisa's novel, and propels the women of Kristoff Village into action when one of their own is physically and sexually violated and when the values that hold the community together are threatened.

Adisa's novel theorizes about cultural resistance in precisely the ways Barbara Christian suggests in "The Race for Theory." Christian makes the following claim: "And I am inclined to say that our theorizing (and I intentionally use the verb rather than the noun) is often in narrative forms, in the stories we create, in riddles and proverbs, in the play with language, since dynamic rather than fixed ideas seem more to our liking" (336). In presenting us with a narrative set in rural Jamaica where time seems to have stopped while the march toward modernity continues on in the rest of the world, Adisa presents her own theories about the ways in which the intervention of modernity might effect negative changes in societies still steeped in tradition. For Adisa, as for Angela Davis, black women are always central to any act of resistance that the black community might contrive to deal with systematic attempts to destroy it throughout history. While Adisa is neither antitechnology nor antiprogress, her novel forces us to deal with certain dire realities that go hand-in-hand with modernity. She reminds us that with the erosion of traditional values that serve specific and necessary functions in these societies, we are left open to certain dangers that are prominent features of modern society, including the proliferation of gratuitous violence and other profligate features of modernity.

As mentioned above, River-mumma is a syncretic figure derived from aspects of West African deities, mythical European water creatures (mermaids), and aligned with other aquatic divinities from diverse traditions. As Lucie Pradel explains: "River Muma is attributed to the double role of sovereign of the waters and precious lodes that are below the waters. The aquatic divinities rival each other with generosity, willingly offering their wealth. Their munificence is equaled only by the love that some of them devote to humans" (*African Beliefs in the New World* 148). In Adisa's text,

River-mumma consolidates female empowerment and creative agency. Through her, Adisa demonstrates that resistance to modernity is compatible with—perhaps even dependent upon—a creolized spirituality. For although the literature aligns "the folk" with Africa, Caribbean folk are, by virtue of history, already interpellated by (and defined against) European modernism. It is through the process of creolization—that both incorporates and resists Eurocentric overdeterminism—that Caribbean peoples are authorized to assert an autonomous identity. In *Writing in Limbo*, Simon Gikandi addresses the process and function of creolization:

> In other words, the slaves' journey from Old World to the New World would open up the African imagination to other temporal and spatial possibilities, while at the same time demanding a new idiom and form. The "modernization" of African cultures in the Caribbean (what has come to be known as creolization) is the process by which exiled Africans set out to develop modernist ways of seeing, knowing and representing their dislocated culture—aware, no doubt, of its aboriginal sources, but motivated by the need to account for new social and historical forms. (14)

The processes through which Adisa's narrative resolves the tensions between modernity (in its most negative, most antithetical manifestations) and tradition echoes Gikandi's definition of a Caribbean modernism that functions in opposition to the epistemic violence of Eurocentric modernism. The modernist anxieties within *It Begins with Tears* also mirror the contradictions inherent to Caribbean subjectivities, which, while never resolved, are dramatized, exposed, and contested within creolized formations. Moreover, in Adisa's work, issues of dominance, deformation, resistance, and creative transformation are worked out through gynocentric social formations that privilege the erotic as a powerful source of resistance and agency.

In Adisa's text, Caribbean women are at once agents of Eurocentric modernity's nihilism and formidable forces of spiritual and cultural resistance against its destructive potentiality. Through the aegis of Oshun and Yemaya's nurturing and healing energies, the syncretized River-mumma represents a space of synergistic transfiguration. River-mumma, the elder priestess Mrs. Cotton, and her trainee Arnella share a consubstantiating relationship that is the source of female empowerment and sexual and spiritual agency. Together with the willing participation of the other women involved in the healing ritual, these three are vested with the power to enact social transformation. Separately, they are powerful, but together they present a formidable challenge to the nihilistic encroachments of modernity as emblematized through the actions of Peggy, Marva, and Grace.

It is not that the men are not visible in the text, but it becomes clear from the very outset of the novel that the plot will center on a community of women and that women will be the active agents and occupy central and formative subject positions in the text. In this way, Adisa's novel mimics the gender division that remains a salient feature of Jamaican peasant society. For as Mrs. Cotton leads the women to the river to enact the healing and resistance ceremony, Mr. Cotton takes the men of Kristoff Village into the bush in a move meant to parallel the women's ceremony. However, Mr. Cotton's ritual does not effect any lasting transformation as the men refuse to open up. It is also Mr. Cotton who makes the pronouncement "change is always nasty," but it is the women's enactment of spiritual resistance against the "nasty" aspects of change that propels acts of transformation and healing within the text.

Despite Angela Davis's warnings against the divisiveness that this kind of polarization of the sexes engenders in the black community, it would be very easy to characterize Adisa's strong, fully developed female characters as matriarchs and the society they inhabit as matriarchal. However, one would be advised to take caution from the African aphrorism "when the lion writes the story, it is never the hunter who comes out as the hero." While it is true that women dominate in Adisa's fictionalized village, the reality of actual village life would most likely demonstrate a division in which both sexes make separate—if not always equal—contributions to the society. In some areas (such as politics), men dominate with or without the sanction and consent of the women. In other spheres, both domestic (the home) and public (the market place), women have total control and wield inexorable power. However, in downplaying the role of the men, Adisa focuses the readers' attention on the autonomy and agency that these women possess.

Adisa's representation of gender separation and division— though it augments and catalyzes female empowerment—also undercuts the narrative's efforts to achieve intersubjectivity and dissolve binaries. Because Adisa cannot resolve this duality into a univocal narrative coherence, she stages it for the reader through textual strategies which oscillate between representing and subverting reciprocal gender ideation. In a conversation with Adisa, she reveals that she considers Kristoff Village a central character and Eternal Valley its alter ego. This formulation works well here, as Adisa seems to represent the realism of gender separation in Kristoff Village while demonstrating She-Devil's resistance to gender division and male dominance in Eternal Valley. One notable exception (in which the narrative appears to unify these two competing imperatives), is in the scene where Desmond joins the women in the healing ritual by licking the pepper from Monica's body.

In addition to contesting and problematizing gender ideation, *It Begins with Tears* privileges the nonrational, or "feelings," over the rational. The "power of the erotic" is the power of women's ways of knowing, being, and doing. In theorizing about the potential for resistance, transcendence, and transformation in women's erotic power, Adisa demonstrates the untapped sources of possibility and empowerment that are available to women who learn to value the unique energy that resides in the female psyche.

5

Power, Eros, and Genocide

Capitalism and Black Female Subjectivity in *The Farming of Bones*

Rituals of Subjection: Re-membering Amabelle

> If the storyteller is, as Edouard Glissant maintains, "the handyman, the djobbeur of the collective soul" (Poetics 69), the transformative production of meaning through narrative must be essential in societies where the soul has been withered by the dead hand of totalitarianism.
>
> Richard F. Patterson, "Resurrecting Rafael: Fictional Incarnations of a Dominican Dictator"

Like the three preceding chapters, this final one examines the healing potential of the erotic. Danticat's *Farming of Bones* provides a useful framework from which to examine the recuperation of black female subjectivity after a historical trauma that took place in 1937, the same year Hurston published *Their Eyes Were Watching God*. In *Farming of Bones*, the female protagonist is a Haitian immigrant named Amabelle Désir. Amabelle is forced to flee Alegría after Dictator Trujillo orders the massacre of Haitian immigrants living in the Dominican Republic. Amabelle is an orphan and the Dominican family she lives with in Alegría is the only family she has known since her parents drowned when she was eight years old. Amabelle's suffering can be usefully compared to Sethe's, and like Sethe she bears the internal and external scars of her trauma. But the comparison with Sethe is relatively easy as both women are traumatized under totalitarian regimes that systematically impose state-sanctioned violence upon their bodies and total abjection of their personhood.[1] But what, if any, are the continuities and discontinuities between Amabelle and Janie? Amabelle and Monica? Does

Amabelle's survival and recuperation hinge on the same factors as the three fictional black women of Morrison's, Hurston's, and Adisa's work?

The purpose of this chapter is to demonstrate that there are clear linkages between these fictional black women and that the consubstantiating forces of spiritual and sexual energy that catalyze the subjectivities of the others also revive Amabelle's. It is fitting that this study begins tracing the emergence of the "new black woman" in literature with Hurston's Janie and ends with Danticat's Amabelle. Hurston's ties with Haiti have been long established, and as numerous critics have maintained, Hurston's tour de force novel was written in Haiti in less than two months. Haiti seems to have provided a fertile breeding ground for Hurston's formidable creativity and literary talent. Lamothe's interrogation of Janie as an Erzulie-figure further establishes the spiritual linkages between Janie and Haitian womanhood. Erzulie, the patron loa of abused, victimized, and lesbian women in Haiti, is the spiritual and ancestral progenitor of both Janie and Amabelle and the aegis through which both characters will effect powerful transformative agency to emerge as triumphant survivors.[2]

Edwidge Danticat's *Farming of Bones* uses a fictional framework to narrate the story of the massacre of roughly thirty thousand Haitians in the Dominican Republic in 1937. Critic Ifeona Fulani suggests that Caribbean authors (such as Edwidge Danticat) are political activists as well as authors, addressing the historical and contemporary issues in their nation-states through their creative work:

> A common feature of the work of this diverse group of Caribbean writers is a profound emotional and intellectual connection to their ancestral islands. Critics note the propensity of Caribbean writers in exile to repeatedly revisit their island of origins via their work. Many Caribbean writers ... seem impelled to address the histories and legacies of colonialism, of capitalism and racism out of a sense of responsibility to their native community and culture. (Fulani 67)

Ifeona Fulani clearly establishes the continuity between the literary output of Caribbean writers and the historical exigencies of the region. In that same vein, Edwidge Danticat's *Farming of Bones* imaginatively recasts the 1937 massacre of Haitian migrant workers in the Dominican Republic. Danticat's novel explores the ways in which culture, ethnicity, and religion were used to damn Haitians to second-class citizenship, and later to deem them annihilable.

The critic Richard Patterson astutely observes in the epigraph above that it is indeed the storytellers (the poets, writers, and artists) who facilitate healing of the collective soul. Danticat's narration of this historical trauma transforms the events of the massacre and its impact upon the Haitian people by breaking the silence surrounding this traumatic event and creating the conditions for collective healing and transformation for the Haitian people.[3] The massacre was an attempt to ethnically cleanse the Dominican Republic of Haitians and Haitian influence, and was ordered by Dominican dictator General Rafael Trujillo, himself the son of a Haitian mother. Claiming that Haitian workers and immigrants were quickly beginning to outnumber Dominicans, some historians argue that Trujillo's acts were not racially motivated, but were driven by concerns over Dominican land and resources that were being used up by Haitian immigrants. Still others recognize the twin issues of economic and racial anxiety as driving forces behind Trujillo's bloody campaign:

> Turmoil in Europe resonated with the Dominican Republic's growing economic difficulties and with Trujillo's own obsession with race and status. By 1937 the Dominican Republic was practically broke, its sugar exports fetching only a penny a pound, one twentieth of the price during the boom a decade earlier. In late September of that year, weeks before the massacre, the Dominican president publicly accepted a gift of Hitler's *Mein Kampf,* whose racial theories he clearly embraced. (Wucker, "The River Massacre" 2)

Danticat makes it clear in *Farming of Bones* that although land and resources were at issue, race or racialism also played a definitive role in Trujillo's decision to exterminate the Haitians. Trujillo's regime formulated a theory of Dominican ethnic superiority over Haitians, aligning Dominican with whiteness and Haitian with blackness, thus creating a hierarchy based on skin color and a fictional myth of origin in which Dominicans were of pure Spanish ancestry, completely "untainted" by African blood.[4] Dominicans, under Trujillo, could erase their African ancestry simply by denying it: "Our motherland is Spain; theirs is darkest Africa, you understand?" (Danticat 260). Haitians, even when they were second- and third-generation residents of the Dominican Republic, could neither abdicate Haitianness nor claim Dominican citizenship. One of the characters in *Farming of Bones* laments the tragedy of generations of displaced people who cannot claim a homeland: "I pushed my son out of my body in this country.... My mother too pushed me out of her body here. Not me, not my son, not one of us has ever seen the other side of the border. Still they won't put our birth papers into our palms so my son can have knowledge placed into his head by a proper educator in a proper school" (69).[5]

Haitians and their descendants were systematically denied the right to Dominican citizenship and the privileges such rights would afford. A small minority of wealthy and middle- class Haitians were allowed to own land, but the majority lived in the Dominican Republic as squatters, not even earning enough to make the journey back across the border to Haiti. These Haitians worked in the sugarcane fields and mills, which were jointly owned by U.S. corporate interests and Dominican landowners. These issues, clearly delineated in Danticat's novel, highlight a nexus between capitalistic interests and the exploitation of Haitian migrant workers in the Dominican Republic in the 1930s.[6]

The Farming of Bones is set in Alegría, a small farming community in the Dominican Republic. The protagonist, Amabelle, is an orphaned Haitian servant girl who works in the household of a respectable, well-to-do Dominican family that boasts of its pure Spanish lineage. Amabelle is the childhood playmate and personal servant of Valencia, the young wife of Senor Pico, an officer in Trujillo's army. Valencia and her father, the distinguished Spanish gentleman from Valencia, Spain, find Amabelle at the Massacre River[7] the same day her mother and father drown there. Although they grow up together and share certain intimacies, their relationship as servant and mistress is firmly established from the beginning of the text. Amabelle clearly knows her place, and both she and Valencia openly acknowledge the supremacy of Valencia's place as the daughter of Señor Ignacio and wife of an officer in the Dominican national army.

The text opens with Valencia about to give birth to twins, a daughter and a son. Amabelle, whose parents were healers and midwives in Haiti, is able to offer midwifery services to Valencia without any prior training. By the time the doctor arrives, Valencia and her two babies are resting comfortably thanks to Amabelle's quick thinking and resourcefulness. Valencia's father rushes to take the news of the births to the twins' father, Pico, who is stationed quite a distance away. Anxious to get to his wife and children, Pico drives recklessly and runs a Haitian cane-field worker off the road with his jeep, killing him on the spot. Pico does not stop to find the body of the man he has slain, nor does he appear remorseful about the accident. The Haitians are, of course, very angry at the death of one of their own, and the incident triggers rumors of other Haitians being killed by Dominicans. But Amabelle refuses to believe any of the rumors, even though her lover, Sebastien, warns her that they may be true.

Amabelle represents many other Haitians who have lived most of their lives in the Dominican Republic and see their destinies as intertwined with that of the country they have adopted. Sebastien tries to convince Amabelle that she is not Dominican, and that her employers are not her family; they do not have her best interests at heart. But besides Sebastien, Valencia and her father are the closest to kin Amabelle knows, since both her parents are dead and she has no memory of relatives in Haiti. Furthermore, Amabelle has spent most of her life in the Dominican Republic. She is as much Dominican as she is Haitian and cannot fathom how that reality could change. What she remembers of Haiti comes to her in dreams and haunting memories. But her Dominican present is her waking reality and an important part of her personal history since it involves the people who have cared for her since she was orphaned, as well as Sebastien, the love of her life.[8]

Useful comparisons can be drawn between Amabelle and Sebastien and the male and female pairings in the work of Hurston, Morrison, and Adisa. In Morrison's Beloved, Sethe has Paul D, while Janie has Tea Cake in Hurston's *Their Eyes Were Watching God*. In Adisa's text, Monica has Desmond; and Angel, Rupert. All four writers seem invested in the recuperation of black heterosexual unions. This could be read both negatively and positively. They appear to promote compulsive heteronormativity, but they also revise a tradition of negative representations of black heterosexuality and inscribe a corrective to the dearth of images of black men and women in sustainable relationships in literature and popular culture.

Furthermore, the presence of intense female bonds in all three works nicely complicates the relational fields of the narratives. After the massacre, Amabelle returns to Haiti and moves in with Yves and his mother. Man Rampadou and Amabelle establish a close union that echoes the relationship between Baby Suggs and Sethe in *Beloved*, and between Monica and Mrs. Cotton in *It Begins with Tears*. Man Rampadou's relationship with Amabelle replaces the mother-daughter bond Amabelle has been missing most of her life. In Adisa's work, Arnella and Valerie are closer to each other than they are to the man they share. Arnella is also a protégé of Mrs. Cotton, the spiritual leader of Kristoff Village. Similarly, when Janie returns to Eatonville, not only does she have Tea Cake's memory, but she also has her best friend and confidante, Phoeby. In a scene that mirrors the reciprocity that inaugurates sustainable relationships, Phoeby gives Janie mulatto rice and takes or shares (listens to) Janie's story.

Like Tea Cake and Janie, Amabelle and Sebastien are more than lovers; they are soul mates, and as close as two individuals can be. It is Sebastien who helps Amabelle to heal from the deep-seated wounds left by the death of her parents. Sebastien is her lifeline, her connection to Haiti, her therapist, and her surrogate parent. Like her, he is from the northern section of Haiti, Cap Hatien, an important site of Haiti's past glory that still holds the ruins of Henri Christophe's palace and citadel. Next to her sometimes unreliable memory, Sebastien is Amabelle's only link to her history and ancestry, a collective and individual past that is complex, troubled, glorious, and quintessentially Haitian, but that she struggles to claim as her own. Theirs is a love that links personal and collective history, country, ancestry, and culture. By placing positive valuation upon her black skin, African nose, and female body, Sebastien teaches Amabelle to value herself as a black woman of African ancestry. He teaches her the necessity of transcending the past, remembering it, reinventing it when necessary, and finding a way to survive it. It is a lesson that Amabelle will carry with her long after she has lost Sebastien—a lesson that will help her to heal from the trauma of unspeakable loss.

The first and most important lesson that Amabelle learns about the relationship between her sexuality and her identity she learns from Sebastien: that she is only herself when she is naked, stripped bare of the maid's uniform that turns her into an object to be used by her master and mistress (2). Echoing the tone of Baby Suggs's sentiments to her congregation in *Beloved*, Sebastien instructs Amabelle that true self-love begins with loving her African body and identity, knowing and accepting the tortured glory of her people's history, and claiming salvation through knowledge of self and community. Their lovemaking is an act of self-revelation, self-reclamation, and self-preservation, black heterosexual loving at its best. Danticat revises the negative trope of black heterosexual relations that has dogged black fiction and popular culture, reinscribing black sexual relations as passionate, completely freeing, deeply expressive, emotive, politically conscious, and spiritually redemptive.[9] But, tragically, fleeting.

Amabelle loses Sebastien to the massacre as events come to a head quickly following the death of Valencia's baby boy. Valencia's son, the oldest and biggest twin, mysteriously dies. Named by his father after the Dominican dictator Raphael Trujillo, Rafi, as he is called for short, is very fair-skinned and has hair that falls in ringlets like his mother's. His sister, Rosalinda, is dark-skinned, and was born both with a caul covering her face and with her umbilical cord wrapped around her neck. Her mother is immediately concerned that the child is "cursed," and worries that she may one day be mistaken for one of Amabelle's people: a Haitian. However, as it turns out, it is not Rosalinda who is cursed, but Rafi, who dies when he is a few days old. As if heralding the massacre, Rafi's death is quickly followed by renewed rumors of Haitians being killed and herded to the border. Amabelle comes to realize that to save herself and Sebastien she must leave Alegría. However, she stays behind to help Valencia, who has begun to hemorrhage following Rafi's death. Amabelle's loyalties are divided, and ironically, her conflicting allegiances save her life.

Sebastien and his sister are forced to leave Amabelle behind as they are herded onto a military truck taking Haitians to the border. Amabelle follows on foot, intent on finding her beloved. She gets swept up in the horrific drama of the massacre, and is forever changed by her near-death experiences, her acts of self-preservation, the horror of watching those close to her killed in cold blood, and the sheer terror of witnessing horrific, unremitting suffering and mass murder at close range.

One of the most dramatic moments in the text occurs when Amabelle and her traveling companions are forced to swallow handfuls of parsley when a murderous throng of Dominican civilians and soldiers force the herb down the throats of the Haitians while goading them on to say "perejil," the Spanish word for parsley. Language becomes the marker of difference because the Haitians cannot pronounce the "j" or trill the "r," and so end up mispronouncing "perejil" as "pewejil" or saying "pesi," the Creole word for parsley. Amabelle miraculously survives the torture, but is maimed in mind and body by the experience. She never finds Sebastien and his sister. They are presumed dead like so many others, and survivors report seeing their corpses. Amabelle returns to Haiti accompanied by Sebastien's best friend, Yves. For the remainder of her life, Amabelle carries physical and emotional scars from the massacre. She does not find love again, and for twenty years she seems completely closed off to the possibility of it. Her life is a series of quotidian rituals that allow her to survive, but never to feel joy. The massacre becomes the only thing she claims as her own. Although the narrative does not dramatize her recovery from the loss of Sebastien or from her experiences as a victim of ethnic cleansing, the text ends on a hopeful note with Amabelle "looking for the dawn" (310).

Within the economic milieu of the novel, the loss of Amabelle and Sebastien's powerful love to capricious historical forces is as wasteful, senseless, and deeply tragic as the massacre itself, which claimed roughly thirty thousand innocent lives.[10] The love between Amabelle and Sebastien, like the history of the black republic of Haiti, reaches epic proportions in its depth, grandeur, beauty, and tragic conclusion, and in this sense, Amabelle can be read as a stand-in for Haiti. Like Amabelle, Haiti is unsure of itself as a nation state and incapable of defending its people against Trujillo's genocidal attempts. Politically and economically unstable with an infrastructure weakened by mismanagement and corruption, slavishly beholden to U.S. corporate and military interests, and thus completely ineffectual against Trujillo's unscrupulous and murderous directives, Haiti does little to hold the Dominican Republic accountable for the massacre. President Vincent of Haiti gives the following reason for his inaction: "Our neighbors have an army of at least 5,000 and they have planes and artillery. It would be madness for us to think of fighting" (Hicks 120). This statement stands in stark contrast to the confidence and courage displayed by Toussaint L'Ouverture and Jean-Jacques Dessalines, who, despite having limited military resources, were victorious against the greatest army of their time, the army of Napoleon Bonaparte.

Like the mixed blessings of Haiti's revolutionary struggle and victory, the dramatic reach of Sebastien and Amabelle's love has far-flung implications for Amabelle's future.[11] Like the massacre, the love she shared with Sebastien will color the rest of her life in drab tones by comparison. Unlike Janie, who can live on the memories of her full but short life with Tea Cake, Amabelle does not get the opportunity to build a life with Sebastien. Amabelle's memories of Sebastien are tainted by the regrets and sense of loss and aborted dreams of a life together that she carries with her into her lonely and difficult future. Yet, in comparing the drama of their love to the drama of the massacre, there are many lessons to be learned. Signs, symbols, and metaphors point to the liberating potential of self-love, self-governance, and accountability.

Voudoun: An Absent Presence

> Erzulie is there in the work by both absence and presence, I guess. She watches over all the women in my stories. She's not openly here this time, however. The goddess of this story is Metrès Dlo, the female spirit of the river, to whom Amabelle dedicates and tells the story.
>
> Edwidge Danticat, quoted in *MaComère: The Journal of Caribbean Women Writers and Scholars*

Given the widespread belief in the supernatural and infusion of spirituality into every aspect of rural life in Haiti, it is curious that Edwidge Danticat[12] makes no explicit references to the Voudoun religion in *Farming of Bones*. In her earlier works such as *Breath, Eyes Memory,* and *Krik, Krak!,* references to Voudoun abound, although Voudoun is not the main focus of either text. Thus, the absence of obvious Voudoun references in *Farming of Bones* is even more curious. Could it be that Danticat does not want mainstream American readers—accustomed to a steady Hollywood diet of misinformation and misrepresentation of the Voudoun religion—to be distracted from the serious nature of this historically based narrative? Perhaps Danticat wants readers to focus on the historical trauma and genocide of the 1937 massacre, rather than on the evidence of Haitian spirituality within the text. But despite her omission, Voudoun infiltrates the narrative, making its presence felt thematically and structurally.

In *Framing Silence*, Myriam Chancy suggests that early twentieth-century travel literature such as William Seabrook's *The Magic Island* and John H. Craige's *Black Bagdad* effectively propagated the notion that Third World spaces and their inhabitants were at once marginal and capable of "embodying" the "evils of the world" (138–39). The Voudoun religion of the Haitian peasant folk—negatively dubbed "voodoo"—with all the attendant stereotypes about the dark arts that this term has come to evoke in American popular media, is perceived as an illicit source of spiritual agency, and is associated with death, darkness, and the devil. Yet Voudoun is recognized by experts as a legitimate source of agency and transformation for the Haitian peasantry, and perhaps even a spiritual reprieve from the abjection of poverty and the oppression of political tyranny. In his ethnographic study *Voodoo in Haiti,* Metraùx explains that the devotees of this indigenous Haitian religion ask of the religion "what men have always asked of religion: remedy for ills, satisfaction for needs, and the hope of survival" (15). However, any kind of power in the hands of the presumed ignorant, the despised, or the marginalized is not admired, but feared. By refusing to announce the presence of Voudoun as part and parcel of Haitian folk philosophy in *Farming of Bones*, Danticat avoids reinscription of the stigmatic, pervasive, and inherent "evil" of voodoo that, for some, might provide a justifiable defense for the spilling of Haitian blood. Rather than announce Voudoun's presence, Danticat signals it in myriad coded ways, and my aim here is to make transparent some of these hidden codes.

The hidden presence of a Voudoun philosophy plays a subtle but significant role in *Farming of Bones*. Danticat's use of symbolism highlights a very specific cultural worldview and shows the relationship between a people's way of thinking and their acts of self-preservation and agency (Weir-Soley, "Voudoun Symbolism in *The Farming of Bones*"). The Voudoun worldview underscores many references to spiritual and physical death, historical and racialized traumas, as well as spiritual resistance, rebirth, and healing within *Farming of Bones*. By omitting any narrative mention of Voudoun, Danticat appears to foreclose its legitimacy as a redemptive spiritual force, as well as its efficacy as a tool of liberation. Indeed, one might be tempted to ask: Where are the loas for Amabelle to call upon? Where is Erzulie, protector of women? Where is Damballah? Ogou? Papa Legba? During the massacre, where is the spirit of the river, Metrès Dlo, and why does she allow her waters to be polluted with Haitian blood? The curious absence of any mention of these deities almost renders these questions extraneous to textual interpretation. Nevertheless, I argue that Danticat finds subtle ways of inscribing Voudoun into *Farming of Bones*, without allowing it to overshadow her central project of capturing the drama and pathos of the massacre of 1937.

Any cursory survey of Haitian peasant religion and folklore will affirm the legitimacy of the Voudoun religion as foundational to the worldview of the Haitian peasants. Metraùx relevantly states: "the ordinary man believes implicitly in magic" (269). Isabel Mayer—one of Trujillo's closest consorts—is said to have given, among her other reasons for hating Haitians, the following evidence of Haitian malevolence: "they know a lot about herbs and botany, and practice sorcery" (Krehn 188). In the early sections of *Farming of Bones*, before the reader has encountered rumors of the massacre, Senor Pico tells his wife, Valencia, that Isabela Mayer is planning a "lavish ball" for Trujillo near the border, and that he "had been given the task of heading a group that would ensure the Generalissimo's safety at the border" (42). Danticat does not take the trouble to fictionalize the name of Trujillo's closest consort.[13] Krehn reveals that it was Dona Isabel's complaint to Trujillo (at a dinner she held in his honor) about Haitians stealing her cattle that was the impetus for beginning the massacre: "he gave orders then and there that every Haitian in the country be butchered" (188). Into her narrative, Danticat inserts this historical figure whose hatred of Haitians was encouraged by her fear of Voudoun.

This is a very calculated move on the part of Danticat as writer and storyteller, and its purpose is both to conceal and reveal. Clearly, the Haitian knowledge of African spiritual practices (and the prevalence of Voudoun worshippers among the Haitian peasantry) figured into Trujillo's decision to purge the Dominican Republic of the scourge of Haitians, and partially accounts for why he was able to convince some Dominicans that Haitians were to be hated and feared.[14] Black magic and sorcery have a powerful hold on our imaginations in Caribbean and Western popular culture.

But, despite Danticat's refusal to foreground Voudoun as the basis for the folk philosophy that undergirds both the conscious and unconscious actions, thoughts and practices of the majority of the Haitian peasants, Voudoun, nevertheless, emerges as an "absent presence" in *Farming of Bones*.[15] Voudoun interpolates the narrative at crucial points in Amabelle's storytelling. These represent formative, life-changing moments for Amabelle, and in each of these moments, Voudoun's hidden presence asserts itself in subtle symbolic glimpses that disrupt the thread of the narrative and allow Amabelle a certain *connaissance* (spiritual power and insight) she does not normally possess.[16] The imagery, metaphors, and symbols of Voudoun are inscribed as narrative tropes that invoke memory, ancestry, culture, history, survival, and continuity and mimetically recall a worldview that is very specific to the Haitian folk.

The form of Danticat's novel also replicates this mimetic framework. Boldface type sets Amabelle's memories, dreams, nightmares, and fantasies apart from her everyday reality, which is represented in regular type. This dual register produces a mimetic rendition of the trope of spirit possession allowing Amabelle access to knowledge and insight she does not possess in everyday life, just as a devotee of Voudoun is invested with divine power and able to dispense sage advice when possessed by a god.[17] Alfred Metraùx explains the dynamics of spirit possession: "Intercourse between the visible and invisible world is easy and constant. The loa communicate with the faithful either by incarnating themselves in one of them, who then becomes his mouthpiece, or by appearing to them in dreams, or in human form" (120). Possession, then, is a double-tiered event in which both gods and men experience a transfiguration: the gods come to earth and are able to experience the joys of the flesh during spirit possession while simple peasants are made divine—if but for a short while—and able to accomplish feats that are impossible for the natural man. Early in the text, Amabelle is represented as naïve, conflicted, and disbelieving with regard to rumors about an impending massacre. She does not believe it can happen until she sees Pico and his men herding Haitians onto the truck to be taken to the border. But the penultimate section of boldface type in the novel reveals a metamorphic transfiguration of the epistemic framework that undergirds Amabelle's consciousness: "I was never naïve or blind, I knew. I knew that the death of many was coming. I knew that the streams and rivers would run with blood. I knew as well how to say 'pesi' as to say 'perejil'" (264). Here, Amabelle is represented as not just linguistically versatile but clairvoyant, possessing even more detailed knowledge and insight than Sebastien. The abrupt shift from naïve servant girl to "knowing" subject approximates the movement from powerless peasant to powerful divinity enacted and performed in rituals of possession. The repetition of "I knew" underscores Amabelle's position as possessor of knowledge, an empowered speaker and subject who made the choice to stay because she had no place or people in Haiti to go back to. Amabelle's concession affirms the displaced "vwayajè" identity of the Haitian migrant workers: wayfarers, belonging in neither the Dominican Republic nor Haiti (56).

The boldface type also reveals Amabelle's imaginative life, dreams, and memories as spiritually developed despite the absence of rituals and prayer in her daily (conscious) life. For example, in one passage Amabelle recounts a memory of when she was ill and her mother was caring for her. She remembers a dream she had in which a doll, made for her by her mother, comes to life and speaks reassuringly to her: "You will be well, again, ma belle Amabelle" (58). The doll, which seems to represent Amabelle's guardian angel, sounds as if she is "speaking from a very tall bottle" (58). In *Haiti, History and the Gods*, Joan Dayan defines how identity is constructed in Haiti: "The petit bon anj or ti bon anj (little good angel), the gwo bon anj (big good angel) and the ko-kadav (body cadaver) constitute the three parts of individual identity in Haitian thought" (67). Dayan continues, quoting from Lorimer Denis's essay "Le Cimetière," "the ti bon anj, a 'guardian' and the source of consciousness, affect and dreams, depend on the loa for protection, for keeping the little good angel steady and bound to the person" (67). Other ethnographers, such as Wade Davis, explain that the "ti bon ange" is a "component of the Voudoun soul that creates personality, character and willpower" and can be captured by a malevolent priest of Voudoun and preserved in a bottle, while the body of the individual, divested of a will, is put to use as a zombie (W. Davis, *Passage of Darkness* 8).[18] The doll Amabelle sees and plays with—whose existence her mother denies—is Amabelle's ti bon ange, coming forth in this critical moment to protect her from a death not meant for her: "It is a sickness we brought home to her from someone else," Amabelle's mother tells her father, "I suppose it might be from the young girl we treated two weeks ago, you remember" (57). Amabelle's ti bon ange is just a little girl who jumps rope and plays with oslès (goat's bones) like Amabelle. Yet her empowering words provide the clue that Amabelle will survive not only the present trauma, but a greater one to come: "I am sure you will live to be a hundred years old, having come so close to death while young" (58). When Amabelle recovers from the fever and tells her mother about the doll, her mother discourages Amabelle's belief in the Voudoun worldview and spirit world: "'there is no such thing and no such doll,' my mother says, 'The fever made you an imbecile'" (58). Thus begins the participation of Amabelle's parents in her spiritual confusion and deformation, a subject I will pursue in detail later.

Linguistic and cultural markers also signify Danticat's encoding of Voudoun on a thematic level. Significantly, the use of parsley as both a linguistic and cultural marker of difference demonstrates Trujillo's obsession with rooting out the folk identity that is linked to African culture as constituted by the Haitian presence in the Dominican Republic. Symbolically, Trujillo and his regime pushed Haitian culture down the throats of Haitians, killing them with it. The parsley (*perejil*) that is stuffed into the mouths of the victims is the agent that links language, culture, religion, and folkways of being with the trauma of the massacre. As Kelli Johnson aptly states: "parsley becomes a new symbol in the collective memory of Haitians—identity, nationalism and death" (87). Why parsley? It is the most commonly used herb, and in Haitian culture especially parsley has many uses: Haitians bathe with parsley, season their food with it, purge their insides, cleanse their bodies, and even wash their dead with it (Danticat 62). In forcing them to swallow it, and killing those unable to say "parsley" in Spanish, Haitian folk culture and death become metonymic. In addition, the Voudoun religion which uses herbs to heal, cure, assist in birth, zombify, and poison also shares a consubstantiating relationship with Haitian folk culture. A powerful component of Haitian folk religion, herbs connote complex religious and social significations. But by inverting the empowering potential of folk culture and reducing parsley to a simple linguistic marker branding Haitians for death, Danticat's novel demonstrates Trujillo's dismissal of the complexly structured, and, for some, mystical codifications that define the socioreligious and political environment of Haiti.[19]

Although Haitians are universally deemed powerless by virtue of economic disenfranchisement, political instability, and corrupt governance, they are far from spiritually impotent. The narrative suggests—if merely by analogy—that underestimating the power and resiliency of Haitian folk culture may have been Trujillo's biggest mistake. Wade Davis mentions that in Haitian Voudoun circles, a victim of human sacrifice is referred to as a "goat without horns" (W. Davis, *The Serpent and the Rainbow* 210). Not coincidentally, upon Trujillo's death, the Haitians in Danticat's novel gleefully rejoice: "*Yo tiye kabrit la! Adye,*" "They killed the goat, Adye!" (267). Regardless of who was eventually held accountable for Trujillo's physical demise, the reference to him as a "goat" suggests that complex spiritual forces precipitated his departure in retribution for taking the lives of Haitians.[20] The reference to Trujillo as a dead two-legged goat underscores a counterhegemonic discursivity of the folk that clearly articulates the following theory: political and economic disadvantages on the part of Haiti should never be construed as spiritual impotence, as the African-centered religion of the folk is still a powerful and potent symbol of agency and survival.

Trujillo was clearly aware of the African spirituality that informs Haitian culture, politics, and religion, but one must recognize how fearful and disdainful Trujillo was of anything African. In fact, I contend that it was the Africanness in Haitians that Trujillo could not abide. Rumored to have worn light makeup to camouflage his African identity, Trujillo mirrors every classic symptom of self-erasure and identity crisis that Fanon delineates in *Black Skin, White Masks*. In *Democracies and Tyrannies of the Caribbean*, William Krehm notes that Trujillo's father was a mulatto horse thief, while his mother was "an ignorant but kindly mulatto" (173). Trujillo's self-hatred may have fueled his obsession with eradicating Haitians and erasing markers of African identity in the Dominican Republic. For Trujillo, purging the Dominican Republic of Haitian folk culture and influence was tantamount to ridding the Dominican Republic (and himself) of Africanness.

But why did Trujillo make language the marker of difference, as Danticat so poignantly dramatizes in *Farming of Bones*? Because skin color alone could not be used: the Dominican population is made up of mulattos, blacks, individuals of various race mixtures, and very few people who would be considered "pure" white outside of the Dominican context. The fact that many dark-skinned Dominicans died in the 1937 massacre suggests that even when blacks were able to say "perejil" correctly, it did not matter. It was Africanness itself that Trujillo was trying to wipe out. The Creole language, unlike Spanish, signifies difference in particularly African ways. Kelli Johnson argues for the dual role of language during Trujillo's mad reign: "a means of control by the regime and a means of resistance and remembering by the people" (85). Nowhere is this more apparent in Danticat's novel than in Odette's counterhegemonic dying utterance in perfect Creole: "*pesi!*" (203). The Creole language transmits the culture, religion, and folkways that Trujillo found threatening to his principal project: creating a new cultural identity based on a fictitious European lineage for himself and the Dominican Republic that would immediately transform the nation's image from primitive (read African) to civilized (read European).

But why would Voudoun, an outsider's religion, be considered such a significant threat to Trujillo's modernizing imperatives? Richard Turits explains that forms of African spirituality had always been practiced—particularly in rural areas—by Dominicans: "And popular Dominican religion, music and idiom had always exhibited forms traceable to Africa and in common with Afro-Haitian practices" (599). Dominicans were clearly aware of the African roots in their cultural practices, even if they refused to acknowledge their blackness in racial terms.[21]

Danticat's first veiled reference to Voudoun occurs at the very beginning of *Farming of Bones* when Valencia gives birth to the twins. According to Métraux:

> twins (marassa), living or dead, are endowed with supernatural power which makes them exceptional beings. In the pantheon they hold a privileged position beside the grands mysteres. Some people would even claim that they are more powerful than the loa. They are invoked and saluted at the beginning of a ceremony immediately after Legba, in some regions, notably Leogane, they even come before him. (146)

In evoking the marassa at the very opening of *The Farming of Bones*, Danticat's text mirrors the ritual sequence of propitiation in some Voudoun circles where the marassa are recognized even before Papa Legba. Narratologically, the presence of the twins foreshadows the caprice, deceit, and horror of the impending massacre. Just as there is never any justifiable reason for the harm the marassa are capable of inflicting (sometimes involuntarily), there is no justifiable reason for the massacre.

In "Re-Membering Hispaniola," April Shemak points out that based on Papi's construction of his daughter's racial lineage, Valencia "serves as a symbolic mother of the Dominican nation whose origins and namesake lie in Spain, not Africa" (90). Shemak exposes the falsity of this construction and declares that the twins really "signify the 'true' diverse racial origins of the Dominican people" (90–91). Shemak's analysis is instructive and does indeed bolster my reading of the Dominican racial and cultural inheritance proffered above. However, not only is Papi's representation of Valencia a false construction modeled on Trujillo's erasure of African identity, but it also denies and erases the common historical origin of the two nations. While Valencia's name evokes Spain only, her body becomes metonymic with the island of Hispaniola, giving birth to twin nations, Haiti and the Dominican Republic. Rosalinda, dark-skinned and smaller, represents Haiti, while Rafael, named after Rafael Trujillo, represents the Dominican Republic and is fair-skinned with straight hair.

In Haitian folklore, twins are aware of the spiritual powers they possess and often use them to punish their parents, family members, and friends for real or perceived slights. Twins are said to hate each other, and therefore have to be watched closely to ensure that they do not hurt or kill one another. Valencia's daughter, who could one day be "mistaken for one of [Amabelle's] people," is born with a caul over her face and the umbilical cord wrapped around her neck (11). As mentioned previously, her mother immediately identifies these signs as evidence of a "curse." According to popular belief, Rafael would have been held responsible for trying to strangle Rosalinda while she was still in the womb, hence the umbilical cord wrapped around her neck. Rafael's death, then, would have been attributed to an act of revenge on the part of Rosalinda.

The almost inexplicable animosity that Trujillo bore toward Haitians replicates and mirrors the capricious and vengeful attitude that Métraux and other experts on Haitian folklore attribute to the marassa, and is reinscribed in Doctor Javier's reaction to the umbilical cord around Rosalinda's neck: "it's as if the other one tried to strangle her" (19). In fact, although Amabelle performs the duties of a midwife for Valencia, the birth of the twins heralds the political repression and annihilation for her people. This is confirmed when Valencia chooses Juana, the Dominican maid, to spend the night with her and the newborns, despite the fact that Amabelle was the one who had assisted in the birth. Amabelle muses on the inequity that inheres in Valencia's choice: "Why Juana? Why not me?" (41).

The death of Kongo's son, Joel (killed by Pico), and the fact that it comes in direct connection to the birth of the twins, is also a signifying event. The twins herald trouble, not just for Amabelle but for all the Haitians in the text. Loved, protected, and feared because of the power they possess, twins are said to share one soul, and so one without the other represents a being without a whole soul. Perhaps their image as mischievous children suggests that a person without a developed soul is not accountable for his or her actions. But, as metonymic representations of the Dominican Republic and Haiti, the fates of the twins are forever linked. Put another way, "the twins are, essentially, one, that which affects one part affects the other and whatever disease or accident may beset one twin is understood to threaten the other; and their violent separation may lead to disaster (Deren 39). Haiti and the Dominican Republic, divided by deep-seated historical conflicts over land, power, individual statehood, and racial identity cannot expect to heal fragmented diplomatic relations with the rest of the world if each cannot make amends with its neighbor, and twin.

Ethnographic studies of Voudoun are replete with references to death, and particularly death under mysterious or accidental circumstances. The mysterious disappearance of Joel's body is another textual moment in which Voudoun is evoked. Joel's father, Kongo, claims that he threw the body back into the ravine because it became too heavy for him to carry back to Haiti. There is no official wake held for Joel, and no one is allowed to view his body. Metraùx, Hurston, Davis, and other ethnographers confirm that Haitian peasants will go to great lengths to protect the corpses of their loved ones because of the fear that a "bokor" (a malevolent priest who practices Voudoun with the left hand) might steal the corpse and use it for nefarious purposes for himself or a client.[22]

Kongo's authoritative textual presence forms the nexus for Voudoun's interpolation of the narrative. Kongo is clearly an elder in the community and he is looked up to by everyone, especially Yves, Sebastien and Amabelle. In Haiti, Kongo was an artist who participated in the ritual life of the community by making masks for carnival. While Kongo's involvement in ritual does not make him a *houngan*, or Voudoun priest, it certainly links him with communal ritual practices. Kongo makes a mask of Joel's face that he gives to Amabelle to keep in remembrance of his son. He casts his mold from the corpse that no one else is allowed to see, an indication that Kongo is visiting the body he claims to have discarded in the ravine. Clearly, Kongo is not afraid to work with the dead, although he does so in secret.

In *Rara! Vodou, Power and Performance in Haiti and its Diaspora*, Elizabeth McAlister states that "the notion of using the recent dead to work operates on at least three levels in Haitian culture" (103). Actions can range from stealing the soul to creating a walking zombie from the dead. However, making a mask from Joel's corpse does not make Kongo a bokor. But his close association with rituals involving the dead, his status as a leader and an elder, and his singularly non-Creolized name (which mnemonically recalls an African identity) clearly align Kongo with Voudoun religious leaders who are themselves repositories of African epistemes.

Similarly, when Sebastien and Amabelle make plans to leave Alegría, Kongo uses cornmeal to draw a "V" on the floor, signaling two different paths: the one they will take to get back to Haiti over the mountains, and the one he will take by staying. He tells them that it is a ritual of protection for their journey that he learned from his grandfather. "He looked up and winked at us. Like a St. Christophe" he said (146). In *Tell My Horse*, Zora Neale Hurston reports that while studying the Voudoun religion in Haiti, she "had some practice in drawing with cornmeal the ververs or signatures of various loa" (164). Kongo's reference to St. Christophe (said with a wink) is a deliberate attempt to camouflage the fact that he is drawing a Voudoun symbol. Kongo's coded reference to the vévé marks the narrative encoding of Voudoun and simultaneously confirms his connection to the old ways, the rituals and beliefs of the folk, and to Voudoun. It also affirms the claims made by many ethnographers that while the Catholic saints are used by Haitians to approximate the loas because of certain superficial associations they bear, saints and loas are not interchangeable. They derive from distinctly different religious systems and embody distinct features, characteristics, and purposes (Desmangles 7–9).

Readers also discover that Kongo was not always called Kongo. He had a different name in Haiti that he refuses to reveal to Amabelle. It is not accidental that the name "Kongo" echoes the nomenclature of the Voudoun loa from the Kongo region of Africa. In *The Faces of the Gods: Vodou and Roman Catholicism in Haiti*, Leslie Desmangles confirms that Voudoun "was brought largely by slaves from the Kongo and Dahomean regions (as well as many other parts) of West Africa to Santo Domingo or Saint-Domingue—as Haiti was called during its colonial period (1492–1804)—and the term voodoo is a deterioration of the Dahomean term vodu or vodun, meaning 'deity' or 'spirit'" (2). Kongo signifies the presence of Voudoun in some very specific ways in this text. Most experts on the Afro-Haitian religion of Voudoun insist that there are two categories of loas. The "cool" and controlled Rada spirits are derived from Dahomey, while the "hot" and out-of-control Petwo spirits are forged in the blood, corruption, and calumny of the New World (Deren 61–62). However, recent scholarship claims that the Petwo and Bizango (secret societies in Haitian Voudoun circles) sects have their roots in the Kongo societies of Central Africa. Elizabeth McAlister quotes one of her informants: "Petwo and Kongo, it's the same path" (87). Kongo's name aligns him with the "hot" Petwo spirits who are said to be aggressive, violent, and impetuous. Kongo's name hearkens back to the ki-Kongo roots of the Petwo spirits, and Kongo, like an ancestral loa, is not to be toyed with.

Just as Joel's death is surrounded by mysterious circumstances, so is the death of Valencia's son Rafael. He simply stops breathing. After the death of her son, Valencia is distraught. She invites the Haitian cane workers to have coffee from her expensive china, and Kongo eagerly participates in this farce. In "Remaking Identity, Unmaking Nation: Historical Recovery and the Reconstruction of Community in *In the Time of the Butterflies* and *The Farming of Bones*," Lynn Chun Ink reads Kongo's acceptance of Valencia's generosity as a conciliatory gesture that proves his lack of anger and desire to form a bond of solidarity with someone who, like himself, has lost a son (805). However, Kongo's gesture is the very antithesis of bonding. Kongo has the upper hand because he seems to possess knowledge of Valencia, himself, and Valencia's role in the greatest tragedy of his life, the death of his son. Valencia, on the other hand, gives no indication that she is aware that Kongo's son was killed by her husband. Kongo assumes a familiarity with Valencia that none of the other cane cutters dare to do. Kongo's stance with Valencia is passive-aggressive hostility parading as kindness. He warns her to watch closely over her daughter so that she does not come to the same fate as her brother, Rafi, who died mysteriously a few days after his birth. While on the surface Kongo's words convey sympathy, they reflect the double-voiced discursivity of the folk that is, at best, ominous. Kongo reaches out his hand to touch Valencia's daughter, at which point Valencia pulls the child away from Kongo's reach and he catches Valencia's hand and kisses it instead. Kongo's verbal and nonverbal warnings to Valencia approximate the stories that abound among Haitian peasants of sudden "unnatural" death. Kongo's posturing is aggressive, and suggests an improbable nexus between them, suddenly made apparent by the death of both their sons under mysterious circumstances. It is not a nexus of shared loss, however, but one that recognizes the disparities in their position and the impossibility of consubstantiality and communality despite the shared grief.[23]

Kongo inserts his body into Valencia's personal space in much the same way as Joel's body was invaded by Valencia's husband. It is a reversal in which Kongo asserts the upper hand. Rafi's death stands out as particularly mysterious, and Kongo's warning seems a veiled threat that is laden with symbolic significance. Did Kongo "send a dead," his son Joel, to take the life of Pico's son? A fair exchange, as the character Mimi said, "a life for a life"? Metraùx argues that "the most fearful practice in the black arts—the one which ordinary people are always talking about, is the 'sending of the dead.' The laying of this spell is always attended by fatal results unless it is diagnosed in time and a capable *houngan* (a priest) succeeds in making the dead let go" (274). Kongo possesses the presence, the bearing, and the sense of personal power that one would expect of a spiritual leader. While he is not identified as a houngan, his role in the community identifies him as a spiritual leader whose stature and authority within the group are unquestionable. He operates within the text as a symbolic houngan or priest, and his character is inscribed as a stand-in for the Voudoun priest figure.

The deaths of Amabelle's mother and father when she is a child represent a second textual moment in which parental figures are implicated in her spiritual underdevelopment. This incident marks another encoding of Voudoun in the narrative.[24] From the standpoint of the Voudoun worldview, the sudden death of Amabelle's parents suggests the presence of malevolent spiritual forces at work in Amabelle's life. It doesn't take a Mambo (a female priestess of Voudoun) to realize that Amabelle needs spiritual intervention. Amabelle's lack of spirituality early in the text and refusal to pray suggests a disconnect brought about by the early death of her parents whose refusal to pay attention to spiritual significations resulted in their deaths. Amabelle remembers and recounts her parents' demise like a mantra she is too traumatized to forget: "in the afternoon, we set out to wade across the river again with our two new shiny pots, it starts to rain in the mountains, far upstream. The air is heavy and moist; a wide rainbow arc creeps away from the sky, dark rain clouds moving in to take its place" (50). Here, Danticat signals the presence of the Voudoun loa Ayida Wédo, symbolized by the rainbow. The rainbow's disappearance is the sign of impending trouble that Amabelle's father misses. Ayida Wédo's signifying presence and subsequent absence are ignored, however, and followed by a personal calamity that could easily have been avoided had Amabelle's father read the signs correctly.

Rivers and waterfalls also signal the presence of Voudoun symbolism in *The Farming of Bones*. References to waterfalls as sites for spiritual pilgrimages and healing abound in Haitian folklore and ethnographic studies. In Haiti, streams, waterfalls, and springs are linked to Damballah and Ayida Wédo, as well as to Erzulie, the goddess of love. In *Tell My Horse*, Zora Neale Hurston describes a spiritual pilgrimage to Saut d'Eau where "the people drape their offerings of colored cotton cords on the sacred tree, undress and climb the misted rocks so that the sacred water may wet their bodies. Immediately many of them become possessed" (231). Hurston's story is reinscribed in *The Serpent and The Rainbow*, which recounts a yearly pilgrimage to Saut d'Eau, where Voudoun worshippers pay tribute to Erzulie. (W. Davis, *The Serpent and the Rainbow* 170).

Amabelle and Sebastien first make love in a cave behind a waterfall in Alegría. Amabelle's first experience of lovemaking is a sacred event that is both personal and communal. The waterfall is located at the source of the stream where the cane workers go to bathe. Spiritual bathing is a sacred act, a ritual that can be communal or personal. We see the importance of bathing communally when Joel dies and the impromptu wake takes the form of the everyday act of bathing that the cane field workers do every morning. On the morning after Joel's death, it takes on a special significance and becomes a spiritual "sending off" for Joel, a moment to discuss his death and the rumors about other Haitians being killed, while paying respect to Joel's father:

> I walked to the stream behind the neighboring sugar mill where the cane workers bathed at daybreak, before heading out to the fields. It was the first day of a new cane harvest. The stream was already crowded, overflowing with men and women, separated by a thin veil of trees. (59)

Amabelle's description of the impromptu wake that takes place in the water renders the stream a sacred space, separated from the secular space of work. The "thin veil of trees" marks the dividing line between men and women, and between the sacred and the secular.[25]

Similarly, the fact that the cave in which Amabelle and Sebastien first make love is located behind the waterfall where the cane workers bathe, is doubly significant. It makes the act of lovemaking an act of joining that solidifies their union with each other and with the community, thus marking the nexus between individual and community. However, what is curious about their first act of lovemaking in the cave is that this celebration of spirit and flesh, the joining together of two bodies and two souls, is filtered through Amabelle's reflections on death. The death of her parents is such a singularly defining moment in her life that everything—even this moment of joyous union with the man she adores—is tainted by the loss of those she first loved. The urgency of Amabelle's lovemaking with Sebastien, the depth of her passion, and her willingness to lose herself in him completely, signals her attempt to recover the security and sense of belonging she lost when her parents died. The light in the cave is magical and sacred, the kind of light Amabelle "wished for on the grave of (her) parents, but now she wishes it also for both Joel and Rafael" (101). The deaths of Joel and Rafael mark the beginning of the harvest of Haitian blood and bones, and Amabelle's wish for sacred light upon their graves becomes a silent prayer for salvation, a supplication for grace and mercy; as before, she is clairvoyant and can foresee the rivers of blood their deaths will herald.

In *The Farming of Bones*, Damballah and Ayida Wédo's presence in the cave when Amabelle first makes love to Sebastien is signaled by the mysterious light, "some memory of the sun, that it will not surrender." (100). Metraùx informs us that in Dahomey, "Dā Ayido Hwedo" is a twin spirit embodying male and female principles. It is necessary to quote here at some length:

> While Mawu, the supreme god, is Thought, Dā is life. He manifests himself "in the world in a number of ways; it is said that there are many Dā, or rather manifestations of Dā, but the chief of them is Dā Ayido Hwedo (in Haiti Damballah-aida-wédo), most commonly seen as the rainbow." He is a being with a dual nature, both male and female. Coiled in a spiral around the earth, he sustains the world and prevents its disintegration. As he revolves around the earth, he sets in motion the heavenly bodies. Because his nature is motion, he is also water. "He may still be recognized today in standing pools which recall the memory of the primordial waters: he is seen cleaving the water like a flash of light." Dā is the creator of mountains and also the excreter of metals. In the latter capacity he partakes of the nature of the sun. Dā was born long before the other vodu. (361)

Because s/he "partakes of the nature of the sun" and "sets in motion the heavenly bodies," Dā is a cosmic force whose presence is central to human existence. Older than the other vodu, this twin force (Dā) was there since the beginning of time, helping God to order the universe and set it in motion.[26] "Dā," "has dual aspects, one male, the other female, and these also are sometimes conceived of as twins.... Together they sustain the world, coiled in a spiral around the earth" (Thompson, *Face of the Gods* 229).

In Haitian Voudoun theology, the duality of Dā is reconfigured as a cosmic pairing of Damballah, the loa represented by a snake, with his wife Ayida Wédo, the rainbow.[27] Dā's presence at the lovemaking of Sebastien and Amabelle marks the centrality of sexuality and spirituality to the wellbeing of individual human beings and to the collective well-being of humanity.

Joined as one in the act of lovemaking that is consecrated by the light that embodies and disseminates Dã's energy, Amabelle and Sebastien undergo a synergistic transfiguration in which they become more than lovers. Their union symbolizes the fusion of male and female essence that is central to the harmony and balance needed to sustain the integrity of the universe. While individually Sebastien and Amabelle are two ordinary people, together they epitomize the potentiality of cosmic order, much like Damballah and his "wife" Ayida Wédo. This partially explains the perfection of their act of lovemaking and the uncanny connection these two share throughout the text.

Narratologically, this means that the moment in which Amabelle and Sebastien are separated in the text marks the beginning of chaos, disharmony, and cosmic imbalance. Their separation is of cosmic importance because it sets in motion a series of traumatic events that will cause their world to disintegrate; it prefigures the fragmentation and disintegration of the Haitian community, and heralds the state-sanctioned slaughter of Haitians that will cause a serious rupture in Haitian/Dominican relations. The trauma of the massacre represents a manmade, "unnatural" disaster that threatens the cosmic order, interrupts the flow of spiritual energy, and eclipses Dã's position as protector and stabilizer. Thus, when Amabelle returns to Alegría twenty-one years after the massacre, she cannot recognize the waterfall as the sacred place in her memory. Damballah and Ayida Wédo's presence is no longer there. Large, imposing, and emptied of its spiritual essence, the waterfall becomes a symbol of Alegría's soulless clamber toward commercialization, modernization, and wealth at the expense of spirituality and humanism.

Again, Danticat repeats the pattern mentioned previously of locating Amabelle's clairvoyance in a passage set apart from the regular narrative. At the moment in which Amabelle seems the most alive—the moment of her first union with Sebastien—she achieves a level of clairvoyance, or *connaissance*, that allows her to foresee both Sebastien's death and the demise of everything she knows of life in Alegría. The references to the death of her parents and her linking of the light in the cave to the light she wishes to be on their graves and on the graves of both Joel and Rafael, foreshadow the events of the massacre (110). In addition, Amabelle's focus on death in her moment of bliss marks the consubstantiality of spiritual *connaissance* and sexual climax, also dubbed "a little death." Life and death, as she knows, are inextricably linked. The birth of Rafael and his sister is a harbinger of Joel's death. In her world, happiness can only lead to its opposite. Glory leads to vainglory. King Henri's citadel lies in ruin at Cap Haitien; a reminder of a past that—though once glorious—is long gone with little hope of a return to its impressive beginning.

Edwidge Danticat also signals the presence of Elegua, or Papa Legba, the loa of the crossroads who governs destiny, chance, and change, to demonstrate Amabelle's deep desire to integrate her inner spiritual life with her outer life that seems devoid of rituals of the spirit. In an interview Danticat discusses the professor who appears toward the end of *The Farming of Bones*. Danticat explains to Renée Shea,

> The professor is just someone who is there, a man who never recovered from the massacre at all after twenty-one years.... So the professor remains a ghost, a different kind of survivor than Amabelle and Yves and the others. He makes himself the guardian of a very painful crossroad and refuses to leave. (Shea 19)

The professor, as guardian of the crossroads, is a Legba figure. Legba is the loa of the crossroads and of communication between the spirit world and the world of humans, and so stands at the in-between places where destiny, fate, and fortune intersect. In *Faces of the Gods*, Robert Farris Thompson describes him as "the Dahomean avatar of the Yoruba orisha Èshu-Elègba, trickster god of communication and contingency, who is alert to lapses of generosity" (174).

In *Flash of the Spirit*, Thompson informs us that Legba has the power to make things happen and multiply ashé, the activating life-force or energy in a person or object (18). He continues by designating this loa "the ultimate master of potentiality" (19). Thus, Legba has to be appeased first before any ritual ceremony can take place, and, if ignored, he "will make a man lose his way" (174). As the one who stands at the intersections of life, Legba is the loa who controls chance, change, and destiny. He is the one who intercedes on behalf of humans before any action can take place. It is no coincidence that Amabelle's first encounter with the professor— the one who makes himself "the guardian of a very painful crossroad"—takes place on the banks of the massacre river before she crosses to the Dominican side to make her peace with history. His kissing her is the transgressive act that seals their connection and signals that Legba grants permission for her mission. Through this personal contact with the spirit of Legba, Amabelle is permitted to cross over and initiate the act that will begin her healing process and reactivate her ashè, which was driven underground first by her parents' deaths and then by the traumatic events of the massacre. Danticat does not make the professor an obviously old and lame man, as Legba is performed in the Haitian imaginary. Critics maintain that in Haitian mythology Legba appears to have passed through a creolization process. In Dahomean mythology, he is a virile young man represented by a large phallus, but in Haitian mythology Legba is an old man and sexually powerless (see Laguerre, *Voodoo Heritage* 45). But the professor's madness is his deformity. As a legba figure, the professor is not just guarding the border of the Dominican Republic and Haiti. He mediates the transitional spaces between madness and sanity, past and present, action and inaction, experience and memory, pain and healing.

Amabelle's return to Alegría ensigns a liberating counterhegemonic critical stance that embodies both her contestation of the continued repression of Haitian migrants and her desire for healing. She risks her personal safety to confront the past, make her peace with it, and surrender it in the telling of her story to Metrés Dlo. Amabelle's ability to tell her own story, instead of having others tell it for her and to her, is a symbol of her revivified spirituality, her psychological healing, and her growth to fully actualized womanhood. The massacre river replaces the waterfall as the sacred space that must heal her. The same river that holds the bones of her murdered people, her drowned parents, and her friend Odette, must be where she goes to find wholeness and healing. At the end of the text, she is lying naked in the river telling her story to Metrès Dlo. Amabelle's ritual bathing is much like the communal bathing that took the place of Joel's wake. This time she is mourning not one but thousands of dead Haitians. The rough pebbles scouring her back enact a ritual cleansing, a laying on of hands by the spirit of the river, Metrès Dlo. Metrés Dlo, the mad professor, and we the readers are the witnesses to Amabelle's self-revelation and to her spiritual and emotional healing.

Danticat's encoding of Voudoun symbolism in *The Farming of Bones* fosters an optimistic reading of the end of the novel, and of Haiti's future. For if Amabelle represents Haiti, her meeting with destiny (embodied by the Legba figure of the mad professor) culminates in a ritual that will facilitate the recovery of Amabelle and of Haiti. Amabelle's decision to confront the past precipitates a series of actions that will eventually enable her to realize her potential, despite the loss of Sebastien. The end of the text finds her expectant and hopeful, "looking for the dawn" (310). However, hers is not a passive stance of waiting for something to change her life. Lying naked in the water, telling her story to Metrés Dlo, Amabelle is affirming a sense of continuity by actively communicating with her gods, reconnecting with her ancestors, reclaiming her sexuality, and coming to terms with her past. Water, a source of renewal, is also the scene of multiple deaths and loss for

Amabelle. To enter such a space as the massacre river demands courage and a willingness to engage with the bitterness of the past in order to move forward into the future. In engaging a critical model that foregrounds the Voudoun worldview, we have access to a mode of interpretation that privileges the continuity between history, text, and cultural context in *The Farming of Bones*.

Recovery and Rebirth: Amabelle's Sexual and Spiritual Healing

> I close the door and lock out the tame night breeze that barely reaches my bare body, naked because Sebastien has made me believe that it is like a prayer to lie unclothed alone the way one came out of the womb.
>
> Danticat, *The Farming of Bones*

In this section, I continue my interrogation of the empowering potential of female erotic energy by explicating the imbrications of sexuality and spirituality in the recuperation of Amabelle's subjectivity after the massacre. Edwidge Danticat links Amabelle's subjectivity to her physical, psychic, emotional, spiritual, and sexual well-being. Amabelle cannot achieve full subjectivity until she begins to heal from the damage done to her psyche, first by the death of her parents, and later by the emotional scars she carries after the massacre, especially the impact of losing her soul mate Sebastien. To heal, to find herself, and to have true self-possession, Amabelle must find God for herself (like Janie tells Phoeby in *Their Eyes*) and relocate her sexuality, even in Sebastien's absence.

Sexuality in the Voudoun religion is tied to spirituality, and female sexual expression is encouraged through ritual and dance, as well as through the figure of Erzulie, the often sexualized Voudoun loa who can "marry" as many men and women as she chooses. On an ideological level, Erzulie's sexual control is empowering to women—even to those who do not serve the loas—precisely because she is a goddess. But Erzulie is not only a sexual goddess. She is the symbol of womanhood and the personification of female beauty. Leslie Desmangles asserts that while Legba and Gede are associated with the phallus, "Ezili represents the cosmic womb in which divinity and humanity are conceived. She is the symbol of fecundity, the mother of the world who participates with the masculine forces in the creation and maintenance of the universe" (131). In other manifestations Erzulie is an elderly peasant woman wracked with pain to incarnate the painful existence of poor black women in Haiti.[28] In all of her manifestations, Erzulie is venerated as a symbol of womanhood, and the Voudoun calendar dedicates three days to her annually (Desmangles 134).

In the postmassacre segments of *The Farming of Bones*, the loss of Amabelle's sexuality and the displacement of her spirituality are linked to her total disempowerment and lack of will. After the massacre, she lives only to work, is disengaged from her surroundings, and indifferent to life and its pleasures. Wade Davis informs us that the malevolent Voudoun priest, called a bokor, "gains power by capturing the victim's ti bon ange—that component of the Voudoun soul that creates personality, character, and willpower" (*Passage of Darkness* 8). It is because it is missing its ti bon ange that a zombie is said to look catatonic. Davis continues: "Robbed of the soul the body is but an empty vessel subject to the commands of an alien force, the one who maintains control of the ti bon ange. It is the notion of external forces taking control of the individual that is so terrifying to the Voudounists" (8). Amabelle's state of apathy and abjection after she returns to Haiti mimics and reproduces the zombie metaphor, and it is through this trope that Danticat continues her encoding of Voudoun as a signatory subtext in this work. Although she is alive, Amabelle experiences "a living death" that belies the affirmation made by the doll—her ti bon ange—on her childhood sickbed, even as it confirms the doll's statement that she will not die (physically) young, but is destined to live to a ripe old age.

Yves shares a fate similar to Amabelle's, but his reconnection to the land suggests the possibility of recovery. Hard physical labor is Yves's way of working through the pain of the massacre. Amabelle, on the other hand, takes on sewing, but this occupation does not suggest creative expression as a mode of healing. Her words confirm that sewing is merely a way to pass the time: "I waited for Doctor Javier's reply by sewing clothes for everyone who came with a piece of cloth and held it in front of me and for my effort offered a few gourdes, a plate of food, and sometimes nothing but a kind grin. Yes, I waited for Doctor Javier's reply by growing old" (267).

Conversely, Amabelle's telling of her story to Metrès Dlo and her surrender to the river spirit as she lies naked in its waters at the end of the text suggest the possibility of healing and the recovery of subjectivity. Spirituality and reawakened sexuality are twinned tropes symbolizing Danticat's recognition of the power of sexuality and a female-centered spirituality for women's empowerment and autonomy.

Amabelle's sexuality—fully developed under Sebastien's expert tutelage—is driven underground after the massacre that seems to have taken her spirit instead of her life. When Sebastien dies, her sexuality dies with him because she has no spiritual self to sustain it. Her one attempt to make love to Yves left "an even bigger void in the aching pit of [her] stomach" (250). Neither she nor Yves can forgive themselves for surviving while Sebastien died, and their attempt at lovemaking only exacerbates their feelings of guilt and bottomless sorrow. Twenty years after the massacre, Amabelle's sexuality remains dormant. This is tragic, as Amabelle's personality when the reader first meets her is informed by a very passionate sexuality that borders on the spiritual, as evidenced in her description of making love in the sacred cave. In the beginning of the text, Amabelle's sexuality, though tied to Sebastien, is never solely dependent upon his presence. When he is alive, she is able to imagine him and visually re-create their sexual encounters even in his absence. As slavery and its vagaries rob Morrison's character Sethe of her sexual authority, so does the massacre rob Amabelle of her sexuality. The horror that the Haitians lived through in that historical episode is embodied by Amabelle's inability to heal and transcend the experience.

To a large extent, Amabelle's passionate surrender to Sebastien when we first meet her in the text is a stand-in for the spiritual grounding she lacks. Sexual love is what informs and animates her personality. So at the end of the massacre, the dried-up shell of a woman that she becomes, the terrible waste of her humanity that makes the latter part of the text so hard to read, yet so impossible to put down, is embodied in the complete absence of Amabelle's sexuality. Readers know that this is a very different woman from the one we first encounter raving about her lover in the first few pages of the book. The postmassacre Amabelle has no substance, no juice, and nothing that reminds us that she is alive, except for the memories and the pain she carries around like totems. Will Amabelle ever recover her personality, reconnect to her spirituality, or find her loas and God?

In the epigraph that begins this final segment, Amabelle refers to lying naked as a form of worship, making a clear connection between her sexuality and her spirituality. However, since she has no gods to call her own, and believes in no gods save Sebastien, she is unable to coherently theorize this relationship (65). What she does tell us about this insight is that it is Sebastien who has revealed it to her. And readers are not surprised since much of what she knows and considers important comes to her through other people. Amabelle is made up of other people's stories, and her subjectivity is informed both by what she has been told and by the stories she constantly retells herself. Sebastien tells her. Valencia tells her. Juana tells her. Her parents tell her. Kongo tells her. Mimi tells her. The sugar woman tells her. Like

Haiti, Amabelle is made up of stories: some great, some tragic. It is when she learns to tell her own stories and construct her own definition of self that Amabelle, like Haiti, finds peace.

When Amabelle helps in the delivery of Valencia's babies, it is the stories told to her or those she overhears from her parents that inform her knowledge of midwifery. She remembers what her father used to say about the importance of regular breathing for women in labor. She remembers her mother saying that after the baby comes out, the baby's "old nest" leaves the body like a second birth (10). It is her memory of this story (she never mentions witnessing a birth) that allows her to save baby Rosalinda after mistaking her for the afterbirth from Valencia's firstborn, Rafi.

Amabelle lives vicariously through stories, but she also learns how to tell stories effectively. She tells the story of Sebastien's hands, worn of their life-lines by years of working in the cane fields, and she tells about the feel of those hands on her body. Readers know Sebastien and begin to love him through the stories Amabelle tells of him. Without her stories, Sebastien is just an ordinary man. In the passages where he speaks for himself, he does not say anything profound or particularly interesting. He is a nice, regular guy who works in the cane fields and is loyal to his friends, but there is nothing special about the Sebastien, who represents himself to the reader through speech. He becomes special thorough Amabelle's recounting of his lovemaking, her retelling of his stories told to her, and his insistence that she rewrite the ending of her parents' story to give herself a happy ending. Even his silences, touches, and philosophical musings as recounted through Amabelle's eyes draw us into his character and make him one of the most memorable men in fiction.

Storytelling and touching, twinned tropes within this text, become metonymic and allow the reader insight into why Sebastien is so important to Amabelle's subjectivity in the beginning of the text. Amabelle tells us that Sebastien has told her that whenever they are not making love (touching) they should be talking (13). Touching, then, is another way of speaking and vice-versa. It is through talking to and touching Sebastien that Amabelle is able to transform her nightmares of her parents' drowning, her memories of Cap Hatien, Henry's Citadel, and her dreams of the sugar woman into a shape that is manageable in the daytime. Talking to Sebastien, touching him, facilitates her ability to live on a sensual and physical plane. It is then that Amabelle seems the most alive.

Danticat also uses speech as a trope of self-possession to show us how Amabelle is able to order her existence and carve out a space for herself in her adopted community of Alegrìa. When she is found by Valencia and Papi on the banks of the Massacre River, her first act of her new life is an act of speech. When Papi asks her to whom she belongs, Amabelle responds by pointing to herself. Valencia reminds her of this moment: "Papi paid one of the boys by the riverside to interpret for him when he asked who you belonged to. And you pointed to your chest and said, yourself" (91). Amabelle's claiming of herself is an act of self-love, a life-affirming act that signals the end of her preoccupation with following her parents into the river of death. It is through speech and gesture that she does so, and her first life-affirming narrative is, therefore, a narrative of self-possession.

However, when she meets Sebastien, Amabelle begins to hope that she can belong both to herself and to someone else. This is why, when asked what she believes in, she can think only of Sebastien. Outside of herself, he is the only person she claims and the only person she allows to claim her. Amabelle recognizes no gods of her own. Her spirituality has been thwarted by too many acts of betrayal. The first betrayal is, of course, her parents' drowning in the Massacre River. The rainbow representing Ayida wédo disappears, thereby abandoning her parents to their fate. Metrés Dlo, the spirit of the river whom her father salutes before entering, also does nothing to prevent their deaths. Amabelle is so traumatized by her parents' untimely deaths that she loses her faith in things of the spirit and has to struggle to regain it.[29]

The second betrayal is Haiti's abandonment of its revolutionary spirit and subsequent abandonment of its people. On the collective and historical fronts, Haiti, as represented by the sugar woman, haunts Amabelle just like the nightmare of her parents dying. The sugar woman is a polyvalent character who registers on multiple symbolic levels. She is linked to Haiti's history of slavery, exploitation, and repression. The muzzle that the sugar woman wears over her mouth is the muzzle that the planters used to place over the mouth of the slaves so they could not steal and eat the sugarcane they were harvesting (James, *The Black Jacobins* 12). The muzzle also represents the slave woman's inability to speak on her own behalf. Haiti is equally voiceless. It cannot fulfill its desire for financial autonomy and political stability, and cannot maintain the promise of its glorious, revolutionary origins.

The sugar woman cannot fulfill even the most basic desire to eat the sugarcane, even as she shortens her life to bring it to harvest. We see her incarnated in the elderly Haitian women bathing in the stream: "one was missing an ear. Two had lost fingers. One had her right cheek cracked in half—the result of a runaway machete in the field" (61). This ancestral memory of a collective past rooted in repression that continues to repeat itself in the present, becomes a personal terror for Amabelle. Amabelle's worst fears materialize in her dreams and are embodied by the historical figure of the sugar woman: the fear of desire unfulfilled, longing, hunger, restraint, physical and psychological repression, bondage, and servitude. Amabelle fears the sugar woman because she does not want to share her fate: silent, repressed, and shackled to the past. Amabelle's subjectivity is informed by both her personal history and her country's history. The sugar woman is the ultimate symbol of defeat because even with the object of desire in her grasp, she can never hope to possess it. The sugar woman is at once Haiti, with its dreams of autonomy and freedom in a perpetual state of deferment, and Amabelle's most terrifying fear, the fear of losing the object of her desire, Sebastien, and thereby losing herself. However, the sugar woman's fate is one Amabelle seems destined to share unless she is able to unshackle herself from the trauma wrought by the massacre.

Amabelle has good reason to be terrified of the sugar woman, who tells her, "I am the sugar woman. You, my eternity." The sugar woman's pronouncement proves prophetic (133). The sugar woman is voiceless because of the muzzle that prevents the clear articulation of her ideas, thoughts, and desires. After the massacre, Amabelle morphs into a silent, repressed, and bitter person. Amabelle is voiceless because the government officials stop writing down the stories before she gets her turn to tell her story. She cannot talk to Yves because neither she nor he can relive the pain of the massacre or forgive themselves for surviving. She cannot talk to anyone else because what is in her heart is too bitter to tell.

Like the sugar woman, Haiti also cannot fulfill the basic demands of statehood: to feed, clothe, and provide housing and healthcare for its citizenry, as well as to provide them with security and protection from lawless insiders and predatory outsiders like Trujillo. Haiti's desire to fully participate on the world stage is as old as the nation itself, forged as it was in 1804 when Haiti first won its freedom from France and became a sovereign nation. The sugar woman's muzzle that prevents her from speaking is an apt metaphor for Haiti's long-repressed desire to be an active participant in world politics rather than a disadvantaged foster child of the international community.[30]

Similarly, Amabelle's desires, dependent as they were upon Sebastien's presence, remain unfulfilled after he disappears. In his absence, she loses all trace of her former self and undergoes a terrifying transformation from a sexually vibrant, erotic being, to a shell of a woman who refuses to be touched by any other man, or by life itself. Silent and asexual, with only sleep and sewing to occupy her life, Amabelle waits for the return of Sebastien even when she has long given up hope that he survived.

Significantly, the sugar woman represents Haiti's bloody history under slavery. The slave woman's muzzle was but one of many excesses in the institution of cruelty that the French masters raised to a new art form. In his groundbreaking work *The Black Jacobins*, C.L.R. James explains the barbaric methods used to keep the slaves in line:

> There was no ingenuity that fear or a depraved imagination could devise which was not employed to break the spirit and satisfy the lusts and resentment of their owners and guardians—iron on the hands and feet, blocks of wood that the slaves had to drag behind them wherever they went, the tin-plate mask designed to prevent the slaves eating the sugar-cane, the iron collar. Whipping was interrupted in order to pass a piece of hot wood on the buttocks of the victim; salt, pepper, citron, cinders, aloes, and hot ashes were poured on the bleeding wounds. Mutilations were common, limbs, ears and sometimes the private parts, to deprive them of the pleasure which they could indulge in without expense. Their masters poured burning wax over their arms and heads, burned them alive, roasted them on slow fires, filled them with gunpowder and blew them up with a match, buried them up to the neck and smeared their heads with sugar so that the flies may devour them. (12)

When juxtaposed against that historically institutionalized cruelty of slavery, Haiti's modern-day excesses of political corruption, the abuse of the people both by their elected officials and by dictators, the siphoning of the nation's money into the bank accounts of the elite, politically motivated gangland-style executions, death by necklace (motor vehicle tires placed on the neck of a victim and set on fire), sexual assaults and rape of women, children, and disempowered men, the pandemic of AIDS and other diseases, the denial of health care and medicine to the masses, contempt for poor people in particular, and human life in general, appear to be part of a continuous cycle of violence orchestrated to break the spirit of the Haitian people. When considering the elite-serving autocratic agenda of Haitian leadership and the interventionist policies of so-called First World nations that refuse to recognize even democratically elected rulers, it is difficult to assess whether Haiti's problems today have undergone any significant changes since the days of slavery (see Dupuy, *Haiti in the World Economy* and *Haiti in the New World Order*). Some of the methods of physical torture have changed, to be sure, but the disregard for black life, especially poor black life, has not changed to any significant degree.

The contempt for human life and disregard for human suffering that is embodied by the sugar woman prefigures Trujillo's genocidal agenda in *Farming of Bones*. Within the world of the text, Amabelle's dream can be interpreted as a warning about the impending suffering of her people, the denial of their dreams and collective desires, and ultimately their deaths en masse. But, much like Baby Suggs in Toni Morrison's *Beloved*, Amabelle is cut off from her spiritual processes and can neither interpret her dreams nor prevent the impending massacre.

Nevertheless, there are narrative moments that link Amabelle's dreams and actions to symbolic associations and foreshadowing of the massacre. As mentioned previously, "the goat without horns" is a reference to human sacrifice, and sometimes to a victim of zombification in Voudoun religious significations. The following song for Erzulie contains lines that are a clear reference to her demand for human sacrifice from one of her devotees: "Ezili, you ask for a goat with two feet/Where could I get it, to give it to you?" (Dayan, *Haiti, History, and the Gods* 116). The goat is first mentioned early in *Farming of Bones*. Before he tells his wife, Juana, and Amabelle of Joel's death, Luis mentions that Pico has brought home a dead goat that he must "cut up and salt tonight" (38). Associated as it is with the night Joel is killed, the goat prefigures Joel's murder, which in turn foreshadows the massacre of the Haitian community. The goat must be attended to immediately, unlike Joel, who lies at the bottom of the ravine where Pico's car threw him.

Amabelle asks for bones from the goat's leg, shaped in the form of dominoes, that she then gives to one of the Haitian children to use in a game of chance. Linked as the goat is to the first known victim, Joel, Amabelle's gesture prefigures the vicissitudes of fortune and history that define the lives of the Haitian migrant community in the Dominican Republic. The goat is also associated with Sebastien, and Amabelle makes this association as she wonders if the murdered cane worker could be her lover:

> I did not stop worrying about Sebastien. As the laughter and Beatrice's effortless Latin phrases echoed from the bedroom, I walked over to the flame tree and peeked at the dead goat Senor Pico had brought home. Near the bloody spot where the goat's nose almost touched the ground lay my sewing basket and Sebastien's still-unfinished shirt. (40)

In the above exchange, Sebastien and Joel are interchangeable. Either of them could have been the victim of Pico's careless driving. Amabelle is the one who dresses Sebastien in life. She also attempts to do the same for Joel in death, by providing clothes for his burial. But it is Joel who draws the first straw for death; he is the one who becomes the sacrificial goat, the first confirmed victim of the massacre in Alegría.

In associating Trujillo's death later in the text with a human sacrifice, the survivors suggest that Trujillo's blood must be spilled as restitution for the many Haitians, like Joel, who were victims of the massacre. This hardly seems to add up numerically, but the point is well made that Trujillo, guilty as he is of the spilling of Haitian blood, must be sacrificed to the cause of justice before there can be any healing of the severed relationship between Haiti and the Dominican Republic. However, as we critique Dominican civilian participation in the massacre, we must place their collusion in this bloody affair within the context of the political repression, intimidation, brainwashing, and sheer terror in which Dominicans were held under Trujillo's leadership.[31] The suffering of Dominicans under Trujillo's reign of terror is referenced in *The Farming of Bones* and poignantly narrated in Julia Alvarez's *In the Time of the Butterflies*. Trujillo's death, then, was a victory for both sides of the island, and suggests the possibility of healing, both on the individual and collective levels, for both nations.

Similarly, through Amabelle's actions toward the end of the text, Danticat gestures toward recovery, and it is these gestures that make the novel less depressing with subsequent readings. What are the signposts? Amabelle's first encounter and subsequent relationship with the professor signals her nascent spiritual rebirth. The women at the riverbank tell her that it is good luck to be kissed by a madman. And Amabelle's spiritual quest in search of self and sexuality is actualized by the transgressive potentiality of Legba. Amabelle's return to Alegría signals a desire for healing. But first she has to confront the past, make her peace with it, and surrender it in the telling of her story to Metrès Dlo. Amabelle's ability to tell her story to the spirit of the river represents the return of her spiritual consciousness, her psychological healing, and the reconstitution of her subjectivity.

Amabelle's parents ignore or fail to read the prefigurative gesture of the retreating rainbow as a sign that it is not safe to cross the river, and it is this legacy of spiritual lassitude that Amabelle must eschew if she is to triumph over her circumstances. According to Judeo-Christian theology, the rainbow is a sign from God that the world after the flood will not again be destroyed by water. As mentioned previously, in Voudoun theology the rainbow signifies Ayida Wédo, wife of Damballah, the snake God. It is not that Amabelle's parents are spiritually underdeveloped. They are spiritual workers, officiating over death, birth, and sickness, and as such, are firmly entrenched in the spiritual network of Haitian peasant culture. But in his haste to get home, Amabelle's father temporarily disconnects from the world of intuition and spiritual insight, or *connaissance*. His judgment is influenced by a Western, linear, concept of time, rather than by the natural cyclicality governing the concept of time that is operational in Afro-religious contexts. Desmangles informs us that "Da is identified not only with the eternal motion of human bodies but also with motion as seen in the cycle of life and death and in the passing of human generations" (125). This cyclical concept of time recognizes the existence of spiritual forces and energies that govern the choices and decisions made by humans.[32] When his wife tells him to wait and watch the current for a while, Amabelle's father responds dismissively: "we have no time to waste" (50). He "reaches into the current and sprinkles his face with the water, as if to salute the spirit of the river and request her permission to enter" (51). But it is too late. He has already committed himself to his fate with a decision that is not spiritually sound. I contend that it is this pernicious error on her father's part that changes Amabelle's destiny forever, and precipitates her spiritual displacement.

However, such displacement does not suggest that Amabelle is resistant to spiritual influence in her conscious life. She does not have an operative spirituality, but she knows something is missing. When she escapes the stray bullet from Valencia's gun as Valencia is engaged in target practice, Amabelle asks Juana which Saint she ought to thank for her good fortune. She is forever seeking a spiritual connection, and her preoccupation with water and waterfalls is at once an acknowledgment of her desire to make peace with her parents' death and a sign of her seeking for spiritual answers in bodies of water. Water, then, is tied to Amabelle's spirituality in significant ways. It is only after she has returned to Alegría that she discovers the real reason for her mission: "Some wishes sound too foolish when uttered out loud. But that is why I have come back to this place, to see a waterfall" (296). It may appear obvious that she is seeking this waterfall because that is where she and Sebastien first made love. But in the *Farming of Bones*, nothing is as simple as it appears. As they stand looking at the waterfall, which looks nothing like Amabelle's memory of it, Valencia states: "I understand why you would come this very long distance to see it. When we were children, you were always drawn to water, Amabelle, streams, lakes, rivers, waterfalls in all their power; do you remember?" (302). Amabelle's preoccupation with water and waterfalls clearly predates Sebastien and is tied both to her spiritual maroonage and to her orphaned status.

Narratologically, it is Valenica who makes the connection between Amabelle's spiritual pilgrimages to water and her search for selfhood: "When I didn't see you, I always knew where to find you, peeking into some current, looking for your face" (303). Amabelle's construction of a self is dependent upon the image she sees reflected back from the literal and symbolic space in which her parents disappeared from her life. Her ontological viability is also tied to the spiritual space occupied by the Voudoun gods who are said to live under the water in the mythical land of "Guineè, Africa, the legendary place of racial origin" (Deren 36). References to waterfalls as sites of spiritual pilgrimages abound in Haitian culture. Zora Neale Hurston describes several of these pilgrimages in *Tell My Horse*. In Haiti, streams, waterfalls, and springs are linked to Damballah and Ayida Wédo, as well as to Erzulie, the goddess of love, and many other water deities both male and female. In *The Serpent and the Rainbow*, Wade Davis describes a yearly pilgrimage to the healing waters at Saut d'Eau where Voudoun worshippers pay tribute to Erzulie (170). Amabelle's attraction to waterfalls links her to the godess Erzulie. Her return to Alegría to seek the waterfall where she first makes love to Sebastian coupled with the unburdening of herself by telling her traumatic story to the spirit of the river suggest that Amabelle's recovery of self and spirit are tied to her reconnection with her spiritual roots.

Although Danticat never mentions Ayida Wédo in *Farming of Bones*, the loa's presence in the cave where Sebastien and Amabelle first make love is signaled by the mysterious light Amabelle describes as "some memory of the sun, that it will not surrender" (100). Clearly, Amabelle's lovemaking with Sebastien in the magical space of the cave is an act of self-celebration, but Amabelle also links it to a sacred act.[33] The following passage from Danticat's text recognizes the spiritual power of place and water, and acknowledges the coterminous relationship between spirituality and sexuality:

> On the inside of the cave there is always light, day and night. You, who know the cave's secret, for a time, you are also held captive in this prism, this curiosity of nature that makes you want to celebrate yourself in ways that the breath in your blood will show you, or the cave will show you, or the emptiness in your bones will show you, in ways that you hope your body knows better than yourself.

> This is where Sebastien and I first made love, standing in this cave, in a crook where you feel half buried, although the light can't help but follow you and stay. (100–101)

The light clearly symbolizes spiritual energy that enshrines the entire act of lovemaking in the realm of the sacred. You, the reader, enter this portion of the narrative and immediately become aware of an otherworldly stillness evoked by the delicate beauty of the language. You are humbled by the sacredness of the love act. And whether or not you are familiar with Damballah or Erzulie, you feel the presence of fecund gods in the "dark green" hush of "wet papaya leaves" and the warm glow of heavenly light (100).[34]

As the goddess of love and sexuality, Erzulie's presence is evoked in Amabelle's joyous abandonment and obvious celebration of her sexuality each time she mentions making love to Sebastien. In other passages, Amabelle is revealed as an active and sensual participant in their lovemaking: "I grab his body, my head barely reaching the center of his chest" (1). And again, "I fall back asleep, draped over him. . . . I can still feel his presence there, in the small square of my room. I can smell his sweat, which is as thick as sugarcane juice when he's worked too much" (3). There is a raw sensuality here that strongly contrasts with the delicacy of the language from the lovemaking scene in the cave. In a synergistic transfiguration, Sebastien's sweat and thick cane juice scent is absorbed by Amabelle, transforming her into an active sexual agent reveling in the lustiness of sexual release and enjoying the heightened sensuality that brings all of her senses into sharp focus. She is sexually aggressive, evoking and reproducing Erzulie's sexual dominance and control.

In the ending of *Farming of Bones*, history surrenders to spirituality as the agent of efficacious and lasting resistance. In a sense, the Massacre River and Henri's citadel serve inverse symbolic purposes for Amabelle. Henri's citadel, a powerful reminder of past glory for Haiti, keeps the history of Haiti's struggle for freedom at the forefront of collective and individual consciousness. But history and the past are not enough to sustain Amabelle. It is to spirituality and the present that she must turn to find her salvation. Through Metrés Dlo, Amabelle must resuscitate her nascent spirituality to harness the strength and the personal power (ashé) she will need to resist complete vitiation by the nihilistic structures of dominance and interpellation that would render her invisible and voiceless like the sugar woman.

The act of telling her story to Metrés Dlo while lying in the Massacre River is a double-voiced symbol of Amabelle's reconnection to her gods, because nudity for Amabelle is a form of worship and telling, a form of touching. This is the spiritual connection for which Amabelle has spent her life searching, and in the moment she finds it she also finds herself, recovers her subjectivity, and makes her peace with history. Amabelle's nakedness symbolizes complete transparency and visibility in this moment that she surrenders the burden of her story to the river spirit. Her lack of shame when the professor walks by and stares at her naked body suggests freedom from traditional gender conventions attending female sexuality and from her own self-imposed sexual maroonage. She is ready to be seen as a sexual being, and ready to act as a free sexual agent.

When Amabelle returns to Alegría to find the waterfall, Sebastien is not there. Neither is Damballah. Nevertheless, this moment evinces the beginning of closure for Amabelle. The Massacre River replaces the waterfall as the sacred space in which she must locate her lost spirituality and in so doing find herself.[35] Valencia confirms that Amabelle is forever looking for her own face in bodies of water, and by the end of the text Amabelle is lying naked in the river telling her story to Metrès Dlo. Amabelle's description of her sexual and spiritual experience makes the link between telling, touching, and healing even more compelling: "the water was warm for October, warm and shallow, so shallow that I could lie on my back in it with my shoulders only half submerged, the current floating over me in a less than gentle caress, the pebbles in the river bed scouring my back" (310).

Besides Metrès Dlo and the mad professor, we the readers are witnesses to Amabelle's telling and to her healing. Amabelle's ritual bathing is much like the communal bathing that was Joel's wake. This time she is mourning not one but thousands of dead Haitians. The rough pebbles scouring her back enact a ritual cleansing, a laying on of hands by the river spirit. As in *Beloved* and *It Begins with Tears*, this laying on of hands is not gentle, but forceful, pulling away all unclean spirits, all negative forces that entrap and threaten to entomb Amabelle in victimhood.

The text ends on a hopeful note, with both Amabelle and the professor "looking for the dawn" (310). And, after all is said and done, hope is Amabelle's best defense against the reification of her status as a zombified figure. No longer repressed into silent victimhood, she has a will, a self, a god, and a friend—the professor—to witness her self-revelation and victorious comeback. Like the historiography of the citadel (burnt to the ground by Henri Christophe himself, rather than risk it being taken by the enemy), the discursivity of Amabelle's surrender theorizes no passive univocal postulation, but a collective reminder that struggle is inevitable, freedom hard-won, victory never certain and perhaps fleeting, but forever possible. What critic Donette Francis says of Sophie in Danticat's *Breath, Eyes, Memory* is also true of Amabelle, another traumatized Haitian woman: "her personal healing and development has collective implications" (86). *Farming of Bones* begins with the name of Sebastien Onius, the man who becomes a symbol of the massacre through Amabelle's recounting of his story and hers. However, the text ends with Amabelle, the survivor of the massacre, revivified from a living death and summoning herself into Haitian historiography as the woman who survived to tell the story. As the stand-in for her nation, Amabelle's survival and victorious transformation symbolize hope for the future of Haiti.

Epilogue

A POEM FOR SARA BAARTMAN

I've come to take you home—
home, remember the veld?
the lush green grass beneath the big oak trees
the air is cool there and the sun does not burn.
I have made your bed at the foot of the hill,
your blankets are covered in buchu and mint,
the proteas stand in yellow and white
and the water in the stream chuckle sing-songs
as it hobbles along over little stones.
I have come to wrench you away—
away from the poking eyes
of the man-made monster
who lives in the dark
with his clutches of imperialism
who dissects your body bit by bit
who likens your soul to that of Satan
and declares himself the ultimate god!
I have come to soothe your heavy heart
I offer my bosom to your weary soul
I will cover your face with the palms of my hands
I will run my lips over lines in your neck
I will feast my eyes on the beauty of you
and I will sing for you
for I have come to bring you peace.
I have come to take you home
where the ancient mountains shout your name.
I have made your bed at the foot of the hill,
your blankets are covered in buchu and mint,
the proteas stand in yellow and white—
I have come to take you home
where I will sing for you
for you have brought me peace.

Diana Ferrus

It is up to us as black women to take our historically beleaguered bodies and images back from the clutches of capitalistic and patriarchal hegemonies. Diana Ferrus, who is of Khoisan descent like Sara Baartman, wrote the above poem while studying in Utrecht, Holland, in 1998. Many believe that it was this poem that catalyzed Nelson Mandela into action to reclaim the remains of his countrywoman from France in 2002. One hundred and ninety-two years after she was taken to Europe under false pretenses, Sara Baartman was brought home and given a proper burial in South Africa. In the words of Dr. Willa Boezak, "It took the power of a woman, through a simple loving poem, to move hard politicians into action."[1]

It was through another poet that I came to know of Sara Baartman. Years before this research was even conceived of, on my way from New York to Boston, I borrowed a book from a friend to read on the airplane. It was Elizabeth Alexander's first collection of poems, *The Venus Hottentot*. I had heard the story before in some undergraduate class, but it had never inhabited any space in my psyche except as an extreme example of the horrors of slavery and colonialism. The reality of Sara's tragic life began to take shape after reading Alexander's poem, "the Venus Hottentot." The poem haunted me for more than a decade. It brought to life this woman—black like me—separated from her family and everything that was familiar to her, suffering untold humiliation and degradation daily from people who saw her only as a scientific curiosity and freak of nature unworthy of human dignity.

I stumbled upon Ferrus's poem while doing research on Sara Baartman for this study. Upon reading Ferrus's poem and the news clippings about the return of Sara's body to her people in South Africa, I felt that I—like Sara and the Khoisan people—had come full circle. One poet's work had compelled me to inhabit Sara's story for more than a decade and contemplate the historical and contemporary ramifications of black women's sexual history in the New World, while another poet's work had allowed me to put the issue to rest.

It was my preoccupation with Sara Baartman that led me to begin interrogating how black women were portrayed in literature and popular culture. Like Candice Jenkins, I understand the impetus behind the "salvific wish": the desire to save black women from such a dishonorable fate. However, the suppression of black female sexuality can never be the answer. In denying our sexuality, we deny our very humanity. In the end, our detractors win. We collude with them in denying ourselves full subjectivity. Our sexuality is God-given to be celebrated, enjoyed, and controlled by us and no one else.

When Sara Baartman agreed to go to Europe, it was with the understanding that she would be able to work for the economic betterment of herself and those she loved.[2] She did not sign up for the abusive treatment she received."[3] She certainly could not have foreseen how her decision would help to shape the development of racist and sexist pseudoscientific discourses vis-à-vis the sexual proclivities of the black woman. Her decision also did not take into consideration the possibility that she was being deceived by "unscrupulous men" who were trying to make their fame and fortune at her expense (Alexander 4–5).

One of the charges made against the "salvific wish" is that it denies black women the agency to control their sexual expression. However, given the demeaning stereotypes about black women that are uttered by some of the women in hip-hop and other arenas of popular culture, how does one differentiate between agency and cooptation?[4] Free sexual expression and sexual exploitation? Can a self-debasing, spiritually underdeveloped consciousness be said to produce agency? Can any barely clad black woman dancing to hip-hop and dancehall be said to claim ownership of her sexuality? What about the women who use the dancehall as a space to act out homoerotic desires? Are they empowered to act upon those desires in the real world and admit homoerotic desires even to themselves?

My preoccupation with the synthesis of sexuality with spirituality originates in the belief that the erotic empowerment Lorde speaks of enables healthy, life-affirming choices. Even agency can be compromised when one is operating out of an unhealthy space, be that space poverty, state-sanctioned violence, political repression, childhood sexual abuse, or whatever exigency may be operative in a woman's life that may cause her to make uninformed or unhealthy choices. Janie Crawford's first marriage was forced upon her by a well-meaning grandmother who was a victim of historical circumstances that severely circumscribed her ability to make life-affirming decisions. Only when Janie is spiritually and sexually whole is she able to operate from a truly "liberating space."

Although a fictional character, Janie represents a model of resistance against both the repression and the exploitation of black female sexuality. Does the lewdly displayed body of the black woman in popular music videos represent freedom of sexual expression or sexual exploitation? The answer seems to reside not in the popular domain but in the literature written by black women. While it is true that black female sexual performance in the arenas of popular culture is potentially subversive, it is in literature that we see a more liberating poetics at work. Characters in black women's texts gesture toward fulfillment by blending a complex spiritual life (God-centered, inner directed, community-building, earth/nature/life-sustaining) with a mature sexual identity that foregrounds their own sexual enjoyment.

Unlike Sara Baartman, they do not volunteer themselves to be on display for someone else's objectifying gaze. Fully conscious of their sexuality, their joyous abandonment is in service to the celebration of (their own) full sexual expression, whether by themselves or in the arms of a consciously chosen lover. With the exception of Janie, who eschews Nanny's brand of wisdom, all of these women seek out spiritual mentorship from older women who represent the vanguard of ancient and powerful spiritual epistemes. One could argue that Janie seeks her council and spiritual mentorship in Erzulie rather than Nanny.

This study proposes that the female characters studied herein—whether born in slavery like Sethe, second generation free, like Janie, sexually liberated like Monica, or survivor of a genocidal massacre like Amabelle—are all engaged in a liberating poetics of eroticism that is predicated on the synthesis of the sexual and the spiritual. Without this balance, the real black women in popular culture can no more achieve full subjectivity than the fictional ones. To be fully liberated, we have to move beyond transgression toward creativity, responsibility, sexual ownership, and sexual authority: we must demand nothing less than full control of our bodies and resources—be they spiritual, economic, sexual, or otherwise. Janie Crawford and her literary progenitors teach us that the power of the erotic is the power to effect positive growth from the inside out, to transform not only our inner lives but our material circumstances, and to access the divine power within ourselves in order to transform our lives and our communities.

Notes

Introduction

1. For example, in *Narrative of the Life of Fredrick Douglass*, Douglass recounts the story of a root given to him by a fellow slave to keep on his body as a talisman that would protect him from the master's whip. Charles Chestnutt's folktales and short stories also show ample evidence of African belief systems.

2. Note, for example, that the first published African-American poet, Jupiter Hammon, wrote the poem "An Address to Miss Phillis Wheatley" to the second published African-American poet, Phillis Wheatley, in 1778, decrying Africa as a "heathen" land from which Wheatley was fortunate to have escaped "thro' the mercy of the Lord" (see *Hammon*, America's First Negro Poet).

3. I am thinking, for instance, of texts such as *Iola Leroy* (Francis Harper); *Incidents in the Life of a Slave Girl* (Harriet Jacobs); and the *Spiritual Narratives* (Jarena Lee, Maria Stewart, et al.); and even *Our Nig* (Harriet Wilson).

4. Critics argue that New World black subjectivity is necessarily fragmented. But as Keizer rightly points out, given the "intolerable conditions" via which such fragmentation was fomented, "there is no reason why they would have celebrated a shattered body or a shattered consciousness" (*Black Subjects*, 44).

5. See Lamothe, "Vodou Imagery, African American Tradition, and Cultural Transformation in Zora Neale Hurston's *Their Eyes Were Watching God*," which makes comparisons between Janie and the Haitian Voudoun goddess Erzulie.

6. See Judylyn Ryan, *Spirituality as Ideology in Black Women's Film and Literature*, for a definition of spirituality "as a combination of consciousness, ethos, lifestyle, and discourse that privileges spirit . . . that is, life-force—as a primary aspect of self and that defines and determines health and well-being" (2).

7. Lamothe identifies Janie as the Voudoun goddess herself, who manifests through Hurston's heroine in multiple emanations, as she does in the Haitian imagination and ritual. She is variously a coquettish mulatta with many lovers, a cold French beauty, or an old black woman from the Haitian working class.

8. See Dayan, "Erzulie: A Woman's History of Haiti."

9. See Shea, "The Hunger to Tell," for an interview with Danticat in which she names Erzulie as both "absence and presence." I coin the term "absent presence" from her usage.

10. See Murphy, *Working the Spirit*, for a definition of *konesans* (*connaissance*) (17).

Chapter 1. The Cult of Nineteenth-Century Black Womanhood

1. See the early nineteenth-century French print entitled *La Belle Hottentot* at www.southafrica.info/ess_info/sa_glance/history/saartjie.htm.

2. Deborah Gray White argues that the very conditions under which black women had to work—bending over in rice fields with their dresses hiked up to their waist to keep them from getting wet or scrubbing floors with their dresses around their thighs to allow free movement and keep the dresses clean—served to convince white men of black women's lack of modesty. She observes that often slave women were forced to wear tattered clothes that exposed their bodies, and this was also held against them as a sign of their sexual impropriety. Black women were also whipped publicly in the nude. These exposures that were a condition of their enslavement—running so contrary to the demand placed on white women to have their bodies fully covered so that no flesh was ever exposed—gave credibility to the myth that black women were more sexual and less moral.

3. In "Black Bodies, White Bodies: Toward an Iconography of Female Sexuality in Late Nineteenth-Century Art, Medicine, and Literature," Gilman reproduces this popular engraving titled *The Hottentot Venus*, ca. 1850.

4. See Hazel Carby's *Reconstructing Womanhood* for an examination of the impact that stereotypical depictions of black female sexuality had on black women's writings in the nineteenth century.

5. In *Narrative of the Life of Frederick Douglass: An American Slave*, Douglass also describes several situations where slaves were murdered by their masters and mistresses for petty offenses:

> The wife of Mr. Giles Hicks, living but a short distance from where I used to live, murdered my wife's cousin, a young girl between fifteen and sixteen years of age, mangling her person in the most horrible manner, breaking her nose and breastbone with a stick, so that the poor girl expired in a few hours afterwards. She had been set that night to mind Mrs. Hicks's baby, and during the night she fell asleep, and the baby cried. She, having lost her rest for several nights previous, did not hear the crying. Mrs. Hicks, finding the girl slow to move, jumped from her bed, seized an oak stick of wood by the fireplace, and with it broke the girl's nose and breastbone, and thus ended her life. (26-27)

6. Giddings contends that black women were blamed not only for their own denigration, but for that of the entire race. She states: "Even the black man's alleged impulse to rape was the Black woman's fault. Historically, the stereotype of the sexually potent Black male was largely based on that of the promiscuous Black female. He would have to be potent, the thinking went, to satisfy such hot-natured women" (*When and Where I Enter* 31).

7. See Carby, *Reconstructing Womanhood* for an explication of Mary's Prince's complicated response to the hypocrisy of the cult of true womanhood (42-43). For Linda Brent's (Harriet Jacobs's) views on her sexual history and the sexual conditions that were forced upon black women during slavery, see 48-49.

8. See, for example, Douglass's account of Christian slaveholders who were the cruelest masters, often punctuating their merciless bloodlettings with biblical scriptures.

9. The sense of agency and empowerment this calling to preach engendered in black women is underscored by Bassard in *Spiritual Interrogations*: "it is within these private encounters with Spirit that African American women often experienced a conferral of personhood denied by larger social constructions of African American and female subjectivity. For it is within this divine dialogue that black women's subjectivity is produced even as her agency is acknowledged and affirmed" (3).

10. See Stewart, "Religion and the Pure Principles of Morality."

11. See also Carla Peterson's *Doers of the Word* for further explication of Stewart's use of Christian doctrine to condemn black people and blame blacks, especially black women, for the degraded condition of the race (70–71).

12. In Stewart, "Religion and the Pure Principles of Morality," the terms used to define the cult of true womanhood are resurrected almost wholesale. She urges black women to be pious, sexually pure, and to remain within their domestic spheres. She further admonishes women to "possess a meek and quiet spirit" and not to "meddle in other men's matters" (6).

13. In *Spirituality as Ideology in Black Women's Film and Literature*, Ryan observes that, similar to her contemporary and mentor David Walker, "Stewart, a woman, inspired even greater hostility among members of the black community, and, it appears, was essentially run out of town because of the perception that her unladylike behavior in speaking in public and the strident tones of her exhortations jeopardized the carefully cultivated image free blacks wanted to preserve" (49).

14. In her essay "The Last Taboo," Paula Giddings observes that during the post-Reconstruction era, sexual exploitation of black women was so pervasive that many were forced to migrate north to escape the threat of rape (454).

15. In addition to the stereotypes of black female promiscuity, black men were also cast as sexual predators and rapists, bent on defiling white women. This stereotype was often the justification used for lynching black men (Giddings, "The Last Taboo," 454).

16. George Schuyler, "Instructions for Contributions," as cited by Henry Louis Gates Jr., in *The Signifying Monkey* (179).

17. Du Bois proposed that the Negro race could only be saved by its exceptional men, whom he dubbed "the talented tenth." Many elite blacks shared his views without considering or critiquing the further marginalization of the folk and of women that was implied by Du Bois's rhetoric of salvation through elitism.

18. For example, in reviewing Claude McKay's novel, W.E.B. Du Bois says that *Home to Harlem* "nauseates me, and after the dirtier parts of its filth I feel distinctly like taking a bath ("Two Novels," 202).

19. Carby argues convincingly that the mulatto character serves as a mediator between the black and white races: "historically the mulatto, as a narrative figure, has two primary functions: as a vehicle for the exploration of the relationship between the races and, at the same time, an expression of the relationship between the races" (*Reconstructing Womanhood*, 89).

20. See Hughes, "The Blues I'm Playing"; and Claude McKay, *Home to Harlem*.

21. See, for example, Carla Kaplan's introduction to *Passing: A Norton Critical Edition*, xix.

22. See Thadious Davis's biography of Larsen for a lengthy critique of Larsen's own elitism.

23. See Thornton, "Sexism as Quagmire."

24. Carby's critique is also leveled at writers like Hurston (and perhaps Toomer) who saw the people as the rural poor. If Larsen saw the people as the urban poor, she certainly did not spend any ink on the issues that concerned them. She focuses on the urban middle-class and wealthy blacks. Her focused critique on the talented tenth only legitimized that group as the only blacks deserving of critical attention. Their laudatory reception of her novels demonstrates their acceptance of her as one of them.

25. There are two versions of the rural folk in *Their Eyes Were Watching God*. The folk in Eatonville vilify Janie and alienate her while the folk in the muck accept her until she shoots Tea Cake. Since the text centers around Janie, the folk are hardly presented romantically. Logan, Nanny, and Joe Starks are all versions of the folk, and all three are represented problematically as are Tea Cake and Mrs. Turner, and others. Carby seems to be suggesting that any representation of the folk that sets them in the rural South is a romanticized representation. But to exclude the rural folk from the literary representation of the entire period and represent only the urban poor would be exchanging one set of problems for another. Certainly, Claude McKay, Langston Hughes, Rudolf Fisher, and many other writers from the period made the urban poor the focus of their poetry and fiction.

26. See Thadious M. Davis's introduction for a full explication of Larsen's class prejudices, affectations, and ambivalence about race. Her ambivalence about class is reflected in the fact that she criticizes the black bourgeoisie while actively seeking their approval and society (4–12).

27. Deborah McDowell notes "the fine line between sexual and religious ecstasy" (*The Changing Same* 85).

28. Larsen's novel received the highest critical acclaim from race leaders such as Du Bois. These were the circles in which she moved and the people who promoted her work. Not only did she share their "salvific wish" (see Jenkins 2002), but it would not have been politic for her to write the kind of narrative that would alienate her friends and supporters.

29. Pfeiffer, "The Limits of Identity in Jessie Fauset's *Plum Bun*," 83.

30. See Michael Awkward's introduction to *New Essays on "Their Eyes Were Watching God"* in which he names Alain Locke and W.E.B. Du Bois as being among the writers calling for respectability in black representation.

31. See Lorde, "Uses of the Erotic: The Erotic as Power," 53.

32. See Carby, *Reconstructing Womanhood*, where she credits Larsen for inscribing Helga as "the first truly sexual black female protagonist in Afro-American fiction" (174).

Chapter 2. Literary Interventions in *Their Eyes Were Watching God*

1. See Naylor, "Love and Sex in the Afro-American Novel," 19–31.

2. See Lamothe, "Voudou Imagery, African American Tradition, and Cultural Transformation in Zora Neale Hurston's *Their Eyes Were Watching God*."

3. bell hooks argues persuasively that black men, white men, and white women failed to recognize that black women did not just occupy the position of blackness and womanness simultaneously, but that the category "black woman" is itself a distinctly separate category with its own set of concerns that may be different from those of black men and white women (see bell hooks, *Ain't I a Woman*, 8; see also Barbara Johnson's essay "Metaphor, Metonymy, and Voice in *Their Eyes Were Watching God*," 54). Johnson argues that because they fail to recognize "black woman" as a category worthy of analogy with other categories, both feminist discourses and black male discourses ignore the existence of black women, even though both discourses foreground the types of oppression that affect black women.

4. See Carby, *Reconstructing Womanhood*, for an examination of the impact that stereotypical depictions of black female sexuality had on black women's writing in the nineteenth century. See also Kaplan, "The Erotics of Talk," 137; Dearborn, *Pocohontas' Daughters*; Hull, *Color, Sex and Poetry*; and McDowell, introduction to *"Quicksand" and "Passing."* All of these critics agree that black women writers applied a kind of self-censure when it came to the issue of black female sexuality, to guard against reinscribing themselves as sexually promiscuous. In addition, during the Harlem Renaissance period, certain subjects were considered taboo or unbecoming by the black male elite, and black female sexuality was chief among these taboos. For a full description of Hurston's inscription of Janie as the Haitian Voudoun goddess Erzulie, see Lamothe, "Voudou Imagery, African American Tradition and Cultural Transformation in Zora Neale Hurston's *Their Eyes Were Watching God*."

5. Robert Haas argues that Janie might actually be going home to Eatonville to die toward the end of the novel ("Might Zora Neale Hurston's Janie Woods Be Dying of Rabies?"). Although the narrative states that Janie was bitten by a rabid Tea Cake, it gives no indication that she is dying or even ill at the end of the text. I do not read this as an omission on Hurston's part, but as an acknowledgment that what matters at this juncture is how full of life Janie appears to be, and how fulfilled she is despite losing the man she dearly loved. Clearly, Janie's sense of self, although shaped by her relationship with Tea Cake, is not dependent upon his physical presence.

6. See Hemenway's argument in *Zora Neale Hurston: A Literary Biography* that *Tell My Horse* was considered a failed ethnographic work in his biography on Hurston.

7. For example, Angela Murray in *Plum Bun* (Jessie Fauset) has a mulatta mother and a black father. Irene, in Nella Larsen's *Passing*, has two African American parents, but is light enough to pass for white when she chooses.

8. As can be observed in *Iola Leroy* and *Incidents in the Life of a Slave Girl*, *Quicksand*, *Passing*, and many other texts written by black writers.

9. See Appiah and Gutman, *Color Conscious*; Helms, *Black and White Racial Identity*; and Gordon and Anderson, "The African Diaspora."

10. See Thaggert, "Racial Etiquette." See also Sherrard-Johnson, "'A Plea for Color.'"

11. She refers to this phenomenon in Nella Larsen's *Passing*, but it is also applicable here.

12. Thaggert's essay suggests that Rhinelander may have encouraged Alice to dress in long sleeves and disguise her color with powder when they were in public.

13. I am thinking, for example, of Peola in "Imitation of Life"; the protagonist in James Weldon Johnson's *Autobiography of an Ex-Colored Man*; and Clare in Larsen's *Passing*.

14. This would not be the first time Hurston appears to reify a convention for the purpose of exposing it. Indeed, she does the same with the convention of marriage. She has Janie marry three times, only to end up proving that marriage, even at its best, can present a real challenge to female autonomy. Even in her best marriage, Janie is subjected to irrational jealousy and physical abuse.

15. In Fauset's novel, Angela Murray cannot feel any attraction to Matthew Henson because he has "bad hair."

16. Sherrard-Johnson argues, in "A Plea for Color," that Larsen's female characters, especially Helga Crane, transgress, transcend, and modernize the tragic mulatta trope (836). However, Helga begins the novel as a tragic figure and ends it even more tragic. Helga, as Sherrard-Johnson argues, points our attention to just how problematic this representation is. But to say she transcends this tragic representation is an overstatement, especially considering how *Quicksand* ends—with Helga in complete abjection.

17. See, for example, Ani, *Let the Circle Be Unbroken*. 40–41.

18. See Gates, "Zora Neale Hurston and the Speakerly Text," 94.

19. See DuPlessis, "Power, Judgment, and Narrative in a Work of Zora Neale Hurston," 112–13.

20. See Willis, *Specifying*, where she explains that although Logan never beats Janie, work on his farm represents the stifling of her dreams and creativity and the suppression of her spirit (46–47).

21. Susan Willis argues that the muck allows Janie and Tea Cake to develop "a truly reciprocal relationship" (48).

22. In *Specifying*, Willis observes that because Janie and Tea Cake are not burdened by "debt and kids," they are able to have an atypical relationship that includes satisfying work, good sex, good food, music, hunting, and other activities that bring them closer as a couple and make life sensual and enjoyable.

23. What Henry Louis Gates reads as a "divided self," I see as an expression of interiority or spiritual awareness (see Gates, "Zora Neale Hurston and the Speakerly Text," 102).

24. See Gates, introduction to *The Signifying Monkey* for his discussion of Esu and the trope of the talking book (xxv).

25. See Boyce Davies's *Migration of the Subject*; and Clark, "Developing Diaspora Literacy and Marassa Consciousness."

26. In "The Race for Theory," Christian suggests that black women have always "creatively theorized" through their works of fiction and drama. Her essay, misread in some camps as antitheory, really advances the notion of a black woman's theoretical language

that parallels Henry Louis Gates's and Houston Baker's readings of black vernacular theories.

27. *Mules and Men* chronicles Zora's folk research in the American South and her experiences studying and learning hoodoo in New Orleans. In *Tell My Horse*, she records her insights on the folk religion of Haiti, Voudoun. For both Hoodoo and Voudoun, Hurston approached her research in a very unconventional way. Ethnographers usually observe and record as an outsider. Hurston became an insider in Voudoun, learning the religion as well as participating in the rituals.

28. As I will explicate later, Lamothe does make the argument that Hurston uses Voudoun to inscribe Janie's character. Janie's resistance to patriarchal mandates can also be seen as a feature of Voudoun's empowerment of women as Mambos (priestesses) and goddesses.

29. See, for example, Fredrick Douglass's narrative, in which he identifies a root given to him by Sandy Jenkins, a fellow slave, to protect him from his cruel master (111). Douglass employs a double-voiced strategy with respect to the power and presence of Hoodoo that is signaled by the root. At first, Douglass dismisses his friend's belief as superstition. Then he indicates that there may be something to the root after he is able to overpower Mr. Covey. Eventually, Douglass attributes his triumph over his master to superior physical prowess, which is tied to concepts of black masculinity. The reader is not sure what to make of the root. Its presence in the text suggests a belief in magic, but does not confirm a coherent spiritual framework as the source of Douglass's newfound power.

30. I disagree with Joyner that the separation between African religions and black expressions of Christianity is as complete as he asserts. What, for example, is speaking in tongues? Alfred Métraux's description of "langage," a noninterpretable (to priests and priestesses as well as to ordinary worshipers) form of communication frequently expressed when a devotee is possessed by a loa, seems identical to the "tongues" of the black church, not only in form but in the silence (and what Metraùx also describes as a kind of embarrassment exhibited by the priesthood when pressed to interpret the "langage" of a possessed) that surrounds its unknowability. I am not suggesting that "langage" is, in fact, uninterpretable. I am merely observing that in Métraux's text, no one seemed to be able to interpret "langage" in the Voudoun circles, which is also the case when people speak in tongues in black churches.

31. In chapter 5 of *Tell My Horse,* Hurston comments on the role of women as "donkeys" in the Caribbean and emphasizes that American women have it easy by comparison. Her delineation of the equality of gender relations in America seems both naïve and contradictory, and is pointed out (Hemenway, *Zora Neale Hurston* 248-49) as one of the analyses that weakens *Tell My Horse*. She also comments on the sexual exploitation of dark-skinned women under the color caste system in Jamaica that reduces them to sexual objects for mulatto or light-skinned middle-class men (Hemenway *Zora Neale Hurston* 228).

32. In *Black Jacobins*, C.L.R. James argues, regarding the Haitian revolution: "Voodoo was the medium of the conspiracy. In spite of all prohibitions, the slaves traveled miles to sing and dance and practice the rites and talk; and now, since the revolution, to hear

the political news and make their plans. Boukman, a Papaloi or High Priest, a gigantic Negro, was the leader" (86).

33. See Washington, "I Love the Way Janie Crawford Left Her Husbands," 28.

34. Lamothe uses the spelling "Ezili." I use "Erzulie" except in quoted material.

35. Desmangles states, in *The Faces of the Gods*, that Erzulie has multiple sexual relationships with both loas and human devotees. Her scandalous sexuality "would be considered disgraceful conduct" (132–33).

36. See Holloway, *Moorings & Metaphors*.

37. C.L.R. James, in *Black Jacobins*, and other critics who write on Haiti represent Voudoun as both a religion and a political tool that can be used for or against the people. For example, in 1804, it was used to help Haitians win the revolution; while Baby Doc used it in the 1980s to control, manipulate, and terrorize the people.

38. In Voudoun parlance, a possessed person is said to have the loa seated in his or her head (see Alfred Métraux 133).

39. See Kaplan, "The Erotics of Talk," in which Kaplan insists that Janie has always had a voice, and was simply in search of the perfect listener to whom she could tell her story (139).

40. Hurston's outgoing nature, acceptance of others, and adaptability is clearly evident in *Mules and Men* and in her autobiography, *Dust Tracks on a Road*.

41. For example, in my reading, when Janie sits under the pear tree observing nature, the "kissing bees" represent her sexual awareness (11).

42. In *Divine Horsemen*, Maya Deren explains that Guinèe is Africa, the legendary place of origin where the loa have their permanent residence (36).

Chapter 3. Contradictory Directives and the Erotics of Re-membering

1. For a full explication of the concept of diasporic literacy, see Clark, "Developing Diaspora Literacy and Marassa Consciousness."

2. Morrison's essay "The Site of Memory" is published in *Inventing the Truth: The Art and Craft of Memoir*, edited by William Zinsser.

3. In "The Site of Memory," Morrison discusses her fidelity to the milieu out of which she writes and in which her ancestors actually lived (111). Elsewhere, such as in the essay "Rootedness," she also acknowledges her desire to revalue ways of knowing that derive from African cosmologies. What I am referring to here is not an attempt to find easy closure, but an attempt to find balance and close the circle, so to speak, since life, in the African worldview, is a cyclical process.

4. See Rody, "Toni Morrison's *Beloved*: History, 'Remory,'" and a "Clamor for a Kiss," 96.

5. Naomi Mandel points to the problematizing of this dedication by critics such as Stanley Crouch, Amy Schwartz, and Emily Budick, who argue that Morrison is trying to signify upon the fact that the African holocaust is not given the same critical attention as the Jewish one. Mandel argues that the very term "sixty million and more" used in reference to the African holocaust is merely an estimate, and that it points to our inability to truly know how many blacks died in slavery and the Middle Passage. Therefore, this estimated figure is, more accurately, a representation of the impossibility of representing

"so vast and devastating a disaster" as American slavery on American soil ("I Made the Ink" 583).

6. See Naomi Mandel's *"I Made the Ink": Identity, Complicity, 60 Million and More*.

7. Frankly, I am also excited at the prospect that African cosmological systems, with their complex epistemological frameworks, richly evocative spiritual traditions, and multilayered (polyvalent) mythos, can potentially provide a common framework of literary images, symbols, and legends for African diasporic writers in pretty much the same way that Greek and Roman mythologies and biblical stories provided a smorgasbord of literary themes and allusions for western writers. And Morrison is the right writer at the right time to be able to legitimate this masterful endeavor.

8. See Richards, *Let the Circle Be Unbroken*, for a more detailed explanation of time in the African context.

9. For diversity and complexity in the way scholars understand these concepts, see the following texts: *Face of the Gods*; *Flash of the Spirit*; *Jambalayah*; *The Way of the Orisa*; *Santeria, From Africa to the New World*; *Working the Spirit*; *Sacred Possessions: Vodou, Santeria, Obeah and the Caribbean*.

10. For decades, African-centered scholars, including Wade Nobles, Leonard Barrett, John Mbiti, Na'im Akbar, Marimba Ani (formerly Dona Marimba Richards), Janheinz Jahn, and Molefi Asante, have been making the claim that interdependence and interconnectedness are central to the African worldview. Similarly, scholars doing ethnographic research on African and New World religions also support the idea that interconnectedness is one of the central tenets of these spiritual traditions. Among these are Robert Farris Thompson, Maya Deren, Joseph Murphy, Joan Dayan, Leslie Desmangles, John Mason, Margaret Fernandez Olmos, and Lizabeth Paravisini-Gebert, to name but a few.

11. I am referring to essays such as Moglen, "Redeeming History in Toni Morrison's *Beloved*"; Fitzgerald, "Selfhood and Community: Psychoanalysis and Discourse in *Beloved*"; Wyatt, "Giving Body to the Word"; and Nicholls, "The Belated Postmodern."

12. See Joyce, *Warriors, Conjurers and Priests*.

13. See Judylyn Ryan's text for an in-depth analysis of the links between African spirituality and black Christianity.

14. See Arlene Keizer's analysis of how African belief systems enabled captive Africans and their descendants to resist Eurocentric hegemony.

15. See, for example, movies such as *Angel Heart*, *The Serpent and the Rainbow*, and *The Believers*.

16. See Métraux, *Voodoo in Haiti*, 120.

17. I explore this issue at length in the introduction of this book and reference it only briefly here.

18. See definitions of creolization proffered by Brathwaite, Glissant, Bernabé, and Confiant, among others.

19. Shango Baptist is prevalent in Trinidad. Pukumina, Zionist, Kumina, and Revivalist are Jamaican versions of creolized religions with African-centered forms of worship and ritual observances. See Leonard Barrett for an explication of African and New World religious practices in Jamaica. In Guyana, worshippers are sometimes called Jordanites.

See Brathwaite, . "Kumina," for an analysis of Kumina religion in Jamaica and Adams for an explanation of Yoruba retention in Guyana.

20. See Barrett, *The Sun and the Drum*.

21. Morrison's repetition of the phrase "at all" parallels the way it is used in Jamaican Creole. In context and meaning, Morrison's text recalls Caribbean usage of this phrase. It is an "ole people" expression—meaning that it is commonly used by the elderly—and denotes deep-seated anxiety as in the context of Baby Suggs's usage.

22. In Gloria Naylor's *Mama Day*, Miranda "reads" eggs to foretell whether or not Bernice will become pregnant.

23. In the Santeria religion, the priestess is called a "Madrina" and has her own religious house and spiritual congregation, known as her "god-children." In Yoruba and Santeria, a "Babalawo" is the highest spiritual leader and only men can hold the office.

24. I adopt this term from Robert Farris Thompson's usage in his book *Flash of the Spirit*. Note also that in the movie *Ghosts of Mississippi*, prosecutor Bobby DeLaughter has a bottle tree outside his young daughter's bedroom window. The child, who is afraid of ghosts, needs this bottle tree to keep evil spirits away. However, the bottle tree seems to stop working for her, and her father is forced to resort to a Dixie-land song that celebrates the values of the old South (which of course, would include the enslavement of black bodies), taught to him by his white southern mother, to comfort the child. Interestingly, this movie that demonstrates white southern racism in its most powerful manifestation—a white man cannot be convicted for killing a black person even if the whole community knows he is guilty—reflects an awareness of the spiritual codes and signs that black America has given to the South, and to America in general. Even more interestingly, the bottle tree as spiritual protection loses its efficacy when placed in the service of a community that neither values African-American bodies nor understands the significance of African-American belief systems.

25. The fact that Sethe names her baby after Amy Denver pretty much says it all.

26. See Adisa, *It Begins with Tears*. River-mumma is a personification of the physical river. However, she has a definitive role as head of a spiritual cadre of women that Adisa constructs. In chapter 3 of this volume, I offer an in-depth analysis of River-mumma's role in the fictional Kristoff Village community.

27. Readers who bristle at my association of this white woman with New World religious figures may well consider the fact that Robert Farris Thompson, one of the leading scholars in the field, and someone who understands African New World religions both as lived realities and as subjects of ethnographic study, is a white American male. In Brazil and Cuba, black skin is (apparently) not a prerequisite for leadership or membership in Santeria and Condomble houses. I am not suggesting that African spirituality is color-blind—though it may very well be—but spiritual power is usually passed down through bloodlines. And because of miscegenation, a spiritual legacy can just as easily be passed down to a white-skinned descendant as to a dark-skinned one. Amy Denver, who, like many enslaved blacks, does not know her father, may or may not have black ancestry. What is incontrovertible is the fact that Morrison clearly aligns her role in the

narrative with that of healers (such as Baby Suggs) and orishas (such as Yemonja and Oshun) who attend women.

28. See Thompson, *Face of the Gods*, for some spectacular representations of New World altars.

29. See Weir-Soley, "Myth, Spirituality and the Power of the Erotic in *It Begins with Tears*." In the poem "Baby Duppy," I explore the connections between Morrison's description of the baby ghost's behavior and the Jamaican belief in vengeful baby spirits who die before their time (*The Caribbean Writer* 9, 21-22).

30. For a discussion of the Jamaican belief in ghosts and haunted houses, see Barrett, *The Sun and the Drum*, 92.

31. See Brathwaite, "Kumina," for a discussion of the role that the silk cotton tree played in Miss Queenie's initiation into Kumina religion (49–51).

32. See Comfort for a discussion of Beloved's power and magic deriving from her discursive liminality (123).

33. Marshall, *Praisesong for the Widow*, explicates the centrality of re-membering the nation dance of one's ancestry and reconnecting with kinship and cultural ties through ritualized dancing, as precursors to spiritual and psychological healing.

34. Keizer argues that the main attributes of an antelope are speed and free movement, and in doing the antelope dance, enslaved Africans can temporarily reverse, "their conditions of physical constraints" (35).

35. See Berthrong for a discussion of Mou Zongsan's views on intersubjectivity as the defining principle in neo-Confucian thought (13).

36. There is clearly a correlation between this idea of bright colors chasing away evil spirits and the idea of decorating trees with brightly colored bottles to capture or chase away evil spirits. The difference is that the glass bottles are also said to capture and hold the spirits of the dead, while the loud colors merely chase them away.

37. See Lamothe, "Vodou Imagery, African American Tradition, and Cultural Transformation in Zora Neale Hurston's *Their Eyes Were Watching God*."

38. See Linda Krumholz, "The Ghosts of Slavery," 108.

39. Quilt historians, such as Giles Wright, Barbara Brackman, Patricia Cummings, and others, refute Tobin and Dobard's theory on the basis that there is no hard evidence to support the links between certain symbols in the quilts and the Underground Railroad. They also note that there is no mention of quilt codes in the slave narratives or oral testimonies of former slaves.

40. Naomi Mandel argues that both the speech and the body of the black subject render her complicit in her oppression: "this interrelation of a complicit speech with a complicit body both invites community and renders it unsustainable" (594).

41. Sethe's success as a storyteller who passes down tales that sustain imagination and nurture memory for her daughters is affirmed and validated by Beloved's eagerness to hear and Denver's desire to retell these stories (see Morrison, *Beloved*, 59, 76).

42. See Thompson, *Flash of the Spirit;* and Thompson, *Face of the Gods.*

43. Milkman must return to his ancestral community to find the threads that will bind him to family, legend, and history, as well as anchor him in the kinship patterns

without which his very survival is in question. What Milkman learns of resistance he must learn through the legends and lessons left behind by his Solomon kinfolk, as well as through Pilate's New World adaptations, which weave elements of the old with the new: her name dangling from a box in her ear, the site of orality. Solomon and his descendants left (for Milkman and newer generations) lessons in flight, transcendence, and transformation.

44. The quotation is mine, not Morrison's.

45. See page 47. In addition to his own ethnographic research in Haiti, Davis carefully identifies established ethnographers of Haitian culture who have contributed to the understanding of Voudoun that he provides.

46. See Dayan.

47. This difference-deviance model is further entrenched with the disturbing memory that haunts Paul D from his postslavery days on the chain gang. He and other black men were forced to perform fellatio on the white prison guards or risk being shot in the head for refusing.

48. See Carden.

49. See Canizares for an explication of animal sacrifice in Santeria religion. He confirms that a black rooster is the ebbø (offering) sacrificed to the god of iron, Ogun (88).

50. See Carby for an analysis of sexual ideology in the nineteenth century (*Reconstructing Womanhood* 20–39).

51. In "Models of Memory and Romance," Carden argues that although we do not see Paul D performing fellatio in the text, "it is clear that Paul D must have endured this violation." She continues, "And because in America he is always subject to the laws of white men—with or without guns—he always occupies this position of powerlessness and coercion" (406).

52. See Laguerre's *Voodoo Heritage* for a description of Erzulie as a jealous lover who requires her servitors to dedicate an entire room in their home to her for ritual lovemaking (71).

53. Sethe's taking to her bed forces comparisons with Baby Suggs, who took to her bed, in my reading, to contemplate resistance strategies. It also reminds this reader of Annie from Jamaica Kincaid's *Annie John*, who, after a long illness (depression) in which she took to her bed for months, emerges with renewed purpose and determination to leave her small island existence and find her place in the larger world.

54. See Lorde, "The Uses of the Erotic."

55. One can make the case that Janie, who is not a mother in Hurston's text, becomes the mother-figure, female ancestor, or literary predecessor to some of the characters inscribed by black women writers, including Morrison's character, Sethe.

56. Erzulie-Dantor is also a mother.

57. Krumholz also sees Beloved as a trickster figure in the African-American tradition.

58. See Canizares for material on the use of herbs and plants. Canizares also states that in addition to being used for stomach ailments, chamomile is also used as a sedative and vaginal wash, which further connects the herb to female sexuality (104).

59. See Canizares on further uses of herbs and plants in the Santeria spiritual tradition (102-3).

Chapter 4. The Erotics of Change

1. See Besson, "Land Tenure in the Free Villages of Trelawny, Jamaica" and "Reputation & Respectability Reconsidered: A New Perspective on Afro-Caribbean Peasant Women," for a full representation of the importance of family land in Jamaican peasant communities.

2. There is some controversy among ethnographers and others experts of Yoruba and Condomble religion as to the orisha or divinity called Yemonja/Olokun. In some of the literature, it is suggested that Yemonja is the divinity who controls the upper reaches of the ocean, while Olokun controls the lower depths. Other critics explain that in Africa, Yemonja is the deity of the Ogun river in Nigeria. See Philip John Meimark, *The Way of the Orisha*, 115-21. Some contend that when Africans of the Ifa religion came into contact with the ocean during the long, hazardous Middle Passage journey, they transformed Yemonja into an ocean goddess. Most experts seem to agree that Yemonja, the quintessential mother-figure and the source of all life, is the orisha who nurtures and protects children. Oshun, the goddess of sexuality and fertility, is the orisha responsible for conception. Yemonja is depicted in art and sculpture with long breasts designating her role as nurturer and quintessential mother-figure.

3. The Jamaican Creole term for women who have the gift of prophecy and discernment. These women are usually elders and pastors in the Zionist, Church of God of Prophesy, Kumina, or Pukumina churches, but "Seeyer" woman can also be found among ordinary women who just have "the gift." Another term that is sometimes used is "Warner" women, as these women will foresee a disaster and parade the streets before daybreak, warning the community of impending doom. "Warning" is sometimes accompanied by a mild form of spirit possession in which the elder seems to be in a state of trance, although she appears clear, articulate, persuasive, and often spellbinding in her exhortations. "Mother" or "Madda" is another popular terminology and designates the protective role (and the authority) of these women who see themselves (and are seen by others) as "Mothers" to the entire community.

4. The model is somewhat like Bakhtin's to the extent that there are many voices in the text, and at least two major contesting schools of thought. At its foundation, there is a quest for unity, but it is a unity that does not turn on homogeneity, but rather recognizes difference as an important constitutive element.

5. In others sections of Jamaica, the Creole phrase in question is "Rain ah fall, sun ah shine, devil and im wife a fight," and not: ". . . devil a beat im wife." This revision recognizes the conflict as a contest between equals, not one in which the woman is the supposed (and "natural") victim.

6. The traditional standard of beauty for women in Jamaica dictated that a stout, voluptuous woman was seen as more attractive than a skinny woman (particularly since coming out of a slave society, being skinny was associated with being starved). This is probably responsible, in part, for the phenomenon that I observe in rural folk culture in

which slight, slender men choose big women as wives. In a physical confrontation, these women could easily overpower their husbands; hence it seems preposterous to assume that men are automatically the aggressors in physical confrontations. See V. S. Naipaul's character Laura, in *Miguel Street*, who frequently beats her husband.

7. In Adisa's novel, the term "peppered" refers to a brutal gang assault (by women) on one woman in which the weapon of choice is hot pepper crushed and rubbed into the victim's private parts. However, the term is also used metaphorically to refer to "tracing matches": heated arguments between women where the tongue is the weapon used by an accomplished verbal expert to apply the "peppering" of words. In such matches, ones' ancestry is often traced as far back as can be remembered or imagined to demonstrate that the opponent's lack of good character is a genetic flaw.

8. In "Kumina," Braithwaite argues that the Kumina religion is a "living fragment of an African religion (mainly Kongo)" (46). Leonard Barrett, in *The Sun and the Drum*, explains that Kumina is from the Twi word *akom*, "to be possessed, and *ana*, an ancestor" (25). "The word Kumina then is from Akom-ana, an ancestor possession cult of the Ashanti people" (25). He later identifies Pukumina as a syncretism of Kumina and Christianity (27).

9. In conversation with Opal Palmer Adisa, I have learned that the similarities between Monica and Sula are not intentional. Intentional or not, however, these similarities should be foregrounded for two reasons. Unlike Sula, Monica survives, and in her living transcends some of the limitations that Sula's refusal of community placed on her spiritual and emotional development. Second, Monica represents a continuity of self-actualized black women characters begun by Zora Neale Hurston with Janie's character in *Their Eyes Were Watching God,* and continued in Toni Morrison's work. Hence, Opal Palmer Adisa's work has its place in a black female tradition that sees fiction as an empowering place from which to work through issues of significant import to the development of black female consciousness and literary tradition.

10. Monica's decision to return to her village signals a yearning to return to tradition. Nevertheless, she has her parents' home completely modernized to suit her acquired taste for the conveniences of a modern home.

11. The culinary adaptation of the Jamaican folk under slavery is a good metaphor through which to understand their ability to resist, transform, or transcend the dominant culture's attempts to eradicate folk culture. I am referring specifically to the fact that ordinary Jamaicans include in their traditional diet various foods considered poisonous: bitter-cassava (which contains a poisonous starch that has to be thoroughly extracted before preparation), ackee (which has been taken off the export list several times because it can be poisonous if harvested too early or improperly prepared), and susumba, considered suspect in Haiti because it is used to cast bad spells. Through historical necessity and traditional wisdom, the folk in Jamaica learned how to extract what is poisonous from these foods and transform what remained into tasty delicacies. Jamaican folk response to ideological threats demonstrates the same level of inventiveness and adaptability: certainly two of the most desirable traits comprising a creolized consciousness.

12. Scholars as diverse as Lawrence Levine, Derek Walcott, Judylyn Ryan, and Carolyn Mitchell maintain that the "Africanizing" of Christianity by blacks in the New World

produced an Afro-Christianity that not only has very distinct features from the original, but that was in effect a form of adaptation and resistance to the imposition of European Christianity upon New World blacks. Scholars of African and New World religions such as Robert Farris Thompson, John Mason, George Brandon, and others have theorized that the survival of African religions in the New World, under systematic attack from postslavery regimes, is the most daring example of slave resistance to European ideological and spiritual domination. Similarly, Jean Besson, Sidney Mintz, Sally Price, and many other Caribbean anthropologists have produced considerable research documenting the almost spiritual importance of family land to the rural peasant class in Caribbean societies. These plots of land were purchased by ex-slaves after emancipation, and the immeasurable sense of value placed on these family plots—which cannot be sold but must be passed down from one generation to the next—exemplifies the importance of property to the descendants of former slaves whose fore-parents were themselves property. But even before they could legally own property, Caribbean slaves used the plots of land that they were given to grow food for their families and to produce surplus food to be sold and bartered. In "From Plantation to Peasantry," Sidney Mintz points out that in rare cases, slaves were able to purchase their freedom with the money they had saved from the sale of these surplus crops. These proto-peasants viewed access to land as the most viable means of resistance against the demoralizing system of slavery. This is evidenced by the fact that they chose to use their very limited free time to take advantage of the only resource available to them which would enable them to gain a modicum of self-respect and independence, and ultimately to purchase the most valued possession of all, their freedom. Adisa's characters are descendants of these proto-peasants and they display the same spiritual adherence to the land and to the values and mores of peasant society.

13. Trickery and cunning are Legba-like principles. The folkloric figure associated with these principles in Jamaica is Brother Anancy, the Ashanti folk hero who uses his wits to outsmart his powerful adversaries. See Leonard Barrett's *The Sun and the Drum* (32). Barrett uses the spelling "Anansi," but both "Anansi" and "Anancy" are used in Jamaican folklore.

14. I'm thinking about critics as diverse as Houston Baker, Simon During, Edward Said, Homi Bhabha, Simon Gikandi, David Lloyd, Lisa Lowe, Saurabh Dube, Gayatri Spivak, Frantz Fanon, and many more. I am well aware that, from time to time, critics refine and revise their arguments, depending on the direction of the critical corpus (for example, claims of competing modernisms or the decentering of European modernity in the context of globalization, etc). However, the essential position held by most critics, with respect to the Eurocentrism of European modernity and its tendency to both hegemonize and homogenize in colonial contexts, is still germane to my discussion of Adisa's text.

15. See Dube, "Introduction: Colonialism, Modernity, Colonial Modernities."

16. It has been observed that Caribbean women novelists tend to write bildungsromans that end just as the female character begins early adulthood, and before she becomes involved in a sexual relationship. However, this pattern is often continued in short story collections. Olive Senior's *Summer Lightning* is one example of this. Sexuality

is either avoided completely or subsumed under "major" thematic issues, thus allowing the writer to avoid dealing with adult sexual issues in the text. In her short story collection, as in this novel, Adisa breaks radically with this pattern as she foregrounds sex and sexuality and women's enjoyment of both.

17. Monica's "work" takes place outside of the narrative. By the time readers meet her, she has already given up prostitution. Monica's prostitution is mentioned because it is antithetical to Judeo-Christian notions of morality—an important tension within this work.

18. The village grocery store is run by Mr. and Mrs. Cotton and there seems to be no need to employ extra help.

19. See Gikandi, introduction to *Writing in Limbo*, for an extended analysis of how Caribbean authors write out of and within this Eurocentric paradigm even as they attempt to critique it.

20. See Rahier, "The Presence of Blackness and Representation of Jewishness in the Afro-Esmeraldian Celebrations of the Semana Santa (Ecuador)."

21. For example, the scene in which Arnella gives birth to her baby takes place outdoors. This is not a traditional practice in rural Jamaica and would only happen if the baby came suddenly while the mother was working in the fields. Traditionally, neither baby nor mother leaves the birth room before eight days. This practice has been traced to West African sources where the baby is not given a name or recognized as a real person until this period of time has passed. Significantly, the name Baby-Girl represents a continuation of this African tradition as her "true" name is withheld from the readers.

22. See Wilson, "Reputation and Respectability," for an analysis of the ways in which rural Caribbean folk place more value on "personal" worth than "social" status as a counterideology to the colonial mind-set that identifies an individual's worth with his material possessions, lifestyle, skin color, and Eurocentric value system.

23. The disease "yaws" induces sores on the feet, mouth, and face of humans, poultry, and other animals.

24. The critic Suzette Spencer reveals her own uneasiness with the negative portrayal of these three women in Adisa's text (see "Shall We Gather at the River?").

25. In "If I Could Write This in Fire, I Would Write This in Fire," Michelle Cliff defines the term "I and I" as a Rastafarian terminology, a concept in "which they combine themselves with Jah," another Rastafarian term denoting God. However, in common Rasta usage "I and I" also refers to "oneness," the interconnectedness between the individual and the collective. "I and I" takes the place of the plural "we" to show the lack of separation between human beings. In all of its combined meanings, then, the pronoun "I and I" refers to humanity's oneness with God and with each other, the most profound sense of intersubjectivity.

26. Sula herself is a revision of Janie as well. Like Janie, Sula has only one close female friend and is ostracized from the community. Like Janie, Sula's sexuality is also problematized (out of balance) in Morrison's text. But unlike Janie, Sula does not claim her spirituality, and is therefore beyond redemption.

27. For the most part, the students who complained were newly converted to Christianity and morally offended by the sexual language of the text. By the time I left Berkeley

in 1999, there was a growing body of born-again Christian groups emerging in the student population particularly among Asian students.

28. According to scholars of the Yoruba religious tradition, there is one supreme deity, sometimes called Olorun and sometimes called Oludumare, who communicates with the human population through his emissaries called orishas. Other scholars point out that the orishas are themselves aspects of God and nature. God is too removed from humans, distant, and unknowable, and has to be broken down into smaller parts to be understood. Hence, Oshun, the river; Yemaya, the ocean; Shango, lightning and thunder; and Oya, the wind, are all aspects of nature and God. These orisha-figures help human beings negotiate their paths in life.

29. For varying interpretations of the orisha Oshun and her defining characteristics, see Bisnauth, *History of Religions in the Caribbean*; Brandon, *Santeria*; Teish, *Jambalayah*; Edwards and Mason, *Black Gods—Orisha Studies in the New World*; Thompson, *Flash of the Spirit*, and *Face of the Gods*; Canizares, *Cuban Santeria*; and Neimark, *The Way of the Orisha*.

30. Yellow roses are also considered Oshun's flower. See, for example, http://tribeofthesun.com/oshun.htm for a listing of symbols associated with this orisha.

31. See Weir-Soley, "Myth, Spirituality, and the Power of the Erotic in *It Begins with Tears*."

32. See Besson, "Reputation and Respectability Reconsidered."

33. As noted earlier, "wood" is supposed to indicate the male sexual organ, but in this case it is deliberately associated with Godfree, Arnella's lover and the father of Baby-Girl.

34. Some of the syncretic religious sects in Jamaica, including the Zionist and Pukumina churches, did not traditionally baptize converts inside a church. Citing the example of John the Baptist in the Bible, they use the river to conduct baptisms. River-mumma, tied as she is to other aquatic deities from West African sources, is already a water spirit. This baptism ritual exemplifies the syncretization of Christianity with West African spiritual traditions in Jamaica. In *The Sun and the Drum*, Leonard Barrett discusses the ritual importance of the "bath" in Revival (Zionist) and Pukumina healing ceremonies in Jamaica.

35. In Claude McKay's poem "Spanish Needle," he reminisces about catching crayfish beneath the stones in the river. According to folk wisdom, precocious preteen girls would also take advantage of the opportunity to place the little river bugs known as bubby-biters on their bare breasts to induce early breast growth.

36. In Adisa's novel, Monica remembers a childhood event in which she went to the river to wash clothes with her mother, and they ended up fishing for crayfish first, delaying their return home (203). Monica's memory of this happy moment with her mother is marred by the violent reaction of her father when they return home much later than planned. Thus Adisa offers up a critique of patriarchal attempts to control women's time, curtail their freedom, and disrupt female bonding.

37. The comb and mirror mark her association with the vain Oshun, the beautiful river goddess of sexuality within the Yoruba pantheon. The blue and white colors in her dress clearly call to mind the nurturing ocean goddess, Yemonja. There is a correspond-

ing Akan deity called "Mama Water" (a name that is used synonymously with "River Mumma" in some parts of the island), who is also a mermaid. Adisa asserts the privilege of her complexly syncretized diasporic identity by combining various sources of African and New World religious symbolism. One of the short stories in *Bake-Face and Other Guava Stories* centers on Yemonja as the "seductive" mistress of the ocean, who has the power to steal fishermen from their earthly wives. It is, in fact, Oshun—not Yemonja—who is said to be the seductress (according to many Yoruba, Santeria, and Condomble experts).

38. For example, stories from the oral tradition in Jamaica suggest that "River Mumma" knows the location of "Paniol Jar" (Spanish Jar), which contains gold and silver treasure that the Spaniards buried when the English invaded the island (see Pradel, *African Beliefs in the New World*).

39. The orisha are closely associated with ecology and human relationships. Inanimate objects are invested with a life force or ashé. Oshun's energy is the river, and through its power Oshun is able to heal. Hence Luisah Teish's observation in *Jambalayah*: "When the doctor fails, Oshun heals with cool water" (122). As priestess-in-training to Mrs. Cotton, Arnella leads the women down to the river to participate in a healing ritual.

Chapter 5. Power, Eros, and Genocide

1. I am comparing the slaveholding South to a totalitarian regime because its ownership of black bodies mimics the complete denial of subjectivity under totalitarian governments such as Rafael Trujillo's.

2. Significantly, Erzulie is also linked to Monica and Beloved (and Desmond, Sethe, and Paul D).

3. I moved to Miami in 1999 to take a university post, and *The Farming of Bones* immediately became a staple on my syllabus. At that time, the vast majority of my Haitian students had never heard of the massacre and expressed surprise that I, a non-Haitian, knew about it. I told them I only found out about it when I read *The Farming of Bones* and urged them to go home and ask their parents about the massacre. Some parents denied that it ever happened. A few said I should mind my own business. It became clear to me that the massacre was still a source of shame for many Haitians. The shame about being a victim of historical trauma is not so unusual. Many blacks in the Caribbean—certainly in Jamaica when I was growing up—were ashamed of slavery and wanted to distance themselves from a slave past. Almost ten years later, I am happy to report that when I teach *Farming of Bones,* the Haitian students know about the massacre, even when no one else in the class does. I believe Edwidge Danticat deserves the credit for this.

4. See Turits, "A World Destroyed," for a discussion of the racial dimension of anti-Haitianism in the Dominican Republic. Turits argues that the forms of anti-Haitianism that can be observed in the Dominican Republic today were not so pervasive before the massacre, and that Dominican national identity "was far from antithetical to or exclusive of Haitians and Haitian culture" (593). Prior to the massacre, the border towns consisted of a "transnational and bicultural frontier" of ethnic Dominicans and Haitians who intermarried or had conjugal relations and got along fairly well (594). He argues further that

Trujillo, in an attempt to construct a unified national identity for Dominicans, relied on a discourse of Dominican separateness and racial difference from Haitians that gave rise to the virulent anti-Haitianism that can be observed in the Dominican Republic today. Turits further contends that the Haitian massacre should be seen as a conflict between two visions of the Dominican national identity, and not as a result of anti-Haitianism in the Dominican Republic prior to the massacre.

5. Hereafter, *Farming of Bones* will be cited parenthetically.

6. Historians such as Michele Wucker are quick to point out that these many of these issues still exist today. Haitians are still migrating to the Dominican Republic to labor—for very little recompense—in conditions approximate to those of slavery.

7. The Massacre River did not earn its name from the 1937 massacre, but from an earlier incident in the eighteenth century when a gang of buccaneers were caught and killed by Spanish troops in this river that borders the Dominican Republic and Haiti (see Hicks, *Blood in the Streets*, 103).

8. Herndon, in "Return to Native Lands, Reclaiming the Other's Language," puts it another way: "In the case of Kincaid and Danticat the migrant either does not want to return to the poverty and lack of resources . . . or cannot be at home without those she has chosen to love" (2). And, in fact, after Amabelle is forced to return, living in Haiti without Sebastien is an almost impossible task. She leaves her heart and soul in her adopted homeland and cannot even summon the energy or desire to reestablish connections with her own extended family.

9. I am thinking about the kind of criticism that was leveled at Alice Walker's *The Color Purple*, for example. See Jenkins, "Queering Black Patriarchy," for an excellent response to Walker's harsh critics. Male critics commented harshly on the negative portrayal of black men. Although Morrison did not suffer the same harsh indictments as Walker, some of the relationships in her novels are also highly problematized. In *The Bluest Eye*, Cholly Breedlove beats his wife and rapes his daughter. In *Sula*, Jude sleeps with his wife's best friend. Similarly—and perhaps even more dramatically—Terry McMillan's *Waiting to Exhale* repeatedly underscores the ugly side of black heterosexual relationships. While I do not criticize these writers for inscribing that very real side of the black experience, the relationship between Amabelle and Sebastien represents a refreshing change and a balanced perspective.

10. Historians disagree on the exact number. Albert Hicks estimates from twenty thousand to twenty five thousand (see *Blood in the Streets* 112.) Michele Wucker estimates the number at thirty thousand ("The River Massacre" 1).

11. After Haiti fought for and won its independence from France in 1804, Haiti actively supported other liberation movements. South American liberator Simón Bolívar was "sheltered" and "funded" by Haiti before he liberated Venezuela, Colombia, Panama, and other South American colonies from Spanish rule (Davis, *The Serpent and the Rainbow* 70). For this reason, Haiti was considered a threat to the United States and other colonial powers. Haiti struggled in isolation as an independent black nation state, surrounded by superpowers that threatened its very right to exist by denying it diplomatic relations. Consequently, the history of the first black republic has been troubled, economically and politically unstable, and bloody. It is a history that records in blood the travails and

triumphs of New World blacks forging selfhood out of the legacy of slavery and colonialism, and the ongoing struggle to define black subjectivities against the metanarratives that labeled them chattel, expendable, subhuman beings existing only for the purpose of advancing the interests of European and American capitalism.

12. Erzulie, the loa of love and passion, is a very complex symbol of Haitian womanhood. Often constituted as a coquettish upper-class fair-skinned Haitian woman, she is sometimes associated with the darker working-class peasant women in her emanation as Erzulie-Dantor. My research renders multiple emanations and conflicting interpretations of this figure, which further confirms her complexity. Danticat, in an interview with Renèe Shea for *MaComère: The Journal of Caribbean Women Writers and Scholars*, responds that Erzulie "watches over all the women" in her stories. She also confirms my reading that neither Erzulie nor other popular Voudoun loas are transparently displayed in *Farming of Bones*.

13. In *Farming of Bones*, Danticat uses Isabela instead of Isabel, but the difference is too slight to hide the identity of the historical figure.

14. Dominican intellectuals and policymakers viewed Voudoun as a threat to Dominican nationality. Its pervasiveness in the Dominican Republic was said to be an impediment to progress and modernity (see Turits, "A World Destroyed, A Nation Imposed" 599).

15. See Renèe Shea, "The Hunger to Tell," for an interview with Danticat in which Danticat says "Erzulie is there in the work by both absence and presence" (19). I adapt the term "absent presence" from her usage.

16. See Murphy, *Working the Spirit*, for a definition of *konesans* (*connaissance*) (17).

17. See Métraux, *Voodoo in Haiti*, 120–24; and Laguerre 161–63.

18. There are variations in the spelling of this word. Unless quoting from a secondary source that uses a different spelling, I use the spelling favored by Maya Deren: ti bon ange.

19. In *The Serpent and the Rainbow* (not to be confused with the horrendously stereotypical and exploitative movie it generated that Davis himself calls "egregious" in an interview with Zach Dundas), Wade Davis agrees with Michel Laguerre that the secret societies of Haiti, such as the Bizango, Zobop, and Macandal, represent a "quasi political arm of the vodoun society charged above all with the protection of the community" (212). Davis argues that these societies are part of a vast underground network that possibly wields as much power as the political regime in Haiti.

20. When Joel is killed in *Farming of Bones*, Pico brings home a dead goat for Luis to prepare for a feast in honor of the birth of his children. The dead goat symbolizes Joel—the first confirmed Haitian victim in this text—and one of thousands who were sacrificed to Trujillo's self-deluding nationalism.

21. See Turits for an analysis of how Dominicans (intellectuals as well as ordinary folk) have historically refused to acknowledge a black identity, even though most Dominicans did not claim whiteness exclusively until Trujillo's regime mandated it (*Foundations of Despotism* 150).

22. All three indicate that the concern over zombification is one reason for the suspicion with which peasants view unexplained or sudden deaths. In addition, the corpses of

people who die from natural causes are also susceptible to malevolent priests and their clients.

23. Ink, in "Remaking Identity, Unmaking Nation," also concedes, after making much of the fact that there should be common ground between Kongo and Valencia, that the bond simply "cannot be" (805).

24. The first is when Amabelle's mother dismisses her dream of the doll and discounts her recollection of the dream as the ranting of an imbecile.

25. In *Face of the Gods*, Thompson calls trees "sentinels of the spirit" and outlines the significance of tree altars and shady groves as sacred spaces designated by Africans and their New World descendants as places of worship that enable spiritual growth and agency.

26. Paul Mercier, "The Fon of Dahomey" as quoted by Robert Farris Thompson in *Face of the Gods* (228).

27. "Ayida Wedo" is the popular spelling in some of the ethnographic representation of its usage in Haiti, while Da Ayido Hwedo is used to designate the original Fon term in Mercier (220). Laguerre spells it Aida Ouedo (32). Deren uses Damballah and Ayida to represent "sexual totality" (116). I will use Damballah and Ayida Wedo unless quoting from a source that spells these terms differently.

28. Desmangles informs us in *The Faces of the Gods* that when Erzulie is thus manifested, her devotees mimic her state of abjection by singing the song "Ezili, I have no bones (to support me)" (132–33).

29. Note that Danticat signals Amabelle's rich spiritual life in childhood before the death of her parents. She plays with her shadow and receives nightmares in which "voices twirl in a hurricane of rainbow colors" and "odd shapes of things rise up and speak to define themselves" (4). Her dream symbolizes the relationship between Damballah and Ayida Wedo. According to Brindha Mehta, Ayida Wedo "fuses with [Damballah] in a kaleidoscopic rain-bow like configuration to embrace a certain totality of union" (see Mehta, "Recreating Ayida-Wèdo," 654). From childhood, Amabelle is already primed for union with Sebastien and for a deep connection with her ancestral spirits.

30. Haiti is, of course, not alone in this. Many other Caribbean nations are also mortgaged to the IMF and the World Bank and exist in a neocolonial relationship to the superpowers, especially America. However, Haiti's continuous lack of political stability severely undermines its economic viability, placing Haiti far behind even other underdeveloped Caribbean nation states.

31. See Wiarda, *Dictator and Development*, for a detailed account of Trujillo's megalomania and the cult of personality he created to augment his power. He renamed every important monument on the island after himself, forced Dominicans to keep a prominent photo of him in their living rooms, and generally held the country in the grip of terror and mind control (Wiarda 124–46). Other historians insist that he demanded mistresses from the daughters of elder statesmen and other upper-class Dominican families. His tendency to foist himself upon beautiful young virgins is also mentioned in Julia Alvarez's novel *In the Time of the Butterflies*. After several generations of this pervasive ideological brainwashing, there were many Dominicans who came to believe that Trujillo was second only to God.

32. African diasporic peoples often use some version of the phrase "nothing ever happens before the time" to signal another way of understanding time that is not dependent upon a clock. Or, put another way, the concept of "black time" usually designates lateness or an inability to recognize linear time. This, according to John Mbiti, is because "the linear concept of time in Western thought, with an indefinite past, present, and infinite future, is practically foreign to African thinking" (21).

33. In *The Serpent and the Rainbow,* Wade Davis explains that the loas live in the "great water" and commute between the mythic homeland of Guineè and Haiti. He further states that they also choose to live in places of great beauty such as "the center of stones, the dampness of caves, and the depths of sunken wells" (172). Vera Rubin also confirms this in her foreword to Laguerre's *Voodoo Heritage.*

34. I have not been able to discover what papaya leaves symbolize in Haiti, but in Jamaica, papayas are symbols of infertility and peasant women often swallow the seeds as contraception. In Jamaican folklore, male papaya trees close to the house are said to promote illness and induce infertility in men. In *Farming of Bones,* "wet papaya leaves" seems to register the lushness and sensuality of the sexual experience. However, the fact that Amabelle does not become pregnant by Sebastien, and her linking of her first sexual experience to death, suggests intercultural links between Haitian and Jamaican folklore. There are intertextual links here as well. Like Janie in *Their Eyes Were Watching God,* Amabelle bears no children from her sexual encounters. As with Janie, Amabelle's childlessness forces the reader to concentrate on Amabelle and her evolving consciousness. Interestingly, the sugar woman morphs into Amabelle's mother the last time she comes to her in a dream. This complicates but does not contradict my reading of her as Haiti, as I think Amabelle's mother also symbolizes the nation of Haiti. It is beyond the scope of my analysis to interrogate this idea fully, but the notion of "mother/mother-country" extant in the critiques of Jamaica Kincaid's *Annie John* are especially useful and applicable.

35. Not only is Metrès Dlo being evoked here as Amabelle's protector in the river, but the Guedes, "the spirits of the dead," are also being evoked. Baron Samedi is a Guede who protects the cemeteries and the Massacre River is a cemetery for many murdered Haitians. See Laguerre for an explanation of the Guedes's role (95).

Epilogue

1. See www.southafrica.info/about/history/saartjie.htm for the full article and poem.

2. Dr. Willa Boezak, a South African activist who fights tirelessly for the rights of the Khoisan people and spearheaded the movement to bring Sara home, has this to say on the matter of Sara Baartman's choice: "She was taken, not against her will, but under false pretenses, by unscrupulous men."

3. Ann M. Simmons, "A South African Native's Homecoming." *Los Angeles Times/World,* Saturday May 4, 2002.

4. See Thulani Davis, "The Height of Disrespect"; Crenshaw, "Beyond Racism and Misogyny"; and Ayanna, "The Exploitation of Women in Hip-Hop Culture."

Works Cited

Adam, Ian, and Helen Tiffin, eds. *Past the Last Post: Theorizing Post-Colonialism and Post-Modernism*. Calgary: University of Calgary Press, 1990.
Adisa, Opal Palmer. *Bake-Face and Other Guava Stories*. Berkeley: Kelsey St. Press, 1986.
———. *It Begins with Tears*. Oxford: Heinemann, 1997.
Akbar, Na'im. "Rhythmic Patterns in African Personality." In *Akbar Papers in African Psychology*, ed. Na'im Akbar, 123–34. Tallahassee, Fla.: Mind Productions and Associates, 2004.
Alvarez, Julia. *In the Time of the Butterflies*. New York: Plume Books, 1995.
Alexander, Elizabeth. *The Venus Hottentot*. Charlottesville: University of Virginia Press, 1990.
Andrews, William and Nellie Y. McKay, eds. *Toni Morrison's Beloved: A Casebook*. York: Oxford University Press, 1999.
Ani, Marimba (Dona Marimba Richards). *Let the Circle Be Unbroken: The Implications of African Spirituality in the Diaspora*. Trenton, N.J.: Red Sea Press, 1994.
Appiah, Anthony, and Amy Gutman. *Color Conscious: The Political Morality of Race*. Princeton: Princeton University Press, 1996.
Auerbach, Nina. "The Rise of the Fallen Woman." *Nineteenth Century Fiction* 35.1 (June 1980): 29–52.
Awkward, Michael. *Inspiriting Influences: Tradition, Revision, and Afro-American Women's Novels*. New York: Columbia University Press, 1989.
———, ed. *New Essays on "Their Eyes Were Watching God."* New York: Cambridge University Press, 1990.
Ayanna. "The Exploitation of Women in Hip-Hop Culture." www.mysistahs.org/features/hiphop.htm.
Baker, Houston A. *Blues, Ideology, and Afro-American Literature: A Vernacular Theory*. Chicago and London: University of Chicago Press, 1984.
———. *Workings of the Spirit: The Poetics of Afro-American Women's Writing*. Chicago and London: University of Chicago Press, 1991.
Baker, William. "William Wilberforce on the Idea of Negro Inferiority." *Journal of the History of Ideas* 31:3 (July 1970): 433–40.
Bakhtin, M. M. *The Dialogic Imagination*. Austin: University of Texas, 1981.
Barrett, Leonard. *The Sun and the Drum*. Kingston: Sangster's Book Store, 1976.
Bassard, Katherine Clay. *Spiritual Interrogations: Culture, Gender, and Community in*

Early African American Women's Writing. Princeton: Princeton University Press, 1999.

Bernabé, Jean, Patrick Chamoiseau, and Raphael Confiant, *Éloge de la Créolité/In Praise of Creoleness*. Translated by M. B. Taleb-Khyar. Paris: Gallimard, 1993.

Berthrong, John. "Love, Lust, and Sex: A Christian Perspective." *Buddhist-Christian Studies* 24 (2004): 3–22.

Berzon, Judith R. *Neither White nor Black: The Mulatto Character in American Fiction*. New York: New York University Press, 1978.

Besson, Jean. "Reputation and Respectability Reconsidered: A New Perspective on Afro-Caribbean Peasant Woman." In *Women and Change in the Caribbean*, edited by Janet Momsen, 15–37. Kingston: Ian Randle, 1993.

———. "Land Tenure in the Free Villages of Trelawny, Jamaica: A Case Study in the Caribbean Peasant Response to Emancipation." *Slavery and Abolition* 5, no. 1 (May 1984): 3–23.

Bhabha, Homi K. *The Location of Culture*. London and New York: Routledge, 1994.

Bisnauth, Dale. *History of Religions in the Caribbean*. New Jersey: First Africa World Press, 1996.

Boyce Davies, Carole. "Mobility, Embodiment and Resistance." In *Black Women, Writing and Identity: Migrations of the Subject*. New York: Routledge, 1994.

———. *Moving Beyond Boundaries: International Dimensions of Black Women's Writings*. Vol 1. New York: New York University Press, 1995.

Boyd, Valerie. *Wrapped in Rainbows: The Life of Zora Neale Hurston*. New York: Scribner, 2003.

Brandon, George. *Santeria from Africa to the New World: The Dead Sell Memories*. Indianapolis: Indiana University Press, 1993.

Brathwaite, Edward. "Kumina: The Spirit of African Survival in Jamaica" *Savacou Working Paper* 4 (1982): 44–63.

Bush, Barbara. *The Slave Woman and Slave Resistance*. Kingston: Ian Randle Press, 1990.

Cambridge, Alrick. "The Beauty of Valuing Black Culture." In *Resituating Identities: The Politics of Race, Ethnicity, and Culture*, edited by Vered Amit-Talai and Caroline Knowles, 91-102. Ontario: Broadway Press, 1990.

Canizares, Raul. *Cuban Santeria: Walking With the Night*. Rochester, Vermont: Destiny Books, 1993.

Carby, Hazel. "The Politics of Fiction, Anthropology, and the Folk: Zora Neale Hurston." In *New Essays on Their Eyes Were Watching God*, edited by Michael Awkward, 71–93. New York: Cambridge University Press, 1990.

———. *Reconstructing Womanhood: The Emergence of the Afro-American Woman Novelist*. New York: Oxford University Press 1987.

Carden, Mary P. "Models of Memory and Romance: The Dual Endings of Toni Morrison's *Beloved*." *Twentieth Century Literature* 45 (Winter 1999): 401–427.

Chancy, Myriam J. A. *Framing Silence: Revolutionary Novels by Haitian Women*. New Brunswick, N.J.: Rutgers University Press, 1997.

Chestnutt, Charles W. "The Goophered Grapevine," *The Norton Anthology of African*

American Literature. Henry Louis Gates Jr., Nellie McKay, and Barbara Christian, eds. 523-32. New York: W.W. Norton & Company, 1997.

Christian, Barbara. *Black Women Novelists: The Development of a Tradition, 1892–1976.* Westport, Ct.: Greenwood Press, 1980.

———. "The Race for Theory." *Cultural Critique* 6 (Spring 1987): 51–63.

———. "Fixing Methodologies." In *Female Subjects in Black and White: Race, Psychoanalysis, Feminism,* edited by Elizabeth Abel, Barbara Christian, Helen Moglen, 363–370. Berkeley: University of California Press, 1997.

Clark, VèVè. "Developing Diaspora Literacy and Marassa Consciousness." *Comparative American Identities,* edited by Hortense Spillers, 40–61. New York: Routledge, 1991.

Cliff, Michelle. "If I Could Write This in Fire, I Would Write This in Fire." In *If I Could Write This in Fire: An Anthology of Literature from the Caribbean,* edited by Pamela Maria Smorkaloff. New York: New Press, 1990.

———. "'I Found God in Myself and I Loved Her, I Loved Her Fiercely': More Thoughts on the Work of Black Women Artists." *Journal of Feminist Studies in Religion* 2.1 (Spring 1986): 7–39.

Comfort, Susan. "Counter-Memory, Mourning and History in Toni Morrison's *Beloved.*" *LIT: Literature Interpretation Theory* 6.1-2 (1995): 121-132.

Conrad, Joseph. *Heart of Darkness.* New York: W.W. Norton & Company, 2006.

Cooper, Carolyn. *Sound Clash: Jamaican Dancehall Culture at Large.* New York: Palgrave Macmillan, 2004.

Crenshaw, Kimberlé. "Beyond Racism and Misogyny: Black Feminism and 2 Live Crew." *Boston Review: A Political and Literary Forum.* http://bostonreview.net/BR16.6/crenshaw.html.

Danticat, Edwidge. *Breath, Eyes, Memory.* New York: Soho Press, 1994.

———. *The Farming of Bones.* New York: Penguin Books, 1998.

———. *Krik? Krak!* New York: Vintage, 1996.

Dash, Michael J. *Culture and Customs of Haiti.* Westport, Ct.: Greenwood Press, 2001.

Davis, Angela Y. *Women, Race and Class.* New York: Vintage Books, 1983.

———. "Reflections on the Black Woman's Role in the Community of Slaves." *Black Scholar* 3, no.4 (December 1971): 2–15.

Davis, Rod. *American Voudou: Journey into a Hidden World.* Denton: University of North Texas Press, 1999.

Davis, Thadious M. *Nella Larsen, Novelist of the Harlem Renaissance: A Woman's Life Unveiled.* Baton Rouge: Louisiana State University Press, 1994.

Davis, Thulani. "The Height of Disrespect." *Village Voice,* March 9, 2004.

Davis, Wade. *Passage of Darkness: The Ethnobiology of the Haitian Zombie.* Chapel Hill: University of North Carolina Press, 1988.

———. *The Serpent and the Rainbow.* New York: Warner Books, 1985.

Dawes, Kwame. *Natural Mysticism: Towards a New Reggae Aesthetic in Caribbean Writing.* Leeds, UK: Peepal Tree Press, 1999.

Dayan, Joan. "Erzulie: A Women's History of Haiti." In *The Woman, the Writer and Caribbean Society,* edited by Helen Pyne-Timothy, 41–66. Los Angeles: Center for Afro-American Studies Publications, 1998.

———. *Haiti, History and the Gods*. Berkeley and Los Angeles: University of California Press, 1998.

Dearborn, Mary. *Pocahontas' Daughters; Gender and Ethnicity in American Culture*. New York: Oxford University Press, 1986.

Derby, Lauren. "The Dictator's Seduction: Gender and State Spectacle During the Trujillo Regime." *Callaloo* 23:3 (2000): 1112–46.

Deren, Maya. *Divine Horsemen: The Living Gods of Haiti*. New York: McPherson, 1953.

Desmangles, Leslie G. *The Faces of the Gods: Vodou and Roman Catholicism in Haiti*. Chapel Hill and London: University of North Carolina Press, 1992.

Douglass, Frederick. *Narrative of the Life of Frederick Douglass*. New York and London: Penguin Books, 1982.

Dube, Saurabh. "Introduction: Colonialism, Modernity, Colonial Modernities." *Nepantla: Views from South* 3.2 (2002): 197–219.

Du Bois, W.E.B. "Two Novels." *Crisis* 35 (June 1928): 202.

DuPlessis, Rachel Blau. "Power, Judgment, and Narrative in a Work of Zora Neale Hurston: Feminist Cultural Studies." *New Essays on "Their Eyes Were Watching God,"* edited by Michael Awkward, 95-123. Cambridge: Cambridge University Press, 1990.

Dupuy, Alex. *Haiti in the World Economy: Class, Race, and Underdevelopment Since 1700*. Boulder, Colo.: Westview Press, 1987.

———. *Haiti in the New World Order: The Limits of Democratic Revolution*. Boulder, Colo.: Westview Press, 1997.

Edmondson, Belinda. *Making Men: Gender, Literary Authority and Women's Writing in Caribbean Narrative*. Durham: Duke University Press, 1999.

———. "Race, Tradition, and the Construction of the Caribbean Aesthetic." *New Literary History* 25 (1994): 109–20.

Edwards, Gary, and John Mason. *Black Gods—Orisha Studies in the New World*. New York: Yoruba Theological Archministry, 1985.

Eyerman, Ron. "Modernity and Social Movements." In *Social Change and Modernity*, Hans Haferkamp and Neil Smelser, eds. Berkeley and Los Angeles: University of California Press, 1992.

Fauset, Jessie Redmon. *Plum Bun: A Novel without a Moral*. London: Pandora Press, 1985.

Fields, Karen. "To Embrace Dead Strangers: Toni Morrison's Beloved." In *Mother Puzzles: Daughters and Mothers in Contemporary American Literature*, edited by Mickey Pearlman, 159-169. Westport, CT: Greenwood Press, 1989.

Fitzgerald, Jennifer. "Selfhood and Community: Psychoanalysis and Discourse in *Beloved*." *Modern Fiction Studies* 39 (1993): 669-87.

Foote, Julia A. J. *A Brand Plucked from the Fire: An Autobiographical Sketch (1886)*. In *Spiritual Narratives: The Schomburg Library of Nineteenth Century Black Women Writers*. New York: Oxford University Press (1988).

Francis, Donette A. "'Silences Too Horrific to Disturb': Writing Sexual Histories in Edwidge Danticat's *Breath, Eyes, Memory*." *Research in African Literatures* 35.2 (2004): 75–90.

Fry, Gladys-Marie. *Stitched From the Soul: Slave Quilts From the Ante-Bellum South*. New York: Dutton Books, 1990.
Fulani, Ifeona. "Caribbean Women Writers and the Politics of Style: A Case for Literary Anancyism." *Small Axe* 17 (March 2005): 64–79.
Gates, Henry Louis, Jr. *The Signifying Monkey: A Theory of African-American Literary Criticism*. New York: Oxford University Press, 1988.
———. "Zora Neale Hurston and the Speakerly Text." In *Zora Neale Hurston's "Their Eyes Were Watching God," A Casebook*, edited by Cheryl Wall, 59–116. New York: Oxford University Press, 2000.
Giddings, Paula. "The Last Taboo." In *Words of Fire*, edited by Beverly Guy Sheftall, 414–28. New York: New Press, 1995.
———. *When and Where I Enter: The Impact of Black Women on Race and Sex in America*. New York and London: Bantam Books, 1984.
Gikandi, Simon. *Writing in Limbo: Modernism and Caribbean Literature*. Ithaca: Cornell University Press, 1992.
Gilman, Sander. "Black Bodies, White Bodies: Toward an Iconography of Female Sexuality in Late Nineteenth-Century Art, Medicine, and Literature." *Critical Inquiry* 12.1 (Autumn 1985): 204-242.
Gordon, Edmund T., and Mark Anderson. "The African Diaspora: Toward an Ethnography of Diasporic Identification." *Journal of American Folklore* 112.445, Theorizing the Hybrid. (Summer 1999): 282–96.
Hall, Stuart. "Negotiating Caribbean Identities." *New Left Review* 209 (January–February 1995): 3–15.
Haas, Robert. "Might Zora Neale Hurston's Janie Woods Be Dying of Rabies? Considerations From Historical Medicine." *Literature and Medicine* 19.2 (2000): 205-228.
Hammon, Jupiter. "An Address to Miss Phillis Wheatley." *Early Negro Writing, 1760-1837*. Ed. Dorothy Porter. Baltimore: Black Classic Press, 1995. 535-537.
Hammonds, Evelyn M. "Towards a Genealogy of Black Female Sexuality: The Problematic of Silence." In *Feminist Genealogies, Colonial Legacies, Democratic Futures*, edited by M. Jacqui Alexander and Chandra Mohanty, 93-104. New York: Routledge, 1997.
Harper, Francis Ellen Watkins. *Iola Leroy*. Boston: Beacon Press, 1987.
Helms, Janet. *Black and White Racial Identity: Theory, Research and Practice*. New York: Greenwood Press, 1990.
Hemenway, Robert E. "The Personal Dimension in *Their Eyes Were Watching God*." In *New Essays on "Their Eyes Were Watching God,"* edited by Michael Awkward. Cambridge: Cambridge University Press, 1990.
———. *Zora Neale Hurston: A Literary Biography*. Chicago: University of Illinois Press, 1980.
Henderson, Mae Gwendolyn. "Speaking in Tongues: Dialogics, Dialectics, and the Black Woman Writer's Literary Tradition." In *Reading Black, Reading Feminist: A Critical Anthology*, edited by Henry Louis Gates Jr., 116-42. New York: Meridian Books, 1990.
Herndon, Gerise. "Return to Native Lands, Reclaiming the Other's Language: Kincaid and Danticat." *Journal of International Women's Studies* 3:1 (2001): 1–9.

Hicks, Albert C. *Blood in the Streets: The Life and Rule of Trujillo*. New York: Creative Age Press, 1946.

Hindman, Jane E. "'A Little Space, A Little Time, Some Way to Hold off Eventfulness': African American Quiltmaking as Metaphor in Toni Morrison's Beloved." LIT: Literature Interpretation Theory. 6 (1995): 101-120.

Holloway, Karla F. C. *Moorings & Metaphors: Figures of Culture and Gender in Black Women's Literature*. New Brunswick, N.J.: Rutgers University Press, 1992.

Hopkins, Pauline. *Contending Forces*. New York: Oxford University Press, 1988.

hooks, bell. *Ain't I a Woman: black women and feminism*. Boston: South End Press, 1981.

———. *Talking Back: Thinking Feminist, Thinking Black*. Boston: South End Press, 1989.

Houchins, Sue E. Introduction to *Spiritual Narratives: The Schomburg Library of Nineteenth Century Black Women Writers*, edited by Houchins. New York: Oxford University Press, 1988.

Hughes, Langston. "The Blues I'm Playing." In *The Norton Anthology: African American Literature*, edited by Henry Louis Gates Jr. and Nellie McKay, 1267–82. New York: Norton, 1997.

Hull, Gloria T. *Color, Sex and Poetry: Three Women Writers of the Harlem Renaissance*. Bloomington: Indiana University Press, 1987.

Hurston, Zora Neale. "How it Feels to Be Colored Me." In *I Love Myself When I am Laughing . . .*," edited by Alice Walker. New York: Feminist Press of the City University of New York, 1979.

———. *Their Eyes Were Watching God*. New York: HarperCollins, 1990.

———. *Mules and Men*. Bloomington: Indiana University Press, 1978.

———. *Tell My Horse: Voodoo and Life in Haiti and Jamaica*. New York: Harper and Row, 1990.

Huxley, Francis. *The Invisibles: Voodoo Gods in Haiti*. New York: McGraw-Hill Book Company, 1969.

Ink, Lynn Chun. "Remaking Identity, Unmaking Nation: Historical Recovery and the Reconstruction of Community in *In the Time of the Butterflies* and *The Farming of Bones*." Callaloo 27:3 (2004): 788–807.

Jacobs, Harriet. *Incidents in the Life of a Slave Girl*. In *The Classic Slave Narratives*, edited by Henry Louis Gates Jr. New York: Penguin, 1987.

James, C.L.R. *The Black Jacobins: Toussaint L'Overture and the San Domingo Revolution* New York: Vintage Books, 1989.

———. "The Presence of Blackness in the Caribbean and its Impact on Culture." In *At the Rendezvous of Victory*, 2118–35. London: Allison and Busby, 1984.

Jenkins, Candice M. "Queering Black Patriarchy: The Salvific Wish and Masculine Possibility in Alice Walker's *The Color Purple*." Modern Fiction Studies 48.4 (Winter 2002): 969-1000.

———. *Private Lives, Proper Relations: Regulating Black Intimacy*. Minneapolis, MN: University of Minnesota Press, 2007.

Johnson, Barbara. "Metaphor, Metonymy, and Voice in *Their Eyes Were Watching God*."

In *Zora Neale Hurston's Their Eyes Were Watching God: A Casebook*, edited by Cheryl A. Wall, 41–58. New York: Oxford University Press, 2000.

Johnson, Kelli Lyon. "Both Sides of the Massacre: Collective Memory and Narrative on Hispaniola." *Mosaic* 36:2 (2003): 75–92.

Joyner, Charles. "'Believer I Know': The Emergence of African-American Christianity." In *African-American Christianity: Essays in History*, edited by Paul E. Johnson, 18-46. Berkeley and Los Angeles: University of California Press, 1994.

Kaplan, Carla. "The Erotics of Talk: That Oldest Human Longing" in *Their Eyes Were Watching God*." In *Zora Neale Hurston's Their Eyes Were Watching God: A Casebook*, edited by Cheryl A. Wall, 137–63. New York: Oxford University Press, 2000.

———, ed. *Passing, Nella Larsen: A Norton Critical Edition*. New York: Norton, 2007.

Keizer, Arlene. *Black Subjects: Identity Formation in the Contemporary Narrative of Slavery*. Ithaca: Cornell University Press, 2004.

Kincaid, Jamaica. *Annie John*. New York: Farrar, 1983.

Krehm, William. *Democracies and Tyrannies of the Caribbean*. Westport: Lawrence Hill, 1984.

Krumholz, Linda. "The Ghosts of Slavery: Historical Recovery in Toni Morrison's *Beloved*." In *Toni Morrison's Beloved: A Casebook*, edited by William L. Andrews and Nellie Y. McKay, 107-25. New York: Oxford University Press, 1999.

Laguerre, Michel S. *Voodoo Heritage* 98. London: Sage Publications, 1980.

Lamming, George. *The Pleasures of Exile*. London: Allison and Busby, 1984.

Lamothe, Daphne. "Vodou Imagery, African American Tradition, and Cultural Transformation in Zora Neale Hurston's *Their Eyes Were Watching God*." In *Zora Neale Hurston's "Their Eyes Were Watching God," A Casebook*, edited by Cheryl A. Wall, 165–87. New York: Oxford University Press, 2000.

Lane, Dorothy. *The Island as Site of Resistance: An Examination of Caribbean and New Zealand Texts*. New York: Peter Lang, 1995.

Larsen, Nella. *Quicksand and Passing*. New Brunswick, N.J.: Rutgers University Press, 1986.

Lee, Jarena. "Religious Experiences and Journal of Mrs. Jarena Lee." In *Spiritual Narratives*, edited by Sue E. Houchins. Oxford University Press, 1988.

Levine, Lawrence W. *Black Culture and Black Consciousness*. New York: Oxford University Press, 1977.

Lorde, Audre. "Uses of the Erotic: The Erotic as Power." In *Sister Outsider*, edited by Audre Lorde, 53-59. New York: Crossing Press, 1984.

Mandel, Naomi. "'I Made the Ink': Identity, Complicity, 60 Million, and More." *Modern Fiction Studies* 48.3 (2002): 581-613.

Mbiti, John S. *African Religions and Philosophies*. Oxford: Heinemann, 1969.

McAlister, Elizabeth. *Rara! Vodou, Power, and Performance in Haiti and Its Diaspora*. Berkeley and Los Angeles: University of California Press, 2002.

McDowell, Deborah E. Introduction to *Plum Bun: A Novel without a Moral*, by Jessie Redmon Fauset. Boston: Pandora Press, 1985.

———. *"The Changing Same": Black Woman's Literature, Criticism, and Theory*. Bloomington: Indiana University Press, 1995.

———. Introduction to *"Quicksand" and "Passing,"* by Nella Larsen. New Brunswick: N.J: Rutgers University Press, 1986.

McKay, Claude. *Home to Harlem*. Chatham, N.J.: Chatham Bookseller, 1973.

———. www.poemhunter.com/claude-mckay.

McKay, Nellie. "Crayon Enlargements of Life": Zora Neale Hurston's *Their Eyes Were Watching God* as Autobiography. In *New Essays on "Their Eyes Were Watching God,"* edited by Michael Awkward. Cambridge: Cambridge University Press, 1990.

Mehta, Brinda. "Recreating Ayida-Wèdo: Feminizing the Serpent in Lilas Desquiron's Les Chemins de Loco-Miroir." *Callaloo* 25.2 (2002): 654–70.

Mercier, Paul. "The Fon of Dahomey." In *African Worlds: Studies in the Cosmological Ideas and Social Values of African Peoples*, edited and with an introduction by Daryll Forde, 210-234. London: Oxford University Press, 1954.

Métraux, Alfred. *Voodoo in Haiti*. New York: Schocken Books, 1972.

Mintz, Sidney, and Sally Price. *Caribbean Contours*. Baltimore: Johns Hopkins University Press, 1985.

Mitchell, Carolyn A. "'I Love to Tell the Story': Biblical Revisions in *Beloved*." In "Reconstructing the Word: Spirituality in Womens'Writing." Special issue, *Religion and Literature* 23:3 (Autumn 1991): 1–42.

Moglen, Helen. "Redeeming History: Toni Morrison's *Beloved*." In *Female Subjects in Black and White: Race, Psychoanalysis, Feminism*, edited by Elizabeth Abel, Barbara Christian, and Helen Moglen, 201-220. Berkeley: University of California Press, 1997.

Morrison, Toni. *Beloved*. New York: Knopf, 1987.

———, ed. *The Black Book*. Compiled by Middleton Harris, with the assistance of Morris Levitt, Roger Furman, and Ernest Smith. New York: Random House, 1974.

———. "Rootedness: The Ancestor as Spiritual Foundation." In *Black Women Writers (1950–1980): A Critical Evaluation*, edited by Mari Evans, 339–45. Garden City, N.Y.: Anchor/Doubleday, 1984.

———. *Sula*. New York: Knopf, 1974.

———. "The Site of Memory." *Inventing the Truth: The Art and Craft of Memoir*. Ed. William Zinsser. Boston: Houghton Mifflin Co., 1987.

———. "Unspeakable Things, Unspoken: The Afro-American Presence in American Literature." In *Toni Morrison*, edited by Harold Bloom, 201-230. New York; Chelsea House, 1990.

Murphy, Joseph. *Working the Spirit: Ceremonies of the African Diaspora*. Boston: Beacon Press, 1994.

———. "Black Religion and Black Magic: Prejudice and Protection in Images of African-derived Religions." In *Religion* 20.4 (October 1990): 323-337.

Naipaul, V. S. *Miguel Street*. London: Penguin Books, 1971.

Naylor, Gloria. "Love and Sex in the Afro-American Novel." *Yale Review* 78 (Autumn 1988): 19–31.

———. *Mama Day*. New York: Vintage Books, 1989.

Neimark, Phillip John. *The Way of the Orisha: Empowering Your Life Through the Ancient African Religion of Ifa*. San Francisco: HarperSanFrancisco, 1993.

Nicholls, Peter. "The Belated Postmodern: History, Phantoms, and Toni Morrison." *Psychoanalytic Criticism: A Reader*, edited by Sue Vice, 50-74. Cambridge: Polity Press, 1996.

Olmos, Margarite Fernandez, and Lizabeth Paravisini-Gebert, eds. *Sacred Possessions: Vodou, Santeria, Obeah, and the Caribbean*. New Brunswick, N.J.: Rutgers University Press, 2000.

Page, Phillip. "Circularity in Toni Morrison's *Beloved*." *African American Review* 26. 1 (Spring 1992): 31-39.

Patterson, Richard F. "Resurrecting Rafael: Fictional Incarnations of a Dominican Dictator." *Callaloo* 29.1 (2006): 223–37.

Peterson, Carla L. *"Doers of the Word": African-American Women Speakers and Writers in the North (1830–1880)*. New Brunswick, N.J: Rutgers University Press, 1998.

Pfeiffer, Kathleen. "The Limits of Identity in Jessie Fauset's *Plum Bun*." *Legacy* 18.1 (2001): 79–93.

Pradel, Lucie. *African Beliefs in The New World: Popular Literary Traditions of the Caribbean*. Translated by Catherine Bernard. New Jersey: Africa World Press, 2000.

———. "African Sacredness and Caribbean Cultural Forms" *Konversations in Kreole: Essays in Honour of Kamau Brathwaite*. Special Issue of *Caribbean Quarterly* 44.1–2. (March-June, 1998): 145–52.

Rahier, Jean. "The Presence of Blackness and Representation of Jewishness in the Afro-Esmeraldian Celebrations of the Semana Santa (Ecuador)." In *Representations of Blackness and the Performances of Identities*, edited by Jean Muteba Rahier. Westport, CT: Greenwood Press, 1999.

Rich, Adrienne. "Compulsory Heterosexuality and Lesbian Existence (1980)." *Journal of Women's History* 15.3 (Autumn) 2003:11-48.

Rody, Caroline. "Toni Morrison's *Beloved*: History 'Rememory,' and a "Clamor for a Kiss.'" *New Literary History* 7.1 (1995): 92-119.

Rubin, Vera. "Foreword" In Michel Laguerre *Voodoo Heritage*, London: Sage Publications, 1980.

Ruffin, Josephine St. Pierre. "Address of Josephine St. Pierre Ruffin." *The Women's Era* 2.5 (August 1895): 13-15.

Ryan, Judylyn S. "Spirituality and/as Ideology in Black Women's Writing: The Preaching of Maria W. Stewart and Baby Suggs, Holy." In *Women, Preachers and Prophets Through Two Millennia of Christianity*, edited by Beverly Mayne Kienzle and Pamela J. Walker, 267–87. Berkeley and Los Angeles: University of California Press, 1998.

———. *Spirituality as Ideology in Black Women's Film and Literature*. Charlottesville: University of Virginia Press, 2005.

Schuyler, George. "The Negro Art Hokum." In *The Norton Anthology of African-American literature*, edited by Henry Louis Gates Jr. Nellie Y. McKay et al., 1170–74. New York: Norton, 1997.

Seaga, Edward. "Revival Cults in Jamaica." *Jamaica Journal* 3.2 (1990): 3–15.

Senior, Olive. *Summer Lightning and Other Stories*. Harlow, Essex: Longman Caribbean, 1986.

Shange, Ntozake. *For Colored Girls Who Have Considered Suicide When the Rainbow is Enuf.* New York: Scribner Poetry/Scribner, 1975.

Shea, Renèe. "'The Hunger to Tell': Edwidge Danticat and the *Farming of Bones*." *Ma-Comère: Journal of the Association of Caribbean Writers and Scholars* 2 (1999): 12–22.

Shemak, April. "Re-membering Hispaniola: Edwidge Danticat's *The Farming of Bones*." *Modern Fiction Studies* 48:1 (2002): 83–122.

Sherrard-Johnson, Cherene. "'A Plea for Color': Nella Larsen's Iconography of the Mulatta," *American Literature* 76.4 (2004): 833–69.

Simmons, Ann M. "A South African Native's Homecoming." *Los Angeles Times/World*, 4 May 2002.

Smith, Barbara. *Home Girls: A Black Feminist Anthology.* New Brunswick, N.J.: Rutgers University Press, 2000.

Sommer, Doris. "Resisting the Heat: Menchū, Morrison and Incompetent Readers." In *Cultures of United States Imperialism*, edited by Amy Kaplan and Donald E. Pease, 407–432. Durham, N.C.: Duke University Press, 1993.

Spencer, Suzette. "Shall We Gather at the River?: Ritual, Benign Forms of Injury, and the Wounds of Displaced Women in Opal Palmer Adisa's *It Begins with Tears*." *Ma-Comére: the Journal of the Association of Caribbean Women Writers and Scholars* 4 (2001): 108–18.

Stewart, Maria. "Religion and the Pure Principles of Morality: The Sure Foundation on Which We Must Build." In *Spiritual Narratives: The Schomburg Library of Nineteenth Century Black Women Writers*, edited by Sue Houchins, 1-84. New York: Oxford University Press, 1988.

Tate, Claudia. *Domestic Allegories of Political Desire: The Black Heroine's Text at the Turn of The Century.* New York: Oxford University Press, 1992.

Teish, Luisah. *Jambalayah.* New York: Harper Collins, 1985.

———. "Women's Spirituality: An Household Act." In *Home Girls: A Black Feminist Anthology.* New Brunswick, N.J.: Rutgers University Press, 2000.

Thaggert, Miriam. "Racial Etiquette: Nella Larsen's *Passing* and the Rhinelander Case." *Meridians: Feminism, Race, Transnationalism* 5:2 (2005): 1–29.

Thompson, Robert Farris. *Flash of the Spirit: African & Afro-American Art and Philosophy.* New York: Vintage Books, 1984.

———. *Face of the Gods: Art and Altars of Africa and the African Americas.* New York: The Museum of African Art, 1993.

Thomson, Jim. "The Haitian Revolution and the Forging of America." *The History Teacher* 34:1 (2000) 19 pars. www.historycooperative.org/journals/ht/34.1/Thomsonhtml.

Thornton, Hortense E. "Sexism as Quagmire: Nella Larsen's *Quicksand*." *CLA Journal* 16.3 (March 1973): 285–300.

Tobin, Jacqueline L. and Raymond G. Dobard. *Hidden in Plain View: A Secret Story of Quilts and the Underground Railroad.* New York: Anchor Books, 2000.

Turits, Richard Lee. *Foundation of Despotism: Peasants, the Trujillo Regime, and Modernity in Dominican History.* Stanford: Stanford University Press, 2003.

———. "A World Destroyed, A Nation Imposed: The 1937 Massacre in the Dominican Republic." *Hispanic American Review* 82:3 (2002): 589–635.

Walcott, Derek. "The Muse of History." In *Is Massa Day Dead?: Black Moods in the Caribbean*, edited by Orde Coombs, 1–27. New York: Anchor-Doubleday, 1974.

Wall, Cheryl. "Passing for What? Aspects of identity in Nella Larsen's Novels." *Black American Literature Forum*, 20.1/2 (Spring 1986): 97–111.

———. *Women of the Harlem Renaissance*. Bloomington: Indiana University Press, 1995.

Washington, Mary Helen. "'I Love the Way Janie Crawford Left Her Husbands': Zora Neale Hurston's Emergent Female Hero." In *Zora Neale Hurston's Their Eyes Were Watching God, A Casebook*, edited by Cheryl A. Wall, 27-40. New York: Oxford University Press, 2000.

Weir-Soley, Donna. "Myth, Spirituality and the Power of the Erotic in *It Begins with Tears*." *MaComére: The Journal of the Association of Caribbean Women Writers and Scholars* 5 (2002): 243–50.

———. "Voudoun Symbolism in *The Farming of Bones*." *Obsidian III* 6.2 and 7.1 (Fall/Winter 2005-Spring/Summer 2006): 167-180.

———. "Baby Duppy." *The Caribbean Writer* 9 (1995): 21-22.

Welles, Sumner. *Naboth's Vineyard: The Dominican Republic, 1844–1924*. New York: Payson and Clark, 1928.

White, Deborah Gray. *Ar'n't I a Woman?: Female Slaves in the Plantation South*. New York: W.W. Norton & Company, 1985.

Wiarda, Howard. *Dictatorship and Development: The Methods of Control in Trujillo's Dominican Republic*. Gainesville: University of Florida Press, 1978.

Willis, Susan. *Specifying: Black Women Writing The American Experience*. Madison: University of Wisconsin Press, 1987.

Wilson, Harriet E. *Our Nig; or, Sketches from the Life of a Free Black*. New York: Random House, 1983.

Wilson, Peter. "Reputation and Respectability: A Suggestion for Caribbean Ethnology." *Man* 4.1 (1969): 70–84.

Wucker, Michelle. "The River Massacre: The Real and Imagined Borders of Hispaniola." www.windowsonhaiti.com/wucker1.shtml 30 June 2006.

———. *Why the Cocks Fight: Dominicans, Haitians and the Struggle for Hispaniola*. New York: Hill and Wang, 1999.

Wyatt, Jean. "Giving Body to the Word: The Maternal Symbolic in Toni Morrison's *Beloved*." *PMLA* 108.3 (May 1993): 474–88.

Index

Absent presence, Voudoun as, 10, 192–209, 227n9, 246n12
Abuse: physical, 55–56; sexual, 121, 122, 124, 130, 131, 136, 238n47
Activists, black female writers as, 11, 185
Adam Bede (Eliot), 16
Adaptation, 90, 117, 152, 153, 240n11. *See also* Resistance
Adisa, Opal Palmer, 4, 5, 11, 78, 96; *Bake-Face*, 142; diasporic literacy of, 141–42; erotic power codified by, 10; feminist agenda of, 146, 162, 163; Judeo-Christian doctrine and, 144–45, 147; mythology use by, 142, 145, 150. *See also It Begins with Tears*
Aesthetics, black female writers', 1–11, 79–80, 227nn1–3
African-American spirituality, 85, 88, 105
African civilizations, Thompson's study of, 82
African cosmology, 87–88; in *Beloved*, 8–9, 79, 81, 83–84, 86, 87–91, 96–97, 117–18, 234n3; chronicling of, 81; encoding of, 7, 61, 203, 208; eroticism implications in, 4–11; hierarchical system in, 84; interconnectedness understanding in, 84–85, 86, 235n10; sexuality in, 41, 64, 89–90; West, 3, 8, 86, 91, 141–51, 240n8. *See also* Syncretization, religious; Voudoun
African culture, 155, 181, 196, 197
African holocaust, 83
Africanness, 196, 197–98
Africans, as subhuman, 13–14
African spirituality, 5–6, 8, 60, 64, 88; Christianity syncretized with, 91, 235n19; color in, 108; Haitian culture informed by, 197; as literary intervention, 83, 235n7; retention of, 88. *See also* Religions
African-Western synthesis, 1, 227n1
Afro-Caribbean spirituality, 142–43

Agency, xiii, 9, 41, 91, 116, 124, 131; death and, 134–35
Agwe, 119
Akbar, Na'im, 84–85
Alegría, Amabelle's return to, 184, 187, 190, 208, 217
Amabelle (character), 184–85, 187–88, 203, 204, 208, 218; clairvoyance of, 195, 206; death of lover, 189, 190, 211; doll of, 195, 196, 210; as Haiti, 191, 208, 222; Haiti homeland of, 188, 245n8; Monica/Janie and, 184–85; parents' death, 203; sexual/spiritual healing of, 209–22; soulmate/epic love relation of, 189, 191; telling of her story to Metrès Dlo, 210
American Voudou: Journey into a Hidden World (R. Davis), 95
Amy Denver (character), 8, 94–95, 96
Anancy, Brother, 152, 241n13
Anatomy, black female, 12–14
Ancestral spirits, 98–99, 101, 102–3, 114; in *Bake-Face*, 142; in *Beloved*, 112–13; dancing to connect with, 105; presence of, 82–83; in *Their Eyes Were Watching God*, 61–62; veneration of, 85
Angel (character), 148; as bridge between modernity/tradition, 156–66; fear of darkness, 157–59
Angela Murray (character), 48–49
Ani, Marimba. *See* Richards, Dona Marimba
Animal sacrifice, 127, 238n49
Antelope, dance of, 105, 237n34
Archetypes. *See* Tragic Mulatta archetype
Arnella (character), 108, 148–49, 171–72; as Oshun/priestess-in-training, 149, 169, 170, 172–75; outdoor labor/birthing of, 149, 163, 242n21
Arts, 108, 141

Assault, on Monica. *See* Peppering
Auerbach, Nina, 16
Autobiography of an Ex-Colored Man (Johnson), 49
Autonomy: *Beloved* and, 117, 123–24, 130; *The Farming of Bones* and, 210; Haiti's desire for, 214, 247n30; Hurston's legacy and, 78; *It Begins with Tears* and, 182; Janie's desire for, 61–62; *Their Eyes Were Watching God* and, 78
Awkward, Michael, 76
Ayida Wédo. *See* Damballah/Ayida Wédo

Baartman, Sara (Saartjie), 3, 11, 13, 223, 224, 226, 248
Baby spirits, 101
Baby Suggs, holy (character), 85, 91, 98, 101–2, 104, 105–6, 169; Christianity of, 104; color contemplation by, 106, 107–8, 112–13; as conjure woman, 115; fixing ceremony of, 112–13, 116, 133, 136; quilt made by, 109, 112–13, 133–34; sexuality wisdom of, 136; spirit of, 115
Bake-Face (Adisa), 142
Baker, Houston, 6, 65–66, 70–71, 117
Bakhtinian model, 143–44, 239n4
Bakongo people, 102, 110
Baptism, 117, 175
Bassard, Katherine, 22, 37
Bathing, 177–78, 221, 244n39
Beauty, 45–46, 97
Beloved (character): arrival of, 121; Denver mobilized by, 134; as Erzulie, 89, 108, 118, 121, 131–40; exorcism/clearing of, 108, 114, 116–17; hypersexuality of, 89, 121; identities of, 9; lesbian aspect of, 132–33; Paul D and, 120–21, 124, 137, 138; possession of, 137; sexual "shining" of, 121, 138; Tea Cake compared to, 132, 138
Beloved (Morrison), 4, 79–140; African cosmology in, 8–9, 79, 81, 83–84, 86, 87–91, 96–97, 117–18, 234n3; ancestral presence in, 112–13; the clearing in, 90, 98, 101, 102, 114, 116, 117, 131–32; cloth in, 97–98; color in, 106–18; ethnography and, 8, 90, 138; fixing ceremony in, 106–18, 133, 136; folk wisdom in, 80; healing in, 114, 115, 116–17, 129; interpretive models for, 83, 85, 86; keeping room in, 113, 116; location of, 112; masculinity in, 121–30; place in, 98–103; quiltmaking in, 108–9, 133–34; slave men's thwarted sexuality in, 121–23; symbols use in, 81–82. *See also* Sethe
Berzon, Judith, 44
Besson, Jean, 173
Bestiality, 121, 122, 123
Bhabha, Homi, 151
Birth of a Nation, 123
The Black Book (edited by Morrison), 8, 80–81
Black communities: physical abuse in, 55–56; role of, 93–94
Black females: anatomy of, 12–14; blues singers, 25; Caribbean women linked with, 8, 105; first sexual protagonist, 33; nude display of, 13; slaves, 15–16, 18–19, 20, 179, 180, 215; stereotypes of, 12, 15–16, 56–57, 72, 179, 180. *See also* Sexuality, black female; Women; Women, black; Writers, black female
Black magic, 97
Black males, 13–14; distortion of sexuality in, 121–23; stereotypes of, 123; writers, 37, 39
Black place, The Bottom as, 99
Blacks, massacre killing of Haitian, 197–98
Blacksmith, in American slave society, 110
Black Subjects: Identity Formation in the Contemporary Narrative of Slavery (Keizer), 1, 3, 79, 90
Black women. *See* Black females; Women; Women, black
Black Women Novelists (Christian), 41, 43–44, 56
Body: Christianity and, 104; revaluing of, 106
Bottle trees, 93, 236n24
The Bottom, 99
Bourgeoisie, black, 18, 24, 26, 27, 36, 50, 230
Boyd, Valerie, 39
Brand, Sethe's mother's X symbol, 110, 111
Branding, 110
Bridges, 103–4
Brown, Kitty, 65

Cambridge, Alrick, 159
Capitalism, slave-based, 21
Carby, Hazel, 15–16, 18, 20, 21, 27; on *Quicksand*, 29–30, 31, 32, 33, 34, 230n24
Carden, Mary, 122

Caribbean, 86, 114, 176; African-American spirituality and, 105; Afro-Caribbean spirituality, 142–43; modernized African cultures of, 181; rural southern spirituality syncretized with, 43; writers from, 153, 154, 185
Cave, lovemaking in, 204, 219–20
Celibacy, 22, 138
Chamomile, 138–39, 238n58
Chancy, Myriam, 192
Character assassination, 17
Christian, Barbara, 59–60, 86; *Black Women Novelists*, 41, 43–44, 56; conversation with, 82; "The Race for Theory," 6, 180; tragic mulatta archetype discussed by, 43–44
Christianity, 21–22, 40, 91, 235n19; black, 2, 23–24, 62, 88, 104, 229n13, 233n30; body viewed in, 104; cult of true womanhood and, 21; Pukumina and, 148, 240n8; resistance tool as, 21–22; sex/sexual expression in African spiritual traditions v., 2, 4–5, 90, 170; slavery and, 21, 104. *See also* Syncretization, religious
Civilizations, Thompson's study of African, 82
Clairvoyance, 58, 195, 206. *See also Connaissance*; Seeyah women (seers)
Clare (character), tragic mulatta, 26–28, 52
Clark, VèVè, 53, 59, 79
"Classing off," Janie's, 66, 70
The Clearing, 90, 98, 101, 102, 114, 116, 117, 131–32
Cliff, Michelle, 77, 109, 242n25
Cloth, 97–98, 106–7, 108, 109–10; healing associated with, 98; quilts, 108–10, 112–13, 133–34, 237n39
Codes of resistance, 113
Collective intersubjectivity, 168, 169, 242n25
Color: in *Beloved*, 106–18; Egungun, 113, 114, 133–34; Erzulie, 107; healing, 108; in *It Begins with Tears*, 168, 171; as life/spiritual agency, 116; in quilts, 108
The Color Purple (Walker), 245n9
Comfort, Susan, 115
Communality: individuation and, 77, 117; quilting as, 108–9
Community, 55–56; elder of, Miss Beryl as, 159–61; healing of, 116–17; individuation and, 77, 117; *It Begins with Tears* and, 144, 159–66, 175–80; outsiders of, 162–66; ritual clearing of Beloved by, 114, 116–17; role of black, 93–94; slave, 179, 180; unrest in, *It Begins with Tears*, 145; well being of, 106, 116. *See also* Intersubjectivity
Conferral of personhood, 37
Conjure, 66, 67, 71, 115
Connaissance, 10, 194, 206, 218
Conrad, Joseph, *Heart of Darkness*, 157
Cooper, Carolyn, xiii
Cornmeal, drawing with, 201
Cosmology. *See* African cosmology; New World cosmologies; West African cosmology
Courtly masculinity, 123, 124
Cows, 51, 121, 122, 131, 136, 238n47
Creation mythology, 64
Creole language, 70, 91, 92, 143, 145, 146, 198, 239n3, 239n5
Creolization, 6, 90, 103, 105, 116, 117, 145, 152, 181, 208
Crossroads: Legba as spirit of, 103–4, 119, 152, 198; X cross symbol of, 112
Cross symbol, Kongo, 110–12
Cuba, orisha worship in, 108
Cuisine, adaptation and, 152
Cult of true womanhood, 15–16, 18, 21, 22–23, 29, 229n12; *Beloved* and, 94, 128; *Their Eyes Were Watching God* in context of, 42
Cultural resistance, black female, 174
Culture(s): African, 155, 181, 196, 197; Haitian, 197; Jamaican, 107, 152, 155, 176, 240nn11–13

Dã, 205, 206, 218
Damballah/Ayida Wédo, 203, 205–6, 219, 247n27, 247n29
Dance, 105, 111, 114, 147, 209, 237n33; antelope, 105, 237n34; hip-hop, xiii, 11, xivn1, 225
Danticat, Edwidge, 5, 11, 198; on Haitian massacre racial issues, 186–87; Hurston's groundwork and, 4. *See also The Farming of Bones*
Darkness, Angel's fear of, 157–59
Davis, Angela, 179, 180
Davis, Rod, 95
Davis, Thadious, 32
Davis, Thulani, xiii, 11
Davis, Wade, 119, 195–96, 197, 246n19

Dawes, Kwame, 155, 157, 162
Dayan, Joan, 8, 64, 120, 195
Dead: sending of, 203; spirit of, 113
Death, 110; agency and, 134–35; in *The Farming of Bones*, 189, 190, 199, 201–2, 203, 206, 211; Monica's v. Miss Madge, 150; orgasm as little, 206; of Sebastien, 189, 190, 211; sex and, 136; Tea Cake's, 51, 76; Trujillo's, 217; unnatural, 202; violent, 86–87; in Voudoun, 200
Deities: lesser, 84. *See also* God; Loa
Denver (character), 97, 113, 115; Beloved's mobilizing of, 134
Denver, Amy (character), 8, 94–95, 96
Deren, Maya, 7, 63
Desmangles, Leslie, 201
Devil/She-Devil (characters), 145–46, 147
Dialectics, of difference, 166–69
Diaspora, 59–60, 180
Diasporic literacy, 79, 86, 87, 93, 98, 109, 141–42
Difference: dialectics of, 166–69; language as marker of, 190
Difference-deviance model, 12–13, 14, 121
Disrobing, forced public, 46–47
Divination, 92–93
Dobard, Raymond, 109, 110, 112
Dog, rabid, 51
Doll, Amabelle's, 195, 196, 210
Double voice, 72
Douglass, Frederick, 18, 80, 228n5, 233n29
Dreams, 75, 88, 188, 194, 195, 216, 232n20, 247n24, 247n29, 248n34; interpretation through, 87
Dualisms, 104, 120, 132, 144–45
Dube, Saurabh, 153
DuBois, W.E.B., 49
Dunlop, William, 13

Ecstasy, religious, 33, 34
Ecuador, rural folk in, 156
Edmondson, Belinda, 154
Egungun (spirit of dead), 113, 114, 133–34
Ejagham, 82
Eliot, George, 16
Elite, 30, 49, 50
Empowerment, 37, 41, 54, 77, 135, 153, 179
Encoding, Voudoun, 7, 61, 203, 208

Epistemology, African-centered, 79
Equality, 49, 70, 74; in marriage, 57, 232n21
Eroticism: African cosmology implications of, 4–11; agency sourced in, 41; black female writers understanding of, 5, 10; corruption of, 169; empowerment from, 37, 41, 77, 135, 153, 179; female bonding, 176, 178; reclamation of, 37; spiritual definition of, 4. *See also* Spiritual-sexual syncretization
Eroticization, of mulatta figure, 46–47
Erotic power, xiv, 68–69, 77, 172, 174, 183; writers' expression of, 5, 10
Erzulie, 7, 8–9, 118, 119, 209–10, 227n7; Beloved as, 89, 108, 118, 121, 131–40; as both principle/embodiment, 119; color associated with, 107; -dantor, 9, 64, 70, 71, 76, 120, 121; emanations of, 70; ethnography on, 138; *The Farming of Bones* and, 209–10; -Freda, 64, 81–82, 120, 121; -ge-rouge, 64, 120, 121; Janie as, 7, 8–9, 69, 70, 185, 227n7; misreadings of, 120–21; object of gaze, 139; pilgrimage to, 219; restorative quality of, 121, 122; sexual desire normalized by, 136; sexuality of, 120, 136, 137; in *Their Eyes Were Watching God*, 7, 8–9, 40, 41, 69, 227n7; three aspects of, 64, 120
Eshu/Ellegua. *See* Legba (spirit of crossroads)
Esmeraldian society, 156
Eternal Valley, 145, 148–49, 150, 182–83
Ethnography: *Beloved* and, 8, 90, 138; Hurston's, 40, 59–60; Jamaican village, 173; Morrison's research, 8; Voudoun, 40, 59–60, 63, 192, 200
Europeans, black women portrayed by, 12–15
Evil spirits, 106–7
Exorcism, 108, 114, 115, 116–17
Exploitation, black female, 3, 11, 46–47; contemporary, xiii–xiv, xivn1, 11
Eyerman, Ron, 151

Face of the Gods (Thompson), 102
Family system, Jamaican, 173
Fanon, Frantz, 120, 197, 241
The Farming of Bones (Danticat), 4, 184–222; form of, 194; impromptu wake in, 204; intertextuality and, 184–85; location of, 187; postmassacre segments of, 210–12, 214; spiritual-sexual syncretization in, 219;

subjectivity formation in, 10; Voudoun in, 10, 192–209, 246n12
Fauset, Jessie, *Plum Bun*, 25, 34–36, 230n28
Female bonding, 176, 178
Females. *See* Black females; Women; Women, black; Writers, black female
Femininity, 59; Erzulie and, 120; Erzulie as symbol of, 209–10; Hurston's depiction of, 42, 231n3; integration/manhood and, 118; Jamaican, 239n6; nineteenth-century ideals of, 45; sexual empowerment opposed to, 54; white, 94. *See also* Cult of true womanhood
Feminism, Adisa's, 146, 162, 163
Fields, Karen, 128
Fire, spirit of, 119
Fishnet full of life, 76–77
Fixing ceremony, Baby Suggs's, 112–13, 116, 133, 136
Flash of the spirit, 93
Flash of the Spirit (Thompson), 82, 110, 125
Folk, 31–32, 53, 230n24; arts, 108; Ecuador, 156; identities, 31–32, 66–67, 74, 230n24; wisdom, 53, 64, 79–80, 176, 233n29
Folklore, 7, 60, 107, 176, 197
Forgiveness, intersubjectivity/community and, 177
Francis, Donette, 222
Freedom, Underground Railroad and, 109, 112, 237n39
Freud, Sigmund, 13
Fry, Gladys-Marie, *Stitched from the Soul*, 109
Fulani, Ifeona, 185

Garner (character), 121–23, 125
Garner, Margaret, 81, 82
Gates, Henry Louis, Jr., 6, 56, 78
Gender: racial oppression and, 5; roles, 164, 172, 176, 182, 243n36
Giddings, Paula, 17
Gikandi, Simon, 181
Gilman, Sander, 12, 13–14, 16
Goat, without horns, 197, 216
God: Dā as, 205, 218; Damballa/Ayida Wédo as, 203, 205, 247n27, 247n29; as inside, 77; of iron/war, 110, 125–27; in *It Begins with Tears*, 147; Judeo-Christian, 119; personal aspects of, 119; Voudoun loas and, 119
Goddess. *See* Loa

Godfree (character), 143, 147, 148, 167, 168, 172
Greek mythology, 117–18
Guineé, 75–76, 137, 234n42

Hair, beauty symbolized by, 97
Haiti, 188, 245n8; Amabelle as, 191, 208, 222; desire for autonomy, 214, 247n30; as first black republic, 245n11; Hurston in, 60, 62, 185, 201, 204; identity construction in, 195; leadership of, 215–16; as sugar woman, 214, 215; Trujillo's dismissal of, 196–97. *See also* Voudoun
Haitian massacre, 10, 184, 185, 191, 206, 245n10; Amabelle's loss of Sebastien in, 190; blacks killed in, 197–98; breaking silence surrounding, 186; Danticat's racial view of, 186–87; *The Farming of Bones* after, 210–12, 214; migration and, 187, 245n6; shame/silence about, 186, 244n3
Haitian revolution, 65, 233n32
Hammonds, Evelynn, 16–17
Harlem Renaissance, 24, 27, 32, 39, 42, 46, 49; black male writers in, 37, 39; Hurston's legacy and, 78; sexual repression in, 33–34
Harper, Frances, 80
Hawthorne, Nathaniel, 16
Healing: in *Beloved*, 114, 115, 116–17, 129; cloth associated with, 98; color associated with, 108; community, 116–17; dancing for, 237n33; Erzulie and, 121; in *The Farming of Bones*, 184, 185, 209–22; in *It Begins with Tears*, 169, 177–78, 182, 244n39
Heart of Darkness (Conrad), 157
Hegemony, 1–11, 227n1, 227n2; *It Begins with Tears* syncretic subversion of, 153–54; modernity and, 152, 241n14
Helga Crane (character), 28–29, 31, 33, 58
Hemenway, Robert, 43, 53
Henderson, Mae Gwendolyn, 167
Heterosexuality, revision of negative tropes of, 189, 245n9
Hidden in Plain View (Tobin/Dobard), 109, 110, 112
High Priestesses, 81, 178
Hindman, Jane, 108–9
Hip-hop, xiii, xivn1, 11, 225
Hitler, Adolf, 186
Holloway, Karla, 5, 6, 61

266 / Index

Holocaust, African, 83
Home to Harlem (McKay), 26
Hoodoo, 8, 53, 60, 62, 65, 66; obsolescence of, 65; slaves' practice of, 233n29; in U.S., 63, 65–66, 70; Voudoun and, 61, 63, 64. *See also* Voudoun
hooks, bell, 55
Horizon, Janie's pulling in to herself of, 76
Horses, possession and, 76, 89
Hottentots, 12–13
Houchins, Susan, *Spiritual Narratives*, 23
Huget, Lydia Gonzàlez, 108
Humans: loa relations with, 75, 145, 194; sub-, Africans viewed as, 13–14
Human sacrifice, 197, 216
Hurst, Fannie, 48
Hurston, Zora Neale, 2–3, 5, 11, 38, 42, 64, 230n32, 231n3; criticism of, 25, 229n18; dialogue with Morrison, 9; empowerment model of, 77; ethnographic research by, 40, 59–60; groundwork laid by, xiv, 7–8, 38; in Haiti, 60, 62, 185, 201, 204; Hoodoo society and, 65–66; legacy of, 42–43, 77–78, 185; literary tradition revised by, 39–40; *Mules and Men*, 42, 55, 60, 62, 63–64, 233n27; subjectivity model in work of, 7–8; *Tell My Horse*, 3, 42–43, 60, 63–64, 203–4, 219, 233n27; Voudoun research by, 40, 60–61, 62, 63. *See also Their Eyes Were Watching God*
Hypermasculinity, 122
Hypersexuality, Beloved's, 89, 121

Iconography, 97
Identities: Beloved's multiple, 9; Cliff's "I and I," 168, 242n25; collective, 74; difference and, 167–69; folk, 31–32, 66–67, 230n24; Haitian construction of, 195; multiple, 70; Trujillo's African, 197. *See also* Racial identity
Ideology, nineteenth-century sexual, 12–38
Illness, Sethe's, 133, 238n53
Imitation of Life, 48
Incidents in the Life of a Slave Girl (Jacobs), 18–20
Independent, 17
Individual-collective identity, 168, 242n25
Individuation, 74, 77, 117
Inferiority, 12–15, 17; Tea Cake's internalization of, 50–51

Infertility, symbol of, 220
Ink, Lynn Chun, 202
Innovations. *See* Postmodern innovations
Interconnectedness, 84–85, 86, 235n10
Interiority, spirituality and, 4, 58, 73
Interpretation: African cosmology as tool for, 85; *Beloved*, 83, 85, 86; books resisting easy, 166; through dreams, 87. *See also* Reading
Interracial marriage, 44
Intersubjectivity, 106, 116, 144, 167, 172; collective, 168, 169, 242n25; forgiveness and, 177
Intertextuality, 8, 9, 59, 118, 129; *The Farming of Bones* and, 184–85; *Mama Day–Beloved*, 103; Monica/Janie/Sula, 168, 242n26; Tea Cake–Beloved, 132, 138
Iola Leroy (Harper), 80
Irene (character), 26, 27
Iron, 110, 125–27
It Begins with Tears (Adisa), 4, 142–83, 242n17, 242n21, 244n39; characters in, profusion of, 143, 144; community and, 145, 159–62; community unrest in beginning of, 145; failings of, 161–62; hegemony subverted in, 153–54; Jamaica setting in, 152; Judeo-Christian doctrine in, 144–45, 147; love triangle in, 167, 168, 172; outsiders/threesome in, 162–66; peppering assault in, 147, 176, 177, 240n7; prostitute in, 167–69, 242n17; resistance/adaptation in, 152, 153, 240nn11–13; as revision of Janie paradigm, 9; spiritual elder in, 169; structure of, 143–44; trajectory of, 148, 150; weather/village relations in, 145; West African cosmology basis of, 141–51; women's spiritual wisdom/sexual subjectivity in, 169–83; writing course student debate over, 170; writing of, 141; Yoruba in, 143, 147, 170–78, 180–81

Jackson, Rebecca Cox, 22
Jacobs, Harriet, 18–20, 21
Jamaica, 105, 152; Adisa's blending of Judeo-Christian doctrine with folk of, 144–45; African culture and, 155; ethnography on village in, 173; femininity in, 239n6; Kumina religion, 6, 148; Pukumina religion of, 6, 92, 148; spirituality of, 153–54; tourism in, 160. *See also It Begins with Tears*
Jamaican culture, 155, 240nn11–13; culinary ad-

aptations and, 152, 240n11; folklore in, 107, 176; resistance and, 152, 240n11, 240n12
Janie Crawford (character), 2, 8, 38, 61–62, 191; childlessness of, 57–58, 232n22; clairvoyance of, 58; "classing off" of, 66, 70; conjuring accusation of, 67; as Erzulie, 7, 8–9, 69, 70, 185, 227n7; kissing friend of, 74–75; marriage to Jody, 57, 67–68, 72–73, 232n20; marriage to Logan, 72; Monica/Sula intertextuality with, 168, 242n26; as prototype for black female writers, 3–4; racial identity of, 44, 46, 47–50; resistance strategies of, 53–55; return to Eatonville of, 74; revised paradigm of, 9; self defense against Tea Cake, 52; sexual awakening of, 39, 40, 68; sexuality of, 42, 67, 231n3, 231n4; spirituality after Tea Cake's death, 76; as spiritual-sexual being, 40–41; subjectivity of, 74; Tea Cake and, 51, 55–56, 58–59, 71–74, 76, 132; Tea Cake's beating of, 51, 74; transformation of, 71, 234n38; transgressive/transcendent heroine, 50; work in the muck and, 57, 70, 74
Jealousy, Erzulie's, 138
Jefferson, Thomas, 14–15
Jenkins, Candice, 12, 15, 18, 34
Jody Starks (character), 50, 57, 67–68, 72–73, 129, 232n20
Johnson, James Weldon, 49
Joyner, Charles, 62, 233n30
Judeo-Christian doctrine: Adisa's revision of, 147; female sexuality negation in, 22–23; God in, 119; *It Begins with Tears*, 144–45, 147; sexual desire/shame and, 21
Jung, Carl, 85–86

Kaplan, Carla, 37, 39
Keeping room, 113, 116
Keizer, Arlene, 1, 3, 79, 82, 90
Kendry, Clare, 58
Khoisans. *See* Hottentots
Kinship ties, 100, 101, 102–3
Kissing friend, Janie's, 74–75
Kongo, 82, 102; cross/cosmogram, 110–12
Krehn, William, 197
Kristoff Village, 159, 182; alter ego of, 182; modernity v. tradition, 151–55. *See also It Begins with Tears*

Krumholz, Linda, 107, 114, 138
Kumina religion, 6, 148

Laguerre, Michel, 63, 137, 139–40
Lamothe, Daphne, 8, 40, 41, 61, 65, 227n7; on Janie as Erzulie, 168, 185
Language: Creole, 70, 91, 92, 143, 145, 146, 198, 239n3, 239n5; as difference marker, 190; maiden, 71–72; spiritual, sexual desire expressed in, 23–24, 33, 56, 229n13
Larsen, Nella, 38, 230n32; *Passing*, 25, 26–27, 46; *Quicksand*, 25, 28–34, 230n24, 230n26, 232n16
Laveau, Marie, 70–71, 81
Leaders, African-American, 24–25, 229n17
Lee, Jarena, 22, 91
Legba (spirit of crossroads), 103–4, 119, 152, 198, 207–8
Lesbians, 132–33, 172
Let the Circle Be Unbroken: The Implications of African Spirituality in the Diaspora (Ani aka Richards), 105
Literacy, diasporic, 79, 86, 87, 93, 98, 109, 141
Literary heroines, women of color excluded as, 45
Literary interventions: African spiritual practices as, 83, 235n7; double voice, 72; narrative, 81; storytelling, 54, 56; *Their Eyes Were Watching God*, 39–78
Little death, orgasm as, 206
Loa (goddess), 5, 40, 118–19; ancestral spirits and, 105, 237n33; *Beloved* references to, 8–9; black female writers' evocation of, 5; God and, 119; human relations with, 75, 145, 194; mouthpiece of, 76; Orishas, 5, 9, 96, 103–4; Oshun, 8, 96, 97–98, 143, 147, 170, 181; saints and, 201; sex, 69; *Their Eyes Were Watching God* signifying of, 59–78; Voudoun, 119; of war, 110, 125; water, 75, 140, 180–81; working-class, 9, 64, 69–70, 71, 76, 120, 121. *See also* Erzulie; God; Spirits; Voudoun
Locke, Alain, 43, 49
Logan (character), 72
Lorde, Audre, 6, 11, 37, 41, 68–69, 78, 117; on erotic power, xiv, 41, 135, 153, 179; on sexual agency, 124; *Sister Outsider*, 4

Lovemaking, 55–56, 204–6; in cave, 204, 219–20
Love triangle, 167, 168, 172
Loving v. Virginia, 44
Lynching, 17, 24, 229n15

MacGaffey, Wyatt, 112
Macon Dead (character), 99
Maddas (mothers/warner women), 91–92, 239n3
Mad dog, of internalized racism, 51, 55
Maiden language, 71–72
Making Men: Gender, Literary Authority and Women's Writing in Caribbean Narrative (Edmondson), 154
Mama Day (Naylor), 103, 104
Mambos (priestesses), 61, 63, 64
Mandel, Naomi, 83, 111, 237n40
Mande people, 108
Marriage: equality in, 57, 232n21; interracial, 44; Janie's, 57, 67–68, 72–73, 232n20; for security, 72
Martha Brae (Jamaican village), 173
Masculinity: in *Beloved*, 121–30; courtly, 123; embodied kindness in, 128; hyper-, 122; through integration, 118, 128; Paul D's, 118, 120, 123, 124–27; revised definition of, 128
Massacre River, 187, 209, 220, 245n7
Matriarch stereotype, 179, 180
Mawu, 205
McAlister, Elizabeth, 200
McDowell, Deborah, 17–18, 25, 28, 33, 34, 36, 58, 82
McKay, Claude, 25, 26, 82, 154
McKay, Nellie, 49, 71
Memory, place and, 101
Mermaid, 96, 176
Metal, 125
Metonyms: *Beloved*, 89; Hoodoo/Nanny, 65; mule/mulatto, 56–57; parsley, 196; sex/death, 136
Métraux, Alfred, 63, 75, 192, 199
Metrès Dlo (character), 210, 220
Middle class, 32, 154, 230n24; *It Begins with Tears* portrayal of, 154, 162; *Quicksand* portrayal of, 32, 50
Middle Passage, 86, 98–99, 104, 137
Midwifery, 187
Migration, Haitian, 187, 245n6
Milkman (character), 99–101

Miscegenation, 44, 48, 236n27
Misreadings, of Erzulie, 120–21
Miss Beryl (character), 159–61
Miss Madge (character), 150
Mister (rooster), 127
Mitchell, Carolyn, 97
Modernity: Angel as bridge between tradition and, 156–66; as hegemonic, 152, 241n14; postcolonial cultures and, 152; resistance/adaptation and, 152, 240nn11–13; tradition v., 142, 149–55, 180, 240n10
Monica (character), 150, 155, 243n36; affair of, 167, 168, 169; Amabelle/Janie intertextuality with, 184–85; Desmond's sexual act of healing for, 178; healing ritual for, 177–78; Janie/Sula intertextuality with, 168, 242n26; peppering assault on, 147, 176, 177, 240n7; sexuality of, 165, 169
Monkey wrench, 110
Montego Bay, 160, 161
Moorings and Metaphors (Holloway), 61
Morrison, Toni, 4, 5, 8, 11; aesthetics of, 80; *The Black Book*, 8, 81; ethnographic research by, 8; Hurston dialogue with, 9; role of place in novels of, 98–103, 112; "Rootedness: The Ancestor as Spiritual Foundation," 79, 83–84, 89; *Song of Solomon*, 87, 99–100, 117; *Sula*, 87, 93–94, 99, 150–51, 168, 240n9, 242n26. See also *Beloved*
Mother: Sethe as quintessential, 135, 238n55; of twins, 198–99
Mother(s), maddas/warner women, 91–92, 239n3
Mrs. Turner (character), 50; cow image of, 51
Muck, 57, 69–70, 74
Mulatta figure: changing definitions of, 44, 231n7; eroticization of, 46–47; Erzulie-Freda as, 64. See also Tragic Mulatta archetype
Mulatto/Mulatta, mule association with, 56–57
Mules, 56–57, 72
Mules and Men (Hurston), 42, 55, 60, 62, 63–64, 233n27; vernacular space in, ruptured, 66
Murphy, Joseph, 97
Musée de l'Homme, 3
Muzzle: female slaves', 215; sugar woman's, 213, 215
Mysticism, 155, 197; Christian religious, 23–24, 229n13

Mythology: Adisa's use of, 142, 145, 150; creation, 64; Egungun, 113, 114, 133–34; Greek, 117–18

Nanny (character), hoodoo and, 65
Narrative interventions, 81
Narrative of the Life of Frederick Douglass (Douglass), 18, 80, 228n5
Narratives. *See* Writers
Natural Mysticism (Dawes), 155, 157, 162
Nature: lesser deities as forces of, 84; sexuality and, 68
Naylor, Gloria, 39, 103, 104
"The Negro Art Hokum" (Schuyler), 49, 50
Neimark, Philip John, 170–71
Neither Black nor White: The Mulatto Character in American Fiction (Berzon), 44
New Age, 106
New Orleans, 65–66, 70, 81
New World: adaptation to, 90, 117; African religions in, 62, 97, 236n27; sex-spiritual division and, 2. *See also* Resistance
New World cosmologies, postmodern innovations and, 141–51
New World religions: color in, 116; rum in, 102; Sethe/Beloved and, 139
Nigeria, 110
Night, 107; fear of darkness, 157–59
Nommo, 54
Norms, conformance with, 159
Nsibidi symbols, 110
Nudity, 139, 177, 208, 209, 210, 211, 220–21; display of black females, 13; as worship, 220–21

Ogoun (spirit of fire), 119
Ogou/Ogun (iron orisha), 110, 125–27
Oral tradition, 100
Orangutans, alleged black female sexual relations with, 15
Orgasm, 34, 68, 171, 206
Orishas (gods/goddesses), 8, 96, 97–98; Cuban worship of, 108; dance to invoke, 105, 114; evocation of, 5, 9; of iron, 110, 125–27; Legba, 103–4, 119, 152, 198, 207–8; Ogou/Ogun, 110, 125–27; past-present linked by, 103–4; Yemonja, 8, 96, 142, 170, 177, 239n2
Oshun, 8, 96, 97–98, 143, 147, 170–71, 176, 181, 243n37; Arnella as, 170, 172–75; color of, 171
Our Nig (Wilson), 21
Oya, 108

Page, Philip, 92
Palma Christi leaves, 64–65
Papaya, 220, 248n34
Parsley, 190, 195, 196
Passage of Darkness: The Ethnobiology of the Haitian Zombie (W. Davis), 119, 195–96
Passing (Larsen), 25, 26–27, 30, 46
Passing, racial, 47
Passion, spiritual, 23–24
Patterson, Richard, 186
Paul D (character), 8–9, 82, 99, 114, 120, 123, 124–27, 136; Beloved and, 120–21, 124, 137, 138; red heart symbol of, 81–82, 120, 137; Sethe and, 128–30, 131
Peasantry, 70, 142–43, 154–55, 173–74, 176, 182; gender roles of, 182; Trelawny, Jamaica, 173. *See also* Folk; *It Begins with Tears*; Proto peasants
Penis, wood as, 143
Peppering (assault), 147, 176, 177, 240n7
Phoeby (character), 78
Physical abuse, in black communities, 55–56
Pilate, song from, 100
Place, Morrison's use of, 98–103, 112
Plague of robins, 87
Plato, Ann, 22
Plum Bun (Fauset), 25, 34–36, 49, 230n28; *Their Eyes* v., 56
Politics of silence, 16–17
Possession, 75–76, 89, 136, 137, 194; in *The Farming of Bones*, 195; self-, 212–13
Postmodern innovations: mythological creativity as, 145; New World cosmologies and, 141–51
Power. *See* Empowerment; Erotic power
Pradel, Lucie, 141, 180
Preachers, black women as, 104, 105–6
Pregnancies, Helga's unwanted, 58
Priest, in *The Farming of Bones*, 203
Priestesses: Arnella as, 149, 169, 170, 172–75; High, 81, 178; in *It Begins with Tears*, 169; mambos as, 61, 63, 64; in training, 92, 149, 169, 170, 172–75; Voodoo, Laveau as, 81
Prince, Mary, 20, 21
Prison guards, slaves and, 124, 130
Professor (character), 207, 208
Progress, black women's late nineteenth-century, 17
Prostitute, in *It Begins with Tears*, 167–69, 242n17

Protagonist, first black female, 33
Proto peasants, 173, 240n12
Psychoanalysis, interpreting *Beloved* through, 86
Public disrobing, black women's forced, 46–47
Pukumina religion, 6, 92, 148, 240n8

Quicksand (Larsen), 25, 28–34, 56, 58, 230n24, 230n26, 232n16
Quilts/quilting, 108–10; Baby Suggs's, 109, 112–13, 133–34; monkey wrench stitched into, 110; Underground Railroad linked with, 109, 237n39

Race: Haitian massacre issues of, 186–87; social class and, 94–95
"The Race for Theory" (Christian), 6, 180
Racial identity, 44, 46, 47–50, 94–95, 159; ambivalence, 47–49, 94, 159; color marker of, 107
Racial oppression, gendered effects of, 5
Racial uplift, 30, 31
Racism, mad dog as symbol of internalized, 51, 55
Rahier, Jean, 156
Rainbow, 203, 213, 217
Rape: of black female slaves, 15–16, 18–19, 20; dialectics of justification for, 15; Europeans' view of black females and, 14–15
Rapists, stereotype of black men as, 123
Ray, 93
Reading: divination as, 92; of texts, 6, 83, 166
Reclaiming, spiritual practices, 79–98
Recursion, text, 69
Recursion/revision, 69
Redfield, Irene, 58
Red Heart, 8–9, 81–82, 120, 137
Redpath, James, 15
Religions: African, 4; African-American, 105; duality in Western, 120; Jamaican, 6, 92, 148; New World African, 62, 97, 236n27; New World's African, 62, 97, 102; Santeria, 92, 96; Thompson's work on African/New World, 82. *See also* Christianity; Spirituality; Syncretization, religious; Voudoun
Religious ecstasy, 33, 34
Renaming, of spiritual practices, 79–98
Repression: black female sexuality, 12, 15–18; West African spiritual practices, 6
Resistance, 90, 117; African cosmology tool for, 81; Christianity as tool for, 21–22; female cultural, 174; female slaves, 179, 180; *It Begins with Tears* and, 174; Jamaican culture and, 152, 240nn11–13; Janie's strategies of, 53–55; keeping room and, 113, 116; modernity adaptation and, 152, 240nn11–13; New World adaptation and, 90, 117; slave strategies of, 107, 117, 174; spiritual, 153; subjectivity and, 3, 227n4
Respectability, 22; sexual expression sacrificed for, 34; writers conforming to standards of, 49
Revision, text, 69
Rhinelander, Alice, 46–47, 232n12
Richards, Dona Marimba, 107; *Let the Circle Be Unbroken: The Implications of African Spirituality in the Diaspora*, 105
Ring game, 100
Rituals, 209; authenticity issues for, 162, 242n21; Baby Suggs's fixing ceremony, 112–13, 116, 133, 136; bathing, 177–78, 221, 244n39; clearing of Beloved, 114, 116–17; color contemplation, 106, 107–8, 112–13, 114; connection of Caribbean/African/West African, 86; dance, 147; exorcism/clearing, 108, 114, 115, 116–17; *The Farming of Bones*, 200; healing, communal, 177–78; *It Begins with Tears*, 162, 242n21; quiltmaking, 108–10; relations shaped by, 107; of subjection, 184–91; survival of, 105
River, 147, 174–75, 176–77, 203, 243n34; bathing in, village women, 177–78, 244n39; -mumma, 96, 176, 180, 181–82; spirit of, 213. *See also* Massacre River
Rody, Caroline, 82–83, 121, 132
Root, Douglass's use of, 80, 233n29
"Rootedness: The Ancestor as Spiritual Foundation" (Morrison), 79, 83–84, 89
Rubin, Vera, 137
Rum, 102
Ruptured vernacular space, Baker's, 66, 117
Rural South: Caribbean spirituality syncretized with, 43. *See also* Folk
Ryan, Judylyn: on Baby Suggs, 91, 104; *Spirituality as Ideology in Black Women's Film and Literature*, 85

Sacred, secular v., 1, 11, 227n2
Sacred spaces, 98, 101–2, 204, 219, 247n25, 248n33

Sacrifice: animal, 127, 238n49; human, 197, 216; sexual expression, 25, 34
Saints, loa and, 201
Salvific wish, 18, 34, 91
Sanchez, Sonia, 78
Santeria religion, 92, 96, 138–39
Scapegoat, 150–51, 240n9
Scholarship, 6
Schoolteacher (character), 105–6, 127
Schuyler, George, "The Negro Art Hokum," 49, 50
Sebastien (character), 204–6; death of, 189, 190, 211; goat association of, 216
Secular: division between sacred and, 1, 227n2; division/integration between sacred and, 1, 11, 227n2
Security, marriage for, 72
Seeyah women (seers), 91, 143, 158, 239n3
Self-knowledge, 77
Self-love, 73, 91, 106, 189, 213
Self-possession, 212–13
Self-respect, xiii
Selvon, Samuel, 155
Sending of dead, 203
Sethe (character), 114–15, 139, 169; allowed to choose sexual partner, 123–24; Amy and, 95, 113; color contemplation ritual by, 114; healing stages of, 114; illness of, 133, 238n53; injuries of, 95; kneel/think-talk activity of, 113; mother's X symbol brand, 110, 111; Paul D and, 128–30, 131; as quintessential mother, 135, 238n55
Sexual abuse, of slaves, 121, 122, 124, 130, 131, 136, 238n47
Sexual coercion, of female slaves, 15–16, 18–19
Sexual desire/expression: *Beloved*'s slave men's thwarted, 121–23; desire to feel, 67; Erzulie's normalizing of, 136; Hurston v. Larsen in representing healthy, 38; object of another's, 67; *Plum Bun* v. *Their Eyes*, 56; price of, 58; in *Quicksand*, 56, 58; sacrifice of, 25, 34; shame over, 20, 21, 128; spiritual language for, 23–24, 33, 56, 229n13
Sexual deviance, 12–15, 16
Sexual empowerment, femininity opposed to, 54
Sexual encounters, spiritual dimensions for, 118–40
Sexuality: African cosmology and, 41, 64, 89–90; agency and, 9, 124, 131; Amabelle's healing and, 209–22; awakening to, first experience, 39, 40, 68; bestializing of, 121, 122; Christianity v. African spiritual traditions view of, 2, 4–5, 90, 170; death and, 136; distortion of black male, 121–23; Erzulie's, 89, 108, 118, 120, 121, 131–40; ideology in nineteenth-century writing, 12–38; Judeo-Christian negation of female, 22–23; nature and, 68; spirituality as separate from, 4, 23; spiritual practice component of, 89–90; subjectivity and, 89–90, 209; threat of, 165; transgressive, *It Begins with Tears*, 166–69; in Voudoun, 64, 209–10; writers' repression/avoidance of, xiv, 22, 153. *See also* Spiritual-sexual syncretization
Sexuality, black female: Harlem Renaissance repression of, 33–34; Hurston's Janie and, 42, 231n3, 231n4; Jefferson's maligning of, 15; politics of silence strategy and, 16–17; *Quicksand*, 33–34; repression of black female, 12, 15–18; *Their Eyes Were Watching God*, 39. *See also* Agency
Sexual repression, climate of, late nineteenth century, 15–18
Sexual totality, Damballa/Ayida Wédo as God and, 203, 205, 247n27
Shalimar, in *Song of Solomon*, 99–100
Shango, 59, 97–98, 108
Shango Baptist church, 91
Shemak, April, 198–99
Sherrard-Johnson, Cherene, 48
The Signifying Monkey (Gates Jr.), 6, 78
Singers, blues, 25
Sister Outsider (Lorde), 4
Slavery, 24, 85, 235n11; African spiritual practices surviving, 88; Baby Suggs on self-love and, 106; Christianity and, 21, 104; recovery from, 9; spiritual practices disrupted by, 85; subjectivity denied by, 84, 111, 127–28; two brands of, 127
Slaves, 21, 215; *The Black Book* chronicles of, 80–81, 233n29; blacksmith, 110; Hoodoo practice by, 233n29; institutionalized cruelty to, 215; resistance/community of, 179, 180; resistance strategies of, 107, 117, 174; sexual abuse of, 121, 122, 124, 130, 131, 136, 238n47; Sweet Home, 107, 121–23, 125

Slaves, female: muzzle on, 215; resistance due to efforts of, 179, 180; sexual coercion of, 15–16, 18–19, 20
Social class, 26–27, 30–32, 230n24; black elite, 30, 50; race and, 94–95; *Their Eyes Were Watching God* and, 66. *See also* Middle class; Working class
Sommer, Doris, 166
Song, from Pilate, 100
Song of Solomon (Morrison), 87, 99–101, 117
Sons of Voodoo, 62–63. *See also* Hoodoo; Voudoun
Sound Clash: Jamaican Dancehall Culture at Large (Cooper), xiii
Space: between physical/spiritual worlds, 103; ruptured vernacular, 66, 117. *See also* Sacred spaces
Spirits: Ayida Wédo/Damballah, 203, 205–6, 247n27, 247n29; babies as, 101; Baby Suggs's, 115; in *Beloved*, 115; of crossroads, 103–4; W. Davis on Voudoun and, 119; of dead, 113; evil, 106–7; of fire, 119; herbs and, 139; hot/cold, 201–2; of river, 213; sea, 140; violent death and, 86–87; writers' use/evocation of, 5. *See also* Ancestral spirits; Loa
Spiritual Interrogations (Bassard), 37
Spirituality: African, 5–6, 8, 60, 64, 83, 88, 91, 108, 197, 235n7, 235n19; African-American, 85, 88, 105; Afro-Caribbean, 142–43; agency, 116; body revaluing and, 106; conferral of personhood from, 37; *connaissance* and, 10, 194, 206, 218; creolized, 90, 103, 105, 116, 181; elder characters', 169; eroticism defined in terms of, 4; Haitian, *The Farming of Bones* and, 192; healing of sexuality and, Amabelle's, 209–22; interiority of, 4, 58, 73; *It Begins with Tears*, 169; Jamaican, 153–54; Janie's, 40–41, 76; limits of, 92; loss and, 76; search for, 218; sexual desire expressed in language of, 23–24, 33, 56, 229n13; sexual encounters in dimensions of, 118–40; sexuality in definitions of, 4–6, 227n6; subject formation requiring, 5, 37; symbols of, 60; undeveloped, 218; women's wisdom/sexual subjectivity and, 169–83. *See also* Spiritual-sexual syncretization; Syncretization, religious
Spirituality as Ideology in Black Women's Film and Literature (Ryan), 85

Spiritual Narratives (Houchins), 23
Spiritual practices: reclaiming/renaming, 79–98; sexuality as component of, 89–90. *See also* Rituals
Spiritual-sexual syncretization, 4–6, 9–10, 37, 153, 227n6; *Beloved*, 140; in *The Farming of Bones*, 219; *It Begins with Tears* and, 169–83; as political act, 41; *Their Eyes Were Watching God* and, 40–41, 58, 60, 68, 73
Stereotypes: black female, 12, 15–16, 56–57, 72, 179, 180; black male, 123; female slave as matriarch, 179, 180; mule, 56–57, 72; pseudoscientific, 15–16
Stewart, Maria, 22, 23, 91
Stitched from the Soul (Fry), 109
Storytelling, 54, 56, 66, 100, 184, 210, 212, 220
Subjection, rituals of, 184–91
Subjectivity, 9–10; formation of, textual representation of, 9–10, 118; Hurston's model for, 7–8; inter-, 106, 116, 144, 167, 168, 172, 177, 242n25; memory and, 101; plural, 167–68; resistant, 3, 227n4; sexuality and, 89–90, 209; slavery as denial of, 84, 111, 127–28; spirituality essential to, 5, 37
Sugar woman, 211–15, 216
Sula (Morrison), 87, 93–94, 99, 150–51, 168, 240n9, 242n26
Sweet Home, slaves of, 107, 121–23, 125
Symbols: Adisa's use of, 142; *Beloved* haunted by, 81–82; dream interpretation and, 87; encoding of, 7; freedom, 112; resistance, 110; spiritual, 60; Voudoun, Danticat's subtle use of, 193
Syncretization, religious, 6, 43, 85, 91, 105, 116, 153–54, 235n19, 243n34; Christianity-West African cosmology, 148, 240n8; Hoodoo-Voudoun, 61; River-mumma as form of, 96, 176, 180, 181–82. *See also* Spiritual-sexual syncretization; Synthesis
Synthesis, African-Western worldview, 1, 227n1

Talented Tenth, 24, 50, 229n17
Talking Book, Gates's, 59
Tate, Claudia, 21
Tea Cake (character), 42, 51, 52, 55–56, 58–59, 71–74, 132, 191, 231n5; Beloved and, 132, 138; death of, 51, 76; inferiority internalization of, 50–51; Janie's beating by, 51, 74

Index / 273

Tell My Horse (Hurston), 3, 42–43, 60, 63–64, 203–4, 219, 233n27
Textiles, 106–7, 109–10
Thaggert, Miriam, 46–47
Their Eyes Were Watching God (Hurston), 39–78, 129, 191; ancestral presence in, 61–62; black female sexuality depicted in, 39; black female writers and, 3–4; central question of, 40; Erzulie in, 7, 8–9, 40, 41, 69, 227n7; healing of division starting with, 2–3; literary interventions in, 39–78; *Plum Bun* v., 56; reviews of, 42; tradition started by, 7; Voudoun in, 40, 41, 59–78, 233n28, 233n61; writing of, 60. *See also* Janie Crawford (character)
Thompson, Robert Farris, 7, 8, 82, 102, 110, 125; on textiles, 106–7
Thornton, Hortense, 29, 30–31
Ti bon ange, 195–96, 210, 246n18
Ti bon anj, 195
Tobin, Jacqueline, 109, 110, 112
Tongues, 76, 82–83, 233n30
Touching, 212, 220–21
Tradition: Angel as bridge between modernity and, 156–66; literary, Hurston's revising of, 39–40; modernity v., 142, 149–55, 180, 240n10; *Their Eyes Were Watching God* starting new, 7
Tragic Mulatta archetype, 25, 26–31, 48, 50, 157–58, 229n19; subversion of, 43–59, 231n7, 232n14
Trees, as sacred spaces, 102
Trelawny (Jamaica), 173
Trujillo, Rafael, 10, 184, 186, 193, 196–97, 216, 244n1, 244n4, 246n13, 247n31; Africanness despised by, 196, 197–98; death of, 217
Twins, 198–200
2 Live Crew, xivn1

Ukara cloth, 110
Underground Railroad, 109, 112, 237n39
United States (U.S.), Hoodoo practice in, 63
U.S. Supreme Court, 44
"The Uses of the Erotic: The Erotic as Power" (Lorde), 68–69

Vagina, in Voudoun, 119
Valencia (character), 187, 198–99
Valrie (character), 171–72
Velvet, pursuit of, 95, 97
Vernacular space, ruptured, 66, 117
Vesey, Denmark, 81
Victorians, and obsession with black female anatomy, 12–14
Violence: domestic, 133; slave beatings, 111; spirits of those killed in, 86–87
Voodoo, 62, 63, 192, 201; Laveau as High Priestess of, 81. *See also* Hoodoo
Voudoun, 7, 40, 59–60, 63, 119, 192, 200; absent presence of, 10, 192–209, 227n9, 246n12; Danticat's first reference to, 198; death in, 200; encoding of, 7, 61, 203, 208; in *Farming of Bones*, 10, 192–209, 246n12; fear of, 194, 246n14; God/loas in, 119; Hoodoo and, 61, 63, 64; Hurston's research of, 40, 60–61, 62, 63; ignorance of, 8; possession in, 75–76, 89, 136; sexuality in, 64, 209–10; in *Their Eyes Were Watching God*, 40, 41, 59–78, 233n28, 233n61; transformation and, 70–71, 234n37; women's role in, 63–64, 233n31. *See also* Erzulie
Vwayajè, 195

Walker, Alice, 77–78, 245n9
Wall, Cheryl, 26–27, 30, 78
War, god of, 110, 125–27
Warner women (Maddas), 91–92, 239n3
Water, 75, 140, 180–81, 208, 218, 219
Waterfalls, 203, 206, 208, 219
Wells, Ida B., 17
West African cosmology, 3, 86; *Beloved*'s characters representing aspects of, 91; *It Begins with Tears* basis in, 141–51; Morrison's use of references to, 8; syncretization of Christianity with, 148, 240n8
West African spiritual practices, 6, 61
Western religions, duality in, 120. *See also* Judeo-Christian doctrine; Religions; Synthesis, African-Western worldview
Wheatley, Phillis, 22
White, Deborah Gray, 15
Whiteness: approximation to, 25; racial ambiguity and, 47
White women, "fall" of black v., 16
Willis, Susan, 57, 232n20
Wilson, Alexander, 15
Wilson, Harriet, 21
Witchcraft, 80–81

Women: acceptance of differences among, 168; Caribbean linking with African-American, 8, 105; conjure, 115; "fall" of black v. white, 16; female bonding of, 176, 178; females cultural resistance, 174; friendship bond between, 172; seeyah, 91, 143, 158, 239n3; as spiritual vanguards/sexual subjects, 169–83; Voudoun role of, 63–64, 233n31; warner, 91–92, 239n3. *See also* Black females; Femininity; Slaves, female; Sugar woman; Writers, black female

Women, black: Europeans' portrayal of, 12–15; "fall" of, 16, 23; literary heroines as never being, 45; mysticism of, 23–24, 229n13; as preachers, 104, 105–6; progress of, nineteenth-century, 17; public disrobing of, 46–47; respectability for, 22, 34, 49

The Women's Era, 17

Wood, 143

Word, power of, 54

Working class, 25, 75; loa of, 9, 64, 69–70, 71, 76, 120, 121; white, 95

Workings of the Spirit (Baker), 65–66, 70–71

Worship, 85, 108

Wrapped in Rainbows (Boyd), 39

Wright, Richard, 43

Writers: ancestral voice of, 82–83; Caribbean, 153, 154, 185

Writers, black female, 12–38; as activists, xiv, 11, 185; aesthetics of, 1–11, 79–80, 227nn1–3; black male v., 37, 39; Christianity used by, 21; constraints on, 37, 49; dilemma of, xiv, 36–37; erotic power expression of, 5, 10; goddess figures evoked by, 5; Hurston's prototype for, 3–4; imitating each other, 78; respectability standards conformed to by, 49; sexuality avoided by, xiv, 22, 153; sexual-spiritual balance sought/expressed by, 4–5; slave narratives of, 21; spiritual narratives of, 23–24; subjectivity of, plural, 167–68

Writers, black male, 37, 39

Writing: course on, student view of *It Begins with Tears* in, 170; *It Begins with Tears*, 141

Writing in Limbo (Gikandi), 181

X symbol, 110, 111

Yemeya, 96, 97

Yemonja (orisha), 8, 96, 142, 170, 177, 239n2

Yoruba cosmology, 59, 82, 92, 103–4, 108, 125, 139; in *Bake-Face*, 142; in *Beloved*, 8–9, 96–97; in *It Begins with Tears*, 143, 147, 170–78, 180–81

Zombies, 119, 195–96, 210, 221

Zone of occult instability, 120

Donna Weir-Soley is associate professor of English at Florida International University. A published literary critic and poet, she is the author of the poetry collection *First Rain* and co-editor of the book *Caribbean Erotic: Poetry, Prose, and Essays.*